CW00730836

A PASSION
FOR RECORDS

Walter Rye (1843–1929)

Topographer, sportsman and Norfolk's champion

Christopher Kitching

Copyright © 2018 Christopher Kitching

The moral right of the author has been asserted.

Apart from any fair dealing for the purposes of research or private study,
or criticism or review, as permitted under the Copyright, Designs and Patents
Act 1988, this publication may only be reproduced, stored or transmitted, in
any form or by any means, with the prior permission in writing of the
publishers, or in the case of reprographic reproduction in accordance with
the terms of licences issued by the Copyright Licensing Agency. Enquiries
concerning reproduction outside those terms should be sent to the publishers.

Matador
9 Priory Business Park,
Wistow Road, Kibworth Beauchamp,
Leicestershire. LE8 0RX
Tel: 0116 279 2299
Email: books@troubador.co.uk
Web: www.troubador.co.uk/matador
Twitter: @matadorbooks

ISBN 978 1788039 215

British Library Cataloguing in Publication Data.
A catalogue record for this book is available from the British Library.

Printed on FSC accredited paper
Printed and bound in Great Britain by 4edge Limited
Typeset in 11pt Minion Pro by Troubador Publishing Ltd, Leicester, UK

Matador is an imprint of Troubador Publishing Ltd

For the countless editors and indexers who, like Walter Rye,
have experienced a passion for records

CONTENTS

PREFACE

Approach

Conventionally, a biography follows its subject's life story chronologically from birth to death. That would have been unhelpful in the case of a man like Walter Rye with fingers in so many pies at once, and perhaps especially unhelpful for the reader who might be interested in one particular aspect of his life: record-breaking athlete; prolific topographer, antiquary and local historian; genealogist and controversialist; champion of the Norfolk Broads and of the preservation of historic buildings; lawyer; family man and of course, not to be forgotten, Mayor of Norwich.

I have chosen instead to begin with just a brief outline of his life followed by a more detailed account of his childhood and youth, but then to let his life story unfold through a series of thematic biographical essays or Tracks, which can be read or dipped into in any order to suit the reader, but through which there is a logical progression towards a wider understanding of the man. Of course the Tracks are not mutually exclusive: they overlap and interweave, although I have tried to keep repetition and cross-referral to a minimum. They are:

Track 1: Professional and family life
Track 2: The sportsman
Track 3: The antiquary
Track 4: The genealogist
Track 5: Publish and be damned
Track 6: Norfolk's champion

The final section picks up on a few further attributes of the man without which our understanding of him would be incomplete, before making an assessment of whether he was indeed, as one of his friends described him, 'OOTB: One Of the Best'.

A note on sources

Any account of the life of Walter Rye must of course start with his *Autobiography of an Ancient Athlete and Antiquary* (1916). Compiled mainly in a rather bitty and compressed style from yearly diaries which do not now survive, it contains almost no references to contemporary events in the wider world, and was privately printed for close friends and family, so was not really intended for wider circulation, although – as with so many of his other publications – he presented copies to the British Museum and certain other public institutions. Due allowance has to be made for the fact that these are the reflections of a man in his mid-seventies thinking he was near to death.

Supplementary information of a semi-biographical nature can be found in several of his other publications, especially *Rubbish and Nonsense* (1887); *A Month on the Norfolk Broads on Board the Wherry, 'Zoe' and its Tender, the Tub, 'Lotus'* (1887); and *The Recreations of a Norfolk Antiquary* (1920, 1922). But revealing incidental information is also scattered throughout his many other publications. Thanks to the combined resources of the British Library, the Norfolk Record Office, the Norfolk Heritage Centre (Norfolk and Norwich Millennium Library), the Guildhall Library (London), and the libraries of the Society of Antiquaries of London and The National Archives, I believe I have seen most of his published work. The News Room at the British Library proved to be an unexpectedly rich source because both London and provincial newspapers widely noticed and reviewed his publications, as well as reporting on his sporting triumphs and some of his more celebrated public engagements, such as his court appearance for the non-payment of his gas bill (triumphant acquittal!), or his protracted campaign for public rights of access to the Broads. A comprehensive collection of cuttings of his newspaper sports columns of the 1870s survives conveniently in a volume he himself presented to the Guildhall Library in London.

Walter's antiquarian notes, the original manuscripts he collected, and his voluminous correspondence – that is to say the letters he received, but only very occasionally his draft replies – survive in bulk at the Norfolk Record Office. It is worth stressing that phrase 'in bulk'. Throughout the years of my research the correspondence had not been systematically sorted and catalogued, but simply boxed in the disorder in which it was found. Making some sense of this vast quantity of material has been one of the imperatives, but also one of the hardest challenges. Individual letters were not numbered within the boxes so, alas, citations could be given by box only. The contents of most boxes were not internally arranged either by writer or by date, but every so often the researcher might find a note in Walter's hand suggesting a date range or alphabetical range of correspondents or topics for a particular bundle. Sometimes, just to make matters worse, this note was separated by one or more boxes in the sequence from the documents to which it referred, suggesting, dare one say, that there was once some kind of order. After the successive shufflings of this material that seem to have taken place, items clearly related by date or correspondent can now be found several, or even many, boxes apart in the series, and an item once enclosed in a letter might now be orphaned elsewhere in the box, or in another box altogether. I can claim to have at least looked through every box of correspondence, but I called a halt to detailed analysis once the additional glimpses of the man afforded by further hours of immersion in this rich but muddled source material proved insignificant. The same collection in Norwich also contains Walter's antiquarian notes, which might well be useful to anyone set on appraising in more detail his work on particular sites or buildings, but for the present purposes I have merely dipped into those.

A word should perhaps be said as to what these sources do *not* reveal. They can be searched almost in vain for insights into his business affairs as a lawyer, his politics, his religious beliefs, or for that matter his tastes in fiction, music or the arts. Did he feel that these were matters too personal to be shared? Nor is there much about Walter as parishioner or next-door neighbour. After qualifying as a solicitor he seems to have been so wrapped up in his legal work, sport and antiquarian studies that he lacked both time and inclination to engage at all actively with the communities in which he lived. And, with the notable exception of the First World War on which he set down forthright opinions in the local press, only rarely do we find in any of his writings more than a passing glimpse of contemporary events outside his own immediate interests. Yet just as the sparse mention of his legal business in the surviving material clearly does not indicate that he did not engage actively and very successfully with that, so it would be equally absurd to assume that he had no particular views on national or local politics, religion, the arts, and so forth: it is just that you must read between the lines to find them.

All of this should serve to warn the reader that the present work cannot claim either to represent the last word on Walter Rye, or to mine every last bit of gold in his large archive. That is good news for anyone who might wish to take up the challenge to dig deeper, and my hope is that this study will at least provide a foundation on which others can build, particularly if resources are ever found to catalogue the collection more fully.

ACKNOWLEDGEMENTS

This work would not have been possible without the kind assistance of many archivists and librarians throughout the decade or more in which it has been in gestation. The Norfolk Record Office has been unfailingly generous in allowing me to see sometimes very large quantities of material in short spaces of time, and my particular thanks are due to Dr John Alban and Susan Maddock there (both now retired).

I should also like to record my gratitude to Peter Rye, Walter's great grandson, for his part in shepherding the Rye archives into the Norfolk Record Office, his kindness in welcoming me to his home to discuss our mutual interest in Walter, and particularly for reading through the entire work in draft, making many useful suggestions, and providing a number of the illustrations. Nor is that the end of my debt to the family, for Anthony, Christopher and Jeremy Rye also provided helpful comments and pointers.

I have benefitted greatly from the insights and expertise of Dr John Alban, Dr Richard Olney and Professor Carole Rawcliffe who read the whole text in draft; of Professor John Beckett who helpfully explained the wider context of Walter's dealings with the Victoria County History; and of Thomas Woodcock, Garter King of Arms, who helped me to a better understanding of the procedure for Walter's grant of arms.

It has been a real pleasure to use the resources of (in London) the British Library, Camden Local Studies and Archives Department, the Guildhall Library, the Society of Antiquaries of London, The National Archives, the VCH archives at the Institute of Historical Research, and Wandsworth Heritage Service; and (in Norwich) the *Eastern Daily Press* archives and the Norfolk Heritage Centre (Norfolk and Norwich Millennium Library). Susan Snell, the archivist at Freemasons' Hall, London, kindly facilitated my research there on the archives of Quatuor Coronati Lodge, and I am obliged to the Lodge's Secretary for permission to consult those. My thanks are also due to Messrs Radcliffes Le Brasseur for confirming the apparent loss of the archives of Messrs Rye and Eyre; to Lynsey Darby, archivist at the College of Arms; and Ruth Frendo of the Institute of Advanced Legal Studies. Sara Barton-Wood kindly shared with me her research on Walter's friend Arthur Patterson. I am also grateful to the respective representatives of Kensal Green Cemetery, the Society of Genealogists, Thames Hare and Hounds, and Westminster City Archives for helpful replies to my enquiries. Thanks to the kindness of the present occupants I was delighted to be able to visit a number of houses formerly occupied by Walter Rye, in particular Winchester House, Putney (Winchester House Club) and Frognal House, Hampstead (Convent of St Dorothy). My wife, Ruth, has been a constant support, indulging my need to 'spend time with Walter', urging this work on to completion, and then living with the consequences by proof-reading the completed text!

Apart from the anonymous photographers or engravers commissioned by Walter for his *Autobiography*, every effort has been made to identify and acknowledge the respective copyright owners and/or custodians of works used in the illustrations, and my special thanks are due to all who kindly supplied, or allowed me to reproduce them.

I am especially grateful to the team at Matador who have seen this book through the press, in particular to Rosie Lowe and to my copy editor Imogen Palmer.

It would be conventional to conclude by saying that any remaining errors are mine alone, but, whilst that would undoubtedly be the responsible course, it would not be Walter's way of doing things!

Christopher Kitching
September 2017

ILLUSTRATIONS

Front cover: Sir James Pennethorne's original design for the Public Record Office, 1851. [The topmost section of the tower with the clock was never built]. *The Builder*, IX, no 453 (1851), p.643.

Frontispiece: Portrait photograph of Walter Rye (early 1900s). *Peter Rye.*

Sketch on title pages of Parts One, Two and Three: Walter Rye at the Amateur Walking Championships, 20 June 1868. *Autobiography.*

Illustrations printed in the text.

[Credits are given in the respective captions]

Plates (centre of volume)

ABBREVIATIONS USED

AAA	Amateur Athletic Association
AAC	Amateur Athletic Club
AQC	*Ars Quatuor Coronatorum*
Arch. J	*The Archaeological Journal*
Autobiog.	Walter Rye, *The Autobiography of an Ancient Athlete and Antiquary* (1916).
BL	British Library
DNB	*Dictionary of National Biography*
EA	*The East Anglian, or Notes and Queries [for Suffolk, Cambridgeshire, Essex and Norfolk]*
EDP	*Eastern Daily Press*
EHR	*English Historical Review*
LAC	London Athletic Club
LMA	London Metropolitan Archives
NA	*Norfolk Archaeology*
NAM	*Norfolk Antiquarian Miscellany*
N&Q	*Notes and Queries*
NBPS	Norfolk Broads Protection Society
NNAS	Norfolk and Norwich Archaeological Society
NRO	Norfolk Record Office
ns	new series
ODNB	*Oxford Dictionary of National Biography*
r.	rector
Recreations	Walter Rye, *The Recreations of a Norfolk Antiquary* (2 vols, Holt and Norwich, 1920 and 1922).
RRS	Walter Rye, *Records and Record Searching*
SSC	Sotheby's sale catalogue

THH	Thames Hare and Hounds
TNA	The National Archives, Kew
TRC	Thames Rowing Club
VCH	The Victoria History of the Counties of England
WR	Walter Rye

PART ONE

STARTING BLOCKS

1
A LIFE IN BRIEF

Education and training

Walter Rye (1843–1929) was the seventh child of Edward Rye (a London solicitor with an office in Golden Square, Westminster and a house in Chelsea) and his wife Maria. He grew up in a rather large but in every sense cold household, and received his initial education at a school which he later condemned as brutal, and which he left, at his own request, at the age of fourteen. The only simple option after that, and the one he adopted, was to join his brother as a junior clerk in his father's legal office. After a while, and again apparently on his own initiative, he went on to improve his education by attending night school at King's College, London, where he acquitted himself well both academically and as a member of the college athletics team. With what was now a distinctly improved general education he was equipped to train as a solicitor, and achieved a pass – though nothing more than that – in his final exams: a weak showing in his criminal law and bankruptcy papers denied him a higher overall grade, and in effect determined the scope of his future legal work. After being formally admitted a solicitor in 1866 when he was twenty-two, he in one sense entered his father's firm, although he actually seems to have worked independently, and his father did not entrust serious cases to him for a further five years. Not long after that, his professional life became even more awkward. His father slowly declined into senility and paranoia, and when he could no longer continue to practise, far from handing the firm on to his son, he made Walter borrow money from friends to buy him out in 1874.

As if work experience, continuing education and legal training were not enough to fill the average youth's day, Walter also found time as a teenager to train as an athlete, to teach at a local Sunday school and at a night school, to develop strong antiquarian interests, and to travel, especially (and extensively) in Norfolk, the county of his ancestors and a place which he would quickly make his own.

Sporting legend

Walter Rye wished to be remembered first and foremost as an athlete. His proudest achievements came mostly in his teens and twenties when, indeed, he became a national champion and record-holder in both walking and running events. He went on to hold high office in several of the most important athletics bodies of his day, and founded a new club, Thames Hare and Hounds, which introduced paper-chasing as an adult sport and earned for Walter the epithet 'Father of Paper-Chasing'. He remained a sporting celebrity throughout his long life, and when he came to write his *Autobiography of an Ancient Athlete and Antiquary* in 1916, the order of words in the title was no accident. Today, however, he is far more widely remembered as one of Norfolk's great antiquaries, and a champion of the city of Norwich and county of Norfolk.

It would be quite possible to write a whole book about Walter the athlete, and doubtless that is what he would have preferred. But it would not give us a rounded picture of Walter the man, which is closer to the aim of the present work. Even in the sporting realm, he was not only an athlete but also a notable cyclist, a passable rower and archer, and an intrepid though not very competent sampler of other sports including cricket, pugilism and shooting, as well as a promoter of the introduction into England of lacrosse. For relaxation he was also a sailor, but not in any competitive sense, because for this activity the physical effort was undertaken by paid boatmen. For a time Walter (sometimes writing anonymously) was also a waspish sports journalist and commentator.

Married life

After a number of unsuccessful amorous adventures he finally married in 1870. Over the next nineteen years his wife Georgina bore him eleven children, one of them still-born and another dying of cancer in infancy, but nine surviving to adulthood. Family and professional life notwithstanding,

Walter somehow managed to keep up – indeed to increase – his sporting and antiquarian commitments; and to his accomplishments as a nationally-rated athlete he would soon add those of a skilled genealogist, topographer and local historian (of Norfolk in particular), with many publications to his name, and a collector of antiquarian books and manuscripts. All of this activity must have drastically reduced the time he had available to spend with Georgina and the family, but he was not a completely absent father, and did make time for the children especially when they were old enough to share his interests in athletics, cycling and sailing. Meanwhile Georgina had her work cut out dealing with her successive children (with the help of servants). Sadly, no sooner had she ceased being a child-bearer than she developed diabetes, a disease that would slowly weaken her over the next two decades until she became a bed-ridden invalid, nursed at home largely by their daughters. Walter too fell victim to a number of serious diseases, any one of which could have proved fatal but from all of which, rather to his surprise, he recovered. Poor health may very well have been among the main factors leading to his taking early retirement from his legal firm, which in 1900 he handed on to two of his sons, Frank and Arthur. Walter and Georgina, with their daughters, then moved from London to Norwich, where Walter had already established a very favourable reputation, and in 1908 he became, by invitation, the city's Mayor. Ever since, he has been hailed as one of Norwich's notables.

Georgina's death in 1910 led to an increasingly lonely existence, as first one and then another of his now grown-up daughters left home. His ever-present sense of his own mortality spurred him on to compile in 1916 an autobiography, which was privately printed mainly for the benefit of his family and friends. He surprised himself and others by living on for a further thirteen years, although by then he was failing physically and much of his literary output in this final period represented a sort of desk-clearing rather than new work.

Antiquary and historian

Edward Rye, Walter's father, was by some accounts rather cold and remote, but there are signs too that he actively opened the young Walter's eyes to aspects of history and the heritage. Of his neglect – benevolent or otherwise – it can at least be said that it provided Walter with the opportunity to delve into his father's extensive library. It also encouraged him and his brothers to develop outside interests including natural history and sport, and through those in turn to make new friends and become more independent of the parental household.

The Rye family had roots in medieval Norfolk, and Walter's keen desire even as a teenager to understand his family's history in context sowed the seeds of lifelong interests in genealogy at large, and in the history, topography and antiquities of Norfolk in particular. From the 1860s, while still in training as a solicitor, he took out a reader's ticket at the Public Record Office. This was less than a decade after the PRO had first opened its tiny search room to the public, and although he was not one of the very first generation of readers he is one of the first whose name we actually know. Here he immersed himself in the archives, trawling systematically through sources that seemed most likely to have a bearing on Norfolk's history – both for his own interest and also acting on commission from others. The records had never been trawled like this before, and for the next three decades Walter made frequent skirmishes through them, copying and abstracting them and publishing transcripts, calendars, lists and indexes for the benefit of a wider public, often at his own expense. In his last two decades, when failing eyesight got the better of him, he employed record agents including at least one of his daughters to check references and undertake new work on his behalf at the PRO.

His strongly opinionated and polemical book *Records and Record Searching* (first edition 1887 and still available in print today) became a national, not just a local, best-seller and a *vade mecum* for generations of scholars and genealogists approaching archival sources for the first time.

A passion for Norwich and Norfolk

He was far from being an 'ex-pat' historian working on his ancestral county at a distance but never venturing there. On the contrary, he had begun to visit Norfolk even as a boy, before he knew much at all about archives, although he took with him a clear understanding of the importance of monumental inscriptions from studying those in Fulham parish churchyard not far from his home. It took no time at all for him to become fixated with Norfolk, and for most of his professional life he would spend every available moment of his holidays visiting that county, which he came to know as well on the ground, mile by mile, as he did from the parchments, inch by inch.

His mission was helped by a precociously sociable temperament. He developed both an ear for listening to and an eye for observing local gossip and folklore, dialect, songs and traditions. Chance conversations over a farm gate or at the local inn often proved as valuable in his overall scheme of things as did his days of copying down inscriptions, or extracts from records.

But Walter, from his very first visit to Norfolk, also began to build up a nexus of more serious friendships, especially among the clergy and antiquaries of the county who might be able to open doors for him into the local sources of history and genealogy. From this arose more enduring friendships than those casual, gossipy encounters, and eventually he gained an entrée into a number of local societies, beginning with the Norfolk and Norwich Archaeological Society (with which, however, he would develop a stormy relationship). As the years went by, he would travel around Norfolk by train and dog-cart, on foot, by bicycle and tricycle. And not least by boat, for he became a keen sailor on the Broads and a notable champion, in print and in the courts, both of their preservation and of the public's right of access to them. He was one of the founders of the Norfolk Broads Protection Society and its honorary solicitor, although in his day some of the wider freedoms he sought for the public were never admitted either by the landowners or by the law.

Walter Rye still figures prominently in the roll of honour of Norfolk antiquaries, on the basis of his very successful *Tourists' Guide to Norfolk* (first edition 1879), his *History of Norfolk* (1885), his massive *Norfolk Families* (1911–1913) and many published studies of individual families, parishes and towns, and his guides to and transcripts of original archival sources for the county. He contributed a number of essays on Norfolk antiquaries to the *Dictionary of National Biography,* and worked for a time on the Norfolk section of the *Victoria County History*, although this latter assignment was brought to a premature end by a combination of his own genuine struggle with failing eyesight and fundamental disagreement with the general editor's vision for the project.

Walter Rye is also remembered as the champion and preserver, in his day, of historic buildings in Norwich that might otherwise have fallen into decay or into the hands of unsympathetic developers. These included Anguish's

House, the Maid's Head Hotel (still, happily, going strong), Bacon's House and the Lazar House. So he was already well known and loved in the city of Norwich by the time he retired there in 1900.

Also in Norwich he joined a number of non-sporting social clubs, including the Woodpeckers Art Club and the Science Gossip Club. And although he professed to being rather shy and nervous as a public speaker, this did not prevent him giving frequent entertaining and sententious lectures on a wide range of topics, often illustrated by lantern slides.

In 1908–9, despite having only recently become politically active and having no previous service on the city council (save on its library committee), and despite also having by then a very sick wife, he was persuaded to stand as a stop-gap candidate for Mayor of Norwich. He was duly elected for what turned out to be a very successful, but to him distinctly stressful and rather dreary, year of office that encompassed a visit by King Edward VII, the first royal visit to the city since the seventeenth century. As a roundel he inserted in a window of the parish church at Lammas has it, he was the 'last Mayor of Norwich', because a Lord Mayoralty was bestowed on the city under his successor, Walter having preferred to be known by the ancient title Mayor.

He bequeathed his large collection of books and manuscripts to the Norwich City Library, of which he was a keen supporter.

Author and controversialist

Like others of the Victorian 'chattering class', Walter Rye had firm and often strongly negative opinions on most things. In what follows I have let him have his own say, first to give the reader a sense of the man, his humour, enthusiasms and pet hates, but secondly to show what some of his friends and contemporaries had to put up with from this master of the put-down! His contentious, often reactionary views were aired not only in his lectures but also in the prefaces, texts and footnotes of many of his publications, and in the correspondence and feature columns of national and local newspapers and quality magazines such as *The Athenaeum*, to which he was a regular contributor. Between 1867 and 1929 Walter Rye published some eighty books, ranging from short pamphlets to lengthy histories. In the same period he authored something like 150 articles. If we add to these the prodigious quantity of articles, notes and letters he wrote to national and local newspapers (of which many cuttings survive, uncatalogued, among his papers), his published writings must have run to several million words. It would be an achievement indeed to read every word of his that survives in print.

His determination to speak out, even to the brink of libel or slander, on matters such as fraudulent claims to antiquity or status by gentry families; false claims to sporting records by athletes; careless research or presentation by antiquaries and historians; the destruction of the heritage by developers and town or city councils; the deplorable effects of tourism; the way in which (as he thought) the labouring class shirked military duties in wartime; and many other highly contentious issues, naturally won him enemies, especially where his remarks became public and personal, as they often did. He once described himself as a 'good hater'. Those he offended included the heads of families whose genealogical descent he publicly questioned; individuals and institutions whose taste or judgement he impugned; and almost anyone (including his supposed friends) who had the temerity to suggest that he had misused or misread the evidence on which his argument depended. He was quick to get his feathers ruffled, and was not one to let matters rest once sparring had commenced, no matter how many rounds it might take, to the irritation not only of his antagonists but also of some of his friends and advisers.

Yet his outspokenness also gained him friends and champions who remained fiercely loyal even when he had bitten off more than he could chew in the latest public controversy. From his surviving correspondence it is clear that to intimates, though he was indeed infuriating and incorrigible, he could also be warm-hearted and kindly, fun-loving and highly sociable. As one of them put it as a joke by writing the letters after his name, he was 'OOTB'. One Of The Best!

Outspoken though he was, on the whole his writings were very well received by reviewers in both the local and the national press and the quality journals. And this solid reputation among his contemporaries cannot be lightly dismissed. To many he was simply a star whose every writing or utterance was eagerly awaited. They were awestruck – and who could blame them? – by his prodigious output and the sheer scale of his endeavour. But for the most part they lacked any real familiarity with the kind of sources he was using, so their judgement on the merits of his work tended to be influenced by secondary factors such as whether he told a good story (which he generally did) or presented his case well (which he sometimes did not).

But before we get swept along by all this adulation there are other things to consider. Although he was often highly critical of other people's mistakes, Walter's own research and writings were far from being the epitome of perfection. And he knew it. Lacking a university education, as a writer he was a proudly self-trained amateur. His publications were for the most part self-funded: very little was, as we would now say, 'peer-reviewed', not least because there were few who could claim to be his peer in record searching. He admitted that his work contained errors of transcription, editing, interpretation and proof-reading. At the very end of his long life he came to understand what others had been telling him for years, that the thread of his argument in his more controversial historical, antiquarian and genealogical writings was sometimes lost in a fog of minute detail that none but he could follow.

Perhaps it is too harsh to judge him by today's standards: the reader must decide. But given all that has changed since Walter Rye's time – the increased professionalisation of the study of history, the great expansion of interest in local history and opening up of countless additional sources, and the honing of research techniques – his interpretations and opinions, his transcriptions, and, yes, even some of his 'facts', can legitimately be scrutinised more robustly than was possible at the time.

Good hater or OOTB, he was still a highly desirable catch for a dinner party – at least, among those who could hold their own against this larger-than-life character. He could also prove a useful ally in public campaigns, especially when it came to preserving old buildings or defending public rights on the Broads. In turn, he himself could be a generous host. He threw lavish parties at his successive London homes, and even to a lesser extent in Norwich and at his rural retreat at Lammas, where space for entertaining was more constrained, particularly after his wife's health went into steep decline.

Walter's image, as a seriously overweight (at times over seventeen stone) and boisterous bon viveur, gossip, humourist and practical joker, shines through these pages, but the picture would not be complete without mention of his gentler side: as a gardener, friend and family man; and his vulnerability, including the continual – and by no means irrational – dread of impending death that stalked him throughout his (actually very long) life of eighty-five years.

Water Rye died in 1929. Obituaries spoke fulsomely of his achievements, and many lamented the passing of a giant whose like would not be seen again. Sadly today that fame has been dulled, except in a few specialist circles. It is high time to give it a polish!

2
ANCESTRY, BOYHOOD
AND YOUTH (1843–1866)

Rye ancestry

Walter Rye traced his paternal ancestry to a certain Edward Rye of Cromer, Norfolk, who had died in 1698. Walter's valiant attempts to establish deeper roots among the medieval Ryes of that county were frustrated, largely owing to the loss of Cromer's earlier parish registers.

From that Edward Rye, the male line descended through five generations, successively in Cromer, Erpingham, South Repps, Barningham Parva and finally Baconsthorpe, until it arrived at Walter's great-grandfather, James Rye who died at Baconsthorpe aged eighty-six in 1829.

Edward Rye senior (1774–1843), Walter's grandfather

James's second son, born in 1774, was Walter's grandfather Edward Rye – let us call him 'Edward senior' to distinguish him from Walter's father, who was also called Edward. Edward senior grew up in Baconsthorpe, and his destiny appeared to lie in the family farming tradition, but he had other ideas and ran away from home, becoming first a collier at Wells-next-the-Sea. Some time later – the record is patchy – he set out to try his fortune in London. It remains a mystery what if any contacts he already had there, but he must have had either friends or extremely good luck, because we next find him established as a wine merchant in the City. In 1800, now formally described as a 'victualler', he was admitted to the Needlemakers Company.[1] Normally admission was by one of three routes: apprenticeship, payment of a large entry fee, or patrimony. The last route clearly did not apply in Edward's case, but since neither of the other two seems much more plausible we can only speculate how he qualified for admission.

The company was thriving when he joined. The names of fifty-four new members were entered in its register for that year,[2] which also shows that if he had attended company functions at all regularly he would have mixed with merchants and tradesmen of every description, although by far the largest number were simply described as 'victuallers' like himself. But as there is no indication that he advanced to the livery or to any office within the company in the twenty-nine years of his remaining life in the City, it may not have played a large part in Edward's business or social life.[3]

Whilst Edward senior was the first of his family to venture to the capital for work, and seems to have quickly put down London roots and before long married and started a family, according to Walter he would frequently return to Norfolk by coach. He loved travel, and even went on mystery tours by coach with his 'great boon companion', Charles Burtt.

Edward's domestic life in London proved very peripatetic. We find him living successively in Glasshouse Street (Regent Street), York Buildings (New Road), Portland Place, Woodstock Street, and Westmoreland Street (Marylebone), before he eventually took the lease of a property in the newly built Quadrant in Lower James Street. This would later house the first office for his son Edward junior (Walter's father) when he embarked on business as a solicitor. Edward senior became wealthy enough to invest in property, and the income generated made him well-to-do. By 1840 he had retired to live in Gloucester Terrace, Park Wall, Little Chelsea, where he died on 21 September 1843.[4]

Edward Rye junior (1803–1876), Walter's father

Edward Rye junior was born on 2 February 1803 and baptised at St Andrew Holborn. He was to be the only surviving child of his parents' marriage: his brother George died tragically in childhood, scalded to death by the steam from a kettle, and his sister Mary also died in infancy.[5] By 1814 at the latest he was a pupil at Mr Mason's Academy in Knightsbridge, where he acquired a good knowledge of Latin and won a silver medal for handwriting. Then, in 1816 – perhaps evidence of his father's influence in the City – a 'nomination' was obtained for him[6] to St Paul's School, where all we know is that his

Edward Rye, Walter's father.
Peter Rye.

handwriting again continued to win him prizes. This was not a skill he would pass on to his son Walter! At some point before or after St Paul's he was sent for a short time to St Omer to improve his French.

At the age of sixteen, in March 1819, he was articled to Thomas Bland of Messrs Jones and Bland at 34 Great Marylebone Street to train as a solicitor. His fellow trainees were Thomas Smith, who would later become Walter's clerk (a 'most eccentric man', according to Walter), and G. W. W. Bramwell (later the prominent judge, Lord Bramwell), who in due course would become Walter's godfather and regular legal confidant. On the completion of his training Edward was admitted solicitor on 19 June 1824 at the age of twenty-one, and set up practice at the Quadrant.[7] The following year he moved out of the parental home to live at 2 Lower James Street, off Golden Square.

Golden Square and King's Parade

In 1828, at St James's Piccadilly, now aged twenty-five, Edward married Maria, the daughter of Benjamin Tuppen, a wealthy Brighton builder, and since she brought as her marriage settlement a nice property portfolio, both his family and his business interests seemed for a while to be on a very sound footing.[8] Maria bore three children in rapid succession: Maria Susan (1829), Elizabeth ('Bessie', 1830), and Edward Caldwell Rye ('EC', 1832).[9] In 1830

Edward bought[10] the lease of 16 Golden Square, which temporarily served as the family's home but doubled as his new solicitor's office, a purpose it would continue to serve for decades to come.[11]

The *Survey of London* has charted the changing social and occupational mix of Golden Square from its origins in the early eighteenth century down to the First World War. The buildings went through successive incarnations, first as residences of gentry and titled persons, then diplomatic residences; later there was an influx of foreign artists and harpsichord and piano manufacturers; and by the time Edward settled there the square was a mix of residences and offices of professional men, with a number of hotels and boarding houses. By 1870 there would be no fewer than sixteen solicitors, but after that their numbers sharply declined and it became a centre of the woollen and worsted trades.[12]

Walter would later remember No. 16 as an old house, panelled throughout.

Cardinal Wiseman had lived opposite and had had his windows broken at the time of the 'No Popery Riots'. Tradition said it had once been the residence of the Spanish Ambassador and that it was the house described by Dickens.[13]

This must refer to the second chapter of *Nicholas Nickleby* (1839). Dickens places Ralph Nickleby's office in Golden Square:

Although a few members of the graver professions live about Golden Square, it is not exactly in anybody's way to or from anywhere. It is one of the squares that have been; a quarter of the town that has gone down in the world, and taken to letting lodgings. Many of its first and second floors are let, furnished, to single gentlemen; and it takes boarders besides. It is a great resort of foreigners. The dark-complexioned men who wear large rings, and heavy watch-guards, and bushy whiskers, and who congregate under the Opera Colonnade, and about the box-office in the season, between four and five in the afternoon, when they give away the orders – all live in Golden Square, or within a street of it. Two or three violins and a wind instrument from the Opera band reside within its precincts. Its boarding-houses are musical, and the notes of pianos and harps float in the evening time round the head of the mournful statue, the guardian genius of a little wilderness of shrubs, in the centre of the square. On a summer's night, windows are thrown open, and groups of swarthy moustached men are seen by the passer-by, lounging at the casements, and smoking fearfully. Sounds of gruff voices practising vocal music invade the evening's silence; and the fumes of choice tobacco scent the air. There, snuff and cigars, and German pipes and flutes, and violins and violoncellos, divide the supremacy between them. It is the region of song and smoke. Street bands are on their mettle in Golden Square; and itinerant glee-singers quaver involuntarily as they raise their voices within its boundaries. This would not seem a spot very well adapted to the transaction of business; but Mr Ralph Nickleby had lived there, notwithstanding, for many years, and uttered no complaint on that score.

… and presumably, neither did Edward or the succeeding generations of the Rye family!

Walter wrote that:

There was a great well in the gardens, which had the most beautifully cool water, but it was closed when the cholera scare was about, as Broad Street, Golden Square, was one of the greatest centres of the disease, and I remembered a black flag hanging out of a window there. Popular rumour ascribed the cholera to the disturbance of the plague pit, which was once at the back of Silver Street, Golden Square.

By 1833 business was booming sufficiently for Edward to take on a partner, John Harris. But this proved financially disastrous and only five years later the partnership had to be broken up. Before those problems, Edward had been able in 1835 to buy a long lease on a house at 14 King's Parade, Chelsea on the Fielder Estate from a distant relative, Mary Caldwell. Two further children would be born there before the 1841 census: Mary Anne (1837, known as 'Mary' or 'Annie') and Charles (1839).[14]

With the collapse of his partnership and the resulting financial losses, the family only remained afloat by drawing on Maria's private fortune, although the situation was temporarily eased when Edward senior died in 1843, leaving substantial property.[15]

Birth of Walter Rye

Our man Walter Rye was born on 31 October 1843, six weeks after his grandfather's death. He reflected in later life that, with Hallowe'en for a birthday and the fact that he was his parents' seventh child, he had every right to have been endowed with extra-sensory perception. But he was sorely disappointed: as far as the supernatural was concerned he would have to make do with recounting (usually de-bunking) folk tales, and sceptically reporting or mocking other people's supposed ghostly experiences.

Just to re-cap, at the time of his birth Walter had five surviving siblings: three sisters (Maria Susan, Elizabeth and Mary Ann) and two brothers (Edward Caldwell Rye, always known as EC, and Charles). The eldest, Maria Susan, was about fourteen. Charles, about whom very little is recorded, was four, and the large age gap between him and Walter may well be explained by the birth of a still-born child in between. Some such event must have occurred if Walter was indeed the seventh child. Charles seems not to have survived to adulthood.[16]

Of Walter's earliest years we know very little, save for a passing reflection that, 'My father being a very studious man and my mother very fond of gardening, I was left chiefly in the hands of an old aunt[17] who spoiled me extremely'.[18] With Walter's arrival and a live-in nurse to add to the existing family, not to mention his father's growing book collection,[19] the shortage of space at No. 14 became acute. Very conveniently the house next door, No. 15 King's Parade, fell vacant, and in 1844 Edward acquired that in addition to No. 14. Within a year of Walter's birth Edward had had a wall knocked through to combine the two properties into one dwelling with a grand total of twenty rooms. Here two further children would be born, Clara Louise (1846), and Francis (known as 'Frank', 1848).

Edward's first priority, in order to provide for his large family, was naturally his legal business, which after the bruising experience of the failed partnership, he guarded rather jealously. Outside working hours his book collection took up much of his time and interest, and perhaps intentionally distracted him from greater involvement in fatherly duties. From the children's point of view this was not necessarily a bad thing: growing up in a house full of books and pictures to which they had ready access was itself a formative influence. But it did mean that the boys largely had to fend for themselves. We shall see below how Walter came to rely especially on his eldest brother, EC, who was ten years his senior, and with whom he spent much time in the outdoors.

In the new scheme of things EC, Walter and Frank were given rooms in No. 15 but their father was still counting every penny and austerity prevailed. The house was left uncarpeted. The windows were ill-fitting and in the winter snow came in through the gaps. Only one fire a week was allowed, and that was in the library so that the books could be consulted in comfort! The boys' rooms had no fireplaces or heat. If there was no serious problem for the books, there certainly was for the human occupants. Character-forming it might have been, but Walter later speculated that these conditions contributed to the consumption that eventually carried off his much-loved brother Frank.

At the time of the 1851 census, all eight children (ranging in age from two to eighteen) were still living at home with Mary Tuppen, the aunt aged forty-five, now described as a living-in governess.

St Peter's Collegiate School

When in his own estimation 'very young', Walter followed EC and Charles at what he described as 'a school of very pretentious character called St Peter's Collegiate School, Eaton Square', a Church of England establishment run in association with it's parent institution, King's College, London. In all probability this came about through the good offices of Revd Charles Kingsley, the evangelical parish priest of St Luke's, Chelsea,[20] who taught at King's College.

Walter guardedly makes no personal judgement on the academic prowess of the then headmaster of St Peter's (which is also confusingly referred to in some sources as King's College School), but quotes a fellow pupil as saying that 'he [the head] had not the qualifications of a fourth-form schoolboy'. As to the man's character, Walter remembered him as 'wantonly brutal and severe to a degree, and… justly hated by all his pupils'. It is sad to reflect how typical this ambience was, even at highly reputed schools at the time.[21]

Perhaps as a result of their shared misfortune, some of Walter's schoolmates became close friends, foremost among them being E. F. Gallaher. Walter spent many hours at the Gallahers' house, and Mrs Gallaher became almost a surrogate mother to him. When, a few years later, Walter first considered applying for a reader's ticket at the British Museum he asked Gallaher to write him a character reference, even though Walter was still aged only seventeen and the minimum age for admittance was eighteen. Passing the burden of this moral dilemma squarely back to Walter, Gallaher advised: 'If when you present this paper in the Reading Room *you are asked whether you are 18 and say no* you will be told to *return when you are 18*. So you will know what to say.'[22]

While Walter was subsequently attending night school at King's College (as we shall see in due course), he met up with another old schoolmate from St Peter's, E. Fitzgerald,[23] who became a walking and rowing companion. Fitzgerald later reported corresponding with 'Gibson', another former pupil of St Peter's, who seems to have been branded by both of them as an inveterate liar. Fitzgerald said he had written to Gibson: 'I take no interest in St Peter's School and my recollection of it may be summed up in two words: "time lost"', to which Gibson had replied that 'Ed Rye' [EC] had lately expressed an opposite opinion. But, Fitzgerald added, perhaps this was another of Gibson's lies.[24]

Walter records that Ekin, the head boy in his day, went on to become a scholar of Exeter College Oxford, and that another of the senior boys, Billy Groves, who was a good friend of Walter's brother Charles and looked kindly on his sibling, became a Cambridge wrangler. Others of Walter's contemporaries eventually became a judge, a Member of Parliament and a town clerk respectively. Richard (Dick) Howlett, whom we shall often meet in this story because Walter stayed closely in touch with him throughout his life, rose to a senior position in the Civil Service Commission. So, however dismal the school may have been in Walter's eyes, it seems to have produced a crop of high achievers.

Entomology and athletics

The Rye brothers' pastimes during their school days included natural history. EC, Walter's role model who would later become a renowned entomologist, introduced him to his own passionate interest in the collection and study of insects and butterflies. They went on walks and expeditions together to gather specimens. EC was also an oarsman and an athlete, and in these pursuits too Walter became his disciple.[25]

Walter quits school and enters his father's legal practice

As Walter entered his teens, he had finally had enough of St Peter's School, and at the age of fourteen begged his father to be allowed to leave. Edward let him have his own way, but then made no further educational provision for him, perhaps feeling that the lad must learn to live with the consequences of his own decisions. He did, however, take Walter on as a junior clerk at Golden Square, where EC was already similarly employed. The two boys used to walk together the three or so miles from Chelsea to the office and back every day, and this no doubt helped develop Walter's passion for 'pedestrianism' (walking as a sport).

Business at Golden Square was evidently less than brisk. There was insufficient work to go round so the boys were paid only a pittance by way of pocket money by their father and were given long breaks to go off and amuse themselves, which provided more opportunities for walking, athletics and natural history, and eventually, when Walter was of an age to obtain reader's tickets at the key libraries, for antiquarian research. As he became more experienced in the legal work, he persuaded his father to pay him *pro rata* for work actually undertaken, which actually proved more remunerative than the previous casual contributions and enabled him to build up some savings. He was probably quite glad to get out of the office, which in winter was unheated unless the boys collected the firm's coal from outside and made their own fires, so they surely felt the cold at work as well as at home.

Even so, all was not gloom, for in addition to family holidays, traditionally taken at Herne Bay, his father (possibly in connection with trips made for business reasons) sometimes took Walter to 'show him antiquities'. On three successive trips in 1857 they visited Salisbury and Stonehenge; Cambridge and Ely; Sandwich, Canterbury and Richborough. In 1859 (noteworthy as Walter's first visit to Norfolk), they went to King's Lynn and stayed at Paradise House with Dr J. V. Hawkins.[26] The following year found them at Winchester, St Cross, Portsmouth (HMS *Victory*) and Netley Abbey.

But then, as Walter became older and more independent-minded, he would holiday on his own, not only to break away from the parental rein, but also to put in some serious walking. In August 1861 he went to Walton-on-the-Naze and walked to Colchester, but found it 'a slow, dull holiday, for I had no companion'. In 1862 he persuaded Dick Howlett to join him in travelling by train to St Albans and walking back.

Returns to night school at King's College

Walter's stipend presumably had to cover lunch, his main meal of the day (for in the evening back at Chelsea supper comprised only a very light snack), so at first there cannot have been a great deal of cash to spare. But gradually, modest savings began to accumulate, which were sufficient to persuade him, of his own volition, to return to formal education by enrolling for evening classes at King's College London on four evenings a week.

These classes had been established for just such students as Walter: young men with only a rather basic education to date, who wanted to prepare themselves for wider opportunities in business, commerce and the professions. They came to the college from day jobs, mainly in the cities of London and Westminster, and as they had to pay their own fees they were well motivated to achieve good results. College rules required them to enrol to study at least five subjects including a compulsory course in Divinity (which therefore had a very large class, under Mr Plumtre). Walter began by studying English, Mathematics and Arithmetic, but branched out later into German and Book Keeping.

At the end of each year there were examinations, and those boys with the highest aggregate scores in their five subjects received prizes. We find Walter receiving a prize for Arithmetic and Book Keeping in the spring of 1862. Dr Jelfe, the Principal, noted at the prize-giving that the students:

> ... were all trained up in habits of business, and so knew how to make good use of their time. This was especially seen in the manner in which they took notes of the lectures, which they treated as they did entries in book-keeping, regularly posting them for future reference in the 'ledger' of their minds.[27]

Academic attainment alone was not sufficient. They also had to prove themselves 'regular and punctual in their attendance on lectures and at the college chapel on Sunday mornings and [to] have brought with them to the examination certificates of good conduct'.[28] It was a distinctly arduous course, but clearly stimulated these young men.

For several years, therefore, Walter would work for his father during the day and then go on to King's in the evenings, already a demanding enough regime. But then, from King's as from Golden Square previously, he would walk home late at night. It is hard to imagine what time was left for recreation, but somehow, as we shall see, he managed to train as an athlete (and indeed to represent King's College at athletics meetings both in London and further afield),[29] and to begin serious antiquarian research, having learnt to read old hands in part through his legal training.

Chelsea Athenaeum

His education, and his grasp of wider affairs, was also extended by occasional attendance at the Chelsea Athenaeum, a sort of debating society run by the Reverend W. W. Robinson of St Luke's Chelsea, whom Walter thought a 'worthy and reverend bore'.[30] What he really thought of Robinson is revealed in a fragment of juvenile doggerel reproduced in his later book *Rubbish and Nonsense*.[31]

> A new hymn to Ye tune of Jerusalem the Golden:
> In Smith Street, King's Road, Chelsea
> The drunkards shall have rest
> For Robinson is going
> Who long hath them opprest.
>
> With tract and dreary lecture,
> With all his might and main,
> Each drunken man and woman
> Long hath he plied in vain.
>
> For though his soup and tickets
> Right willingly they took,
> Ne'er read they of his pamphlets,
> Nor trusted in his book.
>
> Said they 'His Curate Billy'
> Grows fatter every day
> ... *caetera desunt*.[32]

Members of the Athenaeum took it in turn to present a short paper or an argument. When his turn came, Walter prepared a contribution on the

Romans in Britain, only to flunk it on the night and after an attack of nerves persuade another member to read it for him! This nervousness at speaking in public would remain with him throughout his life.

Sunday schools

At about the age of sixteen, no doubt under the influence (but certainly in the footsteps) of his much older sister Maria,[33] Walter volunteered as a Sunday school teacher. How this came about, and how difficult it was, is described in an essay written in 1866, a few years after the events described. Again it was published in *Rubbish and Nonsense*.[34] In it he reflects that from time to time everyone is made aware of his own and other people's sinfulness, and of the need to do something about it. But if the moment for action is not seized, the urge for repentance fades! One Sunday, he heard a young Anglican clergyman preaching on how Sunday schools could help tackle social deprivation and its concomitant ills and counteract the influence of 'half-penny numbers of vile periodicals' which teach that theft is a virtue and adultery a pardonable amusement. Other denominations, said the preacher, were making a better fist of this than the Anglicans. Roman Catholics were 'quietly pushing their way' and making converts even in the foulest districts. Dissenters were working with a will in 'dingy schoolrooms, hot with the breath of plague and disease'. Meanwhile, the Church of England was 'sole laggard in the race'.

Walter examined his conscience. 'Hard worked all day in town, I was fit for nothing in the week-day evenings.' But, feeling perhaps for the first time the moral imperative to do something to improve society, why might he not volunteer for duty as a Sunday school teacher? The opportunity came through the same Mr Robinson of the Chelsea Athenaeum.

In Walter's view, the Sunday school's surroundings were not fit for purpose: 'paint was a tradition, dirt an undeniable fact and whitewash an embodied doubt'. He was immediately put to the test by being given charge of a class whose teacher happened to be absent. Having survived this, he was given a class of his own. Soon the disheartening reality dawned on him that few of the six-to eight-year-old boys in his charge could read or write, and that their powers of concentration were slight. They liked to listen to stories but not to seek out the moral to be drawn from them. So Walter had to devise for himself a way of interweaving instructive morals with the stories as he went along. He discovered that long tracts, or for that matter readings from Scripture, were not the way to engage a boy's mind, and that in any case, as a layman, he himself did not have a sufficient grounding in Scripture to use that resource to fill up the teaching time. Instead, he drew on his own experiences of nature and observation to develop something more inspiring, bringing in on the way 'the advantages of honesty, the danger of theft and lying, kindness to animals, etc.' He did not suppose this would work with the older boys, but it appeared to do the trick with those in his immediate charge.

The different classes all met in the same large hall, where indiscipline was rife. When other teachers in the same room could not keep the attention of their pupils missiles were hurled about. 'In fact, a teacher had to defend himself in much about the same way as a cricketer his wicket'. The scale of the problem was such that one day Walter thought he would count up the number of missiles thrown at him, and collected forty-seven bits of orange peel and pips!

He was highly critical of the lack of any real training for the job, and blamed clergymen-superintendents who appeared to assume that it was the easiest thing in the world to take a Sunday school class, and whose interest was limited to inviting the staff round once in a while for Bible reading followed by 'unpleasant hospitality in the shape of tea and muffins'. He noted too that the clergy tended to show respect to upper-class teachers and be rude to the rest, where in truth all of them needed encouragement. Apart from one who was a postman, and Walter himself a legal clerk, the teachers were all shopmen. He suspected that apathy on the part of the superintendent would soon lead to the break-up of the school.

This socially valuable work was exhausting. 'My work on Sundays,' he wrote, 'is twice as hard as it is on week days – and I am no flaneur, no government clerk.' And the ratio of students to staff was too great for there to be any serious impact on individuals. As soon as class was over he felt he had to escape to the country for long walks to reinvigorate the soul. 'I wish I could tell half the delight I feel in those long walks when I have left the babel of tongues, the hot stifling atmosphere, the thousand petty troubles and disappointments behind me.'

Knowing what it was like to miss out completely on a high school or university education, and therefore to have the cards heavily stacked against you for some walks of life at least, Walter also helped at this time with a very rough night school at Paradise Row, Chelsea, although he has left no account of that. He would later ensure that his own sons did not lack educational opportunity.

Discovering Norfolk

A charming fragment of a diary, also reproduced in *Rubbish and Nonsense*, describes Walter's first solo trip to Norfolk in 1863 when he was nineteen. He rose early, taking an 'affectionate but somewhat hurried farewell of my family who were at the moment in question in different parts of the house'. His knapsack overloaded and very heavy with clothes, books and food and drink for the journey, he took the omnibus from Chelsea, which dropped him about a mile from Bishopsgate Station, so he had to complete this part of his journey on foot, staggering under the weight of his baggage.

With very little money in his pocket, he had to travel third class, which put him in working-class company, on seats 18-inches wide, and gave him an opportunity for people-watching. As a relative novice in rail travel (though he had been on train journeys previously with his father), he mistakenly settled down on a seat facing the engine and next to a window, which seemed best while the train was in the station but as soon as it was under way he was covered in dust and dirt.

The atmosphere on board was good humoured. Everyone, male and female, seemed to smoke, and as soon as the train set off they started eating. All, that is, except Walter who saved his picnic until everyone else had finished theirs. Before long he was engaged in conversation by a 'worthy but slightly troublesome British workman of radical opinions and great fluency of incorrect speech'. Between bouts of conversation, however, Walter managed to read the *Sporting Life* from end to end. All the way from Cambridge to Ely, a 'comic man' entertained the carriage with a story then sang a song critical of Ely's municipal authorities.

The journey to Norwich took in all five and a half hours. On arrival he waited 'till all the lot of nasty common vulgar people who had, like myself, come by the London excursion, had cleared out.' He then found his way on foot to the Market Place and an inn, 'the O...'[35] opposite the Guildhall. Worried that in his dusty and dishevelled state he might be turned away, he said he had just walked from London in two days! He was given a nice quiet room upstairs overlooking the Guildhall, with 'clean bed, gas laid on, etc.' He took tea in the coffee room on the first floor, then dutifully wrote to tell 'the mum' that he had safely arrived. He put his feet up and lit a cigar, 'the worst I ever smoked', before going to the post office, 'enjoying the talk and accent of the passing rustics amazingly'.

Tired from the journey, and with nothing better to do, he decided to have an early night. But he was woken at 4am next morning (Sunday) by men clearing rubbish from the Market Place. Despite the early hour he went for a walk before breakfast, after which he went to the cathedral, 'nearly the best I ever saw', with a prayer book borrowed from the landlord. He observes, 'there are plenty of free seats for paupers like myself, to whom the vergers were perfectly civil'. He was impressed by the sermon, although the preacher kept stumbling over his words. After 'dinner' (lunch) he set off for Baconsthorpe – at road-walking pace, but with occasional stops to note down churchyard inscriptions – to find the graves of his great grandfather and great grandmother. He had hoped while there to inspect the parish registers, but the parish clerk was 'out a-harvesting' with the entire male population, and the rector out for a drive with his wife.

Here the fragment finishes, but from the *Autobiography* we find that on this visit he also had his first meeting with the antiquary John L'Estrange at the Stamp Office in Norwich, who afterwards helped him build on what he already knew of deeds from his legal training to read old documents and understand the language and formulae in which they were written. We shall return to this below.

Father and son

In the *Autobiography* Walter shows every respect for both his parents. He tries to portray his father as a kindly man, but one who was often unwilling to give his sons credit for their achievements. At least for public consumption he described him as a man of 'wide and varied reading', a connoisseur of books and paintings, and a lawyer of good repute to whom many other lawyers turned for advice. Although the record is sparse and sombre, Edward does seem to have given his sons some moderate fatherly encouragement, including access to his library, introductions to famous local people, the trips out of town already mentioned and of course the all-important business openings (albeit poorly paid) when they left school.

The regime both in the office and at home was quite spartan, but later, after bringing up children of his own, Walter seems largely to have accepted as inevitable the austerities of his childhood. Privately he may have harboured harsher feelings.

We catch occasional glimpses of real family bonding, as in that 'affectionate' leave-taking and letter-writing when he went on his first solo trip to Norwich. Few letters of a personal or family nature have survived in his archive at the Norfolk Record Office, but two isolated letters – perhaps deliberately kept as reminders of a happy side in an otherwise fraught relationship – give tiny windows on to the interplay between father and son during Walter's early professional career. The first, in October 1865, when Walter was almost twenty-two, is primarily an account of a holiday taken by Edward and Maria in the north of England, from which bad weather was forcing them to return earlier than planned. A casual postscript ('… Belcher & Metropt.: Any appointment for Wednesday or Thursday will suit very well')[36] suggests that Edward had left Walter (now qualified) in charge of the business diary. The account of the holiday itself is also of more than passing interest, for it suggests in passing that Edward might have been a teetotaller. If so, this was another trait that Walter failed to inherit!

> On Monday we went to Hardwick Hall, distant 16 miles, and saw the noble old Tudor Mansion with its pictures and furniture to great perfection – the carpets being down and everything ready to receive the Duke of Devonshire who was coming the next day, when the House will be closed to the public for six weeks. Visitors come from all quarters and of every degree. Sometimes as many as 700 in a day – most persons enter their names in a book in the Great Hall. I saw the Duke of Argyll had been there not long since. Yesterday (Friday) we took rail to Manchester and spent a pleasant day among the mills and warehouses of the cotton princes. We dined at a grand temperance hotel of the poorest architecture and water. Everything here is on a grand scale… [*They went on to Nottingham Goose fair*]: I had never seen such a sight since the time of our Bartholomew. The Market Place, the largest in England, was full to overflowing, and I should think there will be 50,000 headaches tomorrow tho' many thousands like ourselves came away in sober sadness.[37]

Two years later, we find the second surviving letter, written when the situation was reversed and Edward (the father) was minding the business while his sons Walter and Frank were on their respective summer holidays, Frank with friends in Whitby, and Walter significantly contactable only c/o John L'Estrange at the Stamp Office in Norwich. Edward writes that he is glad Walter has:

> … done Cromer Church even to the foundations thereof and found earlier churches and Ryes. I can only account for the absence of the [fish] by your frightening hum whilst swimming – the fish, naturally taking you for a Rhinoceros, get alarmed and depart the coast – let us hope Frank will catch some in the north.[38]

This seems to show a good-humoured and affectionate side to Edward. But there is no escaping the overall impression of him from Walter's *Autobiography* as a distant and aloof father who showed little sign of open affection.

King's Road

By the time of the 1861 census the Rye family had moved to another pair of adjacent houses, at 284-286 King's Road, Chelsea. The full household

John L'Estrange.
Autobiography.

then comprised Edward (Walter's father, now aged fifty-eight) and Maria (mother, fifty-seven); Maria Susan (thirty-two), EC (twenty-eight), Walter (seventeen), Clara Louisa (fourteen) and Frank (twelve), plus Aunt Mary Tuppen (fifty-eight), a cook and a housemaid. Elizabeth [Bessie] (thirty) and Mary Ann [Annie] (twenty-three) were not present, but were probably only away on holiday on census day. From other evidence it appears that the parents and daughters lived at No. 284 and the sons at No. 286.[39]

*

A reminder to the reader:
From this point on the chapters are arranged in six 'Tracks' covering different aspects of Walter's life. They may be read in any order.

Endnotes

1   WR: *An Account of the Family of Rye* (1876), pp.38, 84. The Company, established by Cromwell in 1656, was one of only two created during the Interregnum, the other being the Framework Knitters. The Needlemakers had no hall of their own but went around those of other Companies: D. J. de C. Henshaw, *The Worshipful Company of Needlemakers, 1656–2006, a commemoration of 350 years.*

2   From the 1820s it would fall into steep decline, and it was almost extinct by 1873.

3   See the registers of freemen and admissions, Guildhall Library, London (CLC/L/NA/C/005-6).

4   He was buried in Kensal Green Cemetery beside his wife, Mary, who had predeceased him in 1840.

5   WR: *An Account of the Family of Rye*, p.38.

6   Through Archdale Palmer, *Autobiog.*, p.6.

7   *Autobiog.*, p.7.

8   It is not recorded where the couple lived for the early years of their marriage. For more background see Marion Diamond, *Emigration and Empire: The life of Maria S. Rye* (1999).

9   Another son, George, died in infancy.

10 From the widow of Archibald Patterson.

11 Walter would later buy the freehold, and eventually transfer it to two of his sons.

12 *Survey of London*, vols 31–32 (pt. 2), pp.138–145 [via British History Online].

13 *Nicholas Nickleby* (1839 edn.), ch.2.

14 For Edward's Sun Fire Insurance policies for both 16 Golden Square and 14 King's Parade in 1837 see LMA, MS 11936/564/1256895-8.

15 Edward senior's wife had predeceased him.

16 He is not mentioned in the 1861 or later censuses.

17 Mary A. Tuppen, his mother's unmarried sister.

18 Diamond, *op. cit.* points out that the aunt was dependent on this employment for survival, her father having diverted his assets to maintain a second wife and family.

19 For accounts of sums spent on books etc. by Edward, 1833–34, see NRO, MC 1632/4.

20 Father of the better-known novelist, also Charles.

21 Even Eton and Westminster were dens of cruelty, bullying and violence: A. N. Wilson, *The Victorians*, p.29.

22 Undated letter in NRO, MS 4691/20/1. The italics represent underlining in the original.

23 Several letters in NRO, MS 4691/20/1.

24 NRO, MS 4691/20/1.

25 As a teenager Walter found family holidays boring. He records one year being on the point of suicide from boredom at the seaside with his sisters, until he was rescued by the arrival of two rowing friends, both of whom had designs on the sisters. [See 'How it happened', in WR, *Rubbish and Nonsense.*]

26 The house was later owned by E. M. Beloe, the historian of Lynn, whose daughter married Walter's third son, FG.

27 *London Daily News*, 19 May 1862.

28 I am grateful to Mr Peter Rye for showing me two certificates of Walter's good conduct and good progress, dated 10 Nov. 1860 and 29 Apr. 1861, in a family album.

29 See for example *Liverpool Daily Post*, 11 Sept. 1865.

30 *Autobiog.* for 1859.

31 WR, *Rubbish and Nonsense*, p.56.

32 'the rest is lacking'.

33 Diamond, *op. cit.*

34 WR, *Rubbish and Nonsense*, pp.26–33.

35 Presumably The Oxford, to which he was to return with Howlett in later years.

36 NRO, MC 1632/2.

37 7 Oct. 1865: NRO, MC 1632/2.

38 13 Sept. 1867: NRO, MC 1632/1.

39 WR, *Rubbish and Nonsense*, pp.56–58 includes an amusing tale of life at King's Road, involving unsuccessful efforts to catch a bluebottle, which was preventing the boys from sleeping.

PART TWO

SIX PARALLEL
TRACKS

TRACK 1: PROFESSIONAL AND FAMILY LIFE

1
A MERE GLIMPSE OF LEGAL LIFE

First steps in the legal profession

As we saw above, Walter's poor results in his Bankruptcy and Criminal Law papers ensured that he achieved only a pass in his final legal exams,[1] and dictated that he would specialise throughout his career in civil, not criminal work, in areas such as divorce and testamentary proceedings, executorships and the handling or stewarding of property, rents and chattels.

Edward's decline

On the whole, his father seems to have picked himself up from the collapse of his early business partnership, but according to Walter he had failed to make the most of the improved financial situation that arose from his own father's (Edward senior's) death. He had succumbed to ill-advised investments 'in the time of the railway mania',[2] and his fortunes plummeted again. After that second shock, in order to protect what little of a financial future there now seemed to be for himself and his family, he introduced austerities into both his office and his household. He became increasingly cautious in business affairs, and suspicious of other people's motives, and his misfortunes perhaps seeded what Walter would later describe as a 'morbid fear of contingencies',[3] which in his declining years seems to have deterred business and eventually soured relations with his family as well. Gradually Edward became more withdrawn, cautious and given to self-doubt, and slipped into senility and a kind of paranoia about his business. It cannot have made for an easy life.

Walter Rye as a young man.
Peter Rye.

That was the brooding atmosphere of the office in which Walter began his career as a solicitor in 1866, and all did not go as smoothly as he could have wished. His father kept him on what sounds like a continuing apprenticeship on back-room duties for a full five years until Walter was in his late twenties before first giving him a meaty legal case of his own in 1871. We know, however, that Walter occupied a separate office from his father at 16 Golden Square, and was not entirely reliant on business handed down by him, but undertook some private practice, and had his own separate entry in the postal directories.[4]

*

Perhaps from a proper sense that these were confidential matters, Walter reveals very little about either his own professional life or his dealings with his father or their respective business clients. The firm's records appear to have been destroyed, so with the exception of a few celebrated cases concerning Norfolk, such as the Town Close case and the Hickling Broad case discussed below, the evidence we have on his legal career is episodic, mainly based on infrequent remarks in the *Autobiography* and scattered press announcements requesting potential claimants of testamentary estates to contact the firm.[5]

One symptom of the difficulties of getting started in business was that it was some years before Walter could afford to buy, as opposed to rent, a family house. And as with most businesses, there were ups and downs. He records, for example, that in what should have been his first big case, in 1872 for the respondent in a divorce suit, he had to make many visits to Tynemouth, Newcastle and Shields, but the case against his client was withdrawn at the last moment, which was in one sense a victory, but perhaps deprived him of a moment of glory in court.

Both professional and personal relationships with his father remained strained right up to Edward's eventual retirement in 1874. One rather sad outcome of Edward's deteriorating mental state was his decision to sell off the greater part of his library on 5–9 May 1873 at Hodgson's Sale Rooms in Chancery Lane. This comprised works of literary, legal and topical interest, some of which had been formative in the self-education of Walter and his siblings. But whilst Walter, by now aged almost thirty, might have been dismayed at not inheriting at least some of this collection, he had the makings of a significant book collection of his own, much of it of an antiquarian nature and of rather different taste from Edward's.[6]

Things were about to get even tougher. Walter records in the *Autobiography* that:

… just at this time was the crisis of my life, for having to buy the practice from my father, who was retiring at the age of 71… I had the greatest difficulty in finding the money to pay him (as he declined to give me credit, having become senile and lost all nerve and belief in himself and anybody), but by the most kind and volunteered help of our counsel, John Caldecott, I did so, only to be met with the further difficulty that my father would not transfer the lease of 16 Golden Square to me. This further difficulty, however, was got over by Sir George Bramwell my father's old friend and co-student voluntarily taking a transfer of it and giving me a sub-lease. I was then at last started on my own account, though I had already practised for some years privately.

Edward eventually died in 1876, leaving nothing to any of his sons, partly because they were each by then set on their respective careers. He did, however, provide handsomely for his wife Maria, leaving her a fortune in excess of £14,000 and all his property.[7] He had already bought a further house at Drayton Terrace, South Kensington for his daughters, and Maria as a widow chose to move there after Edward's death. She lived there for a further six years until her own death in 1882, when she left to her children almost exactly the sum she had inherited from Edward, and named EC and Walter as her executors. The daughters then inherited King's Road in their own right.

We shall see below that the early years of Walter's married life were a struggle financially. Nothing is known of the private income, if any, that Georgina brought to the marriage, although initially she and Walter could not afford to be property owners but lived in rented accommodation.

In spite of these inauspicious beginnings, there are indications from his later lifestyle that Walter's legal business became lucrative, especially in the field of executorships, where he occasionally picked up a residual legateeship. By the mid 1870s he was able to take on his sporting friend W. H. Eyre as a legal partner, and we learn that later they also employed as a junior Eyre's cousin A. F. Willoughby.[8] Move on a further decade and we find Walter and his family leading a rather comfortable life. In 1882 Augustus Jessopp would write:

I am very glad to hear you have had so good a year. You are young enough to make some very good berths for your boys and to make ample provision for yourself besides. It has long been plain to me that there are few better things than a solicitor's business if a man has that happy combination of brains, health and character to carry it on – you have them all and nothing can keep you from professional success as long as you choose to stick to your business. I see you far from the zenith of your career.[9]

Walter and Georgina became owner-occupiers successively of two rather grand houses in Putney and Hampstead. As well as meeting the basic necessities, paying domestic staff and covering the fees for schooling his sons, Walter paid dues for many sporting clubs, bought all the latest bicycles and tricycles, made generous donations to charity, entertained lavishly, subsidised many of his own publications, and bought books and manuscripts at auction and through dealers. He also began to build up a property portfolio in Norwich.

Professional life 1882–1899

Disappointingly, however, for the last two decades of his professional life that sustained this kind of lifestyle up to his retirement in 1899, we know almost as little as about the early years.[10] The main exceptions both relate to Norfolk, where he was by now becoming almost as well known as in London. In 1886, having previously criticised the way in which the commoners of Mousehold Heath had been treated in a lawsuit, he was enlisted as solicitor for the plaintiff in the case of *Stanley v. the Mayor of Norwich*, where he successfully established that the Town Close Estate belonged to the freemen individually and not to the corporation. This involved an immense amount of work assembling all the necessary documents, some of which he later published.[11] The Hickling Broad case is separately discussed in Track 2. In 1895 Walter tried but failed to buy a solicitor's practice in Norwich, an early indication of the way his thoughts were tending.

One incidental insight from successive years of the *Autobiography* is that business often took Walter on long trips from home. He was just as opinionated about some of the places he saw around the country as about Norfolk. Northampton (1883) was a 'filthy hole'. In York (1888) 'the cathedral disappointed me': he was on his way for the first time to Edinburgh, where his attempts to sleep at the Royal Hotel were thwarted by cup-tie supporters. On the Sunday morning he walked round the 'old and very squalid part of the city and noticed more drunken women in that forenoon than I had ever seen in London in a year.' Holyrood was 'a shoddy and poor palace', but Arthur's Seat was grand. Canongate was dirty, dilapidated and disappointing, but this did not stop him rating the city overall as 'the finest one I ever saw'. He almost got more than he bargained for: 'The cabman stopped automatically at a private house and said mysteriously "you'll get it there". On enquiry I discovered that he thought the *raison d'être* for my outing was a search for a shebeen house.' Only a few months later he was in Berwick, shortly after the Tay Bridge disaster further north, and with a gale blowing which led to some trepidation as he crossed the Tweed!

In the autumn of 1889 he enjoyed a business trip to Penrith (Runic crosses), Borrowdale, Darlington, Kirkbank and Gatherly, and back via

Peterborough (staying at the Angel). In 1892 and again in 1893 he returned to Berwick, and in the latter year also visited Exeter, Tavistock, and Hereford where 'the cathedral struck me as very fine, with grand decorated work and excellent porch'. In 1896 it was the turn of Manchester, Bury and Rochdale, 'all three towns dirty and unpleasant'; in 1897 Liverpool and Kettering; in 1898 Canterbury. These and other absences no doubt contributed to a certain stress in his marital relations, which we shall explore below.

Endnotes

1   University of London, Institute of Advanced Legal Studies, A.LSOC 6/6, A.LSOC 10/1. His respective marks were: Common Law 82/150; Conveyancing 124/250; Equity 76/150; Total Essentials 282. Non-essentials: Bankruptcy 22/150; Criminal Law 45/150.
2   p.13.
3   Ibid.
4   *Post Office Directory*, 1869, p.308.
5   *The London Standard*, 20 Jan. 1875 printed a small ad. by WR for those interested in the estate of the late James Blyth to contact him. In 1877 Messrs Rye and Eyre were appointed receivers of rents for 1–2 Rose & Crown Yard and 1–5 Pall Mall Place.
6   *SSC* of this date at the British Library. I am grateful to Dr Christopher Wright for this reference. The sale is described as 'A portion of the miscellaneous library of Edward Rye Esq', with a total of 1,575 items spread over the four days, but it seems likely that some are from sources other than Edward Rye (the cover is ambiguous). The first section, alphabetised by author, is definitely Rye material and includes things such as long runs of various periodicals, the *Edinburgh Review, Blackwoods Magazine* etc., together with political memoirs and biographies. No buyers' names are given. The rump of Edward's collection was sold off at Sotheby's on 10 Aug. 1882. This comprised further literary works including Dickens and Thackeray, and many prints and paintings. Walter secured just a few prints. SSC of this date, BL.
7   Web notes on familytreemaker [Rye].
8   *Autobiog.*, pp.55, 108. In 1890 he records that 'Our junior partner left us to better himself but I doubt if he did.'
9   NRO, MS 4691/23, 28 July 1882.
10   In London he was still engaged on probate and testamentary work. In 1891–92 in the case of *Trau v. Wareham* in Chancery, Rye and Eyre were agents for the sale of two Renaissance statues of Bacchus and Venus, by order of the Court, eventually sold to anonymous buyers. SSC, 20 May 1892, lots 146 and 147.
11   *NAM* 3.

2
LONDON SOUTH OF THE RIVER (1867–1891)

Putney and Roehampton

By the summer of 1867 Walter had finally left the parental home to live closer to his growing athletic and rowing interests with Thames Hare and Hounds and the Thames Rowing Club (TRC) south of the river. The latter club had for a number of years rented a room during the rowing season at the Red Lion, Putney[1], and it was there that Walter now pitched his tent, sharing room 5 with his athlete friend and later legal partner W. H. Eyre. Eyre would go on to join the TRC himself in the following year, and over the next two decades would become one of its legendary oarsmen.[2]

Predictably the Red Lion was the scene of youthful drunken revelry, but for Walter – a thinking man as well as a sportsman – it was altogether too noisy to endure for long, and in 1869 he moved again, this time to rented rooms at the King's Head at Roehampton, which he describes as a charming old partly-timbered house, 'a typical country house inn with a great wych elm and benches in front of it [see Track 2.1]. There I stopped till I walked down the hill to be married at Putney church.'[3]

Marriage

Walter's references to his family and domestic life in the Autobiography and surviving correspondence are, perhaps intentionally, laconic. He made some fun of his own early repeated failures to find a wife,[4] and suggested that when his first engagement fell through he chased any girl who would come

The King's Head Roehampton.
Illustrated Sporting and Dramatic News, 7 Nov 1885.
From Walter's own cutting in NRO

near him and entered into several successive but short-lived engagements. Dick Howlett became impatient at these failed *amours*, and wrote in 1868:[5]

> I won't applaud you yet for taking the plunge, but if it all turns out right I shall be very glad indeed, as you know. (21 August 1868.)

> I am very sorry to hear what you have told me. Advice in such (indeed in *all*) cases is futile. You only know the circumstances as far as they can be known. This I would do, tho', were I in your case – I would make an appointment to meet the father and get at the bottom of the affair. Only last night I shocked somebody by saying that I preferred a moderate sinner to a thorough pietist. I agree with you in thinking that it is the work of the girl's pious relations – pious people, I am convinced, never go to heaven – good people go there. My experience of women has been small and not fortunate – not leading me to trust them over much. (30 October 1868.)

> Why don't you get married and give up all this. '*Quare non venit mihi*

in premio?' saith she of Pulham; but no: you must go on. There is some gad-fly driving you – settling seems with you out of the question. Genealogy and big steeple chases, flirtation with third class girls, and fierce messages to meek Hebrews seem the order of the day. Do find peace somewhere. (3 December 1868.)

In November that same year Walter recorded setting eyes for the first time on Georgina Eliza Sturges, the [adopted] daughter of a Shanghai merchant, George Sturges, of Bishopstoke, Hampshire,[6] but it was to be the following July before Walter and Georgina were formally introduced.[7]

Walter's *Account of the Family of Rye* (1876) describes George Sturges as the son of William Sturges of Bishopstoke and Jane (Lockyer) his wife, and identifies Georgina as George's 'younger' daughter, by Martha his wife, the daughter of John Davis of Bath. But the *Autobiography* (1916), written forty years later, and six years after Georgina's death, describes her as Sturges's 'adopted' daughter. Successive census returns from 1871 record her place of birth as Belfast, Ireland. A family tradition has it that she was actually the illegitimate daughter of an aristocrat's wife, a prominent society figure who somehow concealed the pregnancy and birth, and then had the baby secretly adopted in order to avoid scandal.[8] If this is true, the matter was skilfully concealed, and of course left undocumented. Whether true or not, it begs the same two questions: whether the fact of Georgina's adoption was deliberately kept secret during her lifetime to avoid speculation, and indeed whether Walter even knew of it at the time of the marriage.

As to the context in which they came to meet, Walter reveals only that it was 'through my athletic habits'.[9] Was she a spectator at his sporting events, or were the two perhaps introduced by a mutual sporting friend? Walter was eight years her senior, but love evidently blossomed and the next year they became engaged. Later that summer (1870), with the wedding only a week or so away, Howlett jested: 'You much to be pitied animal… the chains are clanking near and the jailer in sight.'[10]

Walter and Georgina ('Wally' and 'Georgie' to each other) were married at Old Putney church (St Mary's) on 25 August 1870. The witnesses signing the register were Walter's brother Francis and Georgina's adoptive brother Henry George Sturges.[11] The bride and groom honeymooned first at the Old

Norfolk Hotel in St Giles, Norwich, and then moved on to the Belle Vue in Cromer. However, they were not alone for long, for Walter had arranged a cliff-climbing rendezvous with two of his athlete friends, Arthur and Wilfrid Ball. As that sort of activity surely cannot have involved a lady, Georgina's reaction can only be imagined. Was this an early marker on Walter's part that marriage would not stand in the way of his regular outdoor pursuits with old chums? If so, how prophetic it proved!

Wandsworth

No mention is made of any financial assets brought to the marriage by Georgina. Could it be that, in view of her adoptive status, none were provided? At any rate, like many newly-weds, they struggled to find the resources to set up their first (rented) home, at 4 Craven Terrace, Wandsworth, where Walter says they lived very comfortably on his still-small income, with furniture that cost him just under £100. Here, while working during the day in Golden Square and maintaining his sporting interests at the weekends, he somehow also managed to continue his community work, becoming the manager of a Wandsworth night school and helping to sort and describe the parish records.[12] At the nearby Spread Eagle Assembly Rooms he also arranged occasional festivities for Thames Hare and Hounds, which in March 1872 included an entertainment to raise funds for his night school [see Track 2.1].[13]

Walter and Georgina's first child, James Bacon Rye, was born in Wandsworth in July 1871, and when a second child was conceived the following spring they set about looking for a larger house. Walter's first bid, for a house in West Hill, Putney in 1872, was unsuccessful, so they made rather hasty alternative arrangements and moved to Ivy Lodge, North Street, Wandsworth, as tenants and co-residents of Mrs Slater, the mother of Micky and Ben Slater, two of Walter's friends from Thames Rowing Club. Walter describes it as 'a quaint little old house' and Mrs Slater as:

> ... a wonderfully well-bred and well-plucked old lady who had stinted herself after her husband's death to educate and bring up her two sons. She was perhaps the frankest and most pleasant woman I ever knew, and... was a real friend to me and my young wife... We practically lived together as a happy family for some time.

Walter and Georgina seem to have left baby James at home with his nurse while they took an early autumn holiday, again split between Cromer and Norwich, and this time accompanied by Walter's brother Frank. Soon afterwards, on 31 October 1872, their second son, Roger Cubitt Rye, was born. The whole family would return to Cromer the following year to have both James and Roger baptised.[14] Does that suggest that Walter had no strong affinity with the parish church in Wandsworth, or was it simply that he was determined to give his sons the link to their Norfolk heritage that he so prized for himself?

*

Georgina's third pregnancy occasioned a further move, though still within Wandsworth, in 1873, when Walter took a lease of The Limes, Fairfield, from which he evidently commuted to work by train. He described it as:

> … a much larger and charming old panelled house, which then stood in the middle of a fine old fruit garden and orchard surrounded by green fields, nearly opposite Wandsworth Station. The garden had been an old garden for years and each spring brought fresh surprises as old clumps of bulbs and other plants sprang up into life. Round the garden we made a rough little running path.

Two more sons were born at The Limes: Francis (1874) and Arthur (1876), '… and I should probably have stopped there all my life in perfect content among its grand old fruit trees and flower beds. Unluckily, however the hand of the jerry-builder was on it and I had to leave, and its site is now covered by vile little shops and houses.'

So in 1877 the family upped sticks yet again, for 'Church Pightle', 9 St Ann's Hill, Wandsworth, a 'much more pretentious and expensive house' on the high land above the main street. Walter could only afford it because his legal partner Eyre, still a bachelor, agreed to move in and pay his share of the rent. A fifth son, Philip Sparrow Townsend Rye, was born there in 1877, but sadly died almost immediately of liver cancer.[15]

The house, as we might say today, ticked a lot of the right boxes for Walter. It had a nice shrub garden and '2–3 acres of fruit garden running at right angles behind, right down to Allfarthing Lane with a duck pond'. He had a straight path made right down the middle in order to practise archery, another sport he loved but one in which he admitted to being too nervous to perform at all well when anyone was watching. The main feature of the garden, however, was an oval running track 350yds in circumference, which he created as a winter training facility for Thames Hare and Hounds.[16] It was built to a sufficiently high standard to host a public athletics meeting, and included a steeplechase with a water jump. But despite what must have been considerable outlay on this development the family were again destined to move on after only a short stay, because when Eyre moved out in 1878 to get married the rent was too much for Walter alone to afford.

Selhurst

At the age of thirty-five, with a wife and now four children to support, Walter ideally needed to buy a house of his own, but could only afford that by moving further out of London. So in June 1878 the family moved into Niel Lodge, Selhurst, Croydon,[17] where Walter subsequently bought some adjacent houses and land to enlarge his estate. It was to be the family home for about six years. This enabled him:

> … to indulge in my growing gardening tastes by building a long lean-to greenhouse with a south aspect, heated throughout by hot water pipes from a very large boiler stoked into the kitchen chimney which gave an immense draught. Never afterwards did I get such heat in a greenhouse and the result was extraordinary.

We hear little more of Selhurst until a frightening incident four years later, on 10 July 1882:

> The only thing my wife was nervous about was fire, and she was always raising false alarms. So when she woke me this time I merely turned over and told her to wake me when she had found out that it was one of her usual fancies. Two minutes later, I was thoroughly aroused by piercing shrieks, and slipping out of bed to the servant's bedroom found it 'well alight'. The girl having gone to sleep with a lighted candle on her knees while trimming her Sunday hat. With

great presence of mind I rushed downstairs for the garden hose (how often it got between my legs I cannot say, but I was afterwards black and blue from my falls) and hastily attaching it to the bathroom tap soon had the fire 'well in hand'. It was not till the girl who was cowering in the corner began to skip about and yell that I realised I had inadvertently fixed the pipe on the boiling water tap. However, hot water put out fire just as well as cold so no harm was done. My brother and his wife who were in the next room slept right through the whole thing.[18]

Under the year 1883 in the *Autobiography* Walter records without further comment that his wife had a still-born daughter.

Winchester House, Putney

In 1884, Walter was the residuary legatee of the estate of one of his clients and inherited several thousand pounds, which meant he could afford to move back to Putney, where he bought the large and distinguished Winchester House, which still stands on the banks of the Thames. It had been built, according to Walter, in the early eighteenth century for the Huguenot de Ruvigny family.[19] He spent considerable sums improving it, and imported a fine oak mantelpiece he had acquired in Norwich.

The grand scale of Winchester House allowed plenty of space for bringing up the children, but also gave scope for lavish entertainment of friends and neighbours, both indoors and in the garden. On 16 January 1886 a belated

Winchester House, Putney. Vignette by Wilfrid Ball from the title page of Walter Rye, *A Catalogue of Fifty Manuscripts...*(1889). *Author.*

Christmas party was held for children and accompanying parents and friends. To quote the spoof invitation, it was held 'at Winchester House... much against the wishes of its owner'. The 'Tomfoolery' began at 5pm with tea for the children and ended at 10.30pm when, as the invitation said, 'You are requested to leave'! In between there were food, drink, games, dancing ('for those who like it – we don't'), a magic lantern show, a conjuror, hide and seek ('greenhouses and chimnies barred'), and much else. And for those (adults, one hopes!) who had overindulged, 'a live Doctor will be in attendance to book orders for the next Morning – medicine in your own Jugs'.[20]

Programme of the Tomfoolery which will (it is feared) take place at Winchester House, Putney (much against the wishes of its Owner) on Saturday the 16th January 1886

5.0 pm	Children's Tea; followed at 5.30 by Temporary Repletion
5.45	Chinese Banjo Entertainment by Herr Sachs
6.0	Old English Sports in ye Loft including Bobbing for Apples, Nuzzling for Treacled Rolls, Climbing the Greasy Pole, and the real original Putney Roll-Board (?) or Pitch for Towpath Coker Nuts
6.15	Dancing for those who like it (we don't)
6.30	Magic Lantern by Mr de Looker (and Lookers-on)
7.0	'A Most Warrantable Intrusion' by the Brothers Wilson of Her Majesty's Theatre (gallery usually) & elsewhere.
7.45	More dancing for ye Children (the elders will refresh)
8.0	Conjuring by Herr Sachs
8.30	Supper
9.15	Christmas Tree
9.30	Hide & Seek (Greenhouses and Chimnies Barred)
9.45	Snap Dragon
10.0	Sir Roger Tichborne de Coverley
10.30	You are all Requested to Go

[A live Doctor will be in attendance to book orders for the next Morning – medicine in your own Jugs]

The artist Holman Hunt, who became a good friend, lived in what Walter describes as a 'quaint old house' just across the river in Fulham. He too used to throw occasional garden parties, to which Walter and no doubt the family were invited. It was probably on one such occasion that Hunt saw in Walter's eldest son James the perfect face to represent one of the 'choristers' for his painting of May morning on Magdalen Tower.[21] Walter agreed to let James model for him. He also noted as an aside, 'the flowers which formed the garland were from my Putney garden'. [*See plate VIII*]

For Walter the special attraction of Winchester House was a long balcony overlooking the Thames, '... nearly opposite the Bishop's Palace and the start for the university boat race, a fact which made me extremely popular for one day in the year among my friends and clients, though it also mulcted me yearly and heavily for their lunch.'

In 1890 his party watching the boat race extended to 120 people.

At Winchester House, too, he again delighted in the garden. Much of the original garden had been sold off, but there remained a mulberry tree and a May tree. Walter made extensive use of greenhouses to grow roses and tomatoes, and boasted that for several years the sale of his tomatoes paid his coal bills.[22]

The great gas dispute, 1887

He might have wished for even more tomatoes, to pay his gas bills too! For in 1887 he became a minor national hero for refusing to pay a gas bill that he thought out of all proportion to his regular charges. He argued that the meter just had to be wrong, whilst the Wandsworth and Putney Gas Company unsurprisingly argued that its meters could not tell a lie, and issued a summons against him for non payment of £17. The magistrate threw out the case, in part because the official who had checked the meter did not appear to give evidence. The company appealed to another magistrate, with broadly the same result except for the reasonable compromise that Walter should pay what would have been his typical quarterly bill.[23] An interesting point of law was thus established for the first time, that a gas meter might indeed be wrong, a finding that gave fleeting hope to many customers when it was widely reported in local newspapers around the country. As the *Pall Mall Gazette* of 7 December 1887 advised its readers: 'The public will do well to note that, according to this decision, a gas meter's register is only *prima facie* evidence of the amount consumed, which may be rebutted by other evidence.'

Strained relations with Georgina

Further children were born at Selhurst and Putney, and by the time of their twentieth wedding anniversary in 1890 Georgina had just borne the last of their eleven children. One had died in infancy and another at birth, but nine (six boys and three girls) were still alive and at home, the eldest aged nineteen and the youngest just one. This family profile on its own is quite sufficient to explain Georgina's unavailability to join in many of Walter's excursions, which sometimes came at the most inconvenient of moments for the domestic routine.

During a regular working week Walter was out of the house for much of the day, at his solicitor's practice; and business occasionally took him out of London for several days at a time. Antiquarian research, on his own and other people's behalf, and the opening up of his library at Winchester House to visitors,[24] accounted for quite a bit of his leisure time; and attendance at sporting events continued to fill many evenings and weekends. Even when he ceased to be an active athlete he was still regularly in demand as a steward or judge at athletics meetings, a sports journalist and a committee member.

But many of Walter's absences can only be described as purely recreational. The *Autobiography* shows that throughout his married life he spent considerable periods away from home, researching and writing or indulging in the sailing, walking and cycling described in Track 2. He enjoyed an abundantly adventurous and clubbable life, and made many lasting friendships, especially in Norfolk. Sometimes he even spent Christmas and holiday periods in Norfolk without Georgina, staying, or often sailing, with male friends.

What did Georgina make of all this? We rarely hear her voice, certainly not sufficiently to hear her question her role as a loyal wife and uncomplaining child-bearer. But there are unsurprising hints that she began to suffer depression and other illnesses. It is not hard to imagine that for much of the time, with only one or two servants, the children, and sometimes a governess for company, she was lonely in Walter's absence. We can only speculate whether her health would have been better had he been around more to take the strain. It is of course possible that her presence was simply taken for granted in the written account and that she was with him, away from home, on more occasions than are mentioned.[25] On the other hand, even Walter's passing references to 'our' usual summer cruises, with a wide range of friends, seem often to refer to himself and his guests, but not to include Georgina.

The couple did take a holiday together from time to time. In 1876, for example, over Christmas in Salisbury taking some time out to recover after the death of Walter's father, they drove over to Stonehenge in a snowstorm, 'the effect being very weird and lonely'.[26] In 1878 we get just a glimpse of Georgina's real frustration. She complained to Walter that he never took her out to the theatre or on other interesting trips. To make amends he arranged 'a fair record day's amusement' with her in London, taking in the Monument and the Tower in the morning; lunch at Birch's; St Paul's Cathedral, the National Gallery, Westminster Abbey and the Aquarium in the afternoon; dinner at Blanchard's, and finishing with a performance of *Pinafore*. Both must surely have returned exhausted![27]

The purchase of a 'Sociable' cycle by Walter in 1882 [see Track 2] gave Georgina the first real opportunity to share in one of his outdoor activities; and she sometimes accompanied him for as much as a twenty-mile ride. This was also the year of that terrifying fire at Selhurst described above, which provided a timely reminder to Walter of Georgina's courage and feistiness. That September, they went together to Tunbridge Wells. Then in 1884 they briefly became closer for the less happy reason that Walter contracted typhoid, and came to owe his very life to Georgina and his sister Annie who together nursed him back to health. The next year he was again struck down, this time with rheumatic fever, and his recovery was set back by news that his brother EC had contracted smallpox. Georgina, in an act of sacrificial kindness, offered to take her sick brother-in-law in, to a room above her kitchen, but EC's wife wisely foresaw the risk to the whole family and instead he was sent to a smallpox hospital, where alas he later died. Very shortly afterwards, Walter's beloved brother Frank also died and Walter himself had a breakdown. It was a truly terrible year.

After this we find just occasional mention of joint outings for Walter and Georgina, for example to Henley Regatta (1887) and The Oaks horse race (1888, which Walter did not enjoy). In the latter year they also went on a trip to Sheerness and Chatham. Perhaps the most spectacular tour of all was the one they undertook in 1895 to, among other places, Gloucester, Ross on Wye and the surrounding countryside, Bristol via the Severn tunnel, Southampton and Worthing. We know, too, that Georgina did occasionally accompany Walter on his sailing trips, as in 1888 with his friends the Ficklins, and in 1896 on the Broads with their three daughters, Muriel, Frances and Kitty. Sometimes, however, she was put up by friends while Walter went off sailing or in search of antiquities; for example she stayed with the Beloes at Lynn after Hubert's baptism in 1880.

Georgina's illness

It was in 1889 that Georgina was first diagnosed with diabetes, the disease which would eventually kill her some twenty years later. For their respective multiple illnesses and ailments, she and Walter were treated by their Putney doctor, Dr Grun, who became a close family friend. In 1889 Grun and his wife took Georgina off to Ramsgate for a rest cure; and we hear of other similar seaside breaks for her in Brighton (1890, 1899), Hove (1891)[28] Seaton (Devon, 1896) and Southwick (1897). Dr Grun also had a country residence in Selborne, Hampshire (of Gilbert White fame), where Georgina went for a long stay in 1894.

In September 1891, after she returned from the seaside there are signs in one of her few surviving letters to Walter that a degree of tension was developing between them. Without his side of the correspondence we do not know the whole context, but it is clear that there was some dispute over the affections or behaviour of the children; that Georgina was suffering from depression; and that Walter had enlisted the help of his partner Eyre to keep an eye on her in his absence.

She wrote to Walter from their Putney home, to say she was:

> … rather astonished, I must say, this morning to get your letter. You know how excitable I always am at all times but I will do as you wish. Eyre as I told you, took us out on the river, and we enjoyed our afternoon immensely. If the children are to come between husband and wife there is an end to all things. We certainly have been fonder of each other lately and I don't care two straws about other people. I took Frank to the Naval last evening and saw Mrs Barrett in the morning who feels just the same depression that I do so I am not the only one. Remember this – I will try to do my best, but I will not be upset with the boys. With the best love I can give you. Yours ever Georgie. PS I shall not bother to come on Sunday. I had rather have you to myself.[29]

How good it would have been to know what triggered this.

Endnotes

1　G. Page, *Hear the Boat Sing* (1991), p.1.

2　See especially W. H. Eyre, 'The Thames Rowing Club: their methods of training and their victories from 1874 to 1882' in R. C. Lehmann, *The Complete Oarsman* (1908), ch.17.

3　Eyre, however, continued to live in Putney, now sharing with a rowing friend, G. H. Vize; see Eyre, *op. cit.* p.180.

4　WR, *Rubbish and Nonsense*, pp.138–9: '*Mes Larmes*': A funny, self-critical poem about his early loves, ending 'I ne'er get beyond an engagement, So can't be a marrying man.'

5　NRO, MS 4691/19 and especially /21. All those quoted are from bundle 21.

6　WR, *An Account of the Family of Rye* (1876), p.39.

7　*Autobiog.*

8　Information from Jeremy Rye, December 2016.

9　*Autobiog.*, 3 Oct. 1869.

10　16 Aug. 1869: NRO, MS 4691/21.

11　There is little evidence of contact with the Sturges family after their marriage, although Walter, in a sense the 'brother-in-law', returned a favour by acting as a witness to Henry George Sturges's marriage at Holy Trinity, Selhurst on 22 December 1881. Henry's father is there described as 'George Sturges, retired merchant, deceased' (ancestry.com).

12　*Some notes on the Deeds relating to the Parish and other Charities of Wandsworth in the county of Surrey* (Austin and Sons, Hertford, 1881).

13　On the Spread Eagle, see Dorian Gerhold, *Wandsworth Past* (1998), pp.118–9, and *Pubs of Wandsworth* (Wandsworth Paper 23, 2012), p.29.

14　*Autobiog.*

15　He was baptised at St Anne's, Wandsworth, on 14 December 1877 (ancestry.com). 'He was buried in a grave I bought at Putney cemetery [B nos 512–513].' Walter gave the second site for a grave for his brother, EC.

16　*Autobiog*; also J. Ryan (comp.) *The Annals of Thames Hare and Hounds 1868 to 1945*, p.37.

17　*Autobiog.*

18　He did not manage to sell Selhurst until 1900, and then at a ruinous loss.

19　On the origins of Winchester House, see 'Putney's Old Houses' in *Wandsworth Notes*, 3 (1912), p.1, and Dorian Gerhold, 'Did James Baudoin build Winchester House?', in *The Wandsworth Historian*, 69 (1998), pp.16–18.

20　NRO, MS 4691/84/2.

21　*Autobiog.* According to the family, James was the 'chorister' on the extreme left of the painting.

22　Sketch of the house in *Autobiog.*, p.58. See also title page of WR: *A Catalogue of Fifty of the Norfolk Manuscripts in the Library of Mr Walter Rye at Winchester House, Putney* (1889).

23　See, for example, *Lloyd's Weekly Newspaper*, 30 Oct. 1887.

24　See catalogue.

25　In 1895 says he went by train to Selborne with 'GB', but in the next breath he mentions taking the wagonette with one of his sons and Kitty, so they must either have travelled with him or have been down there all the time.

26 *Autobiog.*
27 *Autobiog.*, 9 Sept. 1878.
28 She returned with a nasty cold and bronchitis, NRO, MC 1632/1.
29 16 Sept. 1891: NRO, MC 1632/1.

3
LONDON NORTH OF THE RIVER (1891–1900)

The move from Putney to Hampstead

Walter now decided to leave Putney, but not before stripping Winchester House of an ornate Georgian fireplace which had been commissioned by a previous owner, the Revd Gideon Murray, and which he sold to what is now the V&A:[1]

> After living about seven years at Putney, I got rather tired of it, chiefly on account of the growing noise and blackguardism of the towpath rowdies, and the spoliation of the picturesqueness of the place by the pulling down the old timber bridge, the destruction of the towpath, and felling the trees of the Bishop's Meadows opposite; and having the chance of selling both properties advantageously, I bought a larger and very old-fashioned panelled house at Hampstead called Frognal House which I restored, and in which I passed another seven years or so.

Frognal House (now No. 99 Frognal) had been built about 1740, and retained many period features including extensive panelling and a spacious central hall connecting the ground floor rooms.[2] Its hilltop location offered fine views towards London, and its large garden held great potential for growing flowers and vegetables. A set of drawings and watercolours of the house made by the topographical artist J. P. Emslie in 1889, only a few years before Walter moved in, gives a useful idea of its grandeur, inside and out.[3] It was, in Walter's words, 'a very fine and roomy example of the old Merchant Prince's home, panelled from top to bottom'.

Rather typically of Walter, in the run-up to his definitive move from Putney, he spent (of all days!) Christmas Day 1891 at the empty house, evidently away from Georgina but 'with my sons and Dr Furnivall', and then 'went on to Norwich about the Hickling case for the new year.' Over the coming months he prepared the house for habitation, retaining the old panelling, adding more, and importing two fine mantelpieces from Putney. The eventual move took place on 13 March 1892.

Apart from almost incidental details – such as that tobogganing on the Heath became *de rigueur* in the severe winter the following year – little is recorded in the *Autobiography* of the family's life in Hampstead, or their interaction with the neighbours and the parish.[4] It is quite possible that Walter was too distracted by work (both legal and literary), by establishing and tending his garden, and by attending to Georgina in her illness, to have a lot of time to be a sociable neighbour. As concerns the garden, he records that:

> I moved my span house to it, and used it for an orchard house, being most successful with great trained plum trees from Veitch and Rivers which bore me great crops. I also had a long and very successful house for green figs only, and was seldom without fruit.

In the autumn of 1897 he planted 'some very fine expensive poplars we got from Veitch, about 30ft high, and much good ivy. All thrived extremely well, as we had made the ground up with thick layers of rotten manure'. As at Putney, he also had archery butts set up.

Some large-scale socialising certainly did take place, including summer garden parties and winter indoor festivities. On 19 January 1893 Walter began what by popular demand became an annual event at the house, a children's musical evening:

> … at which we introduced a very fine ghost effect of a slim girl walking downstairs across the old Hall, in the full view of everyone and then disappearing behind a curtain. It was done by cutting

out a panel in a locked door through which she slipped, the panel working with leathern stops which made no noise, and letting her through into a back staircase, the joint being masked by a screwed on picture on the one side and a coat rail on the other. It took a lot of working out successfully, but though repeated yearly was never found out till one of my children gave it away 'in strict confidence' to a schoolfellow.

Nothing could better capture his sense of fun and mischief. It is not recorded who the lucky children (and presumably parents) were who received invitations to this spectacle.

The saga of the wall [*See plate III*]

Between what is now the convent garden and the adjacent property there rises an imposing brick wall, and a restrictive covenant prevents its demolition. The explanation can be found in the following extracts from Walter's *Autobiography* for May 1896:

I heard that the garden next to me... had been let for the erection of flats. I told the buyer, Elsden, a builder, that I should block any lights he might open, and offered to take the ground off his hands, but he defied me'. [The following year] 'by the 28th March the flats next door to me at Hampstead were well advanced, and so was my blocking wall, which was, I believe, the highest independent wall in London, 42ft high and 6ft thick at the bottom. It was of good red brick, neatly black pointed on my side, with handsome three-storied buttresses, and of common white bricks on the enemy's side, where it came within one or two feet of his windows, and I need hardly say blocked all the new lights he had hoped to have created looking over my lawn. This unlooked for irritation enraged him extremely, and he began in return to hang out all sorts of dirty old clothes opposite my house. As I had paid him a considerable sum to build the side wall of his houses in red brick, I could, I think have stopped this, but waited, and when he found he could not let any of his flats he at last pulled them down. The wall and the planting trees cost me nearly £1,000 but it was a work of necessity, as otherwise it would have taken two or three thousand pounds off the value of my two properties.

But even the wall provided no long-term guarantee of freedom from development on the other side, and, as we shall see, the problem subsequently returned and would eventually be among the causes of Walter's quitting London altogether.

Visit by Hampstead antiquarians[5]

In 1897 a group of antiquaries and other interested parties from the neighbourhood created a Hampstead Antiquarian and Historical Society. Walter did not hasten to join, even though a number of his friends including the Quaritches (booksellers of Golden Square) were among the earliest subscribers. However, when he heard that the society was planning a summer outing to the parish church of St John-at-Hampstead just down the road on 23 July 1898 he sensed that this would be a good opportunity to show off to a sympathetic crowd not only his house and garden, but in particular his new high wall, of which he was inordinately proud. A few of his manuscripts and antiquarian objects could be displayed at the same time for good measure. Through the Quaritches, he contacted the society's secretary to invite the entire expedition to tea. The President, Sir Walter Besant, had rather expected the party to conclude at *his* house, but on hearing of Walter's offer he graciously agreed to defer that until a later date. And so an enormous party – seventy were said to have signed up – having visited the parish church and been shown certain interesting archives by the vicar, the Revd S. R. Burnaby, ascended to Frognal House at 4.45 to be greeted by 'Mr and Mrs Rye'. According to the transactions they were hospitably entertained and 'spent a very pleasant time in viewing the quaint old rooms of the house… and in examining the valuable collection of curios laid out for their inspection by Mr Rye'.[6] The curios ('antique culinary implements, old fashioned furniture, needlework, work-boxes… a fragment of a sundial found in the garden') sound distinctly miscellaneous, and were in all probability items mostly found in this or Walter's previous houses; but there were one or two items of more general antiquarian interest including a 'shagreen instrument case formerly the property of Samuel Johnson'. From Walter's manuscript collections there were on display notes of earlier

Norfolk antiquaries including Blomefield, Le Neve, Martin and Norris (see Track 3.1), together with a few original documents. He also prepared for his visitors a set of historical notes on the Frognal neighbourhood itself.

After this invasion – for it was little less – Walter did finally become a subscriber to the society but, perhaps because he was already thinking of leaving Hampstead rather than developing new connections and roots there, its books do not show that he was ever an active participant.

What with parties of athletic friends to watch the boat race in Putney, garden parties there and in Hampstead, children's musical evenings, and so on, we can imagine that, within the limits of her disability, Georgina as well as the domestic staff were called upon to play a major role in entertaining at each successive Rye family home.

A country retreat at Selborne (Hampshire)

In 1893 Walter began his summer holiday either alone or with the children, but certainly without Georgina who joined them later for a few days in the middle of the holiday and then went home. Her symptoms were getting steadily worse. When Dr Grun and his wife again invited her to Selborne in 1894 Walter for a while rented Dorton's Cottage nearby, in Lower Lyth, so that they could all be near neighbours. He loved the place so much that he later bought it.

With or without friends in attendance, Selborne would now become the family's country retreat. Walter made regular use of it, arriving by cycle, or by train and then dog cart. He used it as the springboard for further exploratory outings by tricycle, sometimes with Dr Grun, to locations such as Sutton Place. We also find him lending the cottage to his niece Lily and her husband for their honeymoon, and in 1897 inviting Thames Hare and Hounds on one of their country meets, for which he took along massive provisions. Walter would sometimes be there on his own, but from time to time he took at least some of the children, as in 1898 when he went with ALR and Betty at Easter. ALR developed the same affection for the place as his father and played cricket for the village team.

Walter went for his usual holiday in Norfolk in 1894, leaving Georgina with the Gruns for nursing care. Later in the year she was fit enough to join him in Norfolk for a while. But despite the best that medicine and nursing care could do for her, her condition continued to deteriorate. She was very unwell at the time of their summer garden party in Hampstead in 1895, and the holiday tour (already mentioned) that Walter devised that year was designed in part as a pick-me-up.

Norwich calls

During these Hampstead years Walter began gradually to lay plans for an early retirement to Norwich, a strategy encouraged by the high cost of repair and upkeep of Frognal House, but certainly also by Georgina's increasingly delicate condition. He later lamented:

> I was sorry to part with the Hampstead house for many reasons. Until the builder fiend drove me out of it with his hideous flats I don't know that I remember seeing a nicer old house and garden. No doubt (from the fact that broom and harebell still lingered in its grass), it was two hundred years ago part of the old Heath and had been filched off it when the house was built. Its garden ran up the hill and rose up so high that when I erected a rough wooden gazebo at its top I could see from it the Tower of London, the House of Commons with the Big Ben on the Victoria Tower [sic], clearly enough to check my time with it, just as one could see Windsor Castle from the White Stone pond. It was full of fruit trees, and one white heart cherry of an enormous size ripened bushels of fine fruit yearly, only, however, to be invariably eaten in one night by starlings. Pied flycatchers nested in the cherries on the north wall and annually a pair of hawfinches took toll of my peas. Roses flourished extremely and altogether it was a *rus in urbe* only a furlong or so outside the four-mile radius, and the old red-brick house with its wrought-iron gates had a great fascination for me. Two of my younger children nearly came to untimely deaths there, for, escaping from their nursery, they walked round the house by the narrow parapet (but not knowing the danger came round safely).

He had had his eyes on a number of Norwich houses, and had even made one or two unsuccessful bids. Then, shortly before his planned retirement, **St Leonard's Priory**, at the top of Gas Hill and with extensive views over Norwich, came on the market. To Walter this was highly desirable, and he decided to up sticks. The house was relatively modest, and certainly represented down-sizing compared with Hampstead, but it came complete with medieval ruins. What more could an antiquary ask?

Endnotes

1   Room 53b, case 1. When he left the house the fireplace was too big to go with him. He noted that in 1916 it was 'at the late Sir CB Lawes-Wittewronge's.' Walter had two replicas made, one of which ended up in his house at St Leonard's Priory and the other in Anguish's House, Tombland, Norwich. From 1892 when Walter left, the occupant was the Putney Constitutional Club. Its current successor is the Winchester House gentlemen's club. Two framed deeds in the club's bar when visited, 23 Feb. 2010, showed the plot of ground (1) in 1880 (Norton, Trist, Watney & Co), before WR's purchase, with nice big gardens and (2) in 1884 during his occupancy when the grounds were much smaller. The mulberry tree still survives.

2   *VCH Middlesex*, IX (1989) p.33 notes that it was described as 'lately built' in 1741 when it passed to John Padmore of St Giles in the Fields. Sale particulars prepared in 1933, still described it as 'unspoilt in character and interior design... The interior is panelled throughout and the house is pervaded by an atmosphere of charm and repose characteristic of its period type.' Camden Local Studies Department, H728.3. Since that time the building has been altered and adapted to different purposes. It was the London home of General de Gaulle and his wife during World War II, and was at the time of writing an international student residence run by St Dorothy's Convent.

3   Camden Local Studies and Archives Department, 89.3 Frognal 99.

4   His daughter Kitty was, however, baptised at the parish church on 12 April 1894 (ancestry.com).

5   This account is largely based on the society's archives held at the Camden Local Studies and Archives Department, A/01355, including the minutes, cash book and annual reports for 1898.

6   *Transactions of the Hampstead Antiquarian and Historical Society* (1898), pp.40–43.

4
NORWICH AND LAMMAS (1900–1910)

The move from London to Norwich

When Walter was finally ready to call time on Hampstead, in 1899, his first attempt to sell Frognal House at auction failed and the two properties there were bought in at below the reserve price. In time, however, one sold quite well and the other was let on a repairing lease.[1] Details in the sale prospectus for Frognal House perhaps explain why this very particular house and grounds proved so daunting to prospective buyers:

> A large square old (Queen Anne) red brick detached house, panelled throughout and partly covered with clematis and other creepers, standing in the best part of Frognal in its own walled garden of over an acre. It is one of the six left of the old Hampstead houses… [*its rooms described*]. Sanitary arrangements perfect, having been entirely reconstructed when the present owner bought the freehold, and are so arranged that all pipes etc are carried immediately outside the house and ventilated. The House is within three minutes' walk of the Heath, and the Garden is one of the most secluded, picturesque, and best stocked for fruit in Hampstead, sloping up a steep hill, from the top of which extremely pretty views of the neighbourhood, and over London as far as the Crystal Palace, are obtained. There are two Rose Banks well stocked with choice roses in luxuriant bearing, the garden being mostly on Bagshot sand over London clay. Besides

having a full-sized Tennis Lawn, a 60yds Archery Butt, and a secluded Quoit Ground, there is a south fruit Wall, over 100yds long, very well stocked with choice wall fruit in full bearing, a span-roof Peach and Plum House in full bearing (over 1000 dessert plums having been picked one autumn) and a lean-to Fig and Tomato House with two rainwater tanks. Suitable either for residence or for a very high-class School or retreat [*For lease or sale with adjoining properties*] Two Mantels in Dining-room and Drawing-room, and an old lead Cistern which were inserted by the owner, will be removed.[2]

St Leonard's Priory, Norwich

The hill-top location of St Leonard's Priory and its ancient history strongly attracted Walter. They also rather blinded him to the inconveniences of this exposed site. In eager anticipation of at last putting down some real roots in Norwich he spent considerable time at the 'priory' during 1899 before eventually doing as he had previously done in Hampstead and moving in alone for a while, without even a servant to cook for him, in order to supervise the work necessary to make the house habitable for Georgina and their daughter Kitty to join him.[3]

He records that the family saw the procession to celebrate the relief of Pretoria from a window at the corner of the Market Place:

> ... the effect of the various societies marching with torches down London Street being very fine, though the 'mafficking' was too pronounced. The illuminations were very fine and the lavish flare from the Gas Works startled us greatly as we walked home, for it looked just as though our house was on fire!

In 1900, at the relatively young age of fifty-six, Walter transferred his legal business – at, as he thought, a very beneficial rate – to his third and fourth sons Frank (FGR) and Arthur (ALR), and finally made the move to Norwich. Frank and Arthur at once set about selling the Golden Square property in order to move to another one nearby. To provide some continuity Walter continued to go up to London once a week by the early train from Norwich on a Monday, staying in lodgings with one of the sons (ALR) and returning to Norwich on Tuesday evening. The pretext was in case any of

Walter's old clients wished to see him, but in practice he found this very rarely to be the case and was left clicking his heels:

> I can't say I cared for the Monday–Tuesday journeys to London, for I stayed in lodgings with one of my sons [ALR] in various places, which I think he must have chosen for the express purpose of having the *maximum* of noise with the *minimum* of convenience. One I specially remember was poised over or next door to the GN Railway main line, and the express trains through the night rocked me out of sleep, while another adjoined a milk depot, into which many thousand reverberating milk cans were rolled over granite sets from 2.45am. Still they had the effect of making the Norwich factory hooters comparatively sweet to me each week on returning.

Back in St Leonard's Priory, in 1901 another national event, the death of Queen Victoria, finds passing mention in the *Autobiography*, but almost equal billing is given to the achievement of the first motor car to get up Gas Hill! Over several seasons Walter carried out archaeological digs on the priory ruins and wall, which he proudly showed off to antiquarian friends from Norwich and further afield.[4] In July 1902, he served as tour guide for a large party from the Quatuor Coronati monastic lodge, who came for a weekend's outing to Norwich and the Broads (see Track 6). On the Sunday morning, he invited those who were willing to forgo the pleasure of the cathedral's service to visit him at St Leonard's. Their impressions were later set down in the Lodge's Transactions. They described the house as being:

> … upon the hill which commands the loveliest view of Norwich… An old well, at least five feet in diameter, and sunk over two hundred feet into the rock, is still extant… Mr W Rye had excavated some of the ruins of the church and the precinct wall. They are a great attraction to the student of history.

Georgina and Kitty evidently made an impression too:

> The mistress of the house and her daughter extended a cordial

welcome to the visitors, who carried away with them most grateful recollections of hospitality and kindness.

But the main objects of wonder were Walter's library and antiquarian collection:

> The library of Mr Rye made a deep impression on those who had the good luck of seeing it, and the writer knows of at least one visitor into whose heart stole a feeling of secret envy of the ravishing delights concealed on the bookshelves and in the many treasures of antiquity tastily stowed away in odd nooks and corners of the house.

The tradition of holding annual garden parties continued for a while at St Leonard's Priory, until Georgina became too ill. Walter also invited groups with which he was connected to lunch or tea, including the Science Gossip Club and the Norwich and Norfolk Archaeological Society on one of its outings.[5]

A new country retreat at Lammas

Once Norwich became his principal home, the cottage at Selborne was too remote to serve as a regular country retreat, so Walter looked for another country cottage. In 1901, Rectory Cottage at Lammas, some nine miles from Norwich but with a railway station, came on the market. As he had already identified this village as the home of some of his ancestors,[6] the opportunity seemed too good to miss and he duly bought it. He would use it for the next fifteen years as an escape for himself and his household from the rigours and noise of Norwich life. He transformed the cottage and adjacent old schoolroom into a 'commodious dwelling', in which the long schoolroom became the dining room.[7] It was described by one of his friends, W. G. Clarke, as very atmospheric, with its partially stained-glass windows, a peat fire and furnishings that reflected the taste of a cultured antiquary. Here he entertained people of all walks of life: 'teachers, tailors, auctioneers, farmers, librarians, journalists...' And 'entertained' is certainly the right word, because among friends, just as among his old sporting colleagues, Walter was a brilliant raconteur with a keen sense of humour. After-dinner talk extended well into the small hours.[8]

Not content with individual visitors, Walter frequently entertained crowds at Lammas, and visits are recorded by, among others, members of the Norwich Photographic Society, the Woodpeckers, the Gossips, the Prehistoric Society and the Horticultural Society.

In 1903 he commissioned G. A. King to make armorial quarries of all the owners of Lammas Manor, which he hung in the house. He would eventually give these to the parish church.[9] He bought the adjacent orchard and cottages, and even invited the new rector of Lammas to stay while the rectory was being readied for him.

In most respects life at Lammas was idyllic, and Walter felt so at home that he began making arrangements to be buried there.

St Leonard's Priory begins to pall

Meanwhile, as time went on the toll of inconveniences at St Leonard's Priory began to register even with Walter:

> It certainly was a most interesting site, with its great mysterious well, which I shrewdly suspect to be Roman, its memory of a great Roman coin found in the garden, the ruins of the old priory, and its absolutely unrivalled view down onto the city which lies under it. But it was the most exposed and windy site in the city, and many a night have the gales kept us awake by fiercely beating on the windows and depositing a salt coating carried over the land from the sea. Then again, the way up from the road was terribly steep and bad for a man who thought he had heart trouble, and the soil of the hillside poor in the extreme, to an extent which made good gardening almost impossible, except for poppies, for the manure lavishly applied one week was washed down the steep hill the next week. The giant parsnip or false celery was the only thing which flourished in it, and it did flourish.[10]

In September 1904:

> ... the City Engineer, feeling aggrieved that Gas Hill was being used as a test hill by motor bicyclists and motors, took the extraordinary step of driving in posts and putting up a locked gate

across what was one of the oldest public roads in the city. I had suffered a good deal at his hands since I had been in Norwich, but, to use the words of the irate nobleman when the footman dropped a plate of soup down his neck, 'Great G-- Almighty, this is a little too much', so I threatened him with an injunction, with the result that the posts came down...

After the move from London, every mention of Georgina in Walter's autobiography logs her decline. By 1905 she was in and out of a nursing home and the family's former governess, Miss Seccombe, was re-employed to look after her. Georgina was now pretty well housebound for most of the time, and a brief visit to Lammas with Kitty during warm summer weather was a thing of significance to be recorded.

In 1906 Walter bowed to the inevitable and put St Leonard's Priory on the market, with a view to moving into the centre of Norwich. But if he had potential buyers in mind they were more alert to the site's inconveniences than he had been, and there were no bidders. Eventually, as the need to move became more pressing, he had to sell at a great loss (to the cricketer Knyvet Wilson).

Surrey Street

Walter now moved the household to 28 Surrey Street, Norwich, in the hope that this more central location would be beneficial for Georgina, and spent a considerable sum doing it up. But once again it was a bad buy. It was opposite noisy neighbours, a Girls' Friendly Society hostel where piano playing and riotous behaviour sometimes continued well into the night. Walter and Georgina stuck it out for the duration of his year of office as Mayor of Norwich, 1908–1909, although Walter had to warn the corporation that as his house was now in effect a sanatorium for his sick wife there could be no question of its being used to host mayoral receptions. During 1909 Georgina passed almost into a diabetic coma, and her three sons then living in England came to see her for what they thought would be the last time, although in fact she rallied. But it was a stark signal that these domestic arrangements could not continue, and in 1910 the household moved lock, stock and barrel to Lammas, the doctor and Kitty taking Georgina there by car on 16 April.

Georgina dies

For Georgina, alas, it was already too late. On 6 May 1910 Walter went for a cycle ride alone, and returned to find her 'very bad indeed'. He cycled on to Dr Wright at Coltishall, who motored back instantly 'but found her in a state of collapse and gave us no hope'. Next day she could only just recognise Walter and Bessy, her favourite daughter, and she died early on the morning of Sunday 8 May, aged fifty-eight. The same three sons who had visited her the year before attended her funeral at Lammas on 11 May. Dick Howlett, also by now a widower, tried to console Walter by pointing out that 'the death really took place a year or more ago...',[11] whilst D. M. Roberts wrote: 'under the circumstances it is a happy release after many years of suffering. I know what a tie her extremely long illness has been to you all, and that it was only a matter of time waiting for the end'.[12]

Walter's own epitaph for Georgina was set out in the *Autobiography*:

I will only say that she was both the prettiest and pluckiest woman I ever saw, and was for many years the most devoted mother and nurse to me and her numerous children. She feared nothing, she was always ready to tackle anything – fire alarms, burglar or alleged ghost.[13]

Gardening and the natural world[14]

We found Walter as a boy collecting butterflies and insects with his brother EC. This early enthusiasm fostered a lifelong curiosity about, and love of, the natural world, and he came to observe and write about the flora and fauna around him with almost the same degree of enthusiasm as he did about antiquities. His walking, cycling, sailing and gardening provided endless opportunities to indulge this passion.

In his youth he waxed poetical about the forces of nature:

Have you ever at night, when the bossy clouds like flocks of sheep at play have sported over the face of the moon, been struck with the idea that their silence is unnatural and have, as I have done, listened intently, thinking to catch some faint sound of crashing, like grinding of icebergs as the huge, solid-looking masses pursued and ran into one another? Or have you ever half expected to see them catch fire like light cotton, as they glided over the moon's edge? Or are they both but a madman's fancies?[15]

But even in his old age we read of expeditions like those to Foxley Wood to look for purple emperor butterflies or, on several occasions, with his old friend R. J. W. Purdy to see tame buzzards at Coltishall (1909) or search – as it happened, unsuccessfully – for luminous owls. Walter was a keen observer of birds, and perhaps his greatest joy was to see a hoopoe on his pasture at Lammas in 1907. Out on the Broads from time to time he would come across otters; and of course he saw all manner of wildfowl, which, however, he was by no means averse to shooting and eating. Guests sometimes remarked on the very curious menus to which they were subjected!

Visits to friends often included tours of their gardens,[16] and while at Lammas Walter became a member of the local horticultural society. He records that in 1905 they visited Westwick Gardens and had a 'teetotal feed in a tin room, which later on I supplemented by entertaining to non-teetotal beverages just 105 thirsty gardeners at my Lammas Cottage'.[17]

But generally Walter did not even have to leave his own home for that kind of satisfaction. He deliberately planted flowers that would attract butterflies, moths and other insects.[18] The account above of his successive London houses with their large gardens and greenhouses has already given us an indication of his prowess in cultivating fruit, vegetables and flowers. It was an enthusiasm shared with friends and neighbours, especially after he moved to Norwich, and there is often mention in their letters of the exchange of home-grown produce, flowers or seeds, as well as handy tips on growing.[19] Walter's antiquarian instincts even occasionally extended to the collection of ancient plants for his garden. In 1900, after giving a lecture on woad he was given some woad seeds by Dr Plowright and began to cultivate them, commenting, 'I think I am the only man who grows the still curious glaucous-leaved plant in East Norfolk'.

We should leave the last, eloquent word on the wonders of nature to Walter:

Had I visited the Continent at considerable inconvenience to myself I should never have seen an osprey quartering over Barton Broad, or otters playing like dogs in the dry reeds in the winter at Wroxham, or swallow-tailed butterflies feeding on bramble bloom near Horning Ferry, a spot which with its great history and its paved ford leading to Canute's St Benet's at Holme has always had a great attraction for me beyond the material one of the woodcock and snipe pudding, which I used to have when I often cycled over in the winter to be the solitary guest at the 'Ferry'... Then, since I have been at Lammas I have had the luck to see a hoopoe, a flock of bramblings and the biggest flood for centuries. Who can say it is dull in the country? If I didn't see the luminous owl myself, I certainly caught the worst cold I ever had while waiting to do so. And now I have seen *L. gigantium* (which I can't grow at home at all) grow like a weed, self-seeding at Merton and Westwick, and have acclimatized woad and the wild tulip and have wondered at the chalk hill blue flickering by hundreds at a time on Ringstead Downs. And I have stood, at a low neap tide, on the ruins of Shipden church, a quarter of a mile out to sea and seen the ridges of the old streets and have known old Eccles tower, when it used to stand out of the sands like an old man's last tooth. And how often in my yearly ride or walk round the coast have I enjoyed the flower cliff between Cromer and Runton, mad with the colours of poppies and blue succory before it was all barb-wired and stucco-villa'd, and before the stiff and sickly gardens at Overstrand had replaced the Garden of Sleep.

Endnotes

1 *Autobiog.*, p.111.
2 NRO, MS 4691/86.
3 NRO, MS 4691/79 is WR's portfolio of research notes on St Leonard's Priory, including plans and sketches at various dates, with extracts from original sources. Press cuttings include one of unknown provenance and date headed 'St Leonard's Priory: Mr Walter Rye's new property' ending: 'Interest in the old story of St Leonard's Priory and Mount Surrey House [a disappeared mansion once on the site] no doubt has been revived, owing to the very satisfactory circumstance that the property has just been acquired by Mr Walter Rye, who we may be sure, will turn it to the very best account and throw all possible light on its history. Nothing remains of the building.'
4 For the 1903 excavations, with photographs, see *NA* XV (1904), p.194. For the Quatuor Coronati Masonic lodge visit in 1902 he wrote 'In my capacity as Lay Prior [I] shall be glad to show [the remains] to anyone who cares to come up after breakfast for refreshments before returning to London', *Norwich and the Broads: Itinerary* (1902).

5 *Autobiog.*, p.135.
6 *Autobiog.*, p.1.
7 *EDP*, 25 Feb. 1929, p.4; tribute by the late W. G. Clarke.
8 *Ibid.*
9 D. P. Mortlock and C. V. Roberts, *The Guide to Norfolk Churches* (Lutterworth Press, revised edition, 2007), p.168.
10 He still owned Anguish House, and while living at St Leonard's 'spent as usual a lot of money in putting up a replica of the old oak door there and a wrought iron grill', but in the end it never seemed the right place to live, and he would eventually sell it in 1911.
11 19 May 1910: NRO, MS 4691/22/2.
12 26 May 1910: NRO, MS 4691/14/1.
13 *Autobiog.*, 3 Oct. 1869.
14 For further background on gardening see Stephen Constantine, 'Amateur gardening and popular recreation,' in *J. Soc Hist*, XIV, no.3 (Spring 1981).
15 WR, *Rubbish and Nonsense*, p.21.
16 At F. W. Harmer's in 1904 he found a 'very beautiful river garden, with the wealth of acclimatized water-plants'. In 1913 Purdy drove him to see a garden at Sennowe: 'grandiose in the extreme but vulgar', *Autobiog.*
17 *Autobiog.*
18 In 1912 he recorded seeing four humming bird hawk moths at once on the valerian near his gate.
19 Before he even left Hampstead, Theodore Marsh wrote: 'You are so devoted to Norfolk and all connected with it that I thought you and Mrs Rye would be pleased with a few of our wild lilies of the valley which grow in such abundance in the neighbourhood', 8 June 1898, NRO, MS 10612 folder (1). On other occasions he sent Walter fresh quinces and irises by train, ibid. Dick Howlett sent him 'much gratitude for roses and maidenhair plant and for lucid instructions' (1913), NRO, MS 4691/22. See also, for example, William Smith (a rose and thistles, 2 Nov. 1917); Thomas Nelson (figs and Blenheim Orange apples, 1917); E. Beloe (narcissi and daffodils, 25 Apr. 1922) all in NRO, MS 4691/2.
20 E.g. he took seeds at Crowland Abbey in 1882 (*Autobiog*).

5
WALTER'S HOUSEHOLD

We have seen that between 1871 and 1889, Georgina bore Walter eleven children, of whom six boys and three girls survived to adulthood. For well over twenty years, therefore – from 1871 to the mid-1890s – there was never a time without at least one child under five years old being at home. As the family increased, so did the need for domestic servants, and the snapshots provided by the decennial censuses from 1871 to 1911 show very well how the household grew and shrank according to need. In 1871 before they had any children the Ryes already employed one domestic servant. In 1881, with five children ranging in age from eleven months to nine years, they employed two 'nurse domestics' aged seventeen and eighteen. By 1891, the household had reached its maximum size, with eight or perhaps nine children aged two to nineteen living at home;[1] there was now a cook/domestic aged thirty-six, a housemaid aged twenty-two, a nurse/domestic aged twenty and a scullery maid aged fourteen. By 1901, following the move to Norwich, all the sons had left home, leaving just Walter, Georgina and their three daughters plus a cook and a housemaid. Finally, in 1911 after Georgina's death, the three daughters, aged between twenty-two and twenty-nine, were (for a while longer) still in residence at Lammas, with two servants, a cook/domestic aged twenty-one and a girl aged seventeen who was described simply as a 'servant'.[2]

The first six children were all sons, whereas four of the last five were daughters, so the balance and collective interests of the family shifted quite dramatically after Walter and Georgina's first ten years of marriage. It naturally fell to Walter to take the lead with the boys. Having experienced for himself what it was like to be brought up by a cold, distant father, he took a more direct interest in his own sons' development, providing handsomely for their education, cultivating in them from an early age his own love of rowing, athletics and cycling, and taking them on holidays, even when Georgina was not free to join them. To a greater extent the daughters would be left to Georgina's care, but Walter also encouraged in them too a healthy interest in outdoor pursuits such as cycling and archery.

A number of the children themselves had interesting life stories, but they are covered here only insofar as they directly concerned Walter himself.

Sons

James Bacon Rye, Walter and Georgina's first son,[3] was born in Wandsworth on 22 July 1871. By the time he was of an age to attend school the family had moved to Selhurst, so he was sent first to a preparatory school there and later to Whitgift Grammar School, Croydon, before moving on to St Paul's School, London, where he flourished both academically and in sports. His particular enthusiasm for history was so great that Walter tried to persuade the headmaster to enter him at the earliest possible opportunity for an open scholarship to Oxford. When the head took a more cautious line and recommended waiting a year, Walter called in Dick Howlett as a tutor to cram James to sit for a scholarship anyway. The extra work paid off and he won an open scholarship to Balliol, where he was the youngest candidate in his year.

For a while during his student days there was a serious setback to James's sporting prowess. Dr Grun, fearing that early signs of curvature of James's spine could be serious, prescribed treatment that involved his being 'strung up and put in plaster' for a while, which proved enervating and restricted his mobility. Walter ultimately judged all this to have been unnecessary, and diagnosed the problem as an inherited case of 'student's back', stemming he thought from sitting slouched over books. Both Walter and his father had suffered similar symptoms. With time James recovered well and was back on good sporting form, and to Walter's great joy he won Blues in both athletics and rowing at Oxford, but not at the expense of his academic study for he also gained a First in Modern History in 1892. With Walter for a father he could not hide his light under a bushel. A reporter in the unlikely-sounding source, *Horse and Hound*, wrote on 30 July 1892:

I am very glad to see that Mr JB Rye of Balliol College, Oxford, the eldest son of one of our oldest contributors and esteemed friend, Mr Walter Rye, has taken a first-class. Mr Walter Rye, who is well known in the athletic worlds as President of the Thames Hare and Hounds, and formerly hon. sec. of the London Athletic Club, won the Amateur Walking Championship in 1868; and the son is worthy of his sire, for he got his Blue this year, running in the Inter-'Varsity mile, but his best distance is half a mile, at which he has done several very fine performances.[4]

After graduation James began to train as a lawyer, but also kept up his historical interests, winning the Arnold Prize in 1897, an achievement again celebrated by *Horse and Hound*![5] Walter quite possibly expected him, as the eldest son, to make his career in the family law firm, but his first love was really history and, no doubt after some agonising, by 1902 James had decided that the law was not for him.[6] Walter wrote to Doubleday, the general editor of the Victoria County History to enquire if there might be an opening for James (now aged thirty) on the History.[7] But instead James returned to academic life in Oxford where his rooms would later provide a handy port of call for Walter on his occasional visits to the Bodleian Library or to meet Oxford historians such as C. H. Firth (1903).[8]

Walter's other sons were less academically inclined, and their careers followed different trajectories. **Roger** (b.1872) and **Frank** ('FGR' b.1874) for a while were sent off to Beccles Grammar School in Suffolk. Roger seems to have made little progress there, so Walter removed him to a private school in Burgess Hill. Frank, however, followed the trail blazed by James to St Paul's, as did **Arthur** ('ALR', b.1876). Frank followed Walter into Thames Hare and Hounds, and eventually became the club's Secretary. Walter introduced all three of these sons to the delights of cycling, on a tandem (Roger 1888, Frank 1897) and a triplet (Frank and Arthur 1894). Alone, or with other friends, they also joined him to sail, and on other holiday jaunts to Norfolk and Selborne. The ease with which Walter continues to record meetings with them in his later years, either in London or Norfolk, suggests that they bonded well, although their encounters were not always free from incident, as when, in 1899 'FGR and I attempted some rabbit shooting with unusually disastrous results, which I dare not, even at this date, specify'.

At about the age of twenty, like several of his aunts and one of his uncles, whose example may well have influenced him, Roger decided to seek a living in Canada and married there in 1901. Frank and Arthur meanwhile, unlike James, both persevered to train as solicitors. Indeed, not having been to university they qualified ahead of James, in time to take over Walter's business when he retired. In 1901 very shortly after his brother Roger's wedding in Canada, Frank married Ethel Mary Beloe, daughter of Walter's great friend E. M. Beloe, the historian of King's Lynn. Not to be outdone, Arthur also became engaged at about the same time.

Of the upbringing of Walter's sixth and seventh sons, **Hubert Gould** ('HGR') and **Gilbert Walter** ('GWR' or 'Gilly'), we hear little from the surviving family papers. Hubert was born in 1880 and baptised, like his brothers, at Cromer. In the horrible family crisis of 1884–85 when Walter's brothers Frank and EC both died and Walter himself was seriously ill, Hubert, then aged about five, also fell ill and had to have his lungs aspirated, which was a great concern to his parents. But he survived and indeed went on to become a fit youth and, like his father and brother Frank, a member of Thames Hare and Hounds. Hubert maintained a strong and close relationship with Walter, visiting him regularly in Norfolk while a bachelor and, during Georgina's last illness, bringing home his fiancée, Marjorie.

Gilbert (b.1886) left school at fourteen to try his luck first as a merchant seaman and later as a farmer, but neither venture was a success. After his mother's death in 1910 he and Hubert stayed on briefly at Lammas for a few days to keep a watchful eye on Walter, but shortly afterwards Gilbert emigrated to Australia. A remark by Walter that: 'I parted with him with regret, and my entry in my diary was "A good boy, and one of the three of my children who never said an unkind word to their father", perhaps points to family tensions that do not otherwise feature in the record. Hubert and Marjorie, who continued to live in London, returned to Lammas for the inevitably rather sad Christmas season of 1910, as they did again in each of the next three years, though the spark had gone out of the festivities. Christmas 1912, according to Walter, was a 'very dismal one', and in 1913 'we were all ill and in bed all Boxing Day and Saturday'. Walter in turn went up to London from time to time, to stay with Hubert and Marjorie, typically lunching at Simpson's and visiting exhibitions, and taking the opportunity to touch base with Frank on the firm's business. But age and infirmity, as well as the constraints of war and increasing vexation at London's traffic, soon got the better of him and 1915 proved to be the last year in which these visits were practicable. All the sons who were in England, and their respective wives and children, continued regularly to visit Walter in Norwich.

War service

Walter's three youngest sons, Arthur, Hubert and Gilly all served in, and happily all survived, the First World War. Arthur and Hubert both received commissions, whilst Gilbert earned a war medal as an artilleryman in the Dardanelles but was wounded and had to be repatriated.[9] Frank continued to run the law firm throughout the difficult days of the War while Arthur was away, and there was some friction with Walter over this.[10]

Daughters

Mary Muriel Rye ('Murie'), born at Selhurst in 1881, was the seventh of Walter and Georgina's children, and their first daughter. After her in the family line came Gilbert, and then two further daughters, **Frances Elizabeth** ('Betty/Bess/Bessie') (b.1884) and, after a long gap, **Barbara Valentine Catherine** ('Kitty') (b.1889).

Not to be outdone by the boys, Murie became a competent cyclist and archer. Walter took her up to Smallburgh in 1898 to stay with his friends the Griffiths, with whose daughter she became a good friend. Whilst there she learnt to cycle, and as the year went on she was confident enough to cycle both with Walter and on her own. She was now aged seventeen and looking for something meaningful to do with her life. Walter seized the opportunity to enlist her as a potential reader and researcher on his behalf, and persuaded one of the record agents of his acquaintance at the Public Record Office, Miss Walford, to take her on as an apprentice to learn to read Court Hands. With Georgina's indisposition, Murie served in her place as Walter's Mayoress in 1908-9. After her mother's death, tired of country life, she took a job as a governess in Constantinople in 1911, where her sister Betty joined her in 1912, but this does not seem to have lasted: they were back visiting Walter during 1913 and he records that Murie was undertaking research at the PRO on Chaucer on his behalf and meeting him at Simpson's to discuss it.

Murie married and had a son, Bobby, but apart from that in Walter's archive we have only an isolated letter of August 1928 which finds her in Mar del Plata, Argentina.[11]

About Betty, rather less is recorded. She was born at Selhurst on 7 November 1884. After that the *Autobiography* falls silent about her until she was a teenager, but she can be assumed to have been largely in her mother's company at home. In 1899 (aged fourteen) with her brother Arthur she joined Walter for Easter at Selborne, and later that summer, along with the Griffiths' daughter from Smallburgh, visited the Eyres to watch the Henley regatta. Not to be totally eclipsed by her siblings, in 1900 at the Primrose League Gymkhana she won several prizes including that for the ladies' bicycle race. We know that, with all her sisters, she was still living with her parents in Norwich at the time of the 1901 census; that, with Walter's disapproval, she tried her hand at (paid) gardening (1906);[12] that she had a bulldog pup called Diana (1907); and that she was present with the family at Georgina's death (1910).

Not long after the 1911 census had recorded all the daughters as living with Walter at Lammas, one after another of them left home. We can only guess whether this was simply the result of their individual circumstances and opportunities, or whether it was that, with no Georgina around to command their care and loyalty, and indeed to require nursing, Walter on his own was simply too much to handle. At any rate, with their departure he must surely have felt more isolated. He records rather sadly that Betty was the last to leave, and that with no remaining daughter to keep house for him, he urgently needed to find a housekeeper. The *Autobiography* records that in 1914, Betty came home 'to say goodbye', but does not record where she was going.

Kitty, the last child, was born in 1889 and baptised in Hampstead. She was inevitably with Georgina for much of the time and is recorded accompanying her on trips to Selborne and to the seaside. Evidently either she or a close friend had learnt to drive, for Walter records that in 1910 she had a 'motor spill' and had to be brought home in a cart. After Georgina's death she was the only one of Walter's children to spend the Christmas of 1914 with him at Lammas but she seems, at least for a while, to have left home. When his Scottish housekeeper left him the next year, Walter went up to London on an unsuccessful quest to replace her. Kitty returned to help out, and was once again his only company at Christmas 1915. In the New Year of 1916 she again came briefly and went, but this could not be a permanent arrangement and Walter soon saw that he must leave Lammas and move into lodgings in Norwich. It seems from remarks in Walter's will that eventually Kitty returned to live with him in Norwich and nursed him in his final years.

Endnotes

1   Frank was not recorded as at home on census day.
2   Walter himself was not resident on the day of the census, but is recorded staying in Kensington with his old partner W. H. Eyre and his wife.
3   For further information see George A. Stephens, *Walter Rye: Memoir...* (1929); WR, *Norfolk Families* and *Autobiog.*
4   *Horse and Hound,* 30 July 1892, p.495.
5   *Horse and Hound*, 13 Mar. 1897, p.159. For the prize essay see *EHR* XIII (1898).
6   According to family sources, he may have suffered something of a breakdown over this.
7   VCH Archive, A56 (1902).
8   James married in 1914 and his wife bore him a daughter in 1916. He d. 26 Dec. 1935.
9   In a letter of 26 June 1915 Dick Howlett wrote, 'I congratulate you on Gilly's successful "scrap" with the Germans and coming through unhurt. I always liked that boy.' NRO, MS 4691/16. On 4 Aug. 1916 Ficklin wrote to Walter, 'I am delighted to hear the report you give about Gillie... I am glad also to learn that Hubert had got a Commission and hope Arthur will be equally fortunate and no longer have to salute his younger brother.' NRO, MS 4691/5/1.
10 NRO, MS 4691/2: T. H. Jessupp, a new partner in Rye & Eyre: undated letter (but filed among papers for 1919): apologises for errors in letters sent to Walter... 'Poor FGR I know gets very irritable, and is much overworked but I take what I can off his hands and put up with this irritation; he is certainly loyal to his friends and one of the best fellows in the world. You seem to have – unwittingly probably – rubbed him the wrong way as to the financial position of the firm, and I know you have been anxious but will you let me assure you that we are thoroughly sound... Please keep this all to yourself and burn the letter.' Frank went on to become Mayor of Westminster and an MP, see ODNB.
11 NRO, MS 4691/8.
12 In 1906 Walter says that Bessy, attracted by a specious advert for women gardeners, tried her hand at it – 'a paying idea for the promoters, who get their ground cultivated for nothing while their pupils are supposed to be learning'.

6
WIDOWHOOD AND WAR (1910–1929)

In the wider world – about which one hears so little in Walter's *Autobiography* – winds of change were blowing. In 1910, 'dreading like many others the confiscating legislation of Lloyd George' through the Finance Act and a rampant Land Revenue, Walter sold the ancillary cottages and half his orchard at Lammas by auction, but for the time being retained the main house and the rest of his land there.[1]

On 2 July 1911, he found the Coronation Day festivities for King George V 'rather amusing, especially the helping at the dinner, the rural sports and the stately dancing to a dulcimer'. He rode out to Skeyton hill to try to see the Norwich bonfire, but little was visible. At a pageant next day at Buxton he was 'unconsciously snap-shotted on my machine [tricycle], the result being an excellent likeness'.

Perhaps the most momentous event recorded was the great flood. In August 1912, six inches of rain fell in Norwich in twelve hours, resulting in serious flooding in both the city and the surrounding countryside.

> Owing to the neglect of the Buxton miller in not opening the gates, Buxton bridge was carried away; the water flooding the Anchor of Hope and escaping behind it brought down debris which long blocked the channel by the railway bridge, and carried away many houses and the bridge at Coltishall. Drowned fowls were common and only fetched one shilling each, the natives objecting to eat them because they had not been intentionally killed! I did not share their

views! I drove out to see the mischief which was very great and on the Wednesday only just got over Mayton Bridge (where an old sow had floated down and been caught in the wires) and into Norwich.

All post letters and papers ceased to be delivered at Lammas for some days, as the waters were running like a raging torrent and brought down great lumps of peat etc. with it. Eventually (after many days) a temporary plank bridge was made to the Mill over the fields, but the broken road was not filled up till Mr Sewell liberally gave the earth to do so (in the hole whence it was removed the new schoolmaster's house was built) but I doubt it will last if another similar flood comes.[2]

The onset of war

From at least 1907 Walter had included among his lectures one entitled 'War and the Weapons of War', in which he argued strongly that Britain's defences needed to be readied and maintained against an enemy attack, and that this might include attack from the air. By most of his listeners this was dismissed as scaremongering, and he attracted strong opposition. He records in the *Autobiography* that by 1913 rumours abounded of sightings of German airships. Whilst by no means disposed to give credence to every rumour, he felt this one to be quite plausible: might the Germans perhaps allow Britain control of the sea because they knew they could wipe out any resistance from the air? He wrote on those lines to the *Eastern Daily Press*.

When war was declared in 1914, he was staying briefly with Arthur and Mabel, and records his reactions:

Like most Englishmen I did not at first realise the immense importance of the matter. We could not understand why the Germans, who were in the fair way of annexing all the profitable business of the world by their methodical habits, should want to kill the goose that laid the golden eggs and run enormous risks to gratify a militant taste which we did not think was shared by the common people of Germany. In fact we all thought that as soon as the Emperor insisted on the necessarily immense sacrifices his people would turn and rend him. That a whole nation, men and women alike, could be impregnated with war instincts, and with rabid hate of a country that had never done them any harm, did not strike us as being possible, and that individual soldiers could commit the atrocities they afterwards did seemed absolutely impossible, but time has shown how wrong we were.

In Norwich there were soon signs of a military presence, and certain everyday activities and pastimes including Walter's archery were suspended. His son Gilly was quick to join the army and was at first gazetted to a cavalry regiment, but preferred to serve in the artillery (and did so until he came home wounded, after which he obtained a commission in the London Rifle Brigade). Walter himself, although now aged over seventy, also wanted to do something useful for the war effort, and bought a motor tricar in the hope of being able to serve as a dispatch rider. His offer was turned down! Later, after moving into the centre of Norwich he had the brainwave that as a lifelong indexer he could help families and the authorities to keep tabs on the local wounded by making a card catalogue of all in-patients at the hospital, listed on a daily basis; but the authorities preferred their own methods (and personnel). 'This hurt my feelings,' he wrote, 'as indexing was ever my hobby, and I am sure the scheme would have been useful. It was very hard for a septuagenarian not to be able to do some little thing for his country – however small.' One offer of a more humane nature was accepted, namely that he might donate a piano to an internment camp for aliens. Walter's controversial press column during the war, which stirred great resentment in the agricultural community, is discussed in Track 5.

During 1915 a terrifying new war threat emerged in the almost random Zeppelin bombing raids down the east coast. To Walter these were underhand, less than fair play. The inhabitants of Norwich heard the explosions from the Zeppelin raid on East Dereham where, he felt:

… the inhabitants had gone out of their way to 'ask for it' by having a quasi-fair in the market place, a concert at the town hall and a party at a country house nearby. Having been told by apparently veracious people that my old pargetted cottages there (Bonner's cottages) had been blown to pieces I went over to find they had not been touched, though Mr Barton's house almost opposite had suffered greatly.

One Zeppelin raid hit Lammas and the surrounding district, and he feared it might have done for his archery ground:

The continual flights of the Zeppelins over our neighbourhood convinced me that the Germans had some one showing them lights in the district, but I could not get the authorities to take active measures to detect him, and it is no use now going into the question as the suspect has left the neighbourhood.

On 22 January 1915, Ted Beloe (TB) wrote from Lynn of:

... that blasted buzzing in the sky and intermittent flash and crash enough to wake the dead – one bomb did lodge in the [cemetery] to the south of me and the next in the walks to the north, my next door neighbour's windows were smashed, but neither my house, office, museum, wife, maid servant, ox, ass, nor anything that was mine was hurt. There's an unexploded bomb within 10 feet of the office and another within 100 yards of St Nicholas Chapel – but the one on the docks was a plumper, clean in the middle of the hydraulic machinery which supplies all the power to dock gates, cranes and bridges...[3]

On 5 February, Holcombe Ingleby wrote to Walter from southwest London:

I have traced the Zeppelin right across the country as far as Norwich, and cannot imagine why you were not treated to the same sort of dose as we had in our part of the county, unless the villains had used up all the bombs.[4]

... And three days later:

I have an extraordinary mass of evidence, which proves to the hilt that the Zeppelin in our district was accompanied by two motor cars. The only question really is whether there were not more than this number, and whether they were the same as the motor cars that were guiding the Zeppelin outside Norwich. The Zeppelin at

Brancaster was stated to be so low down as to be little higher than the telegraph wires. At Brancaster Staith the occupants of a motor car actually shouted to the occupants of the Zeppelin. The coast-guard office a little further on endeavoured to stop the car without success. The audacity of the spies on this [occasion] is really incredible. They treated the whole place as if it possessed neither a policeman nor a soldier, and they were perfectly justified in doing so, although the whole of our coast-line at that moment teemed with military.[5]

Walter's way of life was subject to strains and stresses as a result of the war. Anxiety over the fate of his sons serving at the front must have dominated. Archery, as we have seen, was off. The opportunities for tricycle rides were seriously circumscribed. He did manage a few excursions by motor car at the invitation of others, but now they had to take their own picnics, as food was not available in the local inns. On one occasion when he went to London and dined at Simpson's with HGR, he found on his return that 'the old restaurant car had been taken off'.

Although too old to enlist, Walter wrote to local papers exhorting younger men to volunteer without waiting to be called up, because the Germans were unscrupulous and ignored the rules of war. Did he perhaps follow the example of some of his friends by reporting suspicions about individuals thought to be spying?[6]

The move from Lammas back to Norwich

In 1916, with neither daughters nor housekeeper now readily available to care for him, and with his sons away fighting, Lammas was a lonely place. Walter sold Rectory Cottage to the rector himself and moved back into Norwich, renting rooms in a house in Mill Hill Road.[7] His good friend Blanche Featherstone wrote: 'That dear Rectory Cottage, I feel quite sorry you have sold it and what a vandal and a Hun that rector must be to make such drastic alterations. What pleasant times I have had there.'[8]

As he now had no spare room in which to put up friends, anyone, like D. M. Roberts, who wanted to stay had to take lodgings elsewhere in the city.[9] But incredibly, yet again Walter had pitched his tent unwisely! His landlady was a nonconformist, and try as he might he could not get on with her. After six months he was off again, to take up a safer offer of rooms with church friends at 48 Christchurch Road, where he was very comfortable, though still troubled with ill health. Jessie Bannister was probably not jesting when she wrote on 16 September: 'We are very glad to know that you are comfortable with your "good church people": it must have been a terrible experience for you to have fallen among dissenters!' [10]

How long this arrangement lasted is not clear, but by 1919 he had the leasehold of a terraced house at 66 Clarendon Road where he remained until his death ten years later. Jane Hales once went to see him there: 'His house was rather a dismal place off the Unthank Road. It was hard to believe that this stoutish bent old man was once the champion walker of England.'[11]

Kitty, who seems to have returned, had her own bedroom and sitting room. She had let Walter know that she was considering becoming a Roman Catholic nun after his death, and a clause was therefore inserted in his will that if she did so she herself should determine who would receive her share of her father's residual estate. In his declining years of sickness Walter also had both a female and a male servant, Florence Hammond and Charles Hurry.[12] His days of serious outdoor activities were over, and during his own last decade his friends and contemporaries were dying, but we do still occasionally find him taking holidays by the sea,[13] and as we shall see in Track 2 he continued to take part in archery contests.

Tom Copeman recollected in 1973:

> I first met him in May 1919 when he asked me to call on him at his house in Clarendon Road as I had subscribed to his *Norfolk Hand Lists*. Stout and bearded, he was suffering from an attack of gout, one of his legs being heavily bandaged and supported on a stool. Book cases covered the walls of the small front room, and from where I sat I could see anyone who came to the front door. Presently no less a person than the Honorary Secretary [of the Norfolk and Norwich Archaeological Society] was ringing the bell, and I expected to be dismissed. On being told who it was Rye roared, 'Tell him I can't see him now'.[14]

In August 1919 for the second time in his life Walter was the victim of a house fire, which was serious enough to be reported in the *Eastern Daily Press*, though as I have found no mention of Walter's having to move out the damage cannot have been irreparable. George Stephen wrote from Great Yarmouth to commiserate:

> We were very sorry to learn from three sources… this morning that you had an alarming fire at your house. We are afraid that you had a very exciting and worrying time. It is exceedingly fortunate that all your MSS are uninjured, because you would have grieved terribly if anything had happened to them… [15]

With only a tiny city garden, compared with the acres he had been used to, Walter's challenge was to 'get some greenery and colour round me once again'. In an essay on 'A city garden', written in 1920, he reflected that 'life was at first very unpleasant'. The garden was full of builders' rubble under light soil, so he had to excavate in places and bring in new soil 'mixed with road scarpings and horse droppings collected by itinerant boys who supplied me with many pailfuls at a penny a time'. At the age of seventy-seven he lacked the strength to mix loads of compost, even if he had been able to acquire it, so a bit-by-bit approach was the best he could manage. But he was pleased with the end results: showy sweet peas, a grand anchusa (Dropmore Gardens variety), Shirley poppies, bergamot (with red blooms and a sweet smell), white tobacco and blue borage; borders of love-in-a-mist and white and blue rock cress. On the west wall were: a button rambler, blue clematis, *begonia radicans*; outdoor tomatoes; red valerian, nasturtium, globe artichoke, sunflower, marrow, scarlet runners, parsley, mint. In the front garden: purple buddleia, everlasting pea (white), montbretia… Many of these were planted with a view to encouraging butterflies.[16] As late as 1927, when Walter was eighty-three, his gardening skills still amazed his friends.[17]

Endnotes

1   Lammas was not the limit of his property investment. He acquired cottages at Horning (also sold off in 1910 for the same reason), and in 1903 a picturesque double cottage on land at Benspit Hole, which he came to call 'Rye's Folly', because it never brought in sufficient rent to pay its way.
2   *Autobiog.*
3   NRO, MS 4691/16.
4   *Ibid.*
5   *Ibid.*

6 Barrett Lennard wrote on 18 Oct. 1915: 'I went to see the CC [Chief Constable] and he showed me a dossier of the man in question. If he were proved to be a spy he could, of course, be dealt with as any Englishman could be. He could not be interned as a foreigner because his father was a naturalized Englishman and he himself born in England of an English mother. Scotland Yard have gone into his case and do not consider that there is any case against him; and the police watch him. This being so there appears nothing to be done at present unless something more crops up.' NRO, MS 4691/14/2.

7 Blanche Featherstone, 17 Mar., in NRO, MS 4691/5/1.

8 NRO, MS 4691/5/1. The house survives, though in much altered form.

9 NRO, MS 4691/5 letters of 2 May and 27 June.

10 NRO, MS 4691/5.

11 Jane Hales, 'I knew Walter Rye', in *Norfolk Fair*, Aug. 1984.

12 Florence and Charles each received cash bequests whilst Arthur Sexton, his chauffeur and odd-jobs man, was bequeathed all Walter's clothes. See his will of which the original is dated 30 Jan. 1927, with codicil of 2 Aug.

13 G. H. Holley of The Vicarage, Holme Next the Sea, wrote on 9 Nov. 1920 that he might know of someone who could offer rooms to let and 'give you all the fresh air you need in his motor car', NRO, MS 4691/2.

14 EDP, Norwich, Rye file, date stamped 23 Jul. 1973.

15 16 Aug. 1919: NRO, MS 4691/2,

16 WR, *Recreations* (1922).

17 B. Cozens Hardy wrote on 16 May 1927, 'I know of none who makes so much use of his garden space as you do', NRO, MS 4691/8.

TRACK 2: THE SPORTSMAN

1
ATHLETICS

'If a general vote could be taken amongst those qualified to give an opinion on the matter, to decide upon the man who has done most for the promotion of amateur athletics, there is 'no possible doubt whatever' that Walter Rye would be returned at the head of the poll by an overwhelming majority.'

Sydenham Dixon, 1894

The title of his *Autobiography of an Ancient Athlete and Antiquary* (1916) speaks for itself. Walter wanted to be remembered first and foremost as an athlete, and deservedly so. For two decades from his late teens to his mid-thirties he held several national athletics records and became one of the country's most celebrated sportsmen. He frequently won both local and national championships over several different distances, as a runner and as a walker. In later life, when he also came to be much sought after as a championship steward and judge,[1] he remained well known to everyone in the athletics establishment, having risen to prominence in the sport's governing bodies. In our own time he has been assessed as 'the most formidable figure in the athletic world' by 1870.[2]

Pedestrianism[3]
Walter would reflect that his athletic stamina and determination were a survival mechanism in the face of his harsh upbringing.[4] The meagre stipend of a junior legal clerk, paid to him by his father, probably ruled out the regular use of public transport. So, in order to get between home in Chelsea and work in Golden Square, or between work and evening classes

at King's College, walking was the only practical option, as indeed many of his contemporaries found: this was very much an age of walking.

The exercise kept him fit and he rather came to enjoy it. On holiday too, walking enabled him to reach and explore distant antiquarian sites, or to set off to collect entomological and other natural history specimens. Before long this purely functional form of walking turned his thoughts to something more athletic. Under the influence of his elder brother and mentor, Edward Caldwell Rye (EC, as Walter always referred to him), he began to experiment with 'pedestrianism' – i.e. walking as an athletic pursuit – and soon spoke of 'the athletic madness' that had overcome him.[5]

In 1859 (aged fifteen) he recorded walking a mile in eleven minutes 'in my clothes'. In September the same year he had his first long walk with EC, and in November recorded that he had walked the seventeen-and-a-half miles from home to Kingston Bridge and back in three hours fifty-three minutes. But it was not long before he tried running too, and in 1860 (aged sixteen) he records 'the first symptoms of *cacoethes currendi*',[6] after taking on and beating many of his contemporaries at sprints.[7] As he gained in stamina and technique, he challenged others to private walking contests.

His training 'walks', evidently purely in the pursuit of athletic excellence, stretched to punishing lengths. In 1861, the year in which he became eighteen, his many very long walks included one of over thirty-eight miles to collect butterflies, and another of forty-one miles in about ten hours without stopping or sitting down. 'I was very chafed and footsore, but hardly tired. Personally I look upon this as the best performance I ever did.'[8]

Sometimes, like Dickens and others of his generation,[9] he walked at night. In Walter's case it was probably more a physical training exercise than either a cure for insomnia (which he did not log among his ailments), or a means of putting his thoughts in order before writing. Perhaps he knew of Walter Thom's *Pedestrianism; or an Account of the Performances of Celebrated Pedestrians During the Last and Present Century* (1813), with its apologia that: 'Exercise on foot is allowed to be the most natural and perfect, as it employs every part of the body and effectually promotes the circulation of the blood through the arteries and veins.'[10]

On 15 October 1861 a long night walk was, he said, 'made extra melancholy by the incessant tolling of Church bells for the death of Prince Albert'. His favourite Sunday evening walk was a mere twenty-four miles, but he records once walking thirty-seven miles into Surrey on a bitterly cold day 'with six cold mutton sandwiches and a bottle of lemonade as my only refreshment'.[11] His longest recorded walk was an awe-inspiring eighty-six miles in a single day.[12]

Whilst staying at North Walsham on one of his Norfolk breaks, he was once taunted by local lads for his manner of walking; and more knowledgeable commentators in the professional press would later be just as critical of his peculiar style; but it evidently did not prevent him winning competitions.[13]

Rowing

Meanwhile in 1861 Walter first ventured on to the river, presumably again with EC, in a light boat from a boathouse near the Magpie and Stump at the bottom of Oakley Street, Chelsea. A short time later, also with EC, he joined the Thames Rowing Club (the former 'City of London' club)[14] and became proficient enough to win his first race, in 1862, in a coxed pair with his former school friend Dick Howlett at bow and EC as cox.[15] The club met on both Wednesday and Saturday evenings at Simmons boathouse, Putney, and hired a room at the Red Lion. Its historian, Geoffrey Page, notes that in its 'City of London' days the members were mainly clerks and sellers from the rag trade. The change of name marked its determination to become both more competitive and more socially mixed. Like many other sporting clubs of the time, its vigorous social life was part of its *raison d'être*, and included home-spun dramatic entertainments.[16] This was a routine that Walter later carried forward into his own Thames Hare and Hounds. Given his continuing educational commitments in the evenings, however, it seems likely that his rowing sessions were only occasional.

Some forty years later R. C. Lehmann would wax lyrical about rowing: 'The exercise itself is one of the noblest in the world, both in regard to its development of bodily strength and health, and in the lessons of self-restraint and discipline in which its votaries are unconsciously forced to perfect themselves.'[17]

Walter would surely have endorsed that vision of manly sport. But his rowing skill came to be far eclipsed by that of his eventual legal partner, W. H. ('Piggy') Eyre, a man some years his junior. Their friendship began during Walter's bachelor days. Eyre became a member of Walter's Thames Hare and

Hounds (see below), and they shared lodgings in Putney in 1867–8. It was Walter who put him up for the Thames Rowing Club (TRC), in which Eyre would become a legend in his own lifetime.[18] But any enthusiasm on Walter's part for rowing was soon eclipsed by his commitment to athletics; and the absence of all mention of his name from Eyre's account of the TRC's early history rather suggests that Walter never proved himself as an oarsman.[19]

Running

Walter made his first appearance in a public running race in the 300-yards at the Volunteer Fête held at Beaufort House in June 1861, but on that occasion he fell at a turn and came in third. He became a member of the London Athletic Club (LAC) only shortly after its foundation in 1863[20] and regularly records taking part in its championships as both a walker and a runner. In 1863 he entered his first major athletic competition, the Gentlemen Amateurs' Walking Race at Hackney,[21] and led it for much of the way but failed to finish the course because, in his own words, he was 'utterly untrained'. This he was determined to remedy by self-motivated training at the athletic track around the West London Cricket Ground and by more of his long walks, which he would keep up for many years, sometimes alone but often with one or more companions – or challengers if the walk was timed.

He was soon putting himself forward as a challenger to some of the most accomplished athletes of the day, and entered an increasing number of competitions not only in and around London but also in Norfolk and as far afield as Nottingham and Liverpool,[22] representing on different occasions the various clubs of which he was a member: Thames Rowing Club, King's College London Rowing Club (1865 and 1866),[23] the LAC and Thames Hare and Hounds. In the *Autobiography* he quotes extensively from his youthful diaries which recorded almost nothing except details of when, how far and how fast he walked or ran, and where relevant the names of his challengers. Contemporary press reports show that many club athletics meetings at this time were open to the public and attracted large crowds, whose marshalling made great demands on the stewards.

By this means Walter became known to a large sporting public as well as to fellow athletes.[24] At his best he was able to beat some of the finest athletes of the day, including W. G. Grace, E. Hawley, and E. A. Hoare. In a meeting in 1865 he was beaten by Walter Chinnery who was to become the first amateur to run the mile in under four minutes thirty seconds; but then Walter went on to beat his brother, G. T. Chinnery, in what was then the record time for two miles walking, of sixteen minutes twenty-eight seconds.[25] He comments:

> This injudicious exposure of form naturally placed me on the scratch mark for all future handicaps, and from it in 1866 I won a mile handicap in 7.37 (also then the best), in 1867 won the LAC challenge cup, and in 1868 won the championship, easing up in 57.40 having done 23.17 for the first three miles, when I was 200 yards in front.[26]

Sydenham Dixon (1894) summed up Walter's athletics career as follows:

> He was the champion walker of his day, and though, as has been the case with nearly every noted walker, his style of moving was occasionally the subject of unfavourable criticism, there were not two opinions as to the indomitable gameness that pulled him through in so many of his races. Then he could run a mile in what, thirty years ago was very good time; indeed, I can recall no one who would have stood the remotest chance with him in a match to 'run a mile and walk a mile'.[27]

By 1867 (aged twenty-four) Walter was beginning to feel 'too heavy in the legs', and wondered if his best running days might be over, so he resolved to concentrate more on walking, while still entering for the occasional run. In November that year his pride took a fall when he was defeated in a walk by S. P. Smith, 'a very tall, strong man [who] walked fairer than I ever saw a man before or since, and I took it for granted that my walking supremacy was a thing of the past.' But the next year Walter beat him twice, and Smith never challenged him again.[28]

The *Autobiography* is sparse for 1868. 'Business and matrimony', or at any rate its pursuit (and, he might have added, increasing weight) tended to keep him away from the athletics track. Even so, press accounts show that he had no shortage of sporting commitments. For instance, the *Morning Post* of 27 April reported on the Athletic Clubs sports held the previous Saturday at Beaufort House, Walham Green. In the three miles walking handicap:

As Mr Walter Rye and other celebrated walkers were among the competitors, considerable interest was manifested as regards the result… On Rye being ordered off from the scratch he went away in his usual rapid style and at the completion of the first mile he had disposed of Williams and Griffiths and was overhauling Nuan, who at the time was walking well but retired after the sixth lap, two miles, Rye's time now being 15 min. 6 sec. At the eighth round, Mitchell went ahead of Wilkinson and Rye now became third, striving his utmost to overtake the leading men. At the end of the seventh lap Mitchell went in advance of Wilkinson, Rye getting closer to his opponents, but despite his almost superhuman exertions he failed in the desired object and was compelled to be contented with third prize. Rye, whose time we have stated as he only started from the commencement, completed the three miles in the extraordinary quick time of 23 min 5 sec.[29]

Two months later, on 22 June, the same paper reported on the next Athletic Clubs sports at Walham Green. In the seven miles walk only three men started: Walter representing the London Athletic Club, T. Griffiths the City Amateur Athletic Club, and H. M. Wilkinson the Civil Service. The event 'excited great interest among the members of the numerous clubs'… even though a vast number of would-be spectators could not reach the event on account of a review of Volunteers at Windsor. Walter's win, 'in the unprecedented time of 57 min. 40 secs,'[30] was to be repeated in the same event the following year.

Between competitions he continued to train regularly. In 1869 he walked every day from his lodgings (now in Roehampton) to his office in town, and back via the circuit at the West London Cricket Ground where he, the two Chinnerys and E. J. Colbeck were 'practically daily visitors':

Our training refreshment after exercise was invariably half a pint of public house port and an arrowroot biscuit each. Verily we must have all had *dura ilia* with a vengeance. Our usual diet was one big cup of tea and a chop or steak for breakfast, the same without tea but with a half pint of bitter or old ale diluted with three penny-worth of gin for dinner, and the same for supper. The idea was the old-fashioned one (now exploded) of limiting men to two pints of liquid a day. None of us smoked then, and yet we were fairly successful.

At the end of the Civil Service Athletic Sports in June 1869 Walter, who had set himself the challenge of walking two miles in fifteen minutes, 'completed the distance in six seconds under the time'.[31]

Marriage and business notwithstanding, the walks, especially the night walks, continued throughout the next decade, and the *Autobiography* records in 1876 a midnight walk with 'Inman from Putney' round Windsor in the summer. There is a sad aside: 'It is a strange coincidence that both of my chief competitors in these long walks afterwards committed suicide.' After a long day at the LAC on 20 November he was still up for a long night walk: eight hours, with Charlie Talbot, G. A. Bolton and E. C. Otter starting at 12.45am.

The 'Father of Paper-Chasing': Thames Hare and Hounds [*See plate IV*]

Steeplechasing was already a recognised part of the athletics repertoire, but in 1867 Walter put to his fellow members of the Thames Rowing Club (TRC) a proposal for a new kind of sporting challenge: paper-chasing, directly inspired by the account of that sport at Rugby School in *Tom Brown's Schooldays*.

The first 'Thames Handicap Steeplechase' [paper-chase], hosted by the TRC, took place not on a running track but over open country on Wimbledon Common, with the permission of Earl Spencer. In essence, one or more runners (the hares) would set off through open country laying a trail of paper and scent. Then, after a reasonable lapse of time, the pack (the hounds) would set off, with a view to catching the hares preferably before they reached the designated finish, but at least in a better overall time. The hares were selected some time before the meet, and would generally walk over the ground in advance to devise a cunning and challenging route, noting points at which they might lay a false trail for a few yards to delay and confuse the pursuing hounds.

The first event was a shambles, but was still rated great fun by the participants, and as a result a new club, Thames Hare and Hounds (THH), was formed in the following year. Happily, it is still in existence. It was to elevate paper-chasing to a recognised adult sport, the ancestor of modern cross-country, and Walter has been fêted ever since as the Father of Paper-Chasing.

Looking back on all this at the time of Walter's death in 1929, Mr A. Scott, who all those years before had been in charge of the Rugby School archives, recalled:

> ... a little historical detail, of which very few indeed can now have any personal knowledge, that... in the autumn of 1868, Mr Rye wrote to me – we were mutual strangers – on the subject of a running club which he and some friends had in contemplation. At his request I did the best I could to provide him with the general rules and customs of the sport as pursued at Rugby, and shortly afterwards the 'Thames Hare and Hounds' came into being and held their first run. So I do not think that I am far wrong in regarding the celebrated London Club as an off-shoot from the old tree, whose roots probably from time immemorial have been in Warwickshire![32]

As this sport evolved, irrespective of whether hare or hounds won the day, all the participants had an exhausting, often muddy run across hedges, ditches and other difficult terrain, depending on the route taken by the hares. The meetings were frequently held late in the afternoon or at night in order to avoid entanglement with daytime walkers or, worse still, shooting parties, but also to facilitate participation after working hours by young professional men like Walter himself. Writing about paper-chasing in 1889 for a general readership, he described the rules and conventions, including the legitimacy of the hares laying false trails. In the same article he noted that whilst some participants had been teetotallers, he personally could see no harm in drinking alcohol or smoking in moderation.

The *Morning Post* of 14 December 1869 reported a THH meet at which the hares (P. Evans of the LAC and Walter) were allowed fifteen minutes' start before the chase:

They proceeded over the King's Road, cutting in and out by the deep glen, straight past the butts to the rounds, over the Roads farm as the crow flies, thence across a lot of plough into the little valley by the Beverley brook up to some ploughed land, through Coombe wood by a steep path emerging at the back of the conduits, then down the Malden lane across the fields parallel with the railway into Coombe lane, up the new grass roads to the ridgeway by the new church, and past the Wimbledon School ground, running home by way of the common and mill, the distance traversed being 8 miles. Up to this point the 'hares' kept together, when they parted and raced home without being caught, having got about two miles by the start given. Rye came in first in 58 min 37 sec and Evans at 59 min 34 sec...

A significant degree of organisation was required for these paper-chases, from the initial liaison with landowners, to the logistics of getting the participants to the start and watching over and collecting up their kit. Sadly, apart from a few individual items, the club's early archives no longer exist, though important traces of its activity in these early days can be found in press reports of the meetings. A single handwritten circular to members from Walter as Secretary, written on Boxing Day 1871, gives a hint of the organisation involved:

Meetings, held weekly, now usually on a Saturday afternoon or early evening, typically attracted between one and two dozen participants, although the number of signed-up members of the club was considerably more. A bus might be hired to take runners to the start, where they had to 'dress how they could'.[34]

Soon the club appointed an administrator, George Howick, affectionately known as the 'Commissary General', a registrar of births, marriages and deaths in Wandsworth who being also a local corn chandler had horses and carts available to transport men and kit. As a tradesman, he was not himself eligible for membership of Thames Hare and Hounds, which remained a gentlemen's club, but he was a respected and indispensable figure, and was allowed to attend the club's annual dinner.[35]

Walter deservedly earned a reputation for setting hard challenges for the hounds, both in terms of the length of the course and the obstacles and hazards that had to be negotiated:

Our longest run, in which I took the bags with Sydenham Dixon, son of the 'Druid', was in the spring of 1871 over Wimbledon, Cheam (where old Harry Andrews had gone on with bags of fresh scent) round Nonsuch and Epsom (more scent called for), Ewell and so home, the distance being carefully estimated at the time at 23¼ miles. J Scott finishing an easy first in 3hr 16min 30sec.[36]

Table: A summons for Thames Hare and Hounds

Dear Sir

The next run of our club will take place from Roehampton on Saturday next (30th inst) – Hares (Messrs FV Rainsford, Wilfred Ball) will be sent out at 3.20 and Hounds at 3.30.

Your attendance is particularly requested as the smallness of the number on the 16th inst at Hampstead is much to be regretted as damaging the prestige of the Club, & unless Members attend the meets – especially when matches are advertized, there will be little use in continuing the runs in future.

Trusting therefore to see you on Saturday with any friends that you can bring.

I am, yours faithfully,
Walter Rye
Hon. Sec. Thames H&H

P.S. 2.20 train from Waterloo to Putney, & the run will take place however abominably bad the weather may be.[33]

A quarter of a century later, Dixon recollected that although Walter had been outrun in that event by Scott, who had won in a remarkable time, it was not until he had made a gallant fight of it and run the other hare (Dixon himself) 'right off his legs'. He went on with a darkly satirical account of Walter's challenges:

Rye has always had a special fondness for promoting quaint and eccentric contests. One still hears dark rumours of a certain gruesome obstacle race, in which the wretched competitors had to crawl through barrels carefully lined with sharp spikes, to climb cucumber frames set upon end, with an unfair proportion of broken glass remaining in them, and to swim a half-frozen pond. These may or may not be true: but I can personally vouch for the fact that carrying a few pounds of shot does not help a man in winning a steeplechase, and that a mile and a half along the bed of the Beverley, the water varying in depth from 6in to 3ft, is not a pleasant course for a race on a cold December afternoon. Such a terribly hard hitter with both tongue and pen as Walter Rye has always been is bound to make enemies, but those who know him best soon discover his sterling worth, and are honestly proud of possessing the friendship of one of the most sensitively honourable men that ever lived.[37]

The club occasionally opened steeplechasing events to non-members, and the printed advertisement for the twelfth of these, held in January 1873, survives in its archives:

Table: Notice of **Thames Handicap Steeplechase No. 12**

This Race will take place on Saturday, the 18th January, 1873. Distance, 4 miles and 5 furlongs, viz., up and down good roads, to Beverley Bridge, then to the left along the brook for 1 mile and 1 furlong of rough and swampy common, then for ¾ of a mile over the Rounds Farm, chiefly turnips and plough, in and out a sunk road, in and out the defiles straight to Wimbledon Mill, over the Common, and so by the cross roads to the Well House. The Race will be started at 4.15 pm. An Omnibus will meet, at Putney, the 3.25 from Waterloo. The Race is open to any gentleman amateur, and there will be five prizes, viz. 1st prize, Silver Cup, value £6 6s.; 2nd prize, a Claret Jug (presented by W. Rye); 3rd prize, a Cup (presented by J. Buchanan); 4th prize, a Pewter (presented by R. Matthews); and 5th prize, a Pewter (presented by the Commissary-General of the T.H. & H.).

Entries, 2s. 6d. each, close Saturday, 11th January, to W. RYE, Hon. Sec., T.H. & H., Ivy Lodge, North Street, Wandsworth, S.W. [38]

In the weekly paper-chase, Walter was a keen participant, sometimes as hare, sometimes as hound, although he was nothing like as good at this as he was at his pedestrianism, and was rarely named among the winners.[39] He had many thrills and spills, and stored up tales of woe and triumph to entertain for years afterwards. On one occasion he came fifth, 'having been

Thames Hare and Hounds group photograph, 1872. *Thames Hare and Hounds*. Walter centre of back row, with beard.

Thames Rowing Club, Wyfold Challenge Cup winners, 1870. *Thames Rowing Club*. WH ('Piggy') Eyre second from the left.

delayed somewhat by a temporary sojourn in a morass at the bottom of a ravine'.[40] On another:

> … determined to have dry things to run home in, and having to swim the Wandle, I stripped and packed my jersey and knickerbockers into my scent bag and threw it, as I thought, across the river, but unluckily it fell a foot or so short, and I had to grope for the bag in the icy water, re-dress in wet things on the opposite bank, and run home over Wimbledon Common in the teeth of a north wind, only just escaping the hounds, who had found a bridge and who came home dry.[41]

Then there was the time when a renowned runner from the north of England, 'Choppy' Warburton, had signed up to take part. The hounds knew they would never beat him on the flat, so in an attempt to tip the scales in their favour they laid a trail that repeatedly crossed the Hogsmill. But they found that he was just as good a swimmer as he was a runner, and he deservedly beat them![42]

As well as being acclaimed as the Father of Paper-Chasing, Walter can also take credit for finding the first HQ for Thames Hare and Hounds, at the King's Head in Roehampton – recently restored in our day – where from 1866 for a short time he lived in rented rooms:[43] 'The **** at the King's Head Roehampton Bottom was fitted out as a dressing room. There was a fine of 1/- on any member who "uttered the accursed word".'[44]

The trade-off with the (no doubt delighted) manager was that members would adjourn there for food and drink after each gathering. But the company was predictably bibulous and boisterous, so it was not unknown for the entire pack to disgrace itself and run off the 'scent' before the finish, into another public house on the way! Walter describes how the paper-chases would typically end, with a warm bath or a cold douche and, if the weather was cold, a steaming glass of port negus 'taken as a precaution'. Before and after the ensuing meal, the tipple of choice was ginger beer mixed with gin, this 'having probably been found by long experience to best carry off the extra heat of the body caused by a long run'. It sounds a pleasant-enough delusion.

The evenings were rounded off with a sing-song, a card game or, more surprisingly, a spelling bee – the latter introduced by Walter in 1882 as an antidote to card games which, he said, were ruining the club![45] Walter himself delighted in compiling club songs and stories with an element of humour and nonsense.[46]

After he entered his thirties Walter's direct participation in both running and walking began to be thwarted not only by business and family ties but also by poor health. Undeterred, again and again after bouts of illness he would get back into training and attempt a comeback. But he was no longer in the prime of youth, and so he gradually began instead to take his exercise by cycling, whilst taking pride in enthusiastically supporting and recording the athletic achievements of his growing sons.[47] His own final participation in a paper-chasing event was in 1882.

To Thames Hare and Hounds, Walter was not only the founder and inspirer of paper-chasing, but also the life and soul of the club. He was Secretary from its inception to 1870 when he stood down in order to get married, and the new office of President was created for him. But this was a very short-term expedient: he was back again as Secretary in 1871, and the Presidency, which had been very much *ad hominem*, was duly abolished.[48] Then in 1876, on formally taking over the solicitor's practice on his father's death, he did finally resign as Secretary and was once again elected President, an office he would hold right up to his death in 1929 half a century later.[49] At a dinner in 1888 to celebrate the club's twentieth anniversary Walter as the founder was presented with a 'very fine and large silver salver'.[50] As late as 1919 an impassioned call went out from his fellow members for him to attend the club's annual dinner in order to give it a boost after the First World War, but he was then in his late seventies and no longer physically able to travel from Norwich, his home for the past twenty years. The festivities went ahead without him, with those present urging him – unsuccessfully – to write the club's history.[51]

'Old Fylfot'

Walter's good company and zest for jollification both during and after his active athletic career was much valued by club members. An encounter in the course of his antiquarian pursuits with a highly eccentric Londoner,[52] Dr William Thorn, who was obsessed with arcana and mystical symbols, gave Walter the idea of sporting a distinctive *fylfot*, or swastika, on his running vest, a symbol that would also later be incorporated into his coat of arms. In the club he therefore earned the nickname 'Black Fylfot' or 'Old Fylfot'.[53]

The members of Thames Hare and Hounds showed their affection and esteem by subscribing to a 'handsome timepiece' to celebrate Walter's marriage.[54] After he and his wife Georgina settled in Wandsworth, the club held an annual entertainment in the Spread Eagle Assembly Rooms there, and in March 1872 this became a fundraiser for the night school at which Walter taught.[55] When, a few years later, the Ryes moved to a much larger house in St Ann's Hill, Wandsworth, Walter would amply repay them, by converting part of his spacious garden into a running track for the club's use in training, and even for the occasional full meet, and by regularly laying on refreshments for the members at his own expense.

The gentleman amateur

As a solicitor and the son of a solicitor, Walter was certainly seen by most of his contemporaries as a gentleman. He had had to drive himself hard and use his own resources to gain the necessary education and qualifications to confirm this status, and although he did not share the public school or university background of many who supported the notion of the 'gentleman amateur' it certainly coloured his attitudes to both class and sport.[56]

The social and moral attitudes of the day drew a distinction between activities that were suitable for tradesmen and labourers on the one hand, and those fit for gentlemen on the other.[57] When Walter first took up sport (and, not long afterwards, sporting journalism) the social classes generally did not mix – a state of affairs of which he strongly approved. From his public pronouncements on the issue he gained the reputation of being 'anti-tradesman'. This was the more ironic because the very pedestrianism in which he was such an enthusiastic participant had begun as a practical means of having messages delivered by paid runners, and had developed into a substantially working-class sporting activity, with bets often being placed on the outcome.[58] Under Walter's influence, however, Thames Hare and Hounds remained, in the old tradition, a bastion for gentlemen.

Walter wrote passionately and at length about the 'gentleman amateur' ideal, concentrating primarily on athletics, although the same issues applied equally to rowing.[59] Apart from his desire to maintain class segregation in sports, there were two other fundamental principles at stake: that athletic prowess was a manly virtue, a social and health-giving activity offering self-improvement, and was therefore suitable for a gentleman; and that, for a gentleman, physical achievement was its own reward; engaging in sporting activities for financial gain was something to be left for the lower classes.[60] In 1867 he even refused the prize money at a steeplechase in Cromer so that he could demonstrate that he was indeed an amateur.

In 1869 Walter was elected Secretary of the London Athletic Club in succession to Walter Chinnery, but the following year he resigned the post after being out-voted on this very issue of the gentleman amateur.[61] He did not resign his membership of the club itself, and a year later, despite being disillusioned with the new management by the Waddell brothers – who later 'had to fly the country on becoming defaulters as accountants' – he agreed to serve again on a committee looking into the activities of the Amateur Athletic Club (est. 1866), a rival organisation which also promoted national championships, and one on which the LAC then looked down.

Walter maintained his 'gentleman amateur' stance even after many clubs admitted all comers regardless of class. His subsequent friend Dr Frederick Furnivall, who had spent some time trying to save working men from vice and drink, took the opposite view on the grounds that social mingling and indulgence in healthy pastimes might improve their lot both socially and morally.[62] Walter looked on with regret as it became common for spectators to be charged 'gate money' to watch steeplechases, and as participants (at least from *some* clubs) came to expect a share of the takings, a trend he dated from about 1877.[63] 'Pendragon', writing in the *Weekly Dispatch* in July 1877 took a swipe at him: 'Despite all his efforts to get himself mistaken for a gentleman, this enemy of trade is as noticeable now for his onslaughts… as he was in days of yore for the acrobatic contortions he dignified by the name of walking.'[64]

From about 1878, however, Walter began to yield to the growing tide of opinion in the sport that men of all classes should be allowed to participate in paper-chasing events in order to open up the field and the records, although this did not result in any change in membership criteria for Thames Hare and Hounds. The AAC dissolved itself in 1879 after running into a boycott of its national championships over this very issue, and was in effect replaced in 1880 by a new body with membership open to all, the Amateur Athletic Association. Most suspected that Walter would object on principle.

But the promoters of the new association wisely recognised that in spite of fundamental disagreements over the exclusivity of the sport, Walter still carried a lot of clout as both a commentator and a respected practitioner. So they wined and dined him in Oxford well enough for him to agree to stand for election to the AAA, as a representative of Thames Hare and Hounds, one of the ten members of the Association's General Committee.[65]

In the *County Gentleman* of 20 March 1880 Walter finally ate his own words:

> Having been for many years one of the spokesmen of the 'gentlemen amateurs' who have considered, and still consider, that the meeting should be confined to men who are 'gentlemen by profession and education', I am bound in common honesty to admit that there seems to be a growing feeling that in running, walking and jumping contests anyone who has never competed for money or against a professional should be allowed to enter.[66]

Thames Hare and Hounds group photograph, 1898. *Thames Hare and Hounds.* Walter third from right.

In 1881 Walter resigned for a time from the LAC,[67] but remained President of Thames Hare and Hounds and an active committee member of the AAA, of which he was elected a Vice President in 1883. In the same year he was also elected President of the National Cross Country Union.[68]

Dublin

In June 1876 an English athletics team travelled to Ireland for an international competition.[69] Walter – although not a member of the team – accompanied them and was a keen supporter in every sense, bringing to the task his well-honed skills of camaraderie and team-building. He can best take up the story himself:

> We had a rough time crossing, several of our team were very nervous, so I was put forward as a sort of professional buffoon to keep them in spirits. We put up at the Gresham and enlivened the waverers with a series of practical jokes, played chiefly on Winthrop, the 'gentle giant', who was to represent England in the weight-putting and tug-of-war. I affected to doubt his being in proper condition and, having previously slipped a gravy spoon up my leg, just below the knee, got him to try if his muscle was as hard as mine. Then we also thought Slade might beat him in the tug-of-war, and he apparently did so, for he was placed next the door and about half a dozen [hung] on to the end of the rope till the 'giant' was tired out. How we got him to believe that he had insulted his future opponent Daly – how a mythical Daly was supposed to be hunting him for revenge half the night – how he apologised for a sin of which he had never been guilty – is old athletic history, as is the presentation in a carefully closed packing case of a most artistic 'testimonial' when he won the tug-of-war for us, is unfit for publication. [sic] As it was, we won eight out of nine events, the first only falling to Ireland.[70]

Later years

After his official retirement from competitive sport, Walter was still looked up to in the world of athletics as a senior figure, and continued to serve on the governing bodies of a number of clubs and to act as a judge for their competitions. Throughout the 1880s and 1890s while he was still resident in

London, he is regularly noted in the press as attending the LAC and THH annual dinners, where he was cheered as a veteran and a celebrity, and was often asked to give a speech or propose a toast. Even in his declining years he continued to take an interest in his old clubs. He also lent financial support and gave prize medals to new bodies such as the Norwich and Norfolk Athletic Club.[71] 'It is,' wrote Sydenham Dixon in 1894, 'by what he has done, and happily is still doing, for the promotion of sport, rather than by his own performances, admirable as they were, that he will always be remembered.'[72]

'Easterling' of the *Sporting Gazette*

Walter mentions writing on sport for the *Pall Mall Gazette* and the *Sporting Gazette* (later renamed the *County Gentleman*) from at least 1867. His lively, usually waspish column for the latter was at first anonymous, but from 1874 to 1882 appeared under the pseudonym 'Easterling', in which, as he later recalled, 'I enriched the English language with the expressions 'common or garden' and 'obstacle race', the latter form of amusement being originated by me at the Thames sports at Putney'.[73]

We have a testimonial in 1879 as to the success of the *Sporting Gazette* and its team of writers, from the improbable distance of Cape Town, South Africa: 'The present staff is not numerous, but it is capable. Messrs. Nevill Fitt, William Mackay, Walter Rye and Henry Harris have no superiors in their respective lines.'[74]

An unsigned editorial dated 25 January 1873, which if not by Walter was fundamentally influenced by his thinking, reported the findings of a judge in the case of *Wheeler v Hillier* that:

> ... a man may be a very worthy member of society, and a very respectable person, without being a gentleman, in the ordinary acceptation of the word; and that gentlemen have, very naturally and properly, a perfect right to say that they will not – unless they like – associate with a class of men lower in education and manners than themselves.[75]

Most of his Easterling columns, if deliberately provocative and amusing, were nevertheless mainly factual reportage of actual athletics events. For the raw material he was heavily dependent on reports received from others who had attended the events described. When this kind of copy was lacking he worked up his own material to fill the space, and not infrequently this was more controversial in tone. The column gave him a platform to be as critical (and poisonous) as he wished – about individuals just as much as issues. And on occasion, in spite of his legal training, he teetered precariously on the brink of libel, treating the lives and morals of athletes who took part in public competitions as if they were public property – a technique absolutely normal today but less so in Victorian times. As an example we might take an article he wrote about Fred Elborough, winner of five AAC championships. The column included the following: 'I should not be doing my duty if I did not point out that the systematic giving way to habits of inebriation must tell its tale sooner or later, especially on a constitution already undermined by venereal disease.'[76]

He also engaged[77] in a crusade against bogus sporting 'records' set in the USA. His editor allowed one American critic the right of reply, but this only fired Walter up. In the *Sporting Gazette* of 1 April 1882, he wrote:

If one succeeds in getting one's opponent very angry indeed, it is a proof of success. I have been very successful in my dealings with the fervent patriot who defends American records, for this is his peroration: 'There is a rare species of animal known to sporting naturalists as the "Juggins". This creature combines the appearance of a gentleman, the boorishness of a mule, the self-sufficiency of a peacock, the perversity of a pig and the intellect of an earthworm. It is the firm belief of many intelligent athletes that if "Easterling" should die without issue, this tribe would become extinct.'

An element of theatricality is never far absent from Walter's writings! When combined with the adversarial techniques of the lawyer and the competitive spirit of the pugilist and sportsman the results can be explosive. Peter Lovesey wrote about Walter's *Sporting Gazette* column: 'His blend of bigotry and wit was entertaining to read if you were not in the firing line... Sports journalists are not renowned for their discretion, but no modern paper would permit such vitriol.'[78]

Walter cut out and kept a set of those pages of the *Sporting Gazette* on which his articles appeared, and had them (together with other rescued cuttings) bound up and eventually presented to the Guildhall Library in London, where they remain.[79]

Apart from his column in the *Sporting Gazette*, he made a few short contributions on sport to larger publications, including a chapter in his own *Songs, Stories and Sayings of Norfolk*,[80] an essay on 'Paper-chasing and cross-country running' for Montague Sherman's *Athletics and Football*,[81] and an article on Norfolk athletes in the *East Anglian Hand Book* for 1878.

Endnotes

1 As early as 1870 we find him acting as a judge at the King's College Sports Day and the United Hospitals Sports.

2 J. Ryan (comp.), *The Annals of Thames Hare and Hounds 1868 to 1945...* (1968), p.41.

3 In 'Sport on Land and Water' in WR, *Songs, Stories and Sayings of Norfolk* (1897), p.133, he gives a short history of pedestrianism and athletics in Norfolk.

4 EDP, Norwich, archive folder on Walter Rye, 'Mr Walter Rye an athlete'.

5 'The athletic madness was still very strong in me'. (*Autobiog.* for 1861).

6 An insatiable desire to run.

7 *Autobiog.* p.20.

8 *Autobiog.*

9 Another famous walker was Charles Kingsley; see *Charles Kingsley: his Letters and Memories of his Life,* edited by his wife (abridged edn. 2 vols, 1879), I, p.107. For the whole phenomenon see Matthew Beaumont, *Nightwalking: A Nocturnal History of London, Chaucer to Dickens* (2015).

10 Quoted in Beaumont, *op .cit.*, p.245.

11 *EDP*, 25 Feb.1929, p.4: tribute by the late W. G. Clarke FGS.

12 Ibid. Even this fell short of the ninety miles walked in twenty-one hours thirty minutes by Robert Barclay Allardice earlier in the century; Peter Lovesey, *The Official Centenary History of the Amateur Athletic Association* (1979), p.15.

13 WR: *Songs, Stories and Sayings of Norfolk,* p.26; Ryan, *op. cit.*, p.42 quoting *Sporting Gazette* etc.

14 For the early years of the club's history see Geoffrey Page, *Hear the Boat Sing: The History of Thames Rowing Club and Tideway Rowing* (1991); and R. C. Lehmann, *The Complete Oarsman* [with chapters by Eyre] (1st edn., 1908).

15 *Autobiog.*, pp.21, 23. One of his first recorded sporting memories was of watching EC row on the Thames in 1852.

16 Richard Holt comments that sport 'was also a matter of getting on together after the event, a source of polite sociability between equals', *Sport and the British* (1989), p.108.

17 Lehmann, *op. cit.*, p.1.

18 On Eyre's role in the TRC see both Page and Lehmann *opp. cit.*

19 It was not until 1869 that Walter first went out in a wager boat, getting

through Old Putney Bridge at the first attempt (*Autobiog.*, p.32). Despite a lot of effort he never won a race in that category, and later surmised that had sliding seats been invented in his youth these would have better suited his sturdy legs and improved his chances.

20 As the Mincing Lane Athletic Club; LAC from 1866; see Lovesey, *op. cit.*, p.16.

21 An event founded only the year before, by William Price, manager of the athletics track at Hackney Wick, Lovesey, *op. cit.*, p.16.

22 In 1863 he went on from the Liverpool meeting for a very long walking tour of Chester and North Wales with Dick Howlett, described in the *Autobiog.* After another meeting there in 1865 he took the train from Southport, via Peterborough and Ely, to Norfolk.

23 Athletics and rowing complemented one another, as Walter pointed out when responding to the toast 'Our athletic friends' at the TRC's annual dinner in 1868. Many oarsmen habitually kept themselves fit by running during the winter months, outside the rowing season. So it was not a contradiction in terms to represent a rowing club in an athletics competition.

24 Walter won for Norfolk its first amateur championship, 'by winning the seven miles in what was then, but alas not now, world's records, but which have since been eclipsed', WR, *Songs, Stories and Sayings of Norfolk*, ch.10, p.133.

25 *EDP*, 25 Feb. 1929, pp.5–6; Lovesey *op. cit.*, p.16.

26 EDP, Norwich, file on Walter Rye.

27 Some old-time athletes', in *Baily's Magazine of Sport and Pastimes*, 1 Aug. 1894, p.126.

28 *Autobiog.*, p.30.

29 *Morning Post*, 27 Apr. 1868.

30 *Morning Post*, 22 June 1868.

31 *Morning Post*, 17 May 1869.

32 NR, MS 4691/95/1: *The Meteor*, no. 745, 30 Apr. 1929, p.36.

33 THH archives, copies kindly supplied by the club.

34 Shearman, *op. cit.*

35 Ryan, *op. cit.*, p.49.

36 EDP, Norwich, Walter Rye file. Extracts c.1909 under 'Mr Walter Rye as an athlete: "The Father of the Paper-Chase".

37 Sydenham Dixon, 'Some old-time athletes' in *Baily's Magazine of Sport and Pastimes*, 1 Aug. 1894, p.126.

38 None of the club's early cups and trophies survive following a fire in the 1970s.

39 Ryan, *op. cit.*, p.20. The *Sporting Gazette*, 24 Jan. 1873, p.58 summarised the results of all the Handicaps to that date.

40 Ryan, *op. cit.*

41 Ryan, *op. cit.*, p.11.

42 EDP, Norwich, Walter Rye file.

43 Ryan, *op. cit.*, p.41.

44 Ryan, *op. cit.*, p.15.

45 Shearman, *op. cit.*, pp.375–382; *Autobiog.* under 1882.

46 Ryan, *op. cit.*, pp.16–17 and Appendix. Many other sporting clubs indulged

in similar relaxation and socialising. A quadrille specially composed for the Thames Rowing Club by Charles Coote (who specialised in this genre) may be found in the BL.

47 ee Track 1.
48 For a team photograph of 1872 see *Runners' World,* July 2006.
49 Ryan, *op. cit.,* p.18 etc.
50 *Autobiog.,* p.66.
51 NRO, MS 4691/2: letters from Voelcker, Eyre, Oct–Nov. 1919.
52 William Thorn, MD of 87 Harrow Road, *Autobiog.,* p.26. Letters in NRO, MS 4961/6. See also
    http://boards.ancestry.co.uk/surnames.thorn/184.190.1.1.1.1.1/mb.ashx
53 *Autobiog.,* p.25.
54 Ryan, *op. cit.,* p.10.
55 Ryan, *op. cit.,* p.15; NRO, MS 4691/84/2: photographs for 1872, 1873.
56 Lovesey, *op. cit.,* p.31 feels, rather harshly, that a psychiatrist might well conclude this demonstrated a sense of inadequacy on Walter's part that he had not been to university.
57 Ryan, *op. cit.* Lovesey, *op. cit.* p.16. See also Halliday, 'Of Pride and Prejudice: The amateur question in English 19th-century rowing,' in *International Journal of the History of Sport,* IV no. 1 (May 1987). Pamela Horn, *Pleasure and Pastimes in Victorian Britain* (Stroud 1999), p.11, 159 ff.
58 Lovesey, *op. cit.,* p.14.
59 Eric Halladay, 'Of Pride and Prejudice: The amateur question in 19th-century English rowing,' in *International Journal of the History of Sport,* IV, 1 (May 1987), p.39.
60 For a wider discussion of the 'gentleman amateur' question, see Richard Holt, *Sport and the British* (Oxford, 1989), ch.2, especially section 3.
61 '[The Waddells] having brought in a number of non-athletic friends as members of the London AC outvoted me at a General Meeting of the Club on the gentleman amateur question and I resigned the secretaryship, and they taking the Club in hand with lamentable results.'
62 Henry Frowde (ed), *Frederick James Furnivall: A volume of personal record* (Oxford, 1911), introductory essay, and Holt, op. cit., p.109.
63 Shearman, *op. cit,* p.377.
64 Ryan, *op. cit.,* p.42, July 1877.
65 Lovesey, *op. cit.,* p.31. The prime movers in establishing the AAA were all from Oxford University: Clement Jackson, a tutor at Hertford College, and Bernhard R. Wise, president, and Montagu Sherman, former president of the Oxford University Athletic Club.
66 Lovesey, *loc. cit.,* p.31.
67 Over 'the great row about the disqualification of Coston by the buffoon W Waddell'. (*Autobiog.*)
68 Sydenham Dixon noted that after Walter resigned from the LAC the motto adopted by the new ruling powers was 'Get members – gentlemen if you can – but *get members*'.

69 Team photo (without WR) in Lovesey, *op. cit.*, p.25.
70 *Autobiog.*
71 Much of the background is in *Autobiog.* See also Ryan, *op. cit.*
72 *Bell's Life in London and Sporting Chronicle*, 21 Nov. 1868.
73 EDP, Norwich, Water Rye file.
74 *The Lantern*, Cape Town, South Africa, 16 Aug. 1879.
75 *Sporting Gazette* cuttings, 1873–1878, Guildhall Library, London: AN 10.6.3.
76 Lovesey, *op. cit.*, e.g. p.25.
77 Ryan, *op. cit.*
78 Lovesey, *op. cit.*, p.25.
79 *Sporting Gazette* cuttings, 1873–1878: Guildhall Library, London: AN 10.6.3.
80 Agas H. Goose, Norwich, 1897.
81 The Badminton Library (1889), pp.373–384.

2
CYCLING AND MOTORING:

'A great hankering after wheeled progression'[1]

Bicycles

Although he is better known as an athlete, Walter in fact spent considerably more of his life, right up to his seventies, as a cyclist, and managed to gain renown in that field too, winning over a hundred cycling trophies in all, although he left much less record of his competitive than of his social cycling.

As an avid reader of, and contributor to, the sporting press, and as a collector of books about sport – many of which he gave to the Guildhall Library, London, in 1882 – he knew a thing or two about cycling even before he took it up himself. As his enthusiasm grew he would make contacts not only in the sport, but also in the cycle trade, and would get insider tips on the best models to buy. He was eventually adept enough to suggest his own designs and adaptations for cycles.

The first pedal-propelled bicycle, the 'velocipede', had been invented by Michaux in France in 1864. Machines of this type had no chain: the front wheel was connected to the rear by the frame alone, and the driver propelled it using pedals attached directly to the front wheel. It only came on the market in Britain five years later yet, by his own account, in the winter of 1868–69 Walter had already tried to make a version of his own, which he took for a spin on Barnes Common. At this stage, however, his mind was still heavily focused on his first love, athletics. As far as cycling

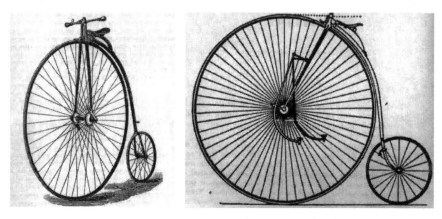

The Ordinary and the Xtraordinary 1879, and Humber tricycles 1886, from HH Griffin, Bicycles and Tricycles of the year … *Veteran Cycle Club Library.*

was concerned he contented himself with commentating on other people's activity. In his 'Easterling' column of 1 August 1874 for *The Sporting Gazette*[2] (there presumably being no athletics meetings that week for him to cover) he reported having watched the Surrey Bicycle Club's race meeting at Kennington Oval. He complimented the organisers on their efficiency, but couldn't resist a side-swipe that 'none of the men seemed what athletic trainers would call fit'. This waspish throw-away remark, so typical of the tone of his column, was belied by the fact that the cyclists kept coming back on to the track for race after race!

The design and engineering of bicycles evolved rapidly, with many companies taking up the challenge to incorporate improvements in their safety, comfort, speed, and efficiency in relation to the rider's effort. Walter saw their potential as a means of transport, but also for physical exercise, and when in 1878 poor health and a growing weight problem put paid to his athletics, he began seriously to consider cycling as his principal means of keeping fit. A number of his friends by then had a bicycle. There was a bewildering range of shapes and sizes to choose from, some with chains or levers to assist propulsion. The 'Safety' bicycle, recognisable in most respects as our idea of a bicycle today, had been put on the market by H. J. Lawson of Brighton in 1873 and was patented in 1879. In 1878, at Lawson's own suggestion, Walter tried out, and possibly acquired, his friend Bob Lowe's lever bicycle, so called because long levers on the back wheel reduced the effort required by the rider. He found it easy to mount, and describes how he got started by sitting on the saddle with his left foot on the ground and pushing on the right treadle. He was impressed by its power when going uphill:

> ... though there was more sway than was pleasant. Yet owing to the smallness of the front wheel one could ride over brickbats with impunity if one held tight. There might have been a great future for it had it been even decently made, but its manufacture was about equal in finish to a servant's cheap iron bedstead, it took immense power to get along.

In later years he would reflect that: '... properly made and fitted with pneumatic tyres, it would still be useful to an elderly man to whom the power of running and jumping into the saddle is gone.'[3]

A good balance on any kind of bicycle did not come intuitively, and it took a while to master a machine. Walter proudly records that after only a little practice on his first bike he was able to ride as far as sixteen miles at one go. He spent the summer holiday of 1878 cycling round Norfolk with S. B. Howlett, Dick's nephew. As it turned out, Walter, although an immensely clubbable man in the right milieu, did not hit it off with his travelling companion, and a series of breakdowns added to the frustrations of the trip. The next year Walter was confident enough of the machine to buy one of Lawson's Safety bicycles for himself, 'but the lever bent at once'. Nothing more is said about it!

His next recorded outing, in 1880, was on what he called the 'high bicycle', or 'Ordinary'. More common than the Safety bicycle, and senior to it in terms of invention, the Ordinary, or 'penny-farthing', an icon of the age, had a huge front wheel and a diminutive rear one. Whereas velocipedes and safety bicycles could be mounted fairly easily, getting up and down from the high seat of an Ordinary usually required either a friend to assist, or a degree of athleticism (or both). Penny-farthings were popular because, in Walter's words, 'their wheels coped relatively well with London's waterlogged and rough road surfaces', but compared with later bicycles they were awkward because they had no freewheel facility, so the rider's feet had to be either on the driving pedals or on the footrests set forward of these. The Singer 'Extraordinary', which Walter purchased only shortly after it came on the market, went on to be one of the two most popular (the other being the Facile). He describes how it worked:

> ... with a long bent treadle, the saddle raking back, the idea being to shift the centre of gravity and remove the possibility of being flung over the handles, for the machine could be ridden over a brick but with no other result than a jolt. It was a beautiful made machine, the first piece of real work I had ever seen.

And with this new acquisition he can really be said to have become a cycling fan. True to form as an athlete, he would test and stretch his own performance. He records, for instance, that he could now get up steep hills and take on rides of up to twenty-four miles.

Tricycles

Without altogether giving up life on two wheels, Walter tried out a tricycle for the first time in 1881 and found it better suited to his age and (now excessive) weight. The first trike he purchased was an Excelsior, and in May 1881 he rode thirty-seven miles on it, with W. J. Winthrop for company, whom he would later describe as 'a good but harum scarum giant, and an excellent companion'.[4] Shortly after this, each of them bought a Delta ('well made but heavy'), which they tested out by riding from London to Norwich and back. So great had Walter's enthusiasm for tricycling now become that in August that year he was off on another tour with Winthrop, this time round East Anglia. But his companion – who seems to have been distinctly accident-prone – ran into a four-wheeled cab and smashed his bike, so the pair of them had to hitch a ride on a fish train to Peterborough to effect the necessary repairs.[5]

In 1882 Walter bought himself a third tricycle, a Meteor, which he found much lighter and more agreeable. But on Whit Monday that year it was on a Fleet ('a much handier machine') that he entered the Norwich Tricycle Race,[6] afterwards taking it back to Liverpool Street by train and then riding all the way to his house at Selhurst near Croydon in the rain. The bug was still with him at the end of the year, when he bought a semi-racing tricycle, a Humber. 1882 was notable for another purchase too, a Sociable, so called because it was designed for two people. For a while he managed to persuade Georgina to accompany him on it, sometimes as far as twenty miles.

It was with old sporting friends such as Winthrop and J. J. Bateman, and with competitive cyclists such as Lacy Hillier ('who kindly gave me much valuable advice as to style and pedalling')[7] that Walter did most of his cycling, both for pleasure and for competition, around the South East and in East Anglia. The competitive spirit acquired during his days as an athlete was never far below the surface of anything he did – from sporting to business activities! He proudly records riding his old Fleet in 1883 up Reigate Hill while Hillier – much more of a cycling expert – riding a Humber, had to get off and walk. And in 1892 Walter boasted of being able to get up Brockley Hill on a trike, which was thought a stiff challenge even for a two-wheeler.

Press reports of the first dinner of the Tricycling Club in 1883 included Walter in a list of names of 'influential gentlemen connected with the sport'. It was a major event, with 150 persons present at the Cannon Street Hotel.

'A Sociable Ride'. Photo ©*British Library Board*. Sketch by GH Edwards, engraved by J Swain, *Illustrated Sporting and Dramatic News*, 1 August 1885, p.528.

The chairman spoke of the 'practical useful nature of the relaxation in which they indulged...' and how it encouraged relaxation for busy men 'by encouraging the development of their mental faculties without an undue exaction on their physical powers'.[8]

In February 1888 Walter records his first ride on another new trike built for him by a Mr Wastnage, which may even have been the one that was still going strong twenty-five years later (see postscript to this section). It was, he said, 'very firm and strong, but the gear too high', but friends and neighbours turned out in force to see the sight.

Trikes now became Walter's normal means of getting around, both in London and in his adopted Norfolk, to visit friends and family or to attend athletics meetings. For a brief while in 1893 he considered transferring his allegiance to a new kind of two-wheeled safety bicycle, but quickly returned to three wheels. After periods of illness, of which there were many, sometimes quite serious, he would exercise on his trike in the hope of building up his strength. When, under doctor's orders, he had to desist, sometimes for months on end, it was a great deprivation. Emerging from one such period of enforced abstinence in 1886 he celebrated by buying a new Cripper tricycle. By 1894 he was finally having some modest success at losing a bit of weight, which he attributed to frequent forays up Petersham steep.

Other members of his family got the cycling bug too. We have already met his wife aboard the Sociable. Walter also records a tandem ride to Lynn and back with his son Roger (1888) on a Cripper, 'a fearfully heavy machine weighing as much as a small motor would now [1916]'. FGR was also introduced to a tandem, in 1897, and a trip with him at Christmas that year was full of incident. Walter seems to have turned the machine over by Hyde Park, and later in the ride a tyre burst so they had to leave the bike for repair and walk to lunch at Bennet's in Mortlake. Two days later he was off on another excursion with 'the boys' to the Red Lion at Barnet. Perhaps the crowning glory was a Triplet ride in 1894 with both Frank and Arthur. His daughter Murie, who to Walter's great joy had also learned to ride, came along on her own bicycle. There were some awkward episodes, as when on one ride with two of his sons he recalled that Arthur was 'so done that he fell off without our missing him, indeed we were unkind enough to say we got on better without him.'

Walter would frequently set off alone for very long cycle rides. In 1897, for example, after taking Georgina to Dr Grun's at Southwick he went on an extended cycling tour into Hertfordshire, Essex and Suffolk. The following year he cycled from his home in Hampstead to Shoreham (Sussex) to inspect what was claimed to be some original crusader chain mail, but it turned out to be a modern replica. He returned by train! The very next month he was off on another long, solitary ride, and this time became lost in Edgware until put right by a friendly tramp.

Cycling trips were not without physical (and some social) danger. The roads were getting more crowded. In their book *Cycling* for the Badminton Library sports series in 1887, Lacy Hillier and Viscount Bury spoke of the regular exodus from London by bike at weekends and holiday periods:

Not only is there a light brigade of young men bent on some favourite country resort forty miles away or more; but steady middle-aged citizens on sober tricycles, some of them on sociable, with wife or daughter at their side, are bound on less distant expeditions… It is better for any young creature with sound limbs and healthy spirits to speed away over heath and downs than to pore over a novel under trees or even play lawn tennis on one eternal acre of grass plot.

In a later book, *Amateur Cycling*, written with W. G. H. Branson in 1893,[9] Hillier was to note (p.15) that: '… many a rider who has taken to cycling solely for the purpose of exercise has found when its novelty has worn off that it has become a necessity to him as an easy and rapid means of transit from place to place.'

Other road users in both town and country could be quite hostile to cyclists: for taking up a wide portion of the roadway and for being prone to accidents that caused delays to others. Even as early as the 1870s, 'road rage' – not, of course, then so called – was well established. Happily it did not often come to the boil as it did on 28 August 1876, when the driver of the St Albans coach lashed out at a passing cyclist with his horse whip, whilst the guard used a weapon that might have come straight from a medieval trial by battle, an iron ball attached to a piece of rope, which he hurled at the cyclist's wheels. Both were apprehended and heavily fined for this outrageous behaviour, which passed into cycling folklore through Hillier and Bury's book.

Of course, Walter himself was not immune from prangs. His Norfolk friend the Revd H. T. Griffith wrote on 17 July 1880, 'Sorry to hear from Mine Host of the Angel that you have gotten a mischief from that Bicycle of yours'.[10] Unfortunately Walter did not give the details of the most mysterious of these mishaps, which he describes as a 'quasi mystic accident' and 'a very eerie experience' at Pulham, Norfolk, in October 1882. Other thrills and spills are reported, some of them routine malfunctions such as a broken chain or a defective treadle. In 1894 he took a Bantam round Elstree but fell off and injured his knee. In 1896, he upturned a new trike weighing only 38lbs, and in the same year, in the course of a fifty-one-mile ride in Norfolk claimed to have 'practically saved the life of an elderly female bicyclist [whose] machine had bolted with her, by letting her run gently into me down Sheringham Hill'.

Cycling – especially in foul weather and sometimes on unmade roads – could (and can) be a very messy business. Walter reckoned that the muddiest ride of his life was that undertaken in December 1894 through flood waters

Walter Rye on his tricycle, early 1900s. *Autobiography.*

in Honeypot Lane at the back of Stanmore Marsh. The water rose over his treadles and he ended up with mud in his pockets: 'I had to have an ostler throw buckets of water over me.' In January 1899 he describes how, while on a trip to visit his sisters, a wind blowing across Hendon Lake lifted his rear offside wheel off the ground, 'an experience I had never before or since – and don't want to have again.' In 1903 (aged sixty), now living in Norwich, he organised a marathon solo trike ride that began from the house of one of his sons in Hampstead and went on to that of another in Oxford. Having left Hampstead he nearly came to grief when his brakes failed in bad weather and he ended up having to jump off at high speed to save himself. That was not all: before the end of the tour he caught a cold and suffered kidney pain. On the way back he reports laconically a contretemps with two female cyclists. (How one would have liked to be an observer!)

Tentative thoughts of motoring

The move to Norwich may well have increased his appetite for cycling, as the open country was closer to home. At any rate, he continued to take regular long rides alone or with friends right up to 1916, and to have occasional knocks and spills, like that at Buxton lock bridge in 1901 which caused him to have his axle widened as an insurance policy. He kept a log, recording for example that in 1900 he went on fifty-five long rides, as opposed to seventy-two the previous year, the difference most likely being explained by the distractions of his house-move to St Leonard's Priory. Even as late as 1913, when he was seventy, he clocked up eighty-three long rides. He made an annual 'autumn tour' in Norfolk, like that in 1901 to Scarning, Swaffham, Lynn, Mundesley and Lammas. He broke his journey by staying with friends or at inns, in this case successively with Augustus Jessopp, with his old school friend Heriot, then at the Clarence at Mundesley, and finally with his antiquarian acquaintance Revd F. Proctor. He would also habitually use his tricycle to reach the destinations of the annual outings of the NNAS to places of interest in the county.

When he went up to London for business or pleasure he sometimes took his trike on the train, and thought nothing of then cycling all the way to his country retreat at Selborne, or to call on his sisters in Hemel Hempstead.

Nevertheless he was not oblivious of motor cars, and he records taking his first motoring trip in 1900, with D. M. Roberts. They were not overly enthusiastic, as the machine they hired proved prone to breakdowns, but it certainly sowed seeds in Walter's mind about motorised power. They would take some time to germinate.

In August 1905 he took his tricycle in to his local repair shop ('WH Morris: Carriages, harnesses and saddlery, Prince of Wales Rd, Norwich', as it said on their letterhead) for re-enamelling, but was told that while it was in pieces it really needed re-plating against a dangerous encroachment of rust.[11] Perhaps this is what encouraged him over the next few months to seek friends' advice on what to do next: buy a new trike, or a quad; have an electric motor fitted to his trike as he had heard of others doing; or – perish the thought – buy a motor car. Another accident in December that year brought matters to a head and provoked Dick Howlett, (who had occasionally accompanied him on a cycling excursion), to write:

> I have been exhorting you not to pound up hills etc. You must of course rest, and you must not get any electric motor. They are all very well until some fine day they give out some miles from home and

then the work that follows is as damaging to the heart as anything can possibly be. I have no knowledge of the electric variety but they are infernal machines one and all.[12]

H. L. Clarke of the Maid's Head in Norwich advised Walter against all options except procuring a second-hand de Dion 6 HP car for around £140.[13] Having weighed it up Walter decided to stick with the tricycle,[14] but he continued to take occasional rides, even tours, in other people's motor cars or with a chauffeur. In 1911 he records several 'botanising' trips with friends, as well as the unpleasant experience of a drive in an open-topped de Dion in a high wind on a cold day to see Thomas Nelson, the head of the Nelson family. He had the consolation of seeing a fine library afterwards, but made alternative arrangements for the return journey. In 1913 he hired a car (and presumably a driver) to take his antiquarian friend Purdy to see the restored Rollesby Hall.

Despite hearing of the sad death of his old friend C. W. H. Dicker in a cycling accident in 1912, he was not put off cycling, though the idea of acquiring some form of power-assisted machine did not fade, as is shown by a long letter of 1913 to his cycle engineer in which Walter discusses the options for developing a machine to his own specification (*see postscript to this section*). It is doubtful that it was ever commissioned. This was the last year in which he was able to make one of his really long cycle rides, for which the full itinerary is given in the *Autobiography*:[15]

Day 1: By train to Hertford – cycle to St Albans for lunch at the Peahen, 'the waiters bitterly complaining of the place being spoiled by the new London motor busses' – on to Hemel Hempstead to see his sisters – then via Box Moor, Chesham, Amersham, Beaconsfield and Woburn, to Little Marlow, where he slept at the Crown.

Day 2: Cycle via Cookham, Maidenhead, Bray, Old Windsor and Chertsey to Walton (where he slept in 'Howlett's haunted room').

Day 3: Cycle to Brooklands, Cobham, Stoke d'Abernon, Leatherhead, Epsom, Cheam and Carshalton to Croydon (where he slept at the Greyhound, 'which had been utterly transmogrified and spoiled').

Day 4: Took the tram to Purley Old Oaks, 'once so pretty, now a mass of shops and villas', then on via Selhurst (where he could only just find his old house) and Thornton Heath ('The whole main road was stinking, vile and overbuilt'), to see his two previous houses in Wandsworth, and the LRC and TRC boat houses, and finally to Barnes where he had a puncture so walked on to a very bad lunch at the Pigeons at Richmond, 'where the rude and overbearing conduct of half a dozen Germans for the first time gave me an idea of unpleasant possibilities', and eventually on again to Eyre's at Kensington Crescent, where he was so dog-tired that he could hardly sleep.

Day 5: A visit to Simpson's and to a 'most ridiculous play founded on *Ivanhoe*, before taking the train home from St Pancras' (sic).

With the onset of war in 1914 Walter seems temporarily to have put aside any idea of buying a motor car and settled instead for a motor tricar. Arthur Sexton (only ever referred to by his surname except in Walter's will) who served as his chauffeur quickly learnt to drive it, and when Walter's hopes of using it to become a wartime dispatch rider came to nothing they put it to purely recreational use. On one occasion Walter had the idea of taking Purdy as 'sitter' to Horning Ferry; but under Walter and Purdy's enormous combined weight it ground to a halt, and the two old chums had to hitch a lift back with Dr Crosse in his large motor, leaving the tricar (no doubt purring quite happily once relieved of the weight) to be brought home by Sexton.

In 1915 Walter finally acquired a second-hand car of his own (the make is not mentioned) from 'Mr Falcon', and used it to take Purdy and others for drives. Sexton, who seems up to this point also to have been also the owner of a pony cart for Walter's use in emergencies, sold off his pony: a new age had dawned.

Still Walter preferred if possible to cycle. Even in 1916, when he was seventy-three, he was undertaking upwards of fifty strenuous rides every year (compared with seventy-six in 1903). Some were purely for pleasure and/or fitness. Others had another purpose such as antiquarianism. He records one trip, with his antiquarian friends Purdy, Daniels and Clarke in

1916 – what a sight, and indeed a challenge to other road users they must have been! They called on a mutual friend, Revd M. Bird of Brumstead, then rode on to Palling 'where we tried to feed on prehistoric food but failed' – was this an aspersion cast upon the offerings of the local hostelry or another of Walter's weird culinary experiments? And so to Waxham Old Hall, 'the most melancholy and deserted place I ever saw'. On more sombre occasions he rode to Hemel Hempstead to visit his sister Maria now lying sick with cancer. He proudly boasts of his fitness compared with that of his sons and other visitors to Norwich, whom he tends to 'see off' on triking exploits even if they have a handicap start. His 'opponents' in such competitions not infrequently gave up exhausted and returned home by train.

In the *Autobiography* he records that 1916 was the year of his last cycle ride. Correspondence from the 1920s shows him going with friends on organised motoring expeditions for picnics, almost certainly in chauffeur-driven vehicles.[16]

*

What happened to all Walter's bicycles and tricycles? It is evident from occasional references to trips on an old one that he stabled several at once, and may even have had quite a collection. Initially, space was probably not a problem, since all the houses he occupied in his London cycling days up to 1900 had very large grounds. The position changed when he moved to a smaller house in Norwich and had to care for his invalid wife. But we also find him selling or handing on used cycles to friends, and acting as middleman for those seeking to acquire a new one. In 1886 he offered his old Sociable – presumably the one on which he and Georgina had previously shared rides, for sale for £6. Griffith, now rector of Smallburgh, Norfolk, successfully bid for this for his daughters, and Walter sent it to him by train. On 20 October he wrote thanking Walter:

> The Sociable arrived in fine order, and has already been used two or three times, nay, once even as far as N. Walsham and back. I have even got into it myself, and hope in time to be able to get about in it comfortably, with one of my girls acting as guide … The arrival of the new 'horse' has created a great stir and excitement amongst

our villagers; for though bicycles are not unknown in the parish, it is quite a novelty for ladies to be seen adopting this newfashioned mode of progression...[17]

That was not the end of the matter. In February the following year Griffith wrote again: 'My girls tell me that they want a guard for their tricycle for the protection of their dresses. We have tried in vain to get what is needed in Norwich; could you oblige me by ordering the right thing from London.'

Another letter, a decade later in 1898, shows how Walter's enthusiasm for getting other people cycling continued. Mary Stanley, writing from Christiania in Norway, thanks him for getting her a bike, but reports anxiously that the cargo ship bringing it has been damaged and has had to put back.[18]

In 1901 he purchased yet another new tricycle, which would last him until his final ride in 1916, and records taking his old one to 'Marsh at Cawston', but rather doubting that Marsh ever used it.

A photograph survives of Walter on his tricycle as an old man with a white beard and country tweed suit. It is apt testimonial to the role of the machine in keeping him alive and fit into his eighties: and this was a man who in his middle years contracted several successive life-threatening diseases and in later years grappled with other serious health issues including bad eyesight and heart disease. He wanted to be remembered above all as an athlete, but perhaps he should really be honoured as a (tri-)cyclist!

POSTSCRIPT

Carbon copy of a letter from Walter Rye to an unnamed cycle manufacturer 11 February 1913: Rye correspondence, NRO, MS 4691/84/3

Dear Sirs

Many years ago (about 15)[19] your Mr Wastnage (whose acquaintance I made through the kind aid he gave me when I was broken down at Stanmore when I was riding out one Sunday morning from my then residence in Hampstead) made me a very excellent tricycle, which I have used continually. It has carried me consistently well and though my weight is never less than 16 stone, and though I have worn out breaks [sic], pedals, and tubes innumerable, the fabric and mechanism is as good as ever, and the machine runs as well as it ever did.

I am now in my 70th year, however, and am greatly tempted by the advertisements I see of a little auxiliary power for long journeys, bad roads and up-hill work.

I hear very well of a gear invented by Mr JE Smith of Gloucester (see advertisement enclosed) but find it cannot be applied to a tricycle without great alterations to the axles, and want your opinion whether it could be applied *at all*. If it can, the only way seems to me to have an entirely new wheel (outside the existing gear case and cogs) over which the band would run. Could this be done so as to leave me free to pedal normally, and only use the extra power when I really want it?

I apprehend it could not go round the front wheel, as that gets out of the straight when steered to the right or left. Nor could it be applied to *one* of the hind wheels as the band would not run parallel to the middle of the machine and would be crooked and possibly affected by steering.

If it were possible I should like the motor gear placed under the present pedals as close to the ground as may be (I am a very careful rider and avoid brickbats instinctively). This would lower the centre of gravity and not take away the space… where I now have a touring bag.

If you can see your way I should like you to make me a new machine embodying the motor from the making (it would hardly be fair to the good old machine to patch it up on to it) and moreover should like some other points considered and also to keep the old machine as a stand by. I don't like side cars at all for many reasons. Of course I am not wedded to the Gloucester motor, but if you know of no better it would seem fair to use it as it gave me the idea.

I am sorry to trouble you with so long a letter, but it is difficult to explain myself more shortly. My anxiety is to keep up my exercise, and I don't want to take on a pure motor till I am so old that I cannot pedal.

    Yours faithfully
    Walter Rye

[PS] I only want a very little extra power – never to exceed 12 miles an hour, not the 30 miles advertised…

Endnotes

1 *Autobiog.*, p.32.

2 *Sporting Gazette* cuttings, 1873–1878, at Guildhall Library, London, AN 10.6.3.

3 Pneumatic cycle tyres were not invented for a further decade, so when Walter first took to the saddle the machines had solid rubber tyres. The ride must have been uncomfortable.

4 *Autobiog.*, under 1912.

5 On another occasion Winthrop ran into a cart-horse in Lynn, damaging his bike, though he was able eventually to catch up with Walter in Norwich. Walter became quite used to putting his machine on a train for the return leg of a long journey even without breakdowns. He briefly set up a Thames Tricycle Club around this time but soon had to abandon it on grounds of ill health. (See J. Ryan [comp], *The Annals of Thames Hare and Hounds 1868 to 1945...* [1968], p.37.)

6 A report in 1885 of his athletic record spoke of his having 'a year or two ago... reappeared, winning three tricycle races at once'. *Illustrated Sporting and Dramatic News*, 7 Nov. 1885, p.177.

7 *Autobiog.*, under 1883.

8 *Bell's*, 23 Dec. 1882.

9 Hillier was the amateur bicycle and tricycle champion at all distances in 1881. Both were members of the London County Cycling and Athletic Club.

10 NRO, MS 4691/4.

11 NRO, MS 10612 folder (1), 5 Aug. 1905.

12 NRO, MS 4691/22.

13 NRO, MS 4691/4, 13 Dec. 1905.

14 Purdy wrote on 31 May 1910, 'I was so glad to hear you are able to enjoy your cycle rides which I feel sure will greatly assist in keeping your health good if not indulged in to excess', NRO, MS 4691/20/2. However, on 27 Aug. 1913 Purdy declined a cycle ride: 'I have had a narrow shave from a motor accident. I have come to the conclusion it would be very silly of me to attempt a journey on my cycle along a road much frequented by the cursed vehicles, or rather their reckless drivers.' NRO, MS 4691/20/2.

15 *Autobiog.*, pp.196–7.

16 A correspondent from Old Catton (signature illegible) wrote on 16 Sept. 1923, 'My wife and all of us will be very glad to accept your offer of a motor jaunt for Sunday 24th' and that they would provide a picnic.' NRO, MS 4691/12. In 1924 Messrs Bussey & Sabberton Bros Ltd, Motor Electrical and General Engineers, Authorised Ford Dealers, told Walter's friend Edwin Southwell JP that they would 'send you the car Mr Rye usually has and which fits his lunch tray and also his usual driver – Rush,' NRO, MS 4691/3. Walter himself was sadly unable to join another elaborate picnic held the next year (NRO, MS 4691/83, letter from Southwell, 8 Sept. 1925).

17 NRO, MS 4691/4.

18 NRO, MS 4691/6

19 Actually twenty-five if this is the same machine from Wastnage already referred to above.

3
SAILING AND THE
BROADS

Rowing and sailing

Messing about in boats, although easily surpassed by athletics and cycling as Walter's main outdoor interests, had a life-long fascination for him. As we have seen, it had begun in London, from 1862 in his first tentative outings on the Thames with EC, and developed in a more competitive phase through his membership of Thames Rowing Club.[1] He took to the water in Norfolk too, first of all as a young and keen oarsman in 1868, when he and Dick Howlett rowed a light coxed pair from Yarmouth on to the Broads.[2] Walter reported with some satisfaction that they spotted only one pleasure craft during the whole trip.

But he was never a man to spend a whole holiday afloat. On the latter occasion, for example, he found time to become infatuated with, and indeed 'temporarily engaged' to a local girl, rather to Dick's disapproval. The liaison was to last little more than a month in all. He spent a few days with her at Lowestoft, where her mother was 'a rabid radical and Dissenter... sharing with my own parents the then prevalent idea that athletics meant pot-housing'.[3] Athletes were not for her!

From his early thirties, Walter fell into the rather different habit of taking a leisurely cruise (with a paid skipper) each autumn on the Broads. The Broads' tranquillity under wide-open skies offered much scope for setting aside the cares of the world through sport and relaxation. When he first came to know the region, in his mid-twenties, organised tourism was in its infancy. Wherries and smaller craft with shallow draught sailed the Broads mainly for commercial purposes, transporting thatching materials and all manner of other goods across the county's winding waterways, whilst wildfowlers took to the water in flat-bottomed punts to stalk and shoot their prey.[4] With deep regret, Walter would see this way of life change drastically in his lifetime. Leisure activities became progressively commercialised as East Anglia was opened up by the railways. And the railway companies themselves first encouraged and later directly sponsored tourism. Seizing on this new seasonal demand, enterprising owners began to convert trading wherries for summer hire. Thus was born the 'pleasure wherry'.[5]

Whilst he was happy to partake of these new leisure services, Walter tended to think of himself as a cut above the regular tourist – more of a pioneer or explorer, perhaps. He could not bear the pollution of his sanctuary with the noise, rowdyism and litter that were the by-products of mass tourism, and the tawdry accommodation and hostelries it spawned. Looking back in later life on his time on the Broads, he was dismayed by the:

> … pretentious vulgarity of waterside bungalows at Wroxham, whose trim lawns with scarlet geraniums and lobelias have replaced the wild vegetation so many loved, by the mere free and easy, if somewhat squalid, settlement at Potter Heigham, and by the bad mixture of boating cottages, and working men's dwellings at Horning Ferry which have combined to destroy nearly all their old world charm.[6]

G. Christopher Davies was at this time famously putting the Broads on the map with his popular writings. With hindsight, this was possibly not always for the best. His book for boys, written about 1876 and entitled *The Swan and her Crew, or the Adventures of Three Young Naturalists on the Broads and Rivers of Norfolk*, whilst primarily (and laudably) intended to excite in young males an interest in natural history, did so in part by encouraging them to destroy the very wildlife and habitats he was urging them to discover. He did not think it wrong, and nor would Walter, to encourage his young readers to collect birds' eggs and nests – the rarer the breed the better – or to shoot and kill wild birds.

Davies was also the compiler of an immensely popular *Handbook to the Rivers and Broads of Norfolk and Suffolk*, which ran to thirty editions before the turn of the century. And by the latter date he too was very conscious of the changes that had been wrought in the local communities. But he was not one for turning the clock back: 'No doubt some of the old *habitués*, who liked to have the whole landscape to themselves [*he might have been addressing this to Walter himself!*] grumble at the change, but the less selfish persons, who happily constitute the majority, do not object to seeing a dozen yachts where formerly they saw but one.'[7] Davies was inclined to place the blame for many misdemeanours on the local inhabitants rather than the tourists: 'The bottle shooters, coot potters and noisy revellers, the swan's egg robbers and grebe destroyers, the persons who use one's boat-houses as luncheon rooms or dust bins are, unfortunately, home products.'[8]

But at the same time he was keenly aware that if the Broads were to remain a haven of peace for all there must be a code of practice to prevent the tourist wrecking the habitat. Accordingly, he drew up his own list of cardinal rules of good conduct.[9]

*

After his marriage in 1870, Walter for a while had to defer any aspiration to become a frequent sailor, in the interests of spending time with his new wife, and soon with his young family as well. But as time went on, with or without Georgina (but more often without), he continued to spend as many holidays as possible in Norfolk, and he would later even be away sailing when at least one of his children was born.[10]

At around the same time he was also having to cope with his father's increasing senility, eventual retirement in 1874 and death in 1876. This all resulted in increased emotional and physical stress, which was accentuated by his increased business responsibilities after buying up his father's legal practice. Escape to Norfolk became more difficult, but all the more imperative for stress-busting when it could be fitted in.

The *Warrior*

In 1878, a full decade after that first Norfolk trip with Dick Howlett, he was finally in a position to procure his own boat, the *Warrior,* from Britcher of Thorpe,[11] and went sailing with his brother Frank, who had recently returned from Canada, and his fellow athlete J. J. Bateman who was to become a firm friend. Britcher provided as the skipper an 'old gardener', with disastrous results. The boat was pursued along the bank by a madman who kept shouting abuse at them until in an unthinking moment Walter suggested that 'the only thing left for [the madman's] father to do was to make him the skipper of a pleasure wherry'! His own skipper overheard, took umbrage at the implied insult to his *métier*, and jumped ship. Walter had no choice but to find another. So at the very outset of his sailing experience he learned from bitter experience the importance of humouring seasoned crewmen and avoiding talk that might cause them offence.[12]

Georgina made one or two trips with him, and in his *History of Norfolk* (1887) Walter records one occasion at Coldham Hall on the Yare when they saw two men fishing:

> ... pulling them out at about six a minute (they caught one hundred and twenty!), and my wife and the skipper meanly went and moored alongside them, hoping to share their luck, and were rewarded, for three hours' labour, with *three*! Of course the successful fishers had baited heavily.[13]

When his sons were old enough Walter would take them along for a sail. Apart from his family, and the hired crew for each trip, he invited as sailing companions in turn a wide range of old school friends, professional colleagues, fellow antiquarians, athletes and other acquaintances: among those mentioned are Revd H. T. Griffith,[14] P. B. Ficklin and his wife, Voelcker, Brooke Little, D. M. Roberts, Warner Herriot and his son Jim,[15] and Walter's cycling companions W. J. Winthrop and Arthur Grimmer.

Illness and family tragedies during the early 1880s

But Walter was not always fit to sail. In the early 1880s both his wife's and his own health were causing concern, and continued to restrict the time available for sailing. In 1882 he managed to fit in a short trip on the *Warrior* with Winthrop and Grimmer. The following year he records laconically that Georgina gave birth to a still-born daughter, and *thinks* he remembers spending that Christmas on the Broads, taking his boys out on a boat, but making little progress for lack of wind. But he adds, 'my memory of this part of my life is almost a blank owing to my attack of typhoid in 1884'. The crisis of 1884–1885, with Walter's illness and eventual breakdown, the deaths of his brothers Frank and EC, and the illness of his son, Hugh, is described below.

On doctor's orders Walter then put work aside and, when he was well enough to contemplate convalescence, turned once again to sailing as the best form of therapy. In a note for the *East Anglian* in 1885 he said he had collected examples of Norfolk dialect 'during the past three months which I have had to spend boating on the Norfolk Broads for the recovery of my health'. One thing he had discovered was that it is not safe to class something as fiction just because it is unlikely, citing as an instance: '... my skipper feeling faint, sick and bilious, early one morning, took rum in his tea and hot stewed eels to his breakfast'.[16]

Friends thought him crazy to tax himself physically like this after a bout of serious illness. Griffith wrote:

Do take care of yourself... the idea of your cruising about these swampy Broads after rheumatic fever does seem to me immensely risky. [*Showing how much he had got the measure of Walter, he added waspishly:*] ... and the Antiquarian world cannot afford to lose you yet, however the rest of humanity might be disposed to contemplate such a contingency with equanimity.[17]

The *Lotus*

Understandably the *Autobiography* is quite sparse at this period. All that it records of his convalescent sailing trip is the purchase in 1885 of the *Lotus*, 'an old round-topped boat with a short jib', and his embarkation on it at Norwich for a long voyage. He does not mention who accompanied him, until in mid-July he breaks off the trip to return to Putney and collect his boys to join him afloat. Altogether, he was on sick leave for twenty-two weeks, and returned to business only briefly in September before doubling back to Norfolk for another short cruise. At Christmas the same year he was afloat again, this time with Brooke Little and Roberts. His companions slept in the boat, 'but I did not, both of them being inveterate snorers'.[18] Further regular sailing trips are recorded in subsequent years, when once again he would typically take an autumn cruise as well as a few days at Christmas. 'I think', he notes, 'mine was the only pleasure boat which regularly put out for the Christmas week'.[19]

Sailcloth and oilskin do not keep out the cold like good thick planking. The last winter I slept out in my own boat – a round-topped 14-tonner – and was as snug and as warm as could be; while the water we had washed up the crockery in after supper froze ¾ inch thick just outside the cabin door.[20]

None of these voyages can be positively identified as the inspiration for Walter's humorous adventure aimed at a popular readership of holiday-makers, *A Month on the Norfolk Broads on Board the Wherry, 'Zoë', and its Tender, the Tub, 'Lotus'*. Published in or about 1887, this pocket- sized book, which became a best-seller, was prettily illustrated by his old athletic friend the artist Wilfrid Ball. It sold for one shilling and sixpence.[21]

In another publication, Walter records that 'great unwieldy' *Zoë* of Norwich was the first expensively fitted up pleasure wherry'.[22] That much at least seems to be fact. The dates of the voyage in the book, however, do not seem to tally with anything in the chronology of his *Autobiography*, nor

Cover illustration by Wilfrid Ball from Walter Rye, *A Month on the Norfolk Broads* [c.1887]. *Author.*

are all the characters readily identifiable; yet so much of it reads like an autobiographical account. Even if it is a semi-fictional and satirical account of tourist life on the Broads, much of the background and quite likely some of the incidents recorded have the ring of authenticity. It includes an account of the acquisition of the *Lotus*, and it does feature some real people, including 'Old Tungate'. B. L. Tungate, a very experienced and good-humoured sailor, already in his mid-seventies, whose fund of sailing stories and anecdotes would provide Walter with much material for miscellanies and after-dinner talk. Although in many respects the two were like chalk and cheese, they stayed together for as long as Walter was able to sail.[23]

Fortunately we have a description of Tungate from a distinctly local source:

> Pore little owd Tungate what used to be a wherry skipper to Mr Walter Rye when he used to sail these waters – he'd tarn in his grave if he could see it. But there, there wouldn't be much for him to tarn. He was what we call a full-size Norwicher. He weighed seven stone and a brick! Them Norwichers allus was little ones.[24]

The *Lotus* is described by Walter as a short-jibbed, 'roomy old tub, half wherry, half cutter of about fourteen tons, drawing 3ft 9in… familiar to the frequenters of the Broads from its curious round top'. He had fallen in love with her at first sight, 'attracted by the wide berths and comfortable cabin', which took his 'luxurious fancy'. But the previous owner had left it in a filthy state so the boat was not ready for immediate occupancy. Layer after layer of paint had to be stripped off to restore the original mahogany to its pristine glory, and then new paint had to be applied, sparingly and according to Walter's own specifications.

Confident enough that his workmen would finish their preparations, he travelled up from London (as the story has it) to board the *Lotus* for its maiden voyage with a party of invited guests. The four berths were assigned respectively to four men identified in the tale only as an Antiquary, a Poet, an Athlete and a Liar. The Antiquary is surely a depiction of Walter himself, the Poet perhaps Dick Howlett (there is reference to the two of them having rowed a paired gig up the North River twenty years before), the Athlete was said to be fresh out of Oxford,[25] and the liar one 'Liar Smith', a reliable stockbroker. In a sense it is immaterial whether or not the story is true: we want it to be, because it says so much of Walter and his humour, and affords precious glimpses of life on the Broads at the time.

As the narrative has it, the trip was nicely fixed up when Walter learnt that an American antiquarian named Grice, with whom he had struck up a correspondence, was to be visiting England with his wife at just the time of the proposed holiday, hoping to trace his Norfolk ancestry. They were persuaded to tag along with the four men, but as there was insufficient room for everyone to sleep aboard the *Lotus* a second boat, the *Zoë*, a large pleasure wherry, had to be hired for the Americans.

Although the Grices were only two, as against the four members of the original party, their boat had to be the larger vessel because – already in danger of becoming the archetypal American tourists – they brought with them unimaginable quantities of baggage, a point on which Walter mercilessly ragged them. Only in this sense was the *Lotus* the 'tender' of the *Zoë*.

When the party arrived at Beccles by train to pick up the boats,[26] Walter found that the new coat of paint on the *Lotus* was still tacky, and the smell too strong to put up with overnight. So instead of sailing immediately they resolved to check in for a couple of nights at the King's Arms, with occasional return trips to the *Zoë* for tea. The ribald foursome soon nicknamed Grice (though not to his face) the 'Fat American', shortened to 'Fataman' to make it sound less offensive if overheard. Mrs Grice consequently became 'Fatima'. Her frequent changes of wardrobe, encompassing a huge range of gorgeous outfits, was a source of endless fascination, while the male foursome (who were, after all, on a sailing holiday) contented themselves with scruffy blazers and flannels.

Only a few of the provisions had been brought with them from London, as there were plentiful supplies of almost everything they needed in Beccles.

Day 2 began with an early morning swim in crystal clear water at the town bathing area in the river, after which the party rowed to 'Ross (or Rose) Hall', an Elizabethan house owned by a former athletics competitor of Walter's who showed them round. On day 3 they decided to go by train to Bungay. 'And oh,' says Walter:

> … if Beccles is sleepy, what words can be used for Bungay? Melancholy reigns supreme. Had I any thought of committing

suicide, and felt a little bit doubtful as to the propriety of doing so, I should certainly stay at Bungay for a while; all doubts would vanish after the third day.[27]

This trip, combined with a disappointing lunch at Loddon, strengthened their resolve to set sail properly the next day, and not to hang around any longer waiting for the paint to dry. So, holding their noses as they passed the Beccles tanneries (to whose stench the townspeople seemed to be innured), they set sail for Yarmouth.

Like the *Warrior* before it, the *Lotus* was patently not the sort of craft that Walter could, or would want to, handle on his own. All the hard work was done by a hired crew of two. For the most part the passengers simply relaxed and let the world go by. Time agreeably ceased to have much meaning. It became difficult to remember what day of the week it was, although even in the middle of a sailing holiday, Sundays were observed, whenever possible, by going to church, 'as all decent boating men ought to do'.

Crucially, having the *Lotus*, and its jolly-boat for excursions, assisted Walter to explore the wilder and remoter parts of his beloved Norfolk: to study the flora and fauna; to make antiquarian sallies with friends (whether they shared his enthusiasm or not) in order to inspect a church or a ruin, or to call on a vicar or rector and request a glance at the parish registers; to meet the locals and study their dialect, stories, songs and way of life. Every one of these experiences was grist to Walter's mill, and sooner or later almost every fragment of gathered information would find its way into print: in popular books, periodicals, newspaper articles or in his autobiographical writings.

The role of crewmen

The crewmen's job was not simply to navigate from A to B, but to make the most of wind and tide so as to avoid becoming stranded in shallow water as the tide fell, and sometimes to extricate the boat from unforeseen difficulties –as when other boats ahead blocked the waterway – and thus safely to make it to the target destination for an overnight stop. With its tall mast and sail, which occasionally had to be lowered to negotiate low bridges, the *Lotus* required skilled handling. There were other advantages to having a paid crew. They could remain on board to keep watch over the boat while the passengers left to buy provisions, or went for an exploratory walk or a row in the jolly-boat.

Some skippers had other trades out of season:

> As a rule they are very hardworking civil men; but some get a bit 'above themselves' through the unwise liberality of Londoners who come down for a week or two, and don't mind living at the rate of £10,000 a year for that time, thus spoiling the men and 'haining' the market for the regular boat-owners.[28]

To Walter the crewmen were a class apart. But as we have seen he had learnt not to tread on their corns, but to give them their own 'space'. He provided them with rum, together with an allowance for beer (which they had to fetch for themselves). For himself and his guests, whisky and soda was the normal tipple. He could never be sure whether the crewmen's advice – for example to stay longer than expected in a given spot, or to sail at a strange hour – was genuinely driven by considerations of wind and tide, or by the desire to reach, or remain at, a favoured hostelry. But Walter was by now canny enough not to challenge their judgement, and advised others against doing so if they wanted to avoid bad blood or unforeseen 'accidents'.

The story has parallels with Jerome K. Jerome's *Three Men in a Boat*, though with more protagonists. Walter recounts adventures and mishaps including a frightening lightning storm, boyish pranks such as rolling a Dutch cheese along the ground, and practical jokes at other people's expense. For example, they engaged one rather garrulous local farmer in conversation, and mentioned the 'antiquarian writings of Walter Rye', without revealing that he was himself one of their party. When the farmer claimed to have read some of these writings, they asked him if he knew Mr Rye personally: 'He said he did, and described that individual to his own face as small and thin, to the intense delight of all the rest of us, who fancied from their ocular vision that he was tall and decidedly stout.'

In fact, by this time the real Walter weighed over seventeen stone! Later the farmer *somehow* slipped off the plank: 'Whether there was any connection between some, doubtless sound, criticism he had ventured on the Antiquary's works, and the eagerness with which the latter volunteered to steady (?) the plank on his departure, is a question we have never yet solved satisfactorily.'

With Walter in charge, the party naturally made compulsory detours to visit churches and ruins. The Americans were keen to take home bits of masonry broken off a genuine English ruin, but Walter kept them in order, at least until they visited one site where bits had already fallen off and he turned a blind eye. He records, however, that the party used some fragments of Roman tile as projectiles to hurl at water rats: 'I mention this fact as it may explain the discovery of undoubted Roman masonry on the banks by Stokesby some day, and thereby save someone from theorizing as to a lost station there.'

But amid all the activities, there was also plenty of time for sheer relaxation: romantic rowing by moonlight, storytelling, and bragging about exploits real and imagined. The *Lotus*'s jolly-boat (which as an oarsman himself Walter could manage very well) provided the means of exploring shallow creeks, and the opportunity for recreational rowing after dinner without the services of the paid crew; or a shooting or swimming spree, sometimes in places where swimming was strictly forbidden: 'It is very wrong to trespass, and I do not countenance trespassing as a rule; but the heat was so great that this sort of sin became an absolute necessity.'[29]

True to form, Walter pulled no punches in recording exactly what he thought of the places he visited. Yarmouth was a 'cheap and nasty place' ('I don't care for the opinion of publisher or artist. I am writing this book – they are not – and this is a free country'). Bastwick church was 'ruined and shamefully dilapidated', nor was it the only one they found in such a state. Prejudice as well as pure observation abound. For example, in the course of a stroll to Horning church they 'noticed with disgust that a settlement of the Salvation Army had been effected in that quiet little village.'[30]

One morning, in order that Grice could seek out his ancestors, the party set off at 5am for a three-hour walk to Barningham. 'Fatima' dressed in an outfit which Walter describes as 'uncommonly nice, but which would have been more in place at a garden party at Marlborough House'. On making an enquiry at a local house as to whether there were still any Grices in the village, they were seen off by an aggressive dog. But the vicar was more hospitable and showed them the parish registers, with some success.

Incidental detail in the book is interesting for local and social history. The local pub, the Three Pigeons, had 'a singularly uninteresting taproom… [with a] noticeable absence of settles, shovel boards and peg pots.' Over the fireplace was a 'quaint painted board':

Those that bring tobacco here
Must pay for pipes as well as beer;
And those who sit before the fire
Must move aside, for I desire
That all my friends as well as you
May see the fire, and feel it too.[31]

He goes on: 'The ornamentation chiefly consisted of grocers' advertising almanacs, wherein lovely, but somewhat bare-necked ladies, garbed in extremely pink dresses and dazzlingly white gloves, were quaffing, with an obviously affected relish, large bumpers of mineral waters concocted in Lower Goat Lane, Norwich.'

Another organised expedition was to see the medieval rood screen at Ranworth, where according to Walter: '…the enormous sprawly feet of the Saints tickled our fancies greatly; they could not, of course, have been done by the same artist who drew the faces, for some of those are simply beautiful and of a style of art one never expects to see in a country church.'[32]

In a later passage we read that 'the sweet chimes of the bells in the new steeple of Thorpe Church, and the flickering flashes of the electric light from Colman's works, helped to please us well'.

Much of the time on the cruise passed smoothly enough, though towards the end of the month Walter and his friends had grown tired of humouring the Americans, especially Fatima, and tempers became frayed. Fatima was 'always on her dignity when not being flattered by someone, and a month is too long to keep on at that game continuously'.[33] But the group parted amicably enough, and the trip did nothing to deter Walter from further sailing. In fact quite the reverse: he was back afloat just a few months later. What it probably did teach him, however, was that he must choose his sailing companions rather more carefully. Fact or fiction, it makes for good entertainment.

*

Christmas 1886 was spent sailing with Plaskett and Brooke Little. They sailed across Barton Broad and Irstead Shoals 'on perhaps the coldest day I ever remember. It was so cold indeed that we could not keep aboard the boat, but turned in at the Great Eastern Railway Hotel at Thorpe.' In the autumn of 1888 Walter remembers running aground at the mouth of Upton Dyke:

We left the man to get her off, and returning at night found her still stuck. We ultimately got her off by anchoring our longest sheet across the river at one end and fixing the other to our tabernacle and laying in wait for the next trading wherry coming down to run into it, which she did to her astonishment but our relief.

The next season was memorable for:

... the roughest passage I ever had down the river, which had overflowed its banks below Acle, and we had to find our course by guess work and noticing the different colour of the water in the deep part. A trading wherry was not as lucky as we, for sailing over a marsh she stuck and a channel had to be dug to get her out...

The *Alma*

During the Christmas holiday of 1890 Walter went to inspect an old trading wherry, the *Alma*, 'once a very fast boat built at Barton'. He then 'drove' with his skipper Tungate to Cley for duck shooting 'with poor success as the cold was intense'. Shortly afterwards he bought the *Alma*, and had it

A pleasure wherry at Coltishall, c.1910. *The Broadland Memories Archive.*

converted into a pleasure wherry. An inventory of items aboard the *Alma*, in Walter's own hand and dated 1 October 1892, gives an idea of the standard of comfort aboard:

Table: Inventory of the *Alma*, 1892

Six large and four small horsehair seats covered red velvet
Four floor rugs
New oilcloth throughout
Four spring mattrasses [*sic*] on frames and four wool mattrasses
Window curtains and bed valances throughout
Four bolsters, eight pillows and three pillowcases
Eight sleeping rugs for saloon and inner cabin and two mens blankets
A two branch candelabra and a red candlestick with shade
Two deck chairs (folding)
Two velvet covered mirrors with candelabra
Iron washstand and fittings
Ten rough bath towels
Watercan, small ditto, and slop pail and 2 chambers – two iron soap stands
New life buoy and new cork fender
Set of new ropes and sheets throughout, 2 cranks
Set of blue tea things complete
One hand basket and two small ditto
Iron tea caddy and (7) dishes and (12) plates[34]
13 knives and 3 spoons (and 8 tea), and 12 forks, carving knife and fork
Box with 1 hammer, screw driver, bedwrench, gimlet and awl.[35]

During the summer of 1891 Walter took his last voyage in the *Lotus* and his first in the *Alma*, with Brooke Little, in both cases measuring the 'tides' on Hickling Broad in connection with the legal action described below for which he became celebrated. This is the only occasion where he definitely mentions undertaking legal business whilst sailing.

The Norfolk Broads Protection Society

With growing public concern about the Broads from local fishermen, sportsmen from further afield, and tourists, the definition of public rights of access assumed some urgency in the eyes of the riparian landowners, who were a powerful vested interest. From at least the early 1880s, some of them had taken to repelling the public by blocking access to 'their' broads with chains or booms, or filling the channel with gravel.[36] In a few instances, as a warning to others of the seriousness of their intent, they took to court even local marshmen who tried to make a living in the disputed waters.[37] From the opposite point of view, that of the public would-be users of the Broads, there were many frustrations. The photographer P. H. Emerson, attempting to capture evidence of life on the Broads, described his own experience:

> On the bank stood a pompous game-keeper, who, when questioned, said no one could go on to the broad because the shooting was let to some gentleman who lived away. Thus this beautiful expanse of tidal water was closed by bars and chains to the innocent recreation of the public because a certain gentleman paid so much to another gentleman for the right to shooting over it, when there is a question as to whether there is any such right at all for any one person more than another. The wild fowl are *ferae naturae*, the water is tidal, and the dike ways, have they not been illegally closed?'[38]

In 1891 Walter acted as solicitor for the defence in a legal action concerning the public right of access to Hickling Broad. At issue in particular was whether the public had any rights to sail, fish or shoot on the Broad. The plaintiffs, a freeholder on the Broad and a shooting tenant, claimed that an Enclosure Award of 1808 allotted both the land and the water, and gave to the freeholders exclusive rights over sailing, fishing and shooting on the Broad. As regards sailing, the landowners quickly lost the argument, because local residents were able to show that sailing had long been openly allowed and indeed that the freeholders had actually encouraged regattas on the Broad. But the argument of the defendant, a marshman, that by virtue of long-standing custom and usage he and his fellows had acquired the right to fish and shoot on the Broad was roundly rejected by the judge.

As he would spell out some years later, with extensive reference to court-roll evidence, in a pamphlet entitled *The Rights of Fishing, Shooting and Sailing on the Norfolk Broads* (1899), Walter was completely in sympathy with landowners' claims to reserved shooting and fishing rights *on their own land*: 'I detest as much as anyone can the rowdy class of visitor who shoots at everything that he sees, from a little grebe to a bullock, and who makes himself a nuisance wherever he goes.'

He accepted that the public had no right to moor or come ashore without the landowner's permission, and even if in practice a blind eye had been turned to shooting from the water he felt that this conferred no rights – certainly no right to come ashore to retrieve the game, and in the Hickling case he tried (unsuccessfully) to persuade his client to drop his claim over shooting rights.

But fishing was a different matter. Here, Walter's argument was that in tidal waters fish were the property of the Crown, not of any individual landowner, and by long-standing custom could be freely taken by all (as long as the fishing were done from a boat). Together with a number of local experts, and a barrister convinced of the strength of the defence case, he was of the view that the natural rise and fall of the water on Hickling Broad was the result of tides, even if the water in the Broad itself remained fresh and not salt.[39] This was the reason why he had spent time on the Broad measuring the rise and fall of the water.[40] The judge agreed that Walter would have had a good case with regard to fishing if the water were indeed tidal, but accepted the evidence of the plaintiff's expert witnesses against this, apparently forbidding Walter to call all the witnesses he had lined up to support his case.[41] The marshman was therefore restrained from both fishing and shooting, and the rights of the plaintiffs under the Enclosure Award were upheld.[42]

Although Walter was disappointed, and to a degree professionally chastened by the outcome, the Hickling Broad judgment did reaffirm the public's right to sail on the Broads in general, and to fish in any waters that could be proved tidal beyond any reasonable doubt. But that was not to be the end of the matter. Press reports take the story on:

> London sportsmen having heard of it, have inaugurated a Norfolk Broads Protection Society; and a defence fund, with over £300 subscribed, has been started, and Mr Walter Rye, a Norwich antiquarian, with two members of the London Court of Common Council upon it. The local piscatorial societies are only too glad to receive city support, as nearly all the Norfolk landlords favour their brethren, though I hear that Sir Edward Birkbeck and Mr JJ Colman – one sitting on each side of the house – are prepared, if necessary, to bring in a Bill dealing with the matter.

The judgement led Walter to become not only a founder member and financial supporter of the Norfolk Broads Protection Society, but also its Honorary Solicitor.[43] The society began almost at once to hold public meetings to rally support for the cause, as well as to make clear the limits of the public rights they were trying to defend: 'While there was no desire to deprive any man of his just rights, they were determined that no man for individual pleasure or profit should deprive the people of their ancient privileges.'[44]

And to many sportsmen and tourists the clarification of public rights implicit in the Hickling judgement was itself a cause for celebration. It earned Walter a rhyme in the magazine *Fun*:

Riparian rapaciousness all a-Rye
The Norfolk Broads, which threatened were of late,
Are now all safe – at least for one more year:
Thus Walter Rye, and others, have borne weight,
So for them *Fun* gives many a hearty cheer.
Anglers and boating men may now descry
A (Norfolk) Broad smile coming thro' that Rye.[45]

The rest of 1891 passed without serious incident on the Broads, but the following year a complaint was laid that Ranworth Broad had now been chained up, and the NBPS appointed Walter, together with Mr Hunt of Yarmouth, to investigate. Walter wrote to the *London Standard* from the *Alma* at Horning on 17 September:

I rowed all over the Broad today, and was not in any way interfered with by the gamekeeper, and have no doubt as to what the result of any litigation would be as the Broad is undoubtedly tidal and there is ample evidence of public rights of way over it.

The autumn of 1892 had already witnessed a hectic sailing and social season:

Our autumn cruise was with the family and one or two visitors, including J. Beloe… Our yearly voyage up the Broads was from 26th August to 9th September, Stephen Wright and a friend were over and the boys and Macfarlane part of the time. My old schoolfellow Heriot and Blyth came down for a week, and with the help of 'Professor Day' we showed them some grand bream fishing off South Walsham Dyke… Afterwards Hunt, Roberts and Reay joined, and we had much pleasant sailing after Stephen Wright deserted and we took Sam Holmes in his stead.[46]

Attempts had also been made to prevent fishing in Barton Broad. Declaring that this too would be resisted, Walter held that the Hickling judgement clearly governed Barton where, as to the existence of a tide, 'there can be no doubt'.[47] Confident that there was more flesh to be picked from the carcass of the Hickling case, and backed by a number of local experts and writers on the Broads, including G. Christopher Davies, Walter set about organising an appeal against the judgement. However, when this was heard in 1893, not only was the initial judgement substantially upheld, but Walter himself was reprimanded for having brought the appeal on 'hopeless' grounds. Lacking the financial wherewithal to take the case to the House of Lords, but at the same time feeling that he must justify his expenditure of the society's funds on an action for which he had been so publicly criticised, he now published privately *The Hickling Broad Case (Micklethwait v Vincent): The Judgment of the Court of Appeal Considered*,[48] emphasising among other things that the case had at least vindicated public *sailing* rights.[49]

Other similar legal actions brought at about this time included one concerning fishing on Walsham Broad,[50] and for decades such issues would continue to bubble up.[51] During his mayoralty of Norwich (1908–1909, see Track 6) Walter used his position to petition for a Royal Commission on the Broads, but Asquith rejected this pending the outcome of an application of the River Conservators for an Order under the Fisheries Act of 1907 to protect them,[52] and nothing came of it.

Endnotes

1 In later life, with no qualms at tackling a new challenge, he struggled unsuccessfully to tame a centre-board craft on the Thames. (*Autobiog.* for 1885.)

2 WR, *The Recreations of a Norfolk Antiquary,* I, 1920, p.7 and *Autobiog.*

3 WR, *Ibid.*

4 Cargoes included coal, sugar, oatcake, groceries, manure, horns, bones and timber: see P. H. Emerson and T. F. Goodall, *Life and Landscape on the*

Norfolk Broads (1886), plate XXIV and p.56 etc. In Davies, *The Swan and her Crew* (c.1876), p.132, the boys are towed by a steam wherry. He later speaks of 'white-sailed yachts with gay-coloured pennants at their mast-heads and laughter-loving pleasure parties on board', p.133.

5   For Walter's own description of wherries and the tourist trade see WR, *History of Norfolk* ch. 14, 'The Broads and Marshes'.

6   WR, *Recreations* as above.

7   *Ibid.* p.xi.

8   *Ibid.* p.xiv.

9   *Ibid.* pp.xv–xvi. For more information on wherries and the Broads see David Bray, *Evolution of the Norfolk Wherry* (nd, c.1980); Roy Clark, *Black-sailed Traders* (1961/1972). On the Broads more generally, see for example, G. C. Davies, *The Swan and her Crew, or the Adventures of Three Young Naturalists on the Broads and Rivers of Norfolk* (London, Frederick Warne & Co., [1876]) and his *Handbook* cited above (Jarrolds' Holiday Series, many nineteenth century editions). See also Norfolk Wherry Trust website.

10 *Autobiog.* for 2 Aug. 1886: During one voyage 'I heard of the birth on 22nd August of my youngest son Gilbert Walter Rye'.

11 WR, *A Month on the Norfolk Broads*, p7; *The Recreations of a Norfolk Antiquary*, I, 1920, p.8; *Autobiog.*

12 WR, *Songs, Stories and Sayings of Norfolk*, p.28.

13 WR, *History of Norfolk*, p.284.

14 NRO, MS 4691/4.

15 NRO, MS 4691/7.

16 *EA*, I, p.132. Some of the dialect expressions he collected are recorded in WR, *History of Norfolk*, pp.281–2.

17 NRO, MS 4691/7.

18 *Autobiog.*

19 WR, *Recreations*, II. In 1886 he took a long cruise [? with Voelcker] in the *Lotus* 'which included a memorable hoax of the Theodore Hook type at Catton'.

20 WR, *History of Norfolk*, p.259.

21 Undated on the title page, published simultaneously in London, Norwich and Yarmouth, and unusually not mentioned in the course of the annual lists of his publications in the autobiography. In 1922, thirty-four years after the maiden voyage of the *Lotus*, Walter would publish another work entitled *Some Notes on the Norfolk Broads*, in which he noted that *A Month...* had 'sold out a large edition almost at once, and is now scarce largely thanks to the sketches by Wilfrid Ball who is now well known in the watercolour world'. The wherry *Zoe* is listed, albeit as a commercial vessel, in Roy Clark, *Black-sailed Traders* (1961/1972), p.237.

22 WR, *Songs, Stories and Sayings*, p.139.

23 He 'stuck to me to the end of my sailing career and was with me when I bought and refitted the *Alma* in 1890'; WR, *A Month on the Norfolk Broads*, p.8. Tungate, of Icehouse Lane, Bracondale, Norwich, was among the

operators recommended to sailors in WR, *History of Norfolk*, p.258.

24 http://www.wherryalbion.com/history/literature/documents/Wherries%20 in%20literature.pdf quoting J. Wentworth Day, *Broadland Adventure*, 1951, p.52.

25 But this is too early a date for it to have been his son J. B. Rye.

26 *Autobiog.* has the 1885 voyage begin at Norwich.

27 WR, *A Month on the Norfolk Broads*, p.6.

28 WR, *Songs, Stories and Sayings*, p.139.

29 WR, *A Month on the Norfolk Broads,* p.79.

30 As Walter is continually bemoaning anything that disturbs the peace of the Broads, it is just possible that the noise of hymn-singing or band, rather than any distaste for the Salvation Army *per se,* lay behind this remark.

31 WR, *A Month on the Norfolk Broads,* p.68.

32 *Ibid.,* p.75.

33 *Ibid.,* p.102.

34 The numbers are added in pencil.

35 NRO, MS 11522.

36 P. H. Emerson, *Pictures of East Anglian Life* (1888), pp.80–81.

37 A press report in July 1891 sets the scene: 'Last winter an old fisherman, named Tubby, was served with an injunction to which he did not appear; it was made absolute, and the man's home was sold up for about twenty-five shillings to pay the cost.' *Nottingham Evening Post* (London column), 15 July 1891.

38 Emerson *op. cit.*, p.80.

39 Walter Rye, *The Rights of Fishing, Shooting and Sailing on the Norfolk Broads* (1899), p.30.

40 *Autobiog.* for 1891.

41 WR, *Songs, Stories and Sayings*, p.141. 'I had them all in Court, and urgently pressed that they should be called, but after hearing a great many the Judge absolutely declined to hear any more of this part of the case.'

42 Multiple copies of the judgment are in NRO, MS11522, which includes further correspondence, press cuttings etc. on Walter's involvement in cases concerning the Broads.

43 *London Daily News*, 1 Aug. 1891, reports that WR has given £100 towards the funds of the NBPS.

44 *London Standard,* 18 Sept. 1891.

45 Quoted in *Sussex Agricultural Express*, 2 Oct. 1891.

46 *Autobiog.* p.78.

47 *London Standard*, 19 Sept. 1892. For correspondence that year with Dr P. H. Emerson on the rise and fall of water in various Broads see NRO, MC 2235/1/25/2 and 3.

48 Printed by A. H. Goose, Norwich, 1893.

49 W. A. Dutt, in his *Guide to the Norfolk Broads* (1923), pp.29–30, felt that the Hickling judgment was quite wrong and that anyone who knew the Broads would recognise that they were indeed tidal.

50 WR, *The Rights of Fishing, Shooting and Sailing on the Norfolk Broads* (1899); for related correspondence on Broads issues see three letters from Dr Emerson, of the wherry *Maid of the Mist* in NRO MC 2235/1/28.

51 Walter continued to be consulted by individuals involved in or contemplating litigation about rights on the Broads. As late as 1924 he was still writing to the press on issues concerning access, following a test case brought at Norwich Shirehall Police Court where the magistrates felt themselves bound by the judgement of a higher court to respect the rights of private owners. (Offprints of an article headed 'Only way to free the Broads' including a letter from WR, *Norwich Mercury* 20 Sept. 1924.) He was still campaigning for a Royal Commission to settle the rights of owners and public once and for all. He concludes despondently that 'the law recognises no such thing as pleasure.' NRO, MS 11522.

52 The *Leicester Chronicle,* 6 Mar. 1909 reported publication of a petition to support the public rights of fishing on the broads. Correspondence, papers and pamphlets concerning the Broads campaign can be found in NRO, MS 11522, and MS 2235/1/25.

4
OTHER SPORTS

Shooting

For better or worse, sailing on the Broads and wildfowl shooting were interlinked activities. Walter was not himself a great shot, and says little about this as a pastime. He certainly knew all the best sites for wildfowl, but so, increasingly, did the whole world. The advent of the railways, as he noted ruefully in his *Tourists' Guide* (which must surely itself have contributed to the problem), made remote areas like the Broads readily accessible and thus multiplied the number of wildfowlers. If they were not shooting birds to eat, they were shooting them to stuff and add to display collections, not only in private houses and museums but even in public houses.[1]

Walter was alert to – but did not have any ready solution to – the conflicts of interest between sport and conservation, and between the amateur and the professional gun. Take, for instance, his description of Breydon in the *History of Norfolk*:

> Given a hard winter… Breydon becomes the happy hunting-ground of all the gun-owners of the district for, from its position and the feeding-ground its long mud-banks afford, it is as good a non-preserved place for fowl as can be found. It is also a special locality for those who take pleasure in exterminating the rare sort of water birds. Luckily, however, the professional shooters, whom you will see stealing along in their slate-coloured punts, look with no great favour on amateur gunners; and I have known them shoot off their

big guns at nothing in particular, just to alarm the ducks rather than let the visitors have a chance.[2]

In 1888 he records entering a pigeon-shooting competition at Sole Street:[3]

> ... but as may be judged from the fact that I secured 10 pigeons (and a pocketful of half crowns) out of 13 with a single gun, the pigeons must have been of a very low class indeed. For want of practice I never could hit flying birds, if strong on the wing.

However, throughout his Norfolk retirement he had keen shots among his friends, who invited him along and regularly presented him with some of their bag if he couldn't make the date.[4] But he did occasionally join them, probably as much to be sociable as to demonstrate any skill on his own part. One friend remarked that Walter was a better shot with a pistol than a shotgun,[5] but perhaps this was not entirely a compliment, for in one of his Norwich lectures he remarked:

> If I have a hobby it is of pistol shooting, which I have sedulously practised for over half a century, during which time I must have shot away hundreds of thousands of cartridges. I have very often shot a pistol at flying birds, but I have never hit or even wounded one – the most I have done is to make a bird wince a bit and change his course.[6]

He became a strong supporter and benefactor of the Miniature Rifle Association in Norwich, as a way of keeping potentially unruly young boys occupied and off the streets. An illustrated lecture he gave on the history of King Street paused over Mountergate Street:

> ... down which, chiefly through the energy of Mr Frank Morgan and the liberality of his firm now stands the capital miniature rifle range... which will be open in a few days and that will be well supported by Citizens generally... Rifle shooting is one of the most fascinating sports possible, and has the extreme advantage that proficiency in it is a very valuable national asset [sic]. A man may

be a crack skittle player, golfer or billiard player but the pleasure he gets out of them is a selfish pleasure and his assiduous practice valueless in case of invasion. These games have not the advantage of general athletes, rowing, cricket or football, which at all events do strengthen the body and clear the mind, or cycling which trains men to be speedy messengers. But this miniature rifle shooting affords a sport which provides for unlimited emulation between individuals and between teams and should appeal to the class of men who at present are satisfied with looking on and yelling ignorant applause and abuse at teams of paid performers who masquerade as Norwich Canaries when there isn't a local man in the whole cage of them. In shooting each man is not only a spectator but a performer...[7]

At different times he also records taking part in clay-pigeon shooting and rook shooting.

Archery

From middle age onwards Walter also became an enthusiastic archer, and had practice butts set up in his gardens at both Wandsworth and Hampstead for recreation. After his retirement he participated in matches in Norfolk with great regularity, sometimes at the rate of several per week in the season, and from 1900 he recorded his scores, achievements and frustrations year by year in the *Autobiography*.

He assessed himself as a good archer when practising alone, but going to pieces when being watched, suffering greatly from the 'nervousness which practically spoiled me as an athlete'. However, archery was evidently something he could enjoy even when his mobility was compromised by his great weight and by sickness. That he could cope with it at all, given the poor eyesight he so often complained of, suggests that it was mainly his near sight rather than distance vision that was affected.

He was formally admitted a member of the two archery clubs of Fakenham & Dereham and of Beeston. The early records of the Fakenham and Dereham club survive. Both men and women were members, and indeed there are signs that it was often the women who were the more proficient. Walter, elected in 1904, became an enthusiastic and regular shooter, though not a high-scoring one and he often did not complete a match. Still, he was sufficiently highly regarded by 1909 to be one of the committee appointed to find a new club President; and it must surely have been through his influence that his friend Prince Frederick Duleep Singh accepted the burden of that office for the year 1909–1910.

Walter was among the handful of members who strove to keep the club going through the rather fallow years of the 1920s once its activities had resumed following the First World War. The club's historian, Eileen Fletcher, records that in 1922:

All scores shot during the season are listed for 16 members and the averages worked out for all except Mr Rye who, it is recorded, 'did not shoot all his arrows at any meeting'.

There is a club tale concerning Walter Rye and practice. It is said that in order to practise his archery, Mr Rye put champagne corks on the ends of his arrows and then used to shoot at the neighbour's cats when they prowled into his garden!…

The following season (1923) Mr Rye claimed that on account of his age and weakness he could no longer shoot 80 yards.[8] On three occasions he simply did not shoot 'the Long' at all; thereafter he shot the ladies distances. Nevertheless he was held in sufficient esteem to be elected onto the committee again after a break of some years.[9]

In his Lammas days, Walter had had butts set up on the green next to his house, but by the 1920s, living in Norwich and now lacking any ground of a suitable size to host one of the club's meetings, as most members did in time, he offered in 1925 to pay instead for the hire of an archery ground in Dereham or Aylsham. At the same time he proposed that members should bring their own picnics to the meetings: 'To my mind these picnics are far better fun than burdening people who are good enough to give grounds with the extra expense of feeding the shooters.'[10]

On 8 August 1925, L. Worthy of the *Norfolk Chronicle* wrote to him: 'I am so glad to note that you are better, and able even to take part in an archery meeting again. There are not many at 82 who can do that.'[11] In fact, Walter continued to shoot with the club for another three years, right up to the Prize Meeting of 11 September 1928, and chaired its AGM that year.

While G. A. Stephen was assembling material for Walter's obituary in 1929, he received a letter from Edward Peake enclosing photographic negatives, which sadly seem not to survive, of Walter at his butts in Lammas:

> The butt was set up on a green beside his house and I saw him make some good shots. He was full of enthusiasm for the sport and had some good yew wood in store for future bows. The particular occasion was a very happy one: WG Clarke, H Halls and myself, with the ladies to keep us from delving too deeply into the stone age. The special dish of the evening was a carp… with a most delectable dressing of wine.[12]

Miscellaneous interests and a few failures

The list of sports in which Walter either demonstrated some prowess or showed real interest goes on, as a few references chosen from different stages of his life will easily demonstrate.[13] By his mid-teens he had acquired a 'competent knowledge' of **boxing** ('sparring') and put it to good use by challenging a youth named Veitch who had always bullied him at school.[14] In 1863 (aged about twenty) he says he was still 'sparring a good deal'. To take an example from his middle years, the particulars of sale for his Hampstead house in 1899 reveal that there was a tennis lawn.

A number of new sports also fired his enthusiasm. On discovering that a member of Thames Hare and Hounds, Dr T. Archer who was a Canadian, had been a member of the Montreal Lacrosse Club, he persuaded THH to make up a **lacrosse** team of its own and invite a Canadian team over in 1876 to play an exhibition series.[15] It was said to be the first sighting of this sport in Britain. Half a century later, in 1918 when Walter was in his mid-seventies, baseball was first demonstrated in Norwich. Neither his advanced age nor the fact that this was wartime stood in the way of his enjoyment. He records that:

> One seldom takes any relaxation nowadays, but I do not feel guilty in admitting that I was one of the very many who saw baseball played in Norwich for the first time the other day for the benefit of a war charity. The game is hard to understand, but inspires the participants

and their friends with maddening enthusiasm, and the players were never at rest for a moment either physically or mentally.[16]

There were a few athletic pursuits that Walter never mastered. He was not a strong swimmer, and on one occasion almost drowned. He tried out cricket just once at the age of seventeen but, as he put it, 'without success'.[17] He was not the first, nor the last, to find golfers' tales full of exaggerations, but noted, 'I cannot speak from my personal knowledge'.[18] And he could never understand people's fascination with horse racing.[19]

The all-round sportsman

Even so, enough has been said throughout Track 2 to illustrate not only Walter's pride and prowess as a sportsman and what it was that fired him, including:

- building up physical fitness and strength, as an honourable virtue in its own right but also as a defence against (and means of recovery from) ill health;
- cultivating skill, discipline and precision;
- giving of one's best, whether as an individual or a team player, against all challengers, and thus aspiring to a place among the greatest;
- doing all this as a dedicated amateur, without thought of financial reward;
- enjoying the wide outdoors and living life to the full;
- keeping out of mischief and making lifelong friends; but in some degree also escaping the confines and chores of family life!

It was an impressive tally, and on all these counts Walter Rye achieved to the full.

Endnotes

1   'In the large room at the Wherry Inn [Oulton Broad] is a most attractive collection of fishes and birds, which have met their death in his locality', G. C. Davies, *The Handbook to the Rivers and Broads of Norfolk and Suffolk*, (29th edition, 1899), p.150. See also Pamela Horn, *Pleasure and Pastimes in Victorian Britain* (1999), pp.96–7. 'Few men would believe the ignoble rivalry that exists between educated men to obtain specimens of rare birds for their

museums', P. H. Emerson, *Pictures of East Anglian Life* (1888), p.86.

2 WR, *History of Norfolk*, p.275.

3 *Autobiog.*, p.63.

4 Horn, *op. cit.*, p.98 notes the extent to which charges for shooting contributed to landowners in Norfolk.

5 'If you shot as well with the gun as you do with the pistol you would take the cake', 26 Oct. 1903, NRO, MS 10612 folder 2.

6 WR, *Recreations*, p.107.

7 NRO, MS 4691/76.

8 This is confirmed by Jane Hales, 'I knew Walter Rye', in *Norfolk Fair,* Aug. 1984: 'The last time I saw Walter Rye was at his archery meeting on a ground [beside] the Fox at Hevingham. He was by then so old and infirm that he had to shoot with the women, as he could not cover the distance for the men.'

9 Elaine Fletcher, *A Norfolk Quiverful: celebrating 100 years of archery in the Fakenham area* (Larks Press, Dereham, 1994), especially p.32.

10 Fletcher, op. cit., p.35

11 NRO, MS 4691/83.

12 NRO, MS 4691/95/2.

13 As an example of his wider interest see his 'Sport on land and water' (chapter 10 of WR, *Songs, Stories and Sayings of Norfolk,* [1897]).

14 *Autobiog.*, p.20.

15 J. Ryan (comp) *The Annals of Thames Hare and Hounds 1868 to 1945…* (1968), p.33. The tour was not a financial success, but a second one in 1883 fared better.

16 'Norfolk and the Great War of 1914 etc.', a scrapbook presented by WR: Norfolk Studies, Millennium Library Norwich, C940.3.

17 *Autobiog.*, p.21.

18 See his lecture on 'The natural tendency of the human race to exaggerate the physical prowess of themselves and their ancestors', (Science Gossip Club, c.1907), in WR, *Recreations*, p.114.

19 In June 1888 he went with Georgina to The Oaks, 'but didn't think much of horse racing, and I don't think went to a race meeting again', *Autobiog.*, p.64.

5
POSTSCRIPT ON HEALTH

It is a paradox that someone who so devoted himself to physical fitness and outdoor activity should also have suffered regular bouts of dangerous ill health. Walter's serious ailments began with dysentery as a teenager, which left him with long-term bowel problems and recurring lethargy and exhaustion. In middle years he went on to contract, at various times, influenza, rheumatic fever and typhoid, and to experience more than one nervous breakdown with its attendant depression. He understood why close friends in similar situations had taken their own lives. Some of his friends thought him, at times, a hypochondriac, and the attention given to his ailments in the *Autobiography* might support this. But he had good reason to worry.

It might be said that disease was a common hazard among men of Walter's generation. But friends like Jessopp and Howlett repeatedly warned him that he was heaping up trouble by his unnecessarily tough physical and mental regimes. Which was cause and which effect? The fear that he could meet an early end was certainly a driving force behind his compulsion to get fit again and to put as much of his research as possible into print at the earliest date.

The substantial food that provided calories for his sport, and the legendary socialising, with more food and alcohol, after sporting events as a youth, help to explain why, despite all his energetic activity – scaled down after his twenties through the demands of professional and family life – he weighed 17 stone by the age of 40. His diet was at times strange, but never less than plentiful ('Epicurean' as he described it). In Norfolk it might include wildfowl from the day's bag: not just pheasant but larks, snipe and even godwit (which he found too oily and unsatisfying), whilst a Christmas dinner was not complete without a roast swan, shared with family and/ or friends, as at Lammas in 1908 with twenty guests while he was Mayor. Walter generally dined well, if not at home then with others, and provided generous hospitality, to individuals but also to large visiting groups, in both London and Norwich.

Certainly the worst crisis came in 1884-5, when first Walter contracted typhoid and nearly died, then his brothers actually did die – Frank from TB and EC from smallpox – and finally his young son Hugh (Hubert) had to have his lungs aspirated. It would have been too much for anyone to bear, and Walter suffered a complete breakdown resulting in long-term sick-leave.

After his retirement, Walter was troubled by a new range of problems: heart disease, decaying teeth, gout and glaucoma. Failing eyesight affected his literary output, as we shall see. And there were other unpleasant side-effects of old age, including on one occasion fainting in the street, and a more general debility which in his seventies led him to invest in a single brougham to get to and from the station. But these were inconvenient rather than life-threatening problems, and until ripe old age he was able to continue tricycling and archery. His doctor's prediction in 1915 when Walter went for a heart check-up, that he could live another fifteen years, was not a bad guess. It was difficult to persuade a man who had repeatedly been very ill that he was not actually dying after all!

TRACK 3: THE ANTIQUARY

1
THE NORFOLK
ANTIQUARIAN TRADITION

As Walter worked his way into Norfolk studies, he quickly became conscious of being compassed about by that great cloud of witnesses, the Norfolk antiquaries from the sixteenth century onwards. From the time of the greatest of them all – Peter Le Neve in the seventeenth and eighteenth centuries – down to Walter's mentor and friend John L'Estrange there was a well-nigh apostolic succession. Walter set about building his own credentials to stand in their shoes: first by his writings on the county, and later, when rising fortunes made it possible, by establishing his own antiquarian collection and even acquiring some of his predecessors' manuscripts and books. He remained loyal to, though not uncritical of, this antiquarian heritage, and on more than one occasion appraised it in print and in lectures.[1] He could also be said to have influenced our own understanding of that inheritance by writing entries for a number of Norfolk antiquaries in the *Dictionary of National Biography*.[2]

He traced the collection and study of the county's antiquities from Robert Kemp, a sixteenth-century herald, through such figures as Sir Henry Spelman, the Revd Anthony Harrison, and Sir Simonds d'Ewes, to Guybon Goddard the deputy Recorder of Lynn (d.1671) whose collections passed partly to Peter Le Neve and partly to Thomas King and Thomas Tanner.

Peter Le Neve (1661–1724), who became Norroy King of Arms and would later be affectionately referred to by Tanner as 'King Peter',[3] was described by Walter as the 'prince of genealogists',[4] and 'simply a marvellously industrious and able man... Whatever he did he did very thoroughly'.[5]

With insider knowledge as an under chamberlain of the Exchequer, he worked indefatigably on the public records, transcribing and abstracting many that were of interest to local history, especially but not exclusively for the counties of Norfolk and Suffolk. Over his lifetime Le Neve amassed a prodigious quantity of notes, many on small scraps of paper and largely unsorted. But he lacked the time or inclination to use this material to write at any length on Norfolk history. Walter, who had often encountered Le Neve's neat handwriting at the PRO, felt that given the disordered state of the records it was 'simply amazing how Le Neve could have got through the amount of work he did... I have more than a suspicion that he gained the good graces of some of the custodians of the records by acting as an amateur calendarer'.[6] In writing up Le Neve for the *DNB*, he concluded that 'all his work was characterised by strictest honesty'.

Thomas Martin (1697–1771)[7] – according to Walter a 'worthy and eccentric' historian – was cast in much the same mould as Le Neve, amassing great quantities of information without ever making much of it himself.[8] He had already become so knowledgeable about the history and antiquities of his native Thetford by his early teens that he was sought out as the local guru by Le Neve himself, and the two struck up a lifelong friendship.[9] A decade or so later Le Neve, as President of the Society of Antiquaries, seems to have sponsored Martin as a Fellow, and later nominated him, along with **Thomas Tanner** (successively Chancellor of Norwich and Bishop of St Asaph) as his executor. In his will Le Neve instructed that his papers of local significance should find a home in a repository in Norwich. But this was overtaken by events. Martin, who was a widower at the time of Le Neve's death, took Le Neve's widow as his second wife, and thereby in a manner of speaking inherited the papers, which he kept at his home in Palgrave (Suffolk), rather to Tanner's dismay. He eventually sold much of this material to Thomas Payne of London.[10]

Francis Blomefield (1705–1752), who would go on to become Norfolk's best-known chronicler, had studied at Caius College Cambridge. His tutor there was Martin's cousin, through whom the two occasionally met.[11] After graduation Blomefield was ordained and was eventually appointed rector of Fersfield, a living purchased by his father to secure him a career and income. This gave Francis in his twenties not only some financial security but also some free time, which allowed his scheme for compiling a topographically-arranged history of Norfolk to take shape.[12] His standing as a local rector opened some doors of clergy and gentry, many of whom not only fed him original documents and information, but also became subscribers to his history. Martin, for his part, gave his near neighbour Blomefield access to his own antiquarian notes and those of Le Neve in his possession, and put him in touch with the Revd Charles Parkin, Rector of Oxburgh, who assisted in the compilation of the history and would eventually become its continuator when Blomefield died having covered only a third of the hundreds of Norfolk.[13]

Central to Blomefield's endeavour was the belief (traceable back to classical authors, and not necessarily religiously motivated) that by recording the noble deeds of earlier generations one might encourage those alive today to emulate them, and conversely that one might avoid the errors and evils of the past by learning what had befallen them.[14] Blomefield was a thorough investigator and a meticulous documenter of his sources. But at the same time he was modest enough to recognise that in the nature of so vast an enterprise he could not possibly have got every detail right. He acknowledged that further evidence which might challenge his conclusions for any parish or manor could well come to light.

And how right he was! The more Walter tested Blomefield's work against his own research, the more he found to criticise. It was in the course of a memoir on Blomefield and his history, in Volume III of the *Norfolk Antiquarian Miscellany*, that Walter first became seriously critical. After an interesting account of the compilation of Blomefield's history, he points out that so many of Blomefield's sources were traceable back to Le Neve that it might better have been called 'Le Neve's History'.[15] And although he regards Blomefield as essentially accurate, and unselfish in imparting his knowledge to others, there are particular areas of weakness. His use of etymology, for example is, according to Walter, 'ludicrous in the extreme'. Blomefield, he says, seems to have had 'water' on the brain, deriving almost every place name from some watery association. And when it came to genealogy – Walter's particular *forte*, of course – Blomefield's critical faculty was absolutely suspended. He swallowed false pedigrees uncritically, 'his pages chronicling as gospel all the ridiculous family histories of the Howards, the Wodehouses, the Cleres and others':

His book, however, is an enduring monument of hard, disinterested work, for it was wholly a labour of love, and as far as the facts chronicled it is usually very trustworthy. It is wonderful indeed how often the searchers in manuscripts of today come across Blomefield's private mark or his beautifully legible handwriting on charters or rolls. A very good point in his character was the unselfish readiness with which he imparted his knowledge to others working in the same field.[16]

It is clear from citations in Walter's writings that he used Blomefield extensively. His overall appraisal[17] was that Blomefield 'was indeed himself a very diligent collector and sorter of deeds and local information, but little more; for his arrangement is devoid of clearness and his knowledge of architecture apparently nil'. (The same was said later of Walter himself!) Blomefield was industrious indeed, but 'neither as able nor as hard a worker as Le Neve'.[18]

At any rate Walter regarded Blomefield's work as infinitely superior to that of his continuator, the **Revd Charles Parkin**, whom he thought 'a most incompetent man'.[19] Parkin's approach was altogether more summary, and from the point at which he took over[20] a lot of the useful detail in the history vanishes, including the depth of the footnotes which are so helpful in Blomefield's work. One particular gap in Parkin's coverage was the monumental inscriptions in churches and churchyards. For the northeast of the county, Walter with several collaborators would later seek to remedy this defect.

The title page of Blomefield's work describes its contents as 'collected out of ledger-books, registers, records, evidences, deeds, court rolls and other authentick memorials'. For references to the public records held in London – other than those few of which transcripts had been published by the likes of Dugdale and Madox – he relied heavily on Le Neve's transcripts, which he described as 'the greatest fund of antiquities for this county that was ever collected for any single county in the kingdom'.[21] Nearer home, he found the records of the Norwich diocese 'the best records that are anywhere extant concerning this county'.[22] Although as a newcomer in the firmament he at first encountered some resistance from the owners of private muniments, eventually he was able to make use of town, parish and manorial records with the compliance of their respective custodians, as well as a large array of private archives and collections, which in some cases included archival documents from dissolved monastic houses.[23]

The role of many local clergy in aiding and abetting Blomefield's work by collecting and transcribing evidence and even writing up whole sections is acknowledged in the Introduction. As well as Parkin these included Dr Henry Briggs (rector of Holt), James Baldwin (r. Bunwell and Carleton Rode) and Charles Barnwell (r. Beeston by Mileham). A number of lay antiquaries are also acknowledged, foremost among them Martin, but also Beaupree Bell jr and Anthony Norris.

Anthony Norris is described by Walter (1889) as the greatest of all recent collectors. His collection had been little known until very recently[24] but in fact Walter found it quite a repository of earlier material. Norris laboured hard but printed nothing, so when Walter wrote his biography for the *DNB* he had to base it largely on 'private information' and on manuscripts in his own possession. After his only son died when he was fifty-one, Norris resolved to dedicate the rest of his life to the history of Norfolk and set to work on East Norfolk, the part of the county least covered by Blomefield. By the time of his death he had produced 1,615 closely written folio pages on the histories of the Hundreds of East and West Flegg, Happing and Tunstead, and five parishes of North Erpingham, the copy for which, Walter says, is now 'ready for the press if the public spirit of the county called for it'. He 'devoted an immense deal of time, trouble and money to compiling what is, in some respects, the most perfect piece of county history ever compiled'.

John L'Estrange we have already encountered as a clerk at the Stamp Office in Norwich, which in effect issued licences to researchers to consult wills there. He was an established antiquary himself but his modest means, and of course his day job, limited his ability to travel beyond the county to further his antiquarian studies. The young Walter met him while on his first research visit to Norwich, and they established a friendly relationship whereby L'Estrange coached Walter in reading old documents and in return Walter transcribed material for him at the Public Record Office.

In Walter's opinion he was 'certainly, since Le Neve, the greatest local collector', and during his early career his industry was 'something abnormal'.[25] He was 'in many respects a very able man', but Walter would later describe him as 'industrious but not a finisher'.[26] He edited twenty-four numbers of *Eastern Counties Collectanea* between January 1872 and December 1873, but his only published work, which Walter regarded as outstanding in its field, was *The Church Bells of Norfolk* (Norwich, 1874). Walter thought of him as a natural contributor when he conceived the *Norfolk Antiquarian Miscellany*, but when L'Estrange held up the entire publication of one number by failing to return his corrected proofs on time Walter did not let their friendship stand in the way of berating him publicly in the volume, saying he was: '... indebted to [him], and I should have been much more so if he had not taken rather more than a year to correct the proofs of it, thereby delaying the publication of this part for just that period.'

Walter would probably not have been so intemperate had he learned in time that his old friend was by then leading a secret, desultory existence, brought to 'hopeless grief [as Walter later discovered] through women and wine'. L'Estrange would later be sentenced to a period of penal servitude for forging the signature of a superior in order to steal stamps worth £1,400, possibly to support these habits. While in prison, he actually penned entirely from memory an article that was eventually published in the next number of the *Miscellany*.[27] At the request of L'Estrange's wife, and in order to start a fund to support her, Walter produced a catalogue of the L'Estrange manuscripts and formally offered them to the Secretaries and Committee of the Norfolk and Norwich Archaeological Society to raise £100 for her benefit. The Society declined to accept them, and before any further decision was taken about the future of the collection L'Estrange died in prison in 1877, aged only forty-one. Walter lamented that L'Estrange's 'deplorable end deprived the county of the man who knew more of its antiquities than any of his predecessors.'[28] Walter *de facto* inherited most of the manuscripts, but was determined to use them to raise money for the destitute widow and her children. He worked up some of L'Estrange's notes and published them in the *Miscellany*, selling individual lots from the collection to those of his friends most likely to be interested.[29] For a time he even took L'Estrange's son into his office in London, but reported sadly that 'he rewarded us by robbing us and running away!'[30] Walter wrote an entry for L'Estrange in the *DNB*, entirely from personal memory.[31]

Endnotes

1 WR, *Index to Norfolk Topography* has a summary of his predecessors. For his lecture of 1889 see WR, 'The unpublished material for a history of the County of Norfolk', reprinted from *Arch. J,* XLVII, p.164; WR, *Tourists' Guide,* p.15.

2 He compiled the biography from his own Le Neve papers, together with others in the British Museum, and from printed sources, with additional help from Athill at the College of Arms.

3 David Stoker (ed.), *The Correspondence of the Reverend Francis Blomefield,* (NRS LV, 1992), p.66.

4 WR, *Tourists' Guide,* p.15.

5 WR, 'The unpublished material...' as above.

6 WR, *Index of Norfolk Topography,* p.x.

7 *ODNB.* Stoker *op. cit.* and David Stoker, 'The ill-gotten library of "Honest Tom" Martin', in R. Myers and M. Harris (eds.), *Property of a Gentleman: The formation, organisation and dispersal of the private library 1620-1920* (Winchester, St Paul's Bibliographies, 1991). Richard Gough, *British Topography,* 2 vols, (1780). His church notes in the Anthony Norris collection were said by Walter to be owned in 1889 by W. R. Kirkpatrick, though Walter had some himself.

8 *NAM* III has a catalogue of Martin's library, reprinted by WR.

9 Stoker, *Correspondence,* as above.

10 Fragments of the collection are in BM Addl MSS and among the Gough MSS.

11 Stoker, *Correspondence,* p.16.

12 *Ibid.*

13 *Ibid,,* p.15.

14 Blomefield, Francis (continued by Parkin, Charles), *An Essay Towards a Topographical History of the County of Norfolk...* (London, 2nd edn, 11 vols, 1805-1810), I, p.xiii.

15 *NAM* III, p.181.

16 *ODNB.*

17 WR, *Index to Norfolk Topography,* p.xiii.

18 WR, 'The unpublished material...' as above.

19 *NAM* III, p.181.

20 Blomefield, *op. cit.,* VI, p.463.

21 Blomefield, *op. cit.,* I, p.xv.

22 Blomefield, *op. cit.,* I, p.xiv.

23 Walter particularly thanked Sir Andrew Fountaine of Narford for access to his collection.

24 WR, 'The unpublished material...'

25 WR, *Index to Norfolk Topography,* p.xvii.

26 WR, 'The unpublished material...', p.5.

27 'He of course having no opportunity of consulting authorities', *NAM* II, ii.

28 WR, *Tourists' Guide,* p.15.

29 NRO MC186/347 includes some material on the sale.

30 *Autobiog.,* p.30.

31 Among other antiquaries mentioned by Walter are John Kirkpatrick, Chamberlain of Norwich d.1728, Benjamin Mackerell, W. Cole, Sir John Fenn Gough, Revd Thomas Kerrich (d.1828), 'the unwearied architecture antiquary', Sir Francis Palgrave, Forby, Cotman, Harrod 'whose sound and able contributions stand out among the weaker papers of historical contemporaries', *Tourists' Guide*, p.15. He lists Munford and Dawson Turner among 'minor lights', and a number of his own contemporaries 'but the existing generation of antiquaries, with two or three exceptions such as Carthew (whose History of Launditch is beyond all praise) is very weak indeed and the County Society is simply stagnating'.

2
THE BRITISH MUSEUM
AND THE PUBLIC RECORD
OFFICE[1]

The British Museum

It was at the British Museum that Walter first began seriously to seek out original documents. He obtained a reader's ticket at the age of eighteen, on 23 April 1862 and used it avidly, but not for long because shortly afterwards a new rule was introduced excluding those aged under twenty-one from readership. By the time he reached that age, attracted by news of the exciting treasures to be found in the Public Record Office (or simply 'the Record Office' or 'PRO'), recently opened off Fetter Lane, he decided to try his luck there instead. It was to be the beginning of a life-long love affair with archives. By 1916, when he compiled his *Autobiography* at the age of seventy-three, even though his PRO visits were over, he still took an active interest in its work and counted himself among its oldest readers.[2]

Exploring the Public Records

The PRO as an entity had come into being in 1838, pursuant to an Act of Parliament which brought under one administration all the fifty or more separate government and legal archive repositories throughout the capital, save for the State Paper Office which remained independent until 1854. The first stone for a new general repository to house the whole PRO was not laid until 1851, but when the first phase of building was almost completed in 1856 the Treasury – doesn't this sound all too familiar in our own day? – withheld funding for two further planned phases of building, and it would be over a decade before those went ahead.[3] The initial accommodation for records, staff and readers was consequently more cramped than was intended. The building, adjacent to the Rolls House off Chancery Lane, was actually entered from Fetter Lane, and when Walter first visited it had a distinctly unfinished air.

First readers at the PRO

News of the records available became public through the annual reports of the Deputy Keeper of Public Records. They contained undreamed-of resources for local and national history, and the process of quarrying them had barely begun.

In the absence of admission registers for the first years little is known of the identity of the readers, but we can make some informed guesses about them. First of all, with seats for only nine readers[4] there were few of them in total. Next, in all probability they did not include many academics. Modern history was yet to be established as an academic discipline at Oxford and Cambridge and few dons or students would meet the admission requirement of sufficient familiarity with both the languages and the scripts of the records.[5] And there were several other reasons why many would-be readers might have been deterred. Even where an academic did possess the necessary skills for admission, penetrating beyond the doors was not for the faint-hearted because it was well known that many of the records were in a filthy condition and poorly described. Then there was the problem of short working hours. There was no artificial lighting in the strongrooms before the advent of electricity, and opening hours were dictated (for the whole year) by the limits of winter daylight, 10am to 4pm. Anyone from outside London was also at a distinct disadvantage in having to bear the cost of transport, and perhaps lodgings. Given all these drawbacks some historians must have concluded that they could not derive sufficient professional capital in the time available to make a visit to the PRO worthwhile, especially if they could find more accessible materials at the British Museum or the Bodleian Library, Oxford. The staff of the PRO would have an uphill struggle in the next generations to encourage more academic readers to make the effort to get to know the records. We might also note in passing that some antiquaries and academics who, to judge by their citations and footnotes, might appear to have had access to the records, had actually consulted not the originals but copies or extracts provided by officials or record agents.[6] And we can be fairly sure that it was these very record agents, some of whom already had long experience of visiting and obtaining transcripts from the various scattered repositories of the previous dispensation, who were the most frequent early users of the PRO.

Walter's induction

Walter first visited the new repository in July 1864, at the age of twenty, while still an articled clerk completing his legal training. It was about six years after the building had opened to the public,[7] but he is nevertheless among the first readers whose name we know for certain, which makes his experiences all the more valuable. It is not clear how fully he met the entry requirements, or whether he had any strings to pull to gain admission, but he was admitted. His legal training had provided him with a modicum of legal Latin and familiarity with some of the scripts. Perhaps he topped this up from self-instruction manuals like Thomas Wright's *Court Hand Revisited* (most recent edition, 1846).

He must have spent a considerable time familiarising himself with the range of available finding aids and getting to know the system for ordering documents.[8] His first impressions were dispiriting. Readers, he said, were seated in a 'long unpleasant room, with low tables and high backless forms which cramped the searcher's legs if he were anything above a dwarf in stature.'[9] Moreover, he must soon have realised that many of the records he would one day have to study were seriously dirty, faded or damaged, and that the writing and form of the ancient documents were rather more difficult than he had envisaged. But we have seen how on his first study visit to Norwich, which came only a few months after his first visit to the PRO, he struck up a friendship with John L'Estrange of the Stamp Office who provided him with just the sort of initial help and encouragement he needed: 'He taught me to read old writing by sending me 17th century deeds to copy, and then returning them with the copies corrected like a school exercise till I got the copy absolutely right.'[10]

The *quid pro quo* was that Walter would transcribe Norfolk material in the PRO for L'Estrange.[11] It was a mutually satisfactory arrangement.

Walter tells us that he reached the PRO each time by walking from Golden Square to Fetter Lane and back in the middle of the day – a strenuous hike, though one for which his walks to and from home and his athletic training had prepared him. His normal routine then was to eat merely a few biscuits in the corridor,[12] although if he was in training for a sporting event and needed energy for the day and evening ahead he called instead at Prosser's in Fleet Street for a lump of cold turbot, two cold sausages, bread and half a pint of bitter. (Could he still stay awake over his documents?) Fortified one way or the other he allowed himself on each visit fifty minutes of transcribing Norfolk records before walking back to the office.[13] Gradually he built up a wide awareness of the relevance of each class of records for Norfolk history, and once he had grasped the language and the often formulaic nature of the documents the battle was half-won. Then, despite being still something of a green-horn, he began to look for ways of putting his findings into print, to assist fellow Norfolk antiquaries who might reasonably be wary of 'the immense bulk of our national records [which] is the greatest hindrance to their use.'[14]

As he became more experienced he cultivated members of the staff. Walford D. Selby, who joined the PRO as a junior clerk in 1867 and over the next twenty years rose to eventual prominence as superintendent of the Literary Search Room,[15] came to be a particular friend. Selby was the founder (1883) of the Pipe Roll Society, and editor of *The Genealogist* (1884–89), to which Walter would frequently contribute.[16] Conversely, Walter would later enlist Selby to publish a guide to the sources for Norfolk history in the PRO.[17] In its preface he noted that most readers found the existing finding aids too bewildering and having 'in nine cases out of ten not the remotest bearing on the particular enquiry'. Thomas's *Handbook*, he said, was 'heavy as suet pudding, and just as indigestible'. Selby therefore began to develop an epitome showing the kind of archival materials available for this one county. He had intended to continue it in a second volume, but was prevented from doing so by his early death.[18]

Early calendars and transcripts

I have written in more depth elsewhere[19] about Walter's pioneering work on three particular categories of records, the Inventories of Church Goods from the time of Edward VI, the Guild Certificates from the reign of Richard

II, and the Feet of Fines. In each case exploratory articles had already been published by earlier Norfolk antiquaries, and John L'Estrange himself had a continuing toe in the door. It is likely that all of these writers had worked from transcripts and extracts provided by staff of the various repositories or by record agents rather than using the original records themselves, whereas Walter set to work to make transcripts directly from the originals.

As they listed items held in parish churches at the time of the Edwardian reformation, the inventories had again become unexpectedly relevant in connection with the ritualist controversies raging in the Church of England in Walter's own day, with their argument over the degree of ornament and ceremony that was acceptable within the law. Walter first entered publicly into this discussion in the columns of the *Church Review*, not essentially with any religious *parti pris* but as a lawyer, pointing out that the mere listing of an item in an inventory was no proof of its *use*; and secondly, as a reader familiar with the originals, noting that where the Commissioners had made *assignments* of church goods so that they might continue in use that was better evidence of their acceptance and use at the time than was any mention in the inventories *per se*.[20]

He went on to publish in 1866 a pamphlet on this subject entitled, *What are the Legal and Advisable Ornaments of the Church of England?*[21] It was his first serious publication, written partly to ingratiate himself with the ritualist brother of a girl for whom he had developed an infatuation, although that was not to last.[22] Walter put himself forward as a 'moderate', standing between the 'Puritan' tradition on the one hand and Anglo-Catholic ritualism on the other. It received a mixed reception, with critics balking at his fence-sitting and his inflated belief in his own opinions on this sensitive subject.[23] He did not return to this subject in later writings, but it was the beginning of a determination, pursued throughout his life, to engage publicly in print on issues of current controversy and whenever possible to cite archival documents in support of his opinions.

As well as transcribing these kinds of documents, he made use of them for his own research, and references to them recur throughout his publications. In 1869, for example, he used the Guild Certificates to write a paper on 'The ancient religious guilds of Bury', which was read in his absence at the historical section of the Royal Archaeological Institute's annual meeting at Bury St Edmunds by the Revd E. Hill and according to press reports was received very favourably.[24]

In the case of the Feet of Fines, considerable groundwork had already been laid by others with regard to Norfolk, but the records particularly appealed to Walter as an aspiring genealogist and topographer because they abounded in the names of people and places. He tried unsuccessfully to persuade the NNAS to commission from him a detailed analysis and index of the Norfolk fines but to his annoyance they (sensibly) asked for something more summary. He was later to concede that there was indeed the scope for summary calendaring, and he found them easy to tackle at speed on that basis, boasting that once he got his eye in he could calendar Fines at the rate of fifty documents per hour.[25] Such was his progress that he finished his transcript and index long before the society was ready to publish it. In fact it was to be 1881 before the first instalment of his *Pedes Finium* eventually appeared in print.[26] He had long since lost patience with the officers of the NNAS, and this delay made matters the more personal.

While waiting, he prepared an interesting note to point the way for others to get to grips with the documents.[27] It shows that he had not only calendared them but made a serious effort to understand them and their value for historical research. He included in the introduction to what became his first published calendar a three-fold worked example of a fine: one set out in Record Type to show the contraction and suspension marks in the original documents, one a Latin transcript with the abbreviations expanded for ease of reference, and one an English translation. For today's reader there are some obvious shortcomings to his methods, but he did at least supply an index of persons and places. A comparison of sample entries from his calendar with the original documents suggests a fair degree of accuracy for the time, and it was to be another seventy years before his work was superseded, when the Pipe Roll Society published full transcripts.[28] By then, understanding of the records had significantly advanced, and the importance of giving full dates and complete lists of the judges and jurors mentioned in the originals (which Walter had failed to do) had come to be realised. But that should not detract from Walter's pioneering achievement, which won very favourable reviews from his contemporaries, including Selby who commended his work as a model of its kind for opening up the records.[29]

It took decades, and prolonged wrangling, for the NNAS to complete the publications of Walter's calendars and indexes to Feet of Fines, but he was able proudly to boast in 1897 that Norfolk was still the only county to have all its fines calendared, 'done in great part by the indefatigable Le Neve, and again recently by the present writer.'[30] We should note in passing that he also calendared the Fines for Suffolk and Cambridgeshire, though with less diligence.

Other sources in the Public Records

It is clear from his published *oeuvre* and correspondence that Walter's research ranged across many more classes of Public Records than those just described. He quickly followed up news of records becoming available for research through the successive *Deputy Keeper's Reports* and the *Calendars* of Public Records, and noted anything that was of special relevance to Norfolk. As many a footnote in his publications, and in his essays for his own *Norfolk Antiquarian Miscellany*[31] show, he was equally at home with Plea Rolls, Patent and Close Rolls, Inquisitions Post Mortem, the State Papers Domestic and Foreign, and numerous other series of records.[32] In short it can be said that Walter Rye became one of the first researchers for *any* county to discover the value of whole categories of untapped public records.

Endnotes

1   For an earlier version of this chapter see Christopher Kitching, 'A Victorian Pioneer in the Records: Walter Rye's *Records and Record Searching* in context', in *Archives*, XXXII, no.119 (Oct. 2008), pp.126–139.

2   *Autobiog.*, p.22.

3   Deputy Keeper's Report [hereafter DKR] 19 (1858), 21, and later reports. For the general progress of building, see successive DKRs. For an overview see Elizabeth Hallam Smith, 'Nine centuries of keeping the public records', in G. H. Martin and Peter Spufford (eds.), *The Records of the Nation* (Woodbridge, 1990). The final phase of building, along Chancery Lane, did not take place until 1892–95.

4   Rye to L'Estrange, 12 May 1865: NRO, MS 4691/24: 'Since I last wrote I have twice been to the Office in the afternoon (the only time I can now get away as I am very busy with legal work), and on both occasions have been unable to obtain a seat in the Search Room, which, by the way, has accommodation for nine only.'

5   There is an early register of permits to see certain documents subject to controlled access (TNA, PRO 6/325). It includes in the 1860s some names to be reckoned with, such as S. R. Gardiner and even Professor Ranke, but does not cover regular readers such as Rye. Writing ten years later, when the PRO

had become more firmly established, Ewald characterised those in the know about its contents as 'the statesman and the judge, the lawyer and the claimant to property, the genealogist and the original historian, the antiquary and archaeologist'.

6   For example, Professor Thorold Rogers, researching the history of prices, persuaded the Treasury to fund more than a year's full-time work by a paid member of PRO staff on his behalf (DKR 25, [1864], vi, and DKR 26, [1865], iv).

7   *Autobiog.*, p.22.

8   Published finding aids then included the successive reports of the Record Commissions, those of the Deputy Keeper with summary lists of newly available materials, and F. S. Thomas's 1853 handbook. There were also unpublished lists and indexes prepared by previous keepers of the records. Only from 1869 would reports on privately-owned muniments be added to this store of information, through the publications of the Historical Manuscripts Commission.

9   WR, *Records and Record Searching* [hereafter *RRS*] (London, 1888), p.103.

10 *Autobiog.* p.30.

11 NRO, MS 4691/11, L'Estrange to Rye, 7 July 1865, in which he thanks him for extracts, sends other material for checking and asks him to search at the PRO for a copy of the Ranworth inventory of church goods.

12 Rye to L'Estrange, 22 Apr. 1865: NRO, MS 4691/24.

13 *Autobiog.* p.25.

14 See, for example, 'Manuscripts in the Public Record Office relating to Norfolk' in *Norfolk Archaeology* [hereafter *NA*], VII, 1872, p.137. He continued his visits to the PRO throughout the next phase of its construction, c.1866–72, which saw the creation of two new reading rooms, respectively for literary and legal searches. For more background see A. C. Ewald, *Our Public Records* (London, 1873), p.24; Christopher Kitching, 'Promoting the Public Records to a nineteenth-century readership: the works of Alexander Charles Ewald (1842–1891)', in *Magazine of the Friends of The National Archives,* XX, no. 3 (Dec. 2009), pp. 5–8.

15 On Selby see *ODNB* and E. Walford, 'The late Mr Walford D. Selby', in *The Genealogist*, ns, VI (1889–90), pp.65–68.

16 See Christopher Kitching, 'Walford Dakin Selby (1845–1889), Superintendent of the Round Room', in *Magazine of the Friends of the National Archives,* XXIV, no.1 (Apr. 2013), pp.18–20.

17 Walford D. Selby (ed.,) *Norfolk Records* (Norwich, NNAS, 1886).

18 As noted elsewhere, he committed suicide in 1889 while suffering a bout of depression after being seriously ill with typhoid. (WR, *Autobiog*, p.69.)

19 Christopher Kitching, 'A Victorian pioneer in the records...'

20 *Church Review* (British Library Newspaper Library) e.g. 30 Sept., 7 Oct. and 14 Oct. 1865.

21 London, 1866.

22 *Autobiog.*, p.25.

23 'An otherwise valuable pamphlet is neutralised for practical good by the obtrusion of the writer's simply arbitrary opinions as to the too much or too little amount of Church ornaments and Ritual,' *John Bull,* 6 Oct. 1866, p.669. 'The writer evidently regards the whole matter as mainly a question of good taste, and his own opinion as a sufficient voucher.' *Ibid.* 16 Feb. 1867, p.118.

24 *Ipswich Journal,* 24 July 1869. *Bury and Norwich Post and Suffolk Herald,* 27 July 1869: 'A very able paper... Mr Rye brought out his points with considerable clearness and brevity'.

25 'This was doubted by the late Mr Muskett, to whom I made the brutal retort I never said *he* could do it.' *Autobiog.* p. 22. The full story is revealed in *EA*, IV.

26 His work on fines appeared in several instalments. *Pedes Finium...* covered Ric. I – John; this was followed by *Short Calendars* covering Ric. I to Edw. I (1885) and Edw. II to Ric. III (1886).

27 WR, 'Feet of fines', in *The Genealogist*, VI, 1882, p.229.

28 PRS, ns, XXVII (1950).

29 For example, *The Genealogist*, ns, III, 1886, p.254, reviewing WR's *Short Calendar of Feet of Fines for Norfolk, part 2, Edw II to Ric III.*

30 WR, *RRS* (1897), p.49. For this work, as for all his editorial work, Walter kept his notes. Many years later when Salzmann revived in *EHR* the question of the earliest feet of fines, Walter told J. H. Round (14 Nov. 1910) that he had a note of an early Norwich fine being recorded on the pipe roll of 35 Henry II. (University of London Library, J. H. Round papers, MS 924/669).

31 A rival to the publications of the NNAS, which he regarded as moribund.

32 WR, *RRS* (1897), p.75. See for example: *EA*, IV (1890–91), pp.23–24 on Inquisitions Post Mortem. *EA*, VI (1895–6) p.46 on subsidy rolls. Even in his eighties he was still keeping up to date with the emerging PRO calendars and maintaining occasional correspondence with the staff. As late as 1927 he refers to the 'valuable calendar of Chancery Warrants' just issued by PRO.

3
OTHER SOURCES

Getting started in Norfolk studies

Encouraged by his first happy trip to Norfolk in 1863, Walter would soon make a habit of spending almost all his summer holidays, and sometimes other breaks as well, in his ancestral county. This allowed him to escape from the pressures of London life and achieve a degree of independence, initially from his parents but later one suspects from his wife and family. More importantly, these breaks enabled him to pursue all his key hobbies at once, with time for cycling and athleticism and for the study of flora and fauna, as well as the history, topography, genealogy and antiquities of the county. Norfolk would also become for him a chosen retreat for convalescence after bouts of serious illness.

These regular visits gave him the opportunity to seek out local sources for the history of the county to supplement those he had found in the PRO. He began with what might be called 'official' records: diocesan, probate, parish and manorial. Following up his first contacts with L'Estrange, he quickly became conversant with the records in many another parish, guildhall and town hall, and with their custodians.[1]

As long as he continued to live mainly in London – and we should remember that this was for more than three decades after he began his researches on Norfolk – progress on his local projects was slower than he wished, because the work was in effect relegated to the status of a hobby. But he made up for this by copious correspondence between visits, by enlisting local help in his absence, and by frenetic bouts of work when he was in the county.

Entrée to the clergy

From Blomefield's example Walter saw how crucial it was to any county historian to establish early contact with the clergy, who were at that date the usual custodians of the parish records. Unlike Blomefield he had the disadvantage of not being a clergyman himself. But he could take comfort in the fact that many clergy were strongly sympathetic to his antiquarian interests, and some were members of the NNAS and other local societies. Walter's copious correspondence amply testifies to his success in engaging with them: he made a number of lasting clerical friendships, and even persuaded some who were not at first fellow-travellers to develop an active interest in antiquities, enlisting them to help gather information for his own books. Some admitted to developing the 'bug' with a vengeance, and to watching others do so.[2]

Once he became known in the county, it was another of his regular pastimes to visit local antiquaries in order to be shown their family muniments or collections of manuscripts or objects.[3]

Monumental inscriptions

Walter once described monumental inscriptions as 'the records of what one may call the little aristocracy of the village: farmer and yeoman... from whom in two or three generations often come the new gentry.'

Blomefield had made a good start on recording the monumental inscriptions of Norfolk, but his continuator Parkin tended to skirt over them unless they were already recorded in Blomefield's notes. In the century between Blomefield and Rye much had happened. Even some of the indoor inscriptions noted by Blomefield in churches had been removed or defaced, whilst worse fates had befallen outdoor monumental inscriptions. Walter therefore sensed the urgency of recording inscriptions before still more were lost. Conversely, since Blomefield's day new inscriptions had been added, which if not recorded might well take the same route to oblivion. As the years went by Walter would see increasing evidence not only of erosion of churchyard inscriptions by the weather but also of deliberate destruction, and he would become highly critical of the 'restorations' of church interiors and the 'tidyings up' of churchyards that had taken place without a thought for this kind of heritage.[4]

It is clear from a contribution he made to *Notes and Queries* in 1862[5] that already by his late teens he had begun noting down the inscriptions in Fulham churchyard near his home. His first serious attempt to assemble this kind of data in Norfolk came with his history of Cromer. He then conceived an ambition to cover the whole of northeast Norfolk, which had not been systematically tackled by Blomefield. Work began with *Some Rough Materials for a History of the Hundred of North Erpingham* (1883). In 1885 he edited and indexed the work of Walter Dew on the *Monumental Inscriptions in the Hundred of Holt*, and later enlisted the Revd A. L. Michell to take forward Dew's work for South Erpingham.[6] Two companion volumes edited by Walter followed, on *Happing* (1886) and *Tunstead* (1891). But it is important to remember that owing to his professional commitments in London he had to rely extensively on input from friends like the Revd H. T. Griffith of Smallburgh and the Revd F. Procter of Witton.[7] For the Tunstead volume Griffith covered eight parishes and five churchyards, and Procter two parishes and two churchyards.

At places like Trimingham and Cromer Walter found inscriptions tiled over. In the previous century Anthony Norris had made copious notes of inscriptions in the hundred of Tunstead, but Walter found that 51 of the 529 church inscriptions in the Tunstead volumes (nearly 10%) although recorded by Norris had already disappeared, including 21 memorial brasses.[8]

In 1923, his eightieth year, Walter crowned his achievement in this field by publishing *Some Monumental Inscriptions in Norfolk before 1600*. This was the culmination of sixty years' work on inscriptions, both sacred and secular, from church monuments, windows, pulpits, doors and seats, from churchyards, and from domestic houses. In order to ensure that it was as complete as possible he trawled afresh the full text of Blomefield, all the manuscript collections in his own library, and (as he put it) 'all the printed topographical material ever published relating to Norfolk', which he estimated at not less than 15,000 pages in all.[9] He dedicated the work to Canon Drake, rector of St John's (Roman Catholic) Church in Norwich, 'who is always ready to share with other students his great knowledge of the history of his Church', out of respect for the 'learning and energy of a straightforward opponent'. A reviewer noted:

> Mr Walter Rye's industry is unapproachable. Last year he was issuing the second part of what he expected would be his last work, and lo!, this year he comes out with a more important work than he has

published for some years past. True, it has taken some sixty years in the compilation, but at last the fruit of his labour is harvested, and another notch has to be added to the score of the many valuable contributions he has made to a fuller and more exact study of byegone East Anglia.[10]

Wider research outside the Public Records

While a resident and night school supervisor in Wandsworth, Walter made the contacts necessary to inspect and list the parish deeds there. In 1872, still in his twenties, we find him among those present for the official opening of the Guildhall Library, London, which suggests he was already becoming well known.[11] He would later donate to it, as well as his own publications, his collection of books on sport, and of press cuttings from his Easterling column in the *Sporting Gazette*. He also mentions consulting archives and manuscripts in other major libraries, including the College of Arms, the Bodleian Library in Oxford,[12] a number of Oxford and Cambridge colleges and the city library and museum in Norwich. His legal work sometimes took him to more distant parts of the country and occasionally gave him the opportunity to drop in at a probate registry, town hall or other public archive repository.[13]

Access to private muniment rooms was altogether more restricted in Walter's day than it is now, but having built up a trustworthy reputation at the PRO and elsewhere he made, as he puts it, 'the antiquarian acquaintance' of Sir Charles Isham, and was invited to his family home at Lamport Hall, Northamptonshire where, after several visits, he edited for publication (1875) the journal of Thomas Isham which became his first major published transcription. His visits there continued, and in his usual way he noted down any passing references to other topics that might subsequently be of use.[14]

In *Notes and Queries* for 1887 we learn that he had been to Lincoln's Inn, having discovered that Maynard MS 84 in its library contained a transcript of the missing Privy Council Register from 1553 to May 1559. 'Why,' he asked, 'are not these registers in the Record Office instead of being practically inaccessible as at present?'[15]

Care for the original documents he studied

In the course of his researches in private muniments, Walter came upon many individual documents that although of some interest, were in poor physical shape. Sometimes he endeavoured to transcribe them so that at least the text might be saved for researchers, and we occasionally catch a glimpse of his robust and surprisingly modern attitude to conservation, as in the case of the first register book of the parish of Old Buckenham.[16] He had first encountered this volume, which was in a very poor physical state, while working on the genealogy of the Preston family, but he later decided to transcribe it for posterity, after persuading his friend Prince Frederick Duleep Singh, who then lived at Old Buckenham Hall in that parish, to put up a significant portion of the cost of publication. Walter described the book as having been wrapped up in brown paper for years endorsed 'illegible', having been exposed in the past to damp: 'quite a third of the paper of which it is composed has rotted away altogether'. He admitted that transcription was very hard work on his eyes, which by this time were already worn out by forty years of close work on records. And he was sure that with more time and perseverance more of the text might be deciphered, but the law of diminishing returns had set in and, in typical fashion he determined to publish it, warts and all. He pretty well admits that he would have applied gall to the ink if he had thought that would help, but that proved impracticable since 'many of the pages are in a state of tinder.'[17] As a temporary preservation measure he inserted cartridge paper between the pages of the original, and in the published transcript exhorted future readers to turn this interleaving, not the original pages, when handling the distressed volume.

In the course of his continuing research he also discovered that early registers of Horsham St Faith's, and those of Aylsham which he had consulted a few years before, had vanished. 'Some day possibly Parliament will wake up to the reality of collecting all these early registers and preserving them from the negligence of many of the clergy.'[18]

Endnotes

1   WR, *Tourists' Guide* mentions a number of records and repositories with which he was already familiar, at Yarmouth (p.57), King's Lynn (pp.99–100) and Swaffham (p.102).

2   Jessopp sought the address of a copyist for Mr Day, the Marquess Townshend's agent, 'who has an Antiquarian craze upon him which may not last long', NRO, MS 4691/23.

3   E.g. Miss Fry's Hornchurch Collection (*Autobiog.*, p.16); Barrett Lennard, 1898: 'and I think impregnated him with antiquarian virus' (*Ibid.*, p.104); Le Strange at Hunstanton 'where I had an interesting time in his record room' (*Ibid.*, 1912).

4   WR, *Some Rough Materials... North Erpingham* (1883), pp.ii-iii.

5   Series 3, II, p.119.

6   Mentioned in the Preface to the *Tunstead* volume.

7   *Autobiog.*, p.117, an 'excellent hardworking antiquary'. Both are kindly acknowledged in the *Happing* volume, p.v.

8   See preface to the *Tunstead* volume.

9   See preface to WR, *Some early English Inscriptions in Norfolk before 1600* (Jarrold, London, [1923]).

10 Review pasted into the copy seen in CCB Library C.3.3.2, which had belonged to Chas G. Chambers.

11 *Autobiog.*, p.39.

12 Not least in order to study the manuscripts left to the library by Bishop Tanner, many of which he had brought from Norwich.

13 In WR, 'Henry Vaughan the Silurist' (*The Herald and Genealogist,* III, [1879], p.33) he reports a visit to the Hereford probate registry where, amid the chaos, he found a MS register which made clear that Vaughan died intestate.

14 Series 7, IV, p.447. Sends a note of a letter of 1559, which he found pasted in a volume at Lamport Hall, concerning a despatch of fruit trees. Jessopp asked him to keep an eye open for material from the years 1640–60 on behalf of S. R. Gardiner, 29 June 1880: NRO, MS 4691/23. Lady Isham was the dedicatee of WR's pedigree of Vaughan of Leominster (now in the BL) compiled from items in her possession, 1876.

15 *N&Q,* Series 7, IV, p. 374.

16 *The First Register Book of the Parish of Old Buckenham in Norfolk, 1560–1649, transcribed, edited and indexed by Walter Rye* (A. H. Goose, Norwich, 1902).

17 *Ibid.*, p.ii.

18 As an aside he notes that he had found a parish register of Bircham Newton among the private papers of the local squire. *Autobiog.*, p.142.

4
RECORDS AND RECORD SEARCHING

After a quarter of a century of researching in both public and private archives, Walter brought together his thoughts and tips for those beginning archival research in his book *Records and Record Searching*. The first edition, published in 1888[1], sold well and a second appeared in 1897.

It is not clear whether this project was entirely his own initiative or was commissioned by the publisher, Elliott Stock of Paternoster Row, perhaps on the recommendation of a third party such as Walford D. Selby of the PRO. This last seems the likeliest scenario, for Selby was simultaneously guiding W. P. W. Phillimore through the Public Records and Phillimore was working on a rather similar book for the same publisher, *How to Write the History of a Family: a Guide for the Genealogist*, which actually appeared shortly before Walter's work. The extent of any collusion within this literary triangle remains unresolved. The two authors were both regular readers at the PRO. Both were London solicitors, Phillimore's office being in Chancery Lane just along from the PRO. And both were keen cyclists. Walter was the older of the two and had been working on the records for rather longer. Phillimore's book shows that he was fully aware of Walter's previous published works. And at least by the time Walter's book reached proof stage he certainly knew that Phillimore's was almost in print, because Selby wrote to him strongly advising him to include an appendix dealing with record publications, on the grounds that this had been done by Phillimore![2]

Curiously, rather than taking cognisance of Phillimore's work when it appeared and incorporating any necessary changes and acknowledgements in his own work before publication, Walter chose simply not to mention it. In a man by then so full of self-confidence this surely cannot have been from any fear that Phillimore's work might highlight shortcomings in his own. But in any case Walter had taken (for him) unusual care over what went into his book. Extensive drafts had been run past learned intermediaries including Selby (PRO), and Dr Marshal (Rouge Croix Pursuivant) and C. H. Athill (Bluemantle Pursuivant) at the College of Arms, in order first to ensure as much accuracy as possible given the current state of knowledge, but also to guard against errors that might have crept in through the speed of his own work. In June 1887, with Walter's proofs in front of him, Selby wrote that he would gladly check those parts relating to the Public Records, hinting tactfully: 'I can see at a glance that you are as always *original* and that the work is excellent, but you produce at such a pace that there must be some slips.'[3]

Two other long-standing friends, both of whom Walter had introduced to the world of antiquarian studies,[4] are also acknowledged as having helped in the book's production.

Whatever his precise relationship with Phillimore, in print the two men remained mutually respectful. Phillimore made special mention of Walter's indexes to Norfolk Feet of Fines: 'Their value to the genealogist may be estimated by the fact that Mr Rye has in these two parts indexed 7,254 documents.'[5] And the acclaim was mutual: a footnote right at the beginning of Walter's *Records and Record Searching*, explained that Phillimore's work was: '… not issued when this chapter was first written, and I have purposely abstained from looking at it except to work some references to it into my index... I need hardly say that it will be most valuable.'[6]

Despite the obvious overlap of content there were clear differences of emphasis, and of target readership. Phillimore's book was specifically aimed at the genealogist, whereas Walter's was pitched at a broader readership and dealt with certain categories of record (such as those relating to land ownership) in greater detail. In the event, the publisher's decision to proceed with both books proved sound, and both became best sellers. The size of Walter's initial print-run is not recorded but he described it as 'somewhat large'.[7]

Most of *Records and Record Searching* concerned the PRO, and the nature and limitations of the finding aids available there, or in print, for each type of record. But it also features the other kinds of repository with which Walter was familiar, and was in effect a *vade mecum* for serious researchers of all kinds. Competent and helpful as a research aid, it was laced with his typically mordant wit, which was not to everyone's liking. It was perhaps only natural that the Master of the Rolls, having been sent a complimentary copy, should commend it; but it was also received with enthusiasm by more detached reviewers:

> There is no limit to Mr Rye's wonderful energy... this handy and instructive volume itself might very appropriately have been lettered 'How to Become an Antiquary'.[8]

> An exceedingly useful handbook for the class of archaeological aspirants. The knowledge of this class of writers is not always equal to their zeal but Mr Rye has done his best to put them in the right way. [*But, noting his failure to take cognisance of Phillimore's book*]... Mr Rye himself has not escaped one weakness of the antiquary, a desire to be original... Surely in compiling a handbook the fear of plagiarism can have no place.[9]

Acknowledging that there might well be shortcomings in the work, Walter invited readers to send him any corrections towards a second edition. When that eventually appeared in 1897 he acknowledged just five people who had taken up his challenge and so, apart from a few interpolations to take account of new finding aids and of his own research in the intervening period, little change to the first edition was necessary. The work was still of sufficient interest to be reprinted in 1969.[10]

Records and Record Searching is written in straightforward, accessible language. Walter was wholly sympathetic to the difficulties researchers were bound to face. It was eminently suitable for beginners, in terms of both the level of understanding assumed and the advice given on research methods. It begins with two 'How to...' chapters: 'How to Compile a Pedigree', and 'How to Write the History of a Parish or other Place'. Each outlines the nature and location of the records most likely to support the research. He sensibly advises would-be genealogists to exhaust family memories and recollections first, and then any evidence such as family Bibles, before turning to published and unpublished archival sources. He warns against placing too much reliance on the uncorroborated recollections of the very old, and against making unjustified connections between people with the same surname.

He seems broadly to have adhered to this strategy in his own work. But what of the following piece of advice? 'Never attempt to theorize or speculate too soon. If you get wedded to a theory you will find yourself unconsciously specially pleading in its favour, and not looking at things fairly.'[11]

How many of Walter's later battles as a controversialist (discussed below) might have been short-circuited if he had really taken this to heart! In similar vein, he urges those writing local histories to stay firmly within the realms of probability and not to damage their credibility by stretching the evidence by unsustainable inferences: 'As you are strong, be merciful. If you can restrain yourself, don't discover that your church is of rather earlier date than St Martin's at Canterbury.'[12]

Later chapters cover, *inter alia*, the archives of land ownership, legal proceeding both civil and criminal, the State Papers, ecclesiastical and monastic records, parish and other local records, fiscal and manorial records. The concluding chapter explains the procedures for access to the main repositories, and includes a note on the best antiquarian booksellers, amongst whom he bestowed the accolade on his friend and neighbour Bernard Quaritch as *facile princeps*.[13] The book is rounded off with informative appendices including transcripts of certain formulaic documents, a list of London cemeteries and classified lists of the Rolls Series, the Calendars of State Papers Domestic and the Historical Manuscripts Commission's reports.

Walter was never reticent about speaking his mind! For example, when he discovered that the Lansdowne MSS at the British Museum contained a key to some of the Feet of Fines in the PRO, he lamented: 'Why the Record Office have not long ago had a transcript of these MSS made and placed on the shelves of the Round Room is one of those mysteries which will probably never be resolved.'[14]

In connection with the manuscript calendars of Patent Rolls he was to remark in 1888 that:

Unluckily... these volumes are not indexed, a fact which terribly discounts their value. If the authorities at the Record Office would only realize the fact that one indexed calendar is worth two unindexed, and that lexicographical indexes could be contracted for out of the office at less than 10s per 1000 references, some improvement would soon take place... The puerility of making alphabetical indexes only out of cut-out slips is most vexatious.[15]

Looking back on his quarter of a century of visits to the Record Office, he felt that both the place and the staff had greatly improved, though the Round Room (in the new eastward extension) was 'a veritable rheumatism trap in winter'. Physical discomfort, however, was soon forgotten by a real devotee of the records like himself, and it is abundantly clear that he remained throughout his life in awe of the sheer volume and diversity of information they contained: '... a mine of material so rich that you could not search a tithe of it if you were to spend a hundred years there.' [16]

What he called 'the bad old days of extortion' (when fees were charged for access) were over, but the rule that only pencils might be used to make notes in the reading rooms he regarded as a 'barbarism'.[17] He raised this with the Master of the Rolls when presenting him with *Records and Record Searching*, but was politely (and properly) told that the MR was 'not disposed to make any relaxation'.[18]

On the other hand, Walter was full of praise for the Record Office staff who 'may be said to be teachers of a record school or university, to the very great advantage of the amateur student.'[19] Towards some of his fellow readers he felt less warmth, and his comments are still relevant in places today:

The gentleman who reads records to himself in a loud voice with chuckling accompaniments expressive of high delight or disgust might be cautioned and disqualified after two cautions. So should the men and women... who think it necessary to talk to the official at the desk for ten minutes at a time, in a high voice which disturbs every reader in the room.[20]

Records and Record Searching dealt with collections outside the PRO with an equal degree of clarity interspersed with occasional (and usually perfectly justified) criticism. Searches by the Society of Parish Clerks for baptismal certificates were, despite the fees they charged, 'often not fruitful'. Diocesan registries were supposed to hold transcripts of parish registers '... but unhappily this cannot be depended on at all. The great majority of clergy and churchwardens have been most remiss in sending in these duplicates.'[21]

And when it came to manorial records, which if found could often be extremely valuable for topographical and genealogical searches:

> Alas, not one manor in twenty has a good series of the rolls, and of these not one in twenty is accessible to the enquirer. Many stewards have the mistaken idea that the old rolls are nuisances, as containing entries which may be used against their lords some day on questions of commons or customs, and very rarely allow anyone to consult them without the special consent of the lord. If this consent is obtained, the office of a busy solicitor (who will of course expect to be paid for the production) is not the place in which an antiquary loves to linger at so much an hour. When, however, the rare opportunity occurs the topographer should never miss it, but setting all other business aside, copy, copy and copy till he has as much as he possibly can.

Endnotes

1 London, Elliott Stock, 1888.
2 NRO, MS 4691/6 (several letters).
3 Ibid., Selby to WR, 6 Dec. 1887.
4 Richard Howlett and Revd Dr Augustus Jessopp.
5 W. P. W. Phillimore, *How to Write the History of a Family: a Guide for the Genealogist* (London, 1887), p.136.
6 *Records and Record Searching* [hereafter *RRS*] (1888), p.1. In his second edition (1897) he added 'but I have since gone through it carefully and am glad to find that the result of our independent work tallies so closely'.
7 *RRS*, (1897), p.ii.
8 *The Genealogist*, ns, V, p.216.
9 *EHR*, III (1888), p.107. This review, although anonymous, has all the hallmarks of J. H. Round.
10 Detroit, Gale Research, 1969.
11 *Ibid.*, p.6.
12 In other words, the oldest church in Engand. Ibid., p.25.
13 *RRS* (1888), p.138.
14 *RRS* (1897), p.52.

15 By 1897 he hoped the Deputy Keeper had this in hand, Ibid., p.114n.
16 *Ibid.*, p.11.
17 *RRS* (1888), p.103.
18 J. J. Cartwright to WR, 6 Jan. 1888: NRO, MS 4691/4.
19 *RRS* (1897), p.119.
20 *Ibid.*, p.127n.
21 *Ibid.*, p.3.
22 *Ibid.*, p.108.

5
NOTES, INDEXES AND CALENDARS

A passion for indexing

Walter was an avid indexer. He advised researchers, 'Never leave an item of newly acquired information unindexed for a day',[1] and set out his own approach as follows:

> Personally I am an enthusiastic indexer, and really do not know any pastime more engrossing or more amusing… Unless a man is a real scientist, it is far better for him to spend his time making indexes, which are of use to many, than making collections which are of interest only to himself.

It was a passion that would stay with him to the end. As late as his eightieth birthday his friend the historian G. R. Potter would send him an amusing postcard quoting *What is an index?* by Henry B. Wheatley, the founder of the Index Society, which was very much in tune with Walter's thinking: 'My friend John Baynes used to say that the man who published a book without an index ought to be damned ten miles beyond Hell, where the devil could not get for stinging-nettles.'[2]

Walter used two alternative indexing techniques. The first involved writing the letters of the alphabet at the head of separate pages in a blank book or on a very large sheet of paper, and entering each index term as it arose. The second involved writing the index terms one after the other, un-alphabetised, on a sheet of paper and then using scissors and paste to rearrange them into alphabetical order. The latter approach of course generated many loose slips which were prone to loss and disorder, but it had the advantage that the slips could later be merged with indexes to other sources to form union indexes.

If he needed an index to enable him later to retrace his own steps, Walter would make one, no matter how crude, and perhaps put it into print. As he remarked more than once about his own books, 'I should have found this compilation very useful to me had I made it before.' He would spend countless hours and days making good the lack of indexes to books and manuscripts, and union indexes to bring together information from a wide range of primary and secondary sources. In due course he would say with little exaggeration that he had indexed every known book and pamphlet relating to Norfolk history.

Published indexes

Walter published a number of (generally short) indexes through the medium of his *Norfolk Antiquarian Miscellany*,[4] but had a grander project in mind to issue a union index of sources for Norfolk history, with references taken from as many published sources as he could identify. This first appeared in 1881 as *An Index to Norfolk Topography* published by the British Record Society's Index Library. Most of the book is arranged alphabetically by place, with the references to each available source marshalled under the place name. The scope was impressive, extracting references from the many descriptions of PRO records detailed in the Deputy Keeper's reports, and incorporating other material from the published finding aids of the British Museum, the Bodleian Library, Cambridge University and Lambeth Palace libraries, the reports of the Historical Manuscripts Commission, articles in *The Gentleman's Magazine, Notes and Queries*, the *Annual Register,* major reference works such as Dugdale's *Monasticon* (1846 edn.) and Le Neve's *Monumenta* (1718). To these were added the first eight volumes of transactions of the Norfolk and Norwich Archaeological Society, and a host of other East Anglian sources.

Starting from the premise that 'any index is better than none', Walter nevertheless admitted that there would be mistakes:

Owing to the great bulk of the MS slips, it was nearly impossible to remember during the process of sorting, which took over a year, whether previous entries, such as those relating to Rising Castle, had been dropped into R. for Rising or C, for Castle Rising... Still, the task is done, so far as I am concerned; and at worst it may serve as an example of bad work, which may encourage collectors for other counties to think, rightly, that they can do much better, and so be of some use, though not that for which it was originally intended.

He also admitted another possible failing, that as he was not at that time resident in the county and had no access to private collections of pamphlets, tracts etc., the bibliographical part was weak. But if his own work were deemed bad, what, he wondered, could be said of the index to Martin's *Suits in the Exchequer?* Or the index to the *Royalist Composition Papers*, which 'seems to have been compiled by someone who was unable to read the bad writing of the seventeenth century'? The index to the Lansdowne MSS at the British Museum was 'very elaborate but most foolishly compiled', and so on. The Bodleian's indexes, however, seem to have been blameless.

A book of that kind was never likely to be a best seller, but its route to publication through the Index Library ensured that it got into the hands of those who could most benefit from it. In addition Walter personally sent copies to his preferred libraries and to personal friends. Griffith summed up the general view when he wrote, 'I stand aghast to think of the amount of toil represented by this modest looking volume.'[5]

The sources requiring indexing naturally continued to accumulate, necessitating a first supplement in 1896,[6] in which Walter referred back to the reception of the original volume:

It was well reviewed, and I think I may say has been of considerable use to those few who seriously interest themselves in the history of Norfolk – probably not less than twenty in number. Financially it was a dead failure and most copies of the edition have been offered for waste paper. [7]

Some three years later[8] there appeared *An index rerum of Norfolk antiquities* – 'of some use to myself if to no one else': 'This little book will, I expect, be the last of my Norfolk Indexes. With its two predecessors[9] it makes 785 pages and they will, I trust, be of use to the rapidly increasing number of students of Norfolk Archaeology.'

Calendars and transcripts of documents in Norwich and Norfolk

While he was resident in London, Walter's work on calendaring documents relating to Norwich and Norfolk was largely confined to the principal sources in the PRO already discussed above, such as the Inventories of Church Goods, the Feet of Fines and the Guild Certificates.[10] Once he retired to Norwich, his attention was more sharply focused on the sources in Norfolk itself, including transcripts and calendars of the parish registers of Old Buckenham (1902) and Lammas (1905), deeds enrolled in the Norwich Court Rolls (1903; 1910: 1915); Norwich corporation material (1902 for Quatuor Coronati Lodge; 1908), depositions before the Mayor and aldermen (1905); the Norwich Rate Book of 1633–34 (1903); an Index to the Red Register of Lynn (1915) and a list of Norfolk plans (1923). *A handbook to the materials available to students of local history and genealogy, arranged in order of date* followed in 1924 and finally, after a long gap, an Index to Marriage Licences in the Consistory Court (1926).

He took a particularly active interest in the Norwich Library and Museum. Determined to make their holdings better known and more useful to scholars, he published in 1907–9 a series of finding aids to the topographical and antiquarian items, and later to the portraits in the library; a list of East Anglian antiquities; a list of biographical works of Norfolk men and women, held by the library and a catalogue of antiquities at the Castle Museum. He made sure that copies of his own works were freely available in the library and eventually catalogued those too (1916).

Endnotes

1   *RRS* (1897), p.16.
2   18 Nov. 1923: NRO, MS 4691/12. 'That the late Mr Phillimore, whose chief *raison d'être* was that of indexing, should have omitted to index each volume as it came out, is as inconceivable as it is unfair to his subscribers…', *Rye's Norfolk Handlists, Second Series*, I (1916).
3   E.g. his rough *index nominum* to Norfolk Feet of Fines in *NAM* II, pt. 1 (1880).
4   For example, to the names of the chief places in Norfolk not being towns or villages, in *NAM* II/I, p.305ff; to the names of the manors mentioned

in Blomefield's Norfolk in *NAM* II/I, pp.285ff. and 'Rough Indexes [sic] Nominum to the Feet of Fines for Norfolk in the reigns of, Hen. VIII, Edward VI and Mary' in *NAM* II/I, p.195ff.

5   NRO, MS 4691/7, 26 June 1882.

6   Combined with his Index to Norfolk Pedigrees.

7   *An index to Norfolk Pedigrees and continuation of Index to Norfolk Topography* (Norwich, Goose, 1896). W. B. Gerish of 15 Thornburn Sq., London SE, wrote on 16 May 1893: 'Are you aware that a large quantity of your valuable work the *Index to Norfolk Topography* is being used at a wayside shop in a small town in Hertfordshire to wrap up pennyworths of fish and fruit?… One would have thought the publishers would have pulped the remainder rather than dispose of it in this way.' When Gerish complained to the British Record Society (Index Library), he was merely sent in return quotes for supplying unbound copies: NRO, MS 4691/4. The following week the society admitted to Walter that they were indeed disposing of some stock, and offered him copies at a discount to give to Norwich booksellers, Ibid., 24 May 1893. A further supplement appeared in 1916 as one of Walter's Norfolk Handlists, covering work published in the thirty-five years since the first volume.

8   The preface is written from St Leonard's Priory which makes the 1899 date just possible, but the BL's copy (011903.i.10) is only date-stamped July 1900.

9   Presumably those to Norfolk topography and Norfolk pedigrees (1896).

10   An exception was his *Calendar of the Freemen of Norwich from 1307 to 1603, (Edward II to Elizabeth inclusive)* (London, 1888), but that was edited from material prepared by John L'Estrange.

6
WALTER RYE'S COLLECTIONS

With a notable book collector for a father, Walter grew up in a house full of books and prints. Sadly, any thought that he might one day inherit his father's collection was dashed when Edward sold most of it off at Hodgson's sale rooms in Chancery Lane in May 1873.[1] Long before that, however, Walter had started acquiring books and manuscripts of his own. We know, for example, that as early as 1863 he owned a manuscript life of the artist John Varley.[2] But by that time he was also becoming familiar with the working practices, as well as the writings, of the earlier Norfolk antiquaries discussed above, and the extent to which these depended on the acquisition and onward transmission of notes and documents. His frequent meetings in his teens and twenties with their modern counterparts confirmed just how much the métier of antiquary still depended on these tools of the trade. So as circumstances allowed he became a collector – of books, original documents and antiquarian material.

Acquisitions

He made many of his purchases on the open market, either by bidding in person at auction or by using agents, in particular Messrs Quaritch whose shop was only a short step away from his own office in Golden Square. Walter's father had been one of Bernard Quaritch's first ever customers, and Walter valued and continued the relationship. The Quaritch family became personal friends of the Ryes, close enough for Walter and Georgina to take 'Mrs and Miss' Quaritch to their country retreat at Selborne in the summer of 1897,[3] and for Walter to travel specially from Norwich to London in December 1899 to attend the funeral of Bernard Quaritch, his 'old friend... a most able man and most kind to me in the way of lending me books and giving me information'.[4]

Examples of his purchases are relatively easy to find, and he made no secret of them. The press reported his purchase of nearly 4,000 letters of the sixteenth and seventeenth centuries at the sale of the Gawdy manuscripts in 1882. He had hopes of publishing these 'in much the same way as Mr Gairdner did the Paston Letters...'[5] At the same sale he acquired papers of previous Norfolk antiquaries including Knyvet and Le Neve. He recorded that another manuscript, which he later published in *Three Norfolk Armouries* (1886) was 'bought by me at the sale of the late Mr D Gurney's books.'[6] At the Frere sale in February 1896 he bought, through Quaritch, further Le Neve and Norris papers, paying, he said, exactly twenty times the sum for which they had changed hands a century previously in 1780.[7] Through these and other purchases Walter assembled a significant collection of the notes of his great Norfolk antiquarian predecessors: Le Neve and Starling from the seventeenth century; Blomefield, Norris and others from the eighteenth; John L'Estrange and Robert John Harvey from his own day.

In addition to antiquaries' notes, his collection came to include original documents relating to Norfolk. In many cases these were items that had at some date been 'borrowed' (by others) and never returned, or had been dubiously purchased (again by others) from a public functionary or institution. Both were sadly common occurrences in his day. He was highly critical of parish clerks and other local officers who had allowed official records to slip out of their custody, and he bought up what he could, sometimes explicitly in order to see them returned to their rightful institutional owner or another appropriate public institution. But some choice items were retained at least temporarily for his own personal use.

Public-spirited purchases were redoubled after his retirement to Norwich. In October 1900 he bought some of the Rough Minutes of the Norfolk and Norwich Hospital 1777–8, which he restored to the hospital.[8] In the case of the Norwich Rate Book of 1633–1634, which antedated the Hearth Tax returns by several decades and was therefore a useful genealogical source, he bought it and transcribed, indexed and published it (1903)[9] before finally giving it to the Corporation of Norwich, whom he described as 'its real owners'. A fabric roll for the Norwich Guildhall for the years 1410–11 he transcribed and copied for his friend Dick Howlett before passing it back to the city.[10] In 1911 he bought at a London auction an address from the people of Norfolk to General Monck, which he gave to the Norwich Public Library;[11] later, at the suggestion of the city librarian, he edited and indexed it with Hamon le Strange. It had been lying, undated, among Townshend heirlooms sold at Sothebys,[12] and was catalogued only as 'apparently to Oliver Cromwell', but was found to be the original manuscript from which a later broadside of the same text with only minor variants was printed. He did not manage to acquire a companion address to Speaker Lenthall that was also in the Townshend sale.[13]

Antiquaries (Walter included) were notorious for 'borrowing' original materials in the course of their research.[14] Some they sat on for an unconscionable period, perhaps hoping some day to have the time to transcribe and edit them (or perhaps, if they were less scrupulous, hoping that in time the owner would forget what had happened to them!). Walter found such strays when sorting out the papers of several of his antiquarian friends after their deaths, and was meticulous in seeing them returned discreetly to their proper owners, even if he first had to buy them to prevent their dispersal in the sale room. In John L'Estrange's library after the latter's death he found and returned the King's Lynn Borough Accounts for 1606–7[15] and some manor court rolls of North Walsham and Thurgarton belonging to the Dean and Chapter of Norwich.[16] After the death of Augustus Jessopp, and with his library already advertised for sale, Walter bought and retrieved several items, some of which belonged to Lord Orford. He was careful to document these transactions, in order to prevent future researchers being confused over provenance. In the case of a deed that he bought and gave to the library at Carrow, for example, he made a 'memorandum to prevent any question arising hereafter as to how it got there'.[17]

By acquiring original documents with a specific view to handing them on, he was setting a new benchmark of probity for future antiquaries. When it came to books, if he ever supposed he might amass a permanent collection worthy of the finest in the county the thought was dispelled when he saw the library at Carrow Abbey in 1889: 'After I had been collecting for some years, in the vanity of my heart I thought that my own collection for the county was a fairly good one; but when I saw this library for the first time I was fairly ashamed of my own.'[18]

Walter himself was allowed to borrow manuscripts from individuals and institutions and even to exchange and copy antiquarian notes, and was generally conscientious in returning them to their rightful owners.[19] However, several records of an official or public nature for which he had not yet found a home at the time of his death are still to be found among the Rye manuscripts in the Norfolk Record Office.

Access to his collection

Throughout his life Walter saw his collection as a resource for others as well as for himself, and from the start he would make items available, by prior appointment and free of charge, to *bona fide* scholars.[20]

By the time his most regular sporting commitments were over, in the mid-1880s, he was generally willing to allow researchers to visit him at home on Saturday afternoons to consult his collection. We first get a real insight into this in 1889, when, while living in Putney, he privately printed a catalogue of his manuscripts in order to make them better known and thus to assist others in their research. Included among the original materials then listed were the original Act book of the Consistory Court of Norwich 1720–1729 written by Thomas Tanner STP: 'very closely written in the worst and most illegible hand I have ever tried to read'; documents relating to the Carpenters' Company of Norwich, sixteenth to eighteenth centuries; and the manor court rolls of Freethorpe.[21]

As Walter's reputation as the fount of all knowledge on Norfolk grew, so did his postbag of antiquarian queries. Incoming letters survive by the hundred if not the thousand among his papers, but of course generally without his replies. If he answered all as fully as we know he answered some, his correspondence alone must have taken up several hours of each day. His initial keenness to help anyone who was genuinely interested in history and antiquities got the better of him. He soon found that correspondents living at remote distances from his successive homes, including some from overseas, had quite unrealistic expectations as to the amount of research he would be prepared to undertake on their behalf, or of the hours at which they might descend upon him. So he set out in the catalogue his own restrictions on access:

Though I am very desirous that the MSS and Indexes described in the following pages should be accessible to all interested in the genealogy and antiquities of Norfolk, it is obviously out of my power to reply to enquiries relating to, or make extracts from them, for any but my personal friends; but they are open to anyone who wishes to use them, and who will give me notice of his intention to call at Putney, any Saturday from 3pm to 9pm.

As the time I can give visitors is necessarily short, anyone wanting to make a long or comprehensive search must kindly do so *through some record agent known to me,* with whom I can arrange as to hours of attendance. (The costs are impossible to predict but a regular search will probably cost a guinea.) I do not and cannot undertake the searches myself. I greatly regret that I cannot promise to make gratuitous searches for unknown correspondents, though on receipt of a stamped envelope I will answer any specific reasonable enquiry.[22]

He might have been writing the rules of one of today's busy public reading rooms!

Those who did consult the collection and/or employ record agents to do so were invariably grateful. Here is one of them:

Pray allow me to say that every person interested in Norfolk history owes you a deep debt of gratitude. I have often been very kindly assisted by you. I hope you will be spared many years to continue your good work. Many years ago you allowed me, when you lived at Putney, to copy part of the will of William Curteys of Necton from a book you had... I copied it easily. I remember you moistened the dryness of my labours by giving me a glass of excellent sherry. Miss Constance Rye finished the copying.[23]

No comprehensive update to the 1889 catalogue seems to have been published after Walter moved on from Putney to Hampstead and then to Norwich. Perhaps he thought better of advertising his wares too widely. Instead, he now tended to publicise new acquisitions in such journals as the *East Anglian*, explaining how he had acquired them and sometimes including extracts or transcripts.[24] Those in the know continued to be allowed access to his successive homes, although we catch only rare glimpses of those who turned up, like the Revd W. P. Holmes of Leicester who came to see the Norris MSS in 1903,[25] and a Mr Tomes and his daughter who came in 1916 to photograph the Martin MSS for his history of Mannington.

Walter allowed – even encouraged – material in his collection to be transcribed for publication by a third party.[26] Exceptionally, he would even lend a manuscript to a trusted individual, as when he let William Hudson borrow L'Estrange's MS transcript of the Norwich Freemen's roll, in 1898.[27]

Enquiries sent to him both at home and at the office in Golden Square extended far beyond the scope of his own collection into history and antiquities more generally. Even so he was usually quite ready to answer. But there was one class of 'researcher' who might well be sent away with a flea in his ear. That was anyone whom he suspected of preparing a pedigree on the flimsiest of evidence. We see this in November 1895 when he retained the carbon copy of a letter he wrote from Golden Square in answer to an enquiry from a Mr Culleton concerning the Kett family pedigree:

> Sir,… In reply to yours of yesterday, I do not feel called upon to help you in any way. Your agency has done so much mischief by disseminating false arms that you must excuse my saying that you are looked upon as a perfect nuisance by every real student of genealogy and heraldry. My Collections have always been at the service of any one desirous of consulting them for his own use, without fee or reward, but it strikes me as the height of impudence on your part to ask me to undertake a laborious search for which you will be paid. I have always made a point of never taking fees for the use of my collection, and your suggestion that I should practically act as your sub-agent is a most offensive one. Your obedient servant.[28]

I have not found Culleton's (no doubt incandescent) reply among Walter's papers, but it provoked a further letter from Walter two days later:

> Sir, In reply to your letter I can only say that your advertisement issued for so many years offering to supply 'your arms and motto' for so many shillings is in my opinion, and in that of every-one who

has ever spoken to me about it, one of the most mischievous and improper advertisements ever issued. You tell ignorant people that you will supply them with *their* arms and motto for a very small fee, which implies that every person in England has a coat of arms and that you can supply each person with his. You must know that this is not the fact, but whether the person who sends you the stamps or Post Office Order has arms or not, you send him something which purports to be 'his' arms. As a Solicitor of some experience I can assure you that if, by doing so, you are not liable to be prosecuted for obtaining money by false pretences, you are sailing very near the wind indeed. No doubt plain speaking is always offensive to the recipient – Nothing can be more offensive than the terms in which the Judge usually sentences criminals, but, as a rule, nothing more deserved. Your offering me payment to help you compile a Pedigree is, considering the sort of reputation you bear in the genealogical world and that I have worked all my life at genealogy without fee or reward, (is) far more offensive to me than anything I have said of you. Your obedient servant, Walter Rye.[29]

A file of unsorted 'antiquarian letters 1922–23'[30] reveals how vast Walter's regular correspondence was even into his ninth decade, and how grateful his correspondents were for the extremely detailed answers he still gave them, the copies of pamphlets he sent, or just the references to other publications where an answer might be found to their query. He left very many satisfied customers, and the range of topics covered is formidable: family history and genealogy; references to documents he has mentioned in print; musical obits and inscriptions; Quo Warranto Rolls at the PRO; the history of individual buildings in Norwich and elsewhere, including the old brewery in King Street; sixteenth-century probate inventories; fossils found in a block of stone; the rights of the public on Martham Broad; the position of ringing chambers in Norfolk churches; Norfolk place names; the history of the swan in England; the legal entitlements of a Lord of the Manor to the foreshore... To these were added general questions worthy of *Brain of Britain*: who was Sir John de Bolewyk? Where was Tierceville? Where might the chantry of Sir Thomas Erpingham be found? And esoteric questions on Sir Thomas Browne's skull or on St

George (in connection with the Honourable Artillery Company and the Royal Toxophilite Society).

*

Sadly, Walter's collection of antiquarian books, which he left to Norwich City Library, was destroyed in the disastrous fire of 1994. By great good fortune, however, his manuscript collection and his own antiquarian notes survived the fire and are now in the Norfolk Record Office.[31]

Objects and antiquities

'Archaeology', in the sense prevailing in the second half of the nineteenth century, embraced the understanding of the past through all tangible remains including sites, objects, artefacts, and even archives. Although Walter's primary interest was in archives, books and manuscripts, his many tours of Norfolk and links with local and national antiquaries led him to develop more rounded antiquarian and archaeological interests. He did not pretend to be a specialist in areas such as philology or toponymy, agriculture or natural history, but saw that a general knowledge of these and similar topics gave crucial underpinning to his wider work.

Whilst he was certainly interested in, and visited, other people's antiquarian collections, unlike many contemporary antiquaries he was not a serious collector of antiquarian objects on his own behalf, although he was not one to miss a bargain and did acquire several objects and artefacts in order to give them to others, especially to the museums in Norwich and Thetford.[32]

Nor was he, in general, active as an excavator of ancient sites and buildings other than his own houses, especially St Leonard's Priory, Norwich; but in his travels around the county he would often make detours to see historic sites for himself or to persuade his travelling companions of their importance, even at risk of life or limb. Dick Howlett recalled that:

> … I think it was in 1868 when boating among the Broads with Rye that I climbed into the bell chamber of Thurne church up a ladder which owned one whole and one broken side and all of whose rungs were loose, and I well remember being rewarded with the sight of a

very ancient bell and with the mystic inscription you have inserted in your book.[33]

As we saw in Track 1, Walter lived in a succession of historically important houses. He would also become famous in Norwich for his passionate interest in saving historic buildings from destruction (see Track 6). He happily engaged in the discussion of antiquities at the Norfolk and Norwich Archaeological Society, and at many a dinner table. And he contributed, and encouraged others to contribute, articles to journals such as his own *Norfolk Antiquarian Miscellany* and the *East Anglian* concerning historic sites and objects, especially if there were any controversy connected with them that he himself could enter into, or preferably demonstrate to be nonsense. He wrote at some length to the *Pall Mall Gazette* on 29 January 1884 concerning a previous contribution on the supposed immuring of nuns, on which he casts doubt.[34] In archaeology, just as in sport and genealogy, he was vigilant against all manner of spurious claims. Romantic notions of secret tunnels set him bristling.

Endnotes

1   The residue was sold at Sotheby's on 10 August 1882, when Walter acquired only a few prints. For 1873 see 36 p.12. The sale catalogue is available at the British Library under the reference [SC] Hodgson 5–9 May 1873. For 1882 see SC nos. 503, 509–10, 522.
2   *Notes and Queries* [154].
3   A return invitation to dinner the following year did not go down so well: 'in the evening to Quaritch's where garlic and herrings did not appeal to me'. *Autobiog.*, 6 Mar. 1898.
4   Quaritch's Commission Books, retained by the firm, begin only in 1884, but thereafter there is passing reference to Walter, e.g. 1890–1995, pp.294, 414; 1895–99 p.117 (Frere sale), 225; 1899–1903 p.388.
5   *Leeds Mercury*, 27 March 1882 quoting the *Athenaeum*.
6   It bears a note on its title 'Copied in Jany 1753 by James Sandcroft'.
7   *York Herald*, 27 Feb. 1896; *Autobiog.*, 17 Feb; *EA*, II, p.343.
8   NRO: NNH 1/43.
9   WR, *The Norwich Rate Book from Easter 1633 to Easter 1634* (1903).
10 *NA* XV, p.164.
11 *Autobiog.*, WR: *An address from the gentry of Norfolk and Norwich to General Monck in 1660*, (1913).
12 19 Dec. 1911 (lot 248).
13 p.28; 'The great labour of transcribing these hundreds of signatures, many of them excessively difficult to read, of arranging them in alphabetical order,

of supplying biographical notices and thereby identifying a large proportion of the individuals, has been undertaken and carried out by Mr Walter Rye. Without his industry and acumen this introduction could not have been written.'

14 Jessopp's perhaps more casual approach to this whole business may be seen from a letter he wrote to Walter in 1885: 'I am sending you some Court Rolls of Manor of Shipden [Cromer] which I think will interest you and which I therefore begged loan of the other day. Watch over them as precious and send them back as soon as may be to encourage the owner to let me have more... I have been ransacking Lord Kimberley's archives. Not very much there and who would have thought of it?' 21 Aug. 1885. NRO, MS 4691/23.

15 Now NRO: KL/C43/5.

16 WR: *A Catalogue of Fifty of the Norfolk Manuscripts in the Library of Mr Walter Rye at Winchester House, Putney, 1889,* no. 41.

17 *EA,* V (1893–4) p.314. He gave some drawings to Thetford Museum, NRO, MS 4691/12 24, May 1922.

18 WR, 'The unpublished material for a history of the County of Norfolk', reprinted from *Arch. J* XLVII, p.1 (1889).

19 Walter borrowed Burnham court rolls from the Walpoles to index, kept his notes on them and returned the originals. In 1914 the vicar of Tunstead called with his wife and left the manor court rolls for WR to go through, with a view to finding a buyer towards the church restoration. WR failed and restored them to the vicar's successor on 2 Feb. 1916. He persuaded several owners to lend him documents for transcription and abstraction, and made copious notes to serve for his future publications. His scrappy notes from the manorial records of Burnham in *NAM* I derived from a time when he had the manorial records on loan. His article in *NA* XV p.1 refers to a MS that J. H. Gurney of Keswick has allowed him to translate.

20 He felt that others should be as open. 'Nearly all these had for generations been selfishly sealed up by the then owners but as they will now be freely open to anyone who may wish to inspect them, and who will write me for an appointment to do so, I have indexed them...' WR, *Norfolk Pedigrees* (1896).

21 WR, *A Catalogue of Fifty...* as above.

22 WR, *Index rerum,* p.101n. 'As an example of *un*reasonable queries I may say that one American sent me 5s in stamps and said he wanted all the Norwich churches searched for about 20 years for a baptism, a commission I declined with thanks.'

23 Lt Col H. Curteis, 27 Sept. 1922: NRO, MS 4691/10. The letter was occasioned by the Colonel's having mislaid Constance's transcript.

24 E.g. *EA,* II, pp.343, 389–92.

25 *Autobiog.,* p.130.

26 E.g. *NA* XV p.94, a copy by L'Estrange of an Elizabethan inventory; same issue p.51 Howlett transcribed household accounts of Kenninghall Palace 1525 from the Thomas Martin collection which WR had at St Leonard's Priory.

27 CA returning the Foulsham Court Rolls which WR has loaned him: will be

nervous till he hears they are safely back, 29 Mar. 1895. NRO, MS 4691/17.

28 7 Nov. 1895: NRO, MS 4691/2.

29 9 Nov. 1895: NRO, MS 4691/2.

30 NRO, MS 4691/10.

31 At one time he considered making the PRO the residuary legatee for his books, see corresp. of 27 May 1915 with Alfred E. Stamp, NRO, MS 4691/2. For his manuscripts see NRO online catalogue under Rye, esp. nos. 1–69.

32 He records, for example, driving to N. Walsham with his son FGR in 1904 to see a carved beam (*NA* XVI, p.76) 'but both being temporarily insane did not buy it for the £5 he asked'. *Autobiog.*

33 12 Sep. 1874: NRO, MS 4691/22.

34 See also *London Daily News,* 10 Mar. 1894.

TRACK 4: THE GENEALOGIST

1
WRITINGS AS A GENEALOGIST

'It is more honourable by far to trace your descent sturdily and clearly to some mediaeval yeoman or tradesman, than by straining coincidences, presuming identities and fudging judiciously, to attempt to hook on to some noble or well-descended family of the same name as yours.'

Walter Rye[1]

Walter's interest in genealogy, and his in-depth knowledge of the sources, began with his natural curiosity about his own roots, and was amplified as he developed a wider interest in the history of Norfolk and its principal families.

In his writings, as in his practice, he insisted that genealogical research must be soundly based on written evidence, whether directly from archives (such as wills or registers of baptism, marriage and death) or family Bibles, or from other tangible sources such as memorial inscriptions. Oral tradition, family legend, and secondary sources such as heraldic visitations (especially those of the Elizabethan period which were to Walter highly suspect) might be taken into consideration but were not trustworthy on their own account and would always be trumped if trusted archival evidence plainly contradicted them. He seems to have conceded that a degree of speculation to fill gaps was inevitable, but only permissible if the results were clearly presented as surmise and not as fact. That, at least, was the theory.

The Rye family

Try as he might, Walter could not trace his own Norfolk pedigree back beyond the late seventeenth century because of the loss of the relevant parish registers for Cromer. He could easily prove that people named Rye were active in the county even before the Norman Conquest, but could not demonstrate any link between them and his own family. He first published his findings, in a series of articles between 1871 and 1874 in *The Herald and Genealogist* and its successor *The Genealogist*,[2] in which incidentally he bemoaned the fact that the town of Rye in Sussex had seriously impeded his progress. It was:

> ... genealogically speaking, the curse of my life, for it gives name to whole broods of Ryes in no way related to the stock whose history I am now relating, who by their numbers render a name, which would otherwise be very uncommon, and easily traced, a comparatively common one in the southern counties.[3]

He later expanded these articles into his privately printed *An Account of the Family of Rye* (1876), which he sent to everyone with the surname Rye whom he knew or suspected to be related, in the hope that they would correct any errors; and he presented copies to strategic libraries including the Society of Antiquaries of London. An anonymous reviewer commended it as a model of good practice, saying that the information:

> ... is recorded with an amount of straightforward simplicity and truthfulness, which we regret to say are rarely (though they always ought to be) the distinguishing characteristics of a genealogist's labours. Mr Rye says in his preface, 'in no case have I assumed any relationships or connections for which I have not actual evidence, preferring to leave an admitted gap of a generation or two, here and there, to confusing and misleading others by assumptions which might, or might not, be correct.' We heartily recommend this account of the Ryes to the attention of all our readers, and especially to those who contemplate publishing their researches relative to any particular family.[4]

Attacks on spurious pedigrees

It was not long before his research began to raise in Walter's mind questions about the authenticity of the supposed pedigrees of many long-established Norfolk families, and it became his mission to expose those in just the same way as he publicly exposed false claims to performance records by athletes.[5]

When he smelt a rat he would set down his findings in print, in genealogical and other magazines, usually without prior consultation with the family concerned, thus in effect throwing down a challenge to them to prove him wrong if they could. Such was his aversion to fraudulent claims to blood, honour, title or possessions, and such his addiction to the sport of deflating them, that he would make remarks and cast aspersions that caused offence by coming close to ridicule or even libel. In later life he would proudly claim that he had spent half a century exposing fraudulent pedigrees.[6] His brashness was not to everyone's taste, and one reviewer prophesied that one day he would be hoist with his own petard.[7] Something else that was not to everyone's taste, especially in Walter's later years, was the nit-picking and tedious detail into which he went to prove his points.[8]

Apart from his own privately-sponsored publications, he continued to write in *The Herald and Genealogist* (edited by J. G. Nichols) and *The Genealogist* (at first edited by George W. Marshall). Selby of the Public Record Office began a new series of *The Genealogist* when he became its editor in 1884. Understandably, he made a point of refocusing the magazine to include more material grounded in the Public Records, and this opened a new door for contributions by Walter, who gained especially honourable mention, first from the editor for always signing his contributions in a field where much similar work was still published under the cloak of anonymity,[9] and then in particular from a younger reader at the PRO, J. H. Round, a gentleman historian whose star was in the ascendant, and of whom we shall hear a lot more shortly.[10]

In a series of articles on 'Doubtful Norfolk Pedigrees' Walter questioned the accepted descents of the families of Howard, Townsend, Walpole, Wodehouse, and Clere of Ormesby.[11] He found the Wodehouse pedigree, for example, 'one of the worst specimens of concoction by Elizabethan heralds that can be imagined'.[12] At various times he castigated Blomefield for swallowing wholesale what the early heralds had said.[13] But at heart he wanted to exonerate Blomefield, who according to Walter had been misled (for example over the Howard pedigree) by 'some courteous herald, duly mindful of the favours of the then great houses'.[14] The Clere of Ormesby pedigree, as set out in Blomefield and elsewhere, was, he said: '... so excellent an example of Elizabethan forgery that it well deserves a place in this series... [*He went on to refer to*] the first ten generations, nine of which there is every reason to believe are the fruits of the imagination of some courtly herald...'[15]

Usually Walter knew he was on sure ground, but occasionally he made silly mistakes himself and had to eat humble pie. For example, he alleged, in effect, that one of the Isham family of Lamport Hall, Northants (which had repeatedly given him hospitality while he studied their archives) 'made a premature appearance' – i.e. was illegitimate. But he was later corrected by a commentator who found that in querying this man's date of birth Walter had forgotten to allow for the year beginning, by the old calendar, on Lady Day.[16]

The reviewer of Walter's *Songs, Stories and Sayings* in *The Genealogist*, who enjoyed the book as a whole, was not convinced by all of Walter's genealogical put-downs:

[He does not] scruple to acknowledge his own mistakes, as in the chapter 'Smiles on their claims of long descent', where he tells us that he formerly wrote that there was plenty of evidence that Sir John Wodehouse was at Agincourt and adds, 'but then I accepted bold statements for evidence more readily than I do now.' After such an admission we cannot avoid the suspicion that some of his criticism may likewise be liable to subsequent correction, and shall not be surprised if he is asked for further proof of his statement that the claim of the Prestons of Beeston, Baronets, to descend from an ardent cavalier is a 'ridiculous fabrication', for we can hardly accept as sufficient the mere fact that Jacob Preston, born 1613, married the daughter of a well-known 'Parliament man' as precluding him from having been, as his descendants allege, present on the scaffold with Charles I.[17]

The Walpole dispute

One further case might serve as a cautionary tale to those interested in Walter Rye's work today.

He began to air suspicions on the Walpole family pedigree in an article in his *Norfolk Antiquarian Miscellany* in 1873.[18] Very quickly he had an irritated reply from the Hon. F. Walpole, complaining that Walter's article was flippant and sneering, and pointing out a fundamental error, namely the unsafe assumption that because a certain Reginald de Walpole of Walpole was mentioned in two undated deeds, the fact of their being undated must place them before the reign of Henry II.[19] Walpole may well have become incandescent when he read Walter's reply:

Sir

I do not know what you mean by calling my paper a 'very flippant publication' or by saying that 'it seems written grudgingly…' I cannot find, after a most careful search, a flippant word, nor a sneer, nor a grudging admission in it and I shall take the opinion of men whose reputation in the antiquarian world cannot be denied whether you are justified in writing to me in the way you have done. Your pedigree has cost me much time and trouble and some little money to work up and I have done my best to elucidate and illustrate it, and the account I have written is an honest and ungarbled one. If you want fiction instead of fact you had better go to some cheap heraldic office where you can no doubt have an illustrious ancestry manufactured for you – and the fact that the early Walpoles were really only very small squireens cleverly burked.[20] I will as requested remove your name from the article and will personally relieve you from your promise to pay for its printing. I send herewith all your books and mss as per list on the other side. My own Robsart collections I shall retain for my own use and they shall certainly never be at the disposal of anyone who can write so ungrateful and uncivil a letter as that which I have received from you. Your obedient servant, Walter Rye.[21]

Walter went on to include the family in his series on 'Doubtful Norfolk Pedigrees' already mentioned. There was no public reaction from the family. But then, in his *History of Norfolk* a decade later, which achieved a much wider readership, he made some careless remarks in passing about Sir Robert Walpole and expressed opinions about his being involved in peculation. In the pages of *Notes and Queries*[22] Henry Spencer Walpole, writing from

Stagbury, Surrey, pointed out simple errors of fact and challenged Walter's opinions, implying that if this one family could be 'singled out for every sort of misrepresentation' in an account in which 'almost every historical fact is incorrectly stated', this did not bode well for the credibility of the *History* as a whole.

Walter should certainly have been more punctilious, and Mr Walpole was quite justified in commenting that there was 'not a shadow of excuse for the random and untrue assertions miscalled facts'. Walter admitted errors,[23] but in his riposte[24] brushed them off as no more than trivial slips for which he had some sort of excuse: 'I may, in justice to myself, say... that I was in bed, recovering from rheumatic fever when I dictated the book, and had not the opportunity of turning up authorities as I should otherwise have done.'

True though this almost certainly was, it does raise fundamental questions over what else might be incorrectly stated in the *History*! He stood by his views on Sir Robert Walpole's ill-gotten gains. He had, he said, privately challenged Mr Walpole to fight that out with him in the pages of the *English Historical Review*. Instead Walpole preferred to embark on a 'microscopic examination of my little book'. The *coup de grâce*, in Walter's estimation, was that no peripheral errors in the *History* in any way undermined the fact that he had 'demolished the apocryphal nonsense... which appears in the peerages'. He suggested that Walpole's (tardy) irritation over that was what really lay behind his challenge. Mr Walpole prudently chose not to reply further, except to impart as if in passing his own scoring punch that before this controversy he had never heard of Walter's *Norfolk Antiquarian Miscellany*.

This case demonstrates very well the need for caution when evaluating Walter Rye's writings today. He seems to have taken the view that publication of his articles and comments, even if that occurred only in a subscription journal with a small regular readership, sufficiently set out his stall to the world, and that it was up to anyone who disagreed with him to be just as *au fait* as he was with such channels of publication, and to respond forthwith in the same or another public arena with observations or counter-arguments. This was, to say the least, disingenuous, for when it suited him to do so Walter publicly admitted that the guaranteed readership for much of his output was minute. We shall see in some of the other controversies he entered into that he repeatedly fooled himself into believing that the lack of a published challenge to his views was a clear demonstration of their wide acceptance. The Walpole case also shows some of the suite of responses Walter used to protect his reputation: admit some errors, claim that they in no way undermine the thrust of the argument, find a plausible excuse for them, and if possible pour scorn and innuendo on the challenger. These and similar tactics he used repeatedly, down to his dying days.

The College of Arms

Walter was a regular correspondent of the College of Arms, exchanging notes, publications and even some original documentary records with successive heralds including Stephen Tucker (Somerset) and Charles Athill (Bluemantle, later Richmond). For much of the time the relationship was entirely amicable. Walter occasionally put them in touch with suitable record agents to work in the PRO, and on at least one occasion was himself asked to undertake while in Norfolk some confidential research for the college on a pedigree.[25] The heralds were full of enthusiasm for his genealogical and topographical output, which of course was of immediate assistance in their own work. In 1882, for example, Athill thanked Walter for his *Index to Norfolk Topography*: 'Of the value of such a work to the Antiquary and Genealogist there can be no doubt. I consider it a matter for regret that the public interest in such a compilation should have been so small as to necessitate publication thro' a Society.'[26]

In 1884 Athill congratulated Walter on the appearance of the latest part of his *Norfolk Antiquarian Miscellany* and added that Garter King of Arms, Sir Albert Woods, wanted to become a subscriber to that series and also to Walter's publications on monumental inscriptions.[27]

From time to time, especially when Walter was having one of his recurring tantrums over the enormities of Elizabethan heralds, relations with the college became frosty. The college was naturally sensitive to any suggestion that its own current work might in any way be tainted by aspersions against its Tudor predecessors, and it would not engage publicly in print with Walter lest that in any way undermine the college's reputation and indeed the heralds' livelihood. Relations reached a low point for a while after Walter had retired to Norwich. After one broadside from Walter, Athill wrote on 3 March 1903:

It would be a little difficult for me to correct your paper because we evidently view the matter from entirely different standpoints… It does seem to me a little unfair and a little un-English, to be continually 'going for' an institution which never 'goes for' anyone… and is honestly striving to do its best.

But the rumpus seems to have blown over, and amicable relations were restored when Walter privately made it clear that his criticism did not extend to the present day College of Arms or it heralds.

In 1891 he edited for the Harleian Society (vol. XXXII) the heraldic visitations of Norfolk for 1563 and 1613. Although the notes and transcripts on which this was based were prepared by others, it still required major editorial effort on his part. It ran to 375 pages, with 44 pages of index. But Walter saw it only as a temporary work of reference for scholars:

… pending the issue of a future volume or volumes[28] in which I hope to reprint the whole in a narrative form, with large additions from the Collections of Le Neve, Martin, Norris and L'Estrange which are now in my library, and which are in the process of being carefully indexed.

He also observed that:

… an elaborate edition of the Visitation of 1563 has been in the Press for the Norfolk and Norwich Archaeological Society for nearly thirty years, but as it has been issued at the average rate of thirty-one pages per year only, it is clear that no one now living will live to see its completion, so the present Volume will serve as a temporary stop-gap for a good many years.[29]

Walter's own grant of arms [See plate V]

In 1898, as he was approaching retirement, Walter applied to the College of Arms for a coat of arms for himself.[30] He stated openly that he could only give properly documented ancestry back to Edward Rye of Cromer in 1698, but added that he had good reason to believe he was descended from the medieval Ryes of Hingham, Norfolk, and wondered if some allusion to that could be entered in his grant of arms. However, desiring to go down in history primarily as an athlete, he proposed as his own arms:[31] ARMS: '*Gu* on a *bend arg* between *2 ryestalks or 3 fylfots.*' CREST: 'A dexter arm habited *gu* holding in its hand a standing cup *or*'. MOTTO: '*Sui victoria indicat regam*', which he explained as follows:

> The fylfots I used to wear on my jersey when I was walking champion a generation ago, and the standing cup is meant to represent the championship cup I once held. The motto is that which my cousins the Suffolk Ryes (of Halesworth) used in their bookplates about 100 years ago, and is meant to refer to the remark Eudo de Rye, 'dapifer', is supposed to have made to the Conqueror when he warded off the blow aimed at his predecessor and reproved the king for his temper. I don't think any of the above infringes the existing coat or motto of anyone.

He need not have worried unduly about his incomplete pedigree, for it was a problem shared by many applicants, and was covered by the common formula applied by Athill as Walter's agent for the grant,[32] expressed thus: '... being uncertain of Armorial bearings pertaining to his family and unwilling to use any without lawful authority [he asks for] such arms and crest as may be proper to be borne by him and his descendants.'

The coat of arms finally registered, apart from being set down (again, no doubt, by Athill) in more precise heraldic language, was exactly as specified by Walter: 'Gules on a bend argent between two ears of rye stalked leaved and slipped or, three crosses cramponne sable'. In working up the final design and content for the crest and motto, however, Athill (or possibly Woods as Garter) down-played Walter's sporting theme and gave priority instead to his work as an antiquary, so that the crest displayed not a sporting cup but an hour glass... 'on a wreath of the colours a cubit arm erect holding an hour glass in bend sinister all proper', with the motto *Tempora mutantur*. As even Walter must surely have admitted this was far less open to challenge than any allusion to an unproven ancestor.

Norfolk Families (1911–13)

Altogether Walter spent half a century researching the history of Norfolk families, and encouraging others to do so, especially the many clergy he met who had an interest in genealogy or who could be persuaded to copy out monumental inscriptions to preserve them for posterity.[33]

He brought together most of his findings in *Norfolk Families*, a work of some 1,100 pages, published in 1911–13, which he admitted had caused him 'great trouble', and significant financial loss as he sold it to his subscribers at the price agreed when he had originally planned it as a work of 720 pages. Dedicated to his friend and fellow antiquary:

> ... His Highness Prince Frederick V Duleep Singh as a slight acknowledgment of the great help he has given me in this work, and especially for having revised my proof sheets, I dedicate it in the hope it may be of some service to him and to all others who like himself take an intelligent and critical interest in Norfolk pedigrees.

This work, however, like much of Walter's output, must today be used with caution, as even he conceded that it was riddled with errors, some due to the printer's not being able to read his 'very illegible handwriting', some to his own carelessness in checking the proofs, and some to the inaccuracy of the information supplied to him by the families contacted.[34]

Tom Copeman, writing in the *Eastern Daily Press* on 23 July 1973, said: 'Who but Rye could have brought out such a monumental work as *Norfolk Families* and separated the sheep from the goats by using heavier type for those whose pedigrees he considered genuine? What a howl went up from those he described as "pompous members of insignificant families".[35]

Whatever errors Walter may have perpetrated in his genealogical research, it is clear that it was in general an honest effort based on an unmatched knowledge of both primary archival and secondary printed sources. To give some idea of his range, in the course of his published genealogical work he cited archival sources from the PRO such as the Norfolk Feet of Fines, the Inquisitions Post Mortem and the Subsidy Rolls and Pipe Rolls; local records such as the Tallage Rolls of Lynn; manuscripts in the British Museum and the Bodleian Library; and visitation records at the College of Arms. Among printed sources cited were Blomefield, Collins Peerage (which he regarded with suspicion), the *Abbrevatio Placitorum*, the *Dignity of a Peer*, and Dashwood's *Ancient Seals at Stow Bardolph*. So this is no lightweight skirmishing into unfamiliar territory. Few families that were the target of his barbs had the skill or knowledge necessary to challenge him, but the sparsity of criticism alone is not a safe indicator as to the reliability of the work.

*

The main genealogical controversies into which Walter entered, concerning the descents of Chaucer and Becket from Norfolk families, and the ancestry of the Styward family and of Oliver Cromwell, are discussed in the next chapter.

Endnotes

1   *RRS* (2nd edn, 1897), p.11.
2   *The Herald and Genealogist,* VI (1871) p.33; VII (1873) p.249; and VIII (1874) p.401; and *The Genealogist,* I, pp.67, 122.
3   *The Herald and Genealogist* VI, p.39.
4   *The Genealogist,* II, p.32.
5   But he was prepared to defend any claims he thought genuine, e.g. WR, *Tourists' Guide* under Merton, p.115: 'Lord Walsingham is, I think, the only Norfolk landowner who holds by descent land granted to an ancestor by William I.'
6   WR, *Two Cromwellian Myths* (1925), p.3.
7   *The Genealogist* reviewing his *Songs, Stories* etc., of which chapter 8 was entitled, 'Smiles on their claims of long descent'.
8   Copious genealogical notes survive in his archive at Norfolk Record Office, with a few strays elsewhere such as notes on Bacon of Baconsthorpe (in WR's own hand) and Vaughan of Leominster at the British Library.
9   *The Genealogist,* III (1879).
10   Was it just an oversight that when Selby wrote his last contribution as editor in 1889 Round, but not Rye, was among those whom he thanked by name? *The Genealogist,* ns, V, intro. Under Selby's successor, Keith W. Murray, Walter very rarely contributed to the magazine, which however did contain regular reviews of his works, but this may simply have been because by then he had a better outlet for his findings in his own publications.
11   *The Genealogist,* II, p.337; III, pp.78–9, 129; IV, p.99.
12   *The Genealogist* III, p.129.
13   E.g. *NAM* III (1887), p.181.
14   *The Genealogist,* II, p.338.
15   *The Genealogist,* IV, p.99; this critique was also to find a place in his *Tourists' Guide,* 1885 edn., p.85–6.
16   *The Genealogist* III, p.250n. and riposte p.300. For a fuller picture of his dealings with the Isham family see Sir Thomas Isham, Walter Rye and Robert Isham (eds.), *The Journal of Thomas Isham, of Lamport... from 1st Nov. 1671 to*

30th Sept. 1673 (Norwich, Miller and Leavins). 'Isham family memoranda', in *The Genealogist,* II (1878), p.241. and III, pp.241–250.

17 Ns, XIV (c.1898), p.139.
18 'Evidence of the early pedigree of the family of Walpole'. *NAM* I, pp.267–284.
19 *The Genealogist,* III, p.79.
20 Presumably, socially elevated, as in Burke's Peerage etc.
21 WR to Hon. F. Walpole, 25 Apr. 1873: NRO, MS 4691/82.
22 *N&Q* 1887 (series 7, IV), pp.221–2.
23 Walpole did not marry the daughter of a Lord Mayor. He was not 'Prime Minister' in 1708. Wolterton was built by Lord Walpole. The 'grey lady' was Dorothy, Lady Townshend not 'Townsend' and not Lady Walpole… and so on.
24 *N&Q* 1887 (series 7, IV) pp.289–290.
25 Tucker to WR 18 Apr.1884: NRO, MS 4691/17.
26 Athill to WR, 14 June 1882, NRO, MS 4691/17.
27 Ibid., 24 Jan. 1884.
28 It never materialised, perhaps for want of subscribers.
29 When the Harleian Society came to publish the Visitation of 1664 (vols. 85–86, 1933–34, ed. A. W. Hughes Clarke and A. Campling) some sixteen genealogies prepared by Walter were included. Before his death he had also allowed the society to make photographic plates of drawings for coats of arms at this visitation from a book then in his possession, made for Le Neve. By the date of publication this had been gifted by Walter to the Norwich Public Library (see editorial note to vol. 86).
30 This section is based on Athill Papers at the College of Arms and the College of Arms Register of Grants of Arms, vol. LXX (1897–1899).
31 College of Arms, Athill papers, XIX, p.402.
32 I am most grateful to Thomas Woodcock, Garter King of Arms, for help with this section, especially in explaining the agent's role.
33 See for example copies of letters to Revd M. C. H. Bird about Cubitt genealogy, 29 Jan. and 4 Feb. 1889: Norwich Library, C. Rye OS.
34 WR, *Norfolk Families* (1913), pp.iii–iv.
35 EDP archives, Norwich, Rye file.

Walter Rye in his robes as Mayor of Norwich, 1908-1909. *Peter Rye.*

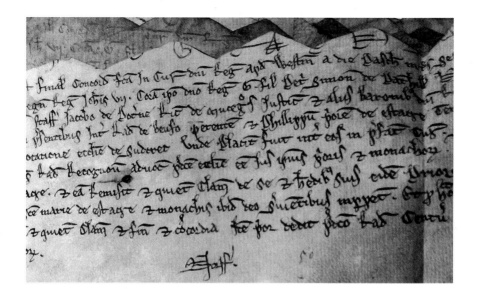

Examples of documents explored by Walter Rye at the Public Record
Office. (a) Feet of Fines (TNA, CP 25/2/1/154/25); (b) Inventories of
Church Goods, (TNA, E117/6/17). *Crown copyright.*
The National Archives.

Frognal House, later famous as the wartime HQ of General de Gaulle:
(a) Exterior today. *London Remembers: www.londonremembers.com*; (b)
Walter Rye's 40ft-high wall. *Author, with thanks to St Dorothy's Convent.*

Thames Hare and Hounds in action, 1869. *Illustrated London News, from an original page in the author's possession.*

Walter Rye's arms: (a) Grant of Arms. *College of Arms, MS Grants, LXX, p.318. Reproduced by permission of the Kings, Heralds and Pursuivants of Arms*; (b) Adapted for use in his memorial window, Lammas church. *Author.*

Norwich buildings bought by Walter Rye: (a) The Maid's Head Hotel. Watercolour by Walter Hayward Young, 1908. *The Maid's Head Hotel;* (b) Bacon's House, Colegate Street. *Keith Edkins.*

Woodpeckers Art Club entertainment programme, Strangers' Hall,
Norwich, 6 Feb. 1902. NRO, MS 4691/84/2. *Author's photograph from an
anonymous original in the Rye Papers,
by kind permission of Norfolk Record Office.*

W Holman Hunt, 'May Morning on Magdalen Tower'. *Photo ©Birmingham Museums.* Walter Rye's first son, James Bacon Rye, modelled as the 'chorister' depicted on the extreme left.

2
THREE GENEALOGICAL CONTROVERSIES

At various times in the course of his genealogical research Walter attempted to claim Norfolk roots for a number of historical celebrities. They included amongst others Thomas Becket[1] and Geoffrey Chaucer. In both cases his findings have been discredited or overlooked, and are not cited today. As his research methods and their limitations were essentially similar in each case, a brief study of the Chaucer case must suffice here.

Was Chaucer a Norfolk man?

Some uncertainty remains even now around Geoffrey Chaucer's birth. For well over forty years (from 1881 to his death), Walter suspected, and sought to prove beyond any doubt, that Chaucer was a Norfolk man. This, to his own satisfaction at any rate, he did. Friends and acquaintances, though apparently few others, tended to be persuaded by his arguments, but he recorded with gratitude that even some of his weightier opponents gave him every encouragement to proceed. Whether he was right or wrong, the openness with which he disclosed and discussed his sources and invited others to challenge them, was well respected by contemporaries.

On reading that an anonymous medieval writer and the author of a missing chronicle of King's Lynn had suggested that Chaucer might have been born there, Walter's antennae began to twitch. The Chaucer scholar and editor F. J. Furnivall, whom Walter described as 'my good friend', but of whom he could equally be scornful,[2] would have none of it, and the Lynn historians of the day, especially his good friends the Beloes, father and son, were also sceptical. Walter decided it was incumbent on him to resolve this from original sources at the PRO and elsewhere because, he said, 'a local antiquary naturally dislikes a strange cock scratching successfully on what he considers his own dunghill.'[3]

He revealed his provisional findings in a letter to *The Athenaeum* and article in *The Academy* of 29 January 1881. We can let a representative of the local press take up the story:

> The latest Chaucer find is by Mr Walter Rye, a solicitor in Golden Square. He has not trusted, as Mr Furnivall did, to Sir Harry Nicolas' having exhausted the old printed indexes in the Record Office, but has turned to the *Index Nominum* in the *Abbreviatio Placitorum*, found there the names Richard, Robert, Mary and John le Chaucer, p.354, looked up the reference and had out the document they noted, the *Coram Rege* Roll of 19 Edward II, AD 1325–26. This discloses the fact that John Chaucer – no doubt John, the poet's father – was the son of Robert Chaucer and not of Richard Chaucer who married Robert's widow. Also that this Robert Chaucer had a house in Ipswich, so that with Chaucer at Norwich and Gerard le Chaucer at Colchester... the poet's family probably belonged to the Eastern counties.[4]

This was not a matter in which many had the necessary skills to engage, although discussion continued sporadically for years, with Walter repeating his position in his own *Norfolk Antiquarian Miscellany*[5] and then, again in *The Academy*, on 30 January 1886 and in the *Life-records of Chaucer* for 1886 where, however, he admitted that his conclusions were still very tentative, and where, in editorial footnotes, Furnivall robustly countered many of his hypotheses.[6] Jessopp, however, wrote to Walter congratulating him on his latest discoveries: 'such a very satisfactory extinguisher (pro hac vice) of that inflated fool Furnivall. My blessing upon you!'[7]

Professor J. W. Hales, in his *DNB* entry on Chaucer published the following year, acknowledged Walter's role in establishing that Chaucer could not have been born in 1328 as previously believed. But as to his Norfolk connections, all he would say was that 'undoubtedly the evidence in favour of London preponderates at present'. From time to time other writers advanced claims for Chaucer's being born elsewhere in the country, which Walter proceeded to rebut, albeit with arguments that could equally have been turned against his own work – such as not placing too much trust in circumstantial evidence.[8]

With the publication of the 1900 edition of the *Life-records of Chaucer* for the Chaucer Society, R. E. G. Kirk as general editor noted that 'in modern times Mr Walter Rye did his best to prove that Chaucer belonged to Lynn in Norfolk', but concluded that Chaucer's parentage had now been definitely established from a deed rooting him firmly in the family tenement in St Martin Vintry in London.[9] However, Walter was not persuaded, and it was something that remained unresolved right up to the First World War when, fearing his own imminent death, he set about printing his 'final' words on a number of controversies in which he had been engaged. His *Chaucer, a Norfolk Man* was issued on subscription in 1915, but by then his views were, if not discredited, at least marginalised. The take-up for this book in wartime was pitifully small, and despite determined advertising readership was largely limited to his immediate friends, but he continued for years afterwards to send copies to anyone who expressed an interest.[10]

Walter always acknowledged that much of his argument was based on coincidences such as documentary sightings of the name 'Chaucer' without the positive proof that they could be tied unambiguously to the right individual. He was too conscientious to make much of an occasional coincidence of names, 'but when there are many scores of them the odds against their being accidental increase'.[11] As in several other controversies, much of his argument was forensic, for example analysing variant forms of place and personal names encountered in the documents, in what to most readers was baffling detail. For all that, the *Library Association Record* for October–November 1915 still featured it among the Best Books of the Month and believed that 'his claim for [Chaucer's] Norfolk origin is very substantial, and cannot be ignored. If it is accepted by literary historians, Mr Rye's clues will open up a fertile field for his biographers.'

We find Walter as late as 1927 criticising G. C. Coulton for not being convinced, but that in itself led Walter to a belated realisation that:

> Where I have hitherto been wrong is that I over-proved my case, and my readers got wary of my details. My greatest friend frankly told

me that he could not see the wood for the trees, and I now feel he was right. It was the fault of my clumsy authorship that the public, and especially the local antiquaries, did not understand the strength of my case.[12]

It is difficult to find any mention whatever of Walter's views in modern writings on Chaucer, but at least it may be said that anyone interested can retrace his steps through the documentary evidence.[13]

The Steward (Styward) pedigree and Oliver Cromwell's alleged descent

In about 1883 Walter's friend and neighbour Bernard Quaritch alerted him to a sixteenth-century pedigree of the Steward family, which had been found bound up with a copy of Upton's *Libellus de Officio Militaris*. It had been copied in 1572 by Somerset Herald from a previous copy made by Baddesworth in 1458. One aspect of the pedigree, which had been accepted as authentic by Carlyle, was that it suggested Oliver Cromwell had been of royal descent, although initially its main interest for Walter was for the genealogy of the Steward (Styward) family.

With Quaritch's permission Walter transcribed the Steward genealogy and published it in 1884 in *The Genealogist*.[14] He then began to study the text in more detail and to research the background before publishing another article the following year, also in *The Genealogist*,[15] in which he explained that his research in the PRO did not corroborate the pedigree. He speculated amusingly on the state of mind of someone who would forge a pedigree, and concluded that Cromwell '... really sprang *ex parte materna* from a Norfolk family, probably of illegitimate descent and certainly of no credit or renown, which had been settled at Swaffham long before the alleged Scottish ancestor is supposed to have landed in England.'

Quite probably this research never came to wide attention at the time. But certainly no representative of the Steward family felt equipped to take issue with it, for there the matter rested for almost forty years. Then, in 1922, Sir Henry Steward of Chilworth, Surrey, firmly but politely challenged Walter's conclusions,[16] and set out a detailed rebuttal, hoping, as he wrote to Walter, that:

… on reconsideration of the case you may see good reason to change or qualify some of the conclusions at which you had formerly arrived. It is a good deal, I know, to ask of a man who has committed himself to a conclusion so uncompromisingly as you have done in this case; but although I think there has been some element of prejudice I also believe (if I may take the liberty of saying so) that honesty is the badge of your work and that you will take whatever course your sense of justice dictates.

In return Walter sent him references to follow up, but Steward, who was just setting off for Italy, lacked the time to take this further. On his return the following year, admitting that he had since done no further research, he asked what Walter might have to say in his own defence, and politely enquired: '[what course] I should pursue in seeking a revision of the conclusions on this subject which appear to have been widely accepted upon the faith of your judgment.'

Walter's draft reply, which is rather difficult to read given the state of his aged handwriting by this date, survives: Steward, he says, should set out his case publicly. (He was confident he wouldn't make much of a fist of it anyway, as he had not even troubled to follow up the references Walter had sent him.) In this exchange Steward comes across as a reasonable man, Walter as a pathetic old bull agitated at the sight of what he took to be a red rag! Steward still wanted satisfaction but, having never met Walter, probably did not know exactly what he was taking on. In what forum, he asked, could they argue it out? He did not favour the press: 'The modern tendency of some newspapers to substitute themselves for the regular tribunals in contemporary judicial proceedings is of doubtful value.'

When Walter replied somewhat curtly that he was not prepared to enter into discussion with an independent arbitrator, Steward prepared a careful demolition of Walter's 1865 article, and of J. H. Round's support for it. He copied this to Round himself, again stressing that he was anxious to avoid putting it in the hands of the press, and that he was really appealing to Walter to be reasonable and justify his own conclusions: 'I do not as yet conclude that Mr Rye has no answers to make; because I realise with much regret that he is now limited in strength by the infirmities of age and of failing eyesight.'

Walter replied in exasperation: 'I regret that I have no time to read, let alone reply in detail [to] your voluminous letter… Instead of criticizing why do you not get some *record* evidence… ?'

Yes, replied Steward, his letter was voluminous but 'I can assure you that it is not in a spirit unfriendly to yourself personally, still less vindictive.' Walter had 'rendered notable service in genealogical research' by exposing flaws in parts of the Steward pedigree, and for that even the family had cause to be grateful, 'but unhappily you allowed yourself to be carried away, and without much further inquiry or consideration you committed yourself to an assault upon the good faith and character of the family… with vigour but without direction.'

More correspondence followed in 1923 and 1924, in which Steward did indeed produce further evidence, from family wills. Walter again responded, but only with the ever less convincing argument that he did not have time to reply in detail. In 1925, in a book entitled *Two Cromwellian Myths*, he brought together his earlier articles on this and the Squire Papers, playing what he always thought to be his trump card, namely that his original arguments, carefully set out in print, had never been publicly challenged. But, he noted, 'one who is named Steward' had for some months been plaguing him with 'enormously long letters' on the subject. 'I offered to let him take copies of all my own material to enable him to go further into the matter, but this offer he declined.' So Walter had decided to publish what he knew.

> I hardly hope to convince my opponent, but I think I shall everyone else. I cannot set forward his own view, for he has practically intimated that if I do so or use any of the statements he has made to me privately he will restrain me by injunction… Were I younger I should probably be able to show this more clearly, but at 82 one has no time to spare getting up one's case thoroughly.

This did not stop him setting out his points in numbered form and truly tiresome detail 'so that the present champion of the tale may answer them in detail if he can'. But it understandably bored reviewers and readers in equal measure. Friends like Prince Frederick Duleep Singh, however, stood by him, hoping he might win this war of words.[17] But Steward's reply was to give a paper, later published in the proceedings of the Cambridge Antiquarian Society,[18] in which he found fault with both Walter's research method and specific details of his presentation. Among other things he accused him of citing information from the British Museum's catalogue instead of the original document to which it referred; confusing two families both called Steward who lived at the same time in Swaffham; and using phrases such as 'there can be little doubt' as a substitute for real evidence. He remained both respectful and friendly to Walter throughout. J. H. Round, he said, had properly described Walter as an eminent expert in his field, but:

> … however eminent a genealogist might be, he cannot come to a right conclusion without knowing the facts; and however expert he might be he cannot know the facts without reference to the recognised sources of information… An expenditure of one or two hours of time and of four or five shillings in money at Somerset House would have established… beyond doubt the order of descent… [19]

Steward laid down his pen with the thought that if his argument did not now convince Walter: 'I shall to that extent be disappointed, but at the same time shall be satisfied that I have done all I can to make the facts of the case plain and clear.'

No further reply from Walter has been found!

The Squire Papers

In *The Academy*, 1885, a distinguished Cambridge historian, W. Aldis Wright, re-opened a can of worms about what became known as the 'Squire Papers'.

Forty years previously, the historian Thomas Carlyle had received a letter from a certain William Squire who claimed to have in his possession a series of letters and journal extracts inherited from his ancestors, 'written by one who rode with Oliver Cromwell in the Stilton troop'. Squire sent Carlyle a number of alleged extracts which he claimed to have transcribed painstakingly from faded and crumbling original documents. The fact that he wrote in unpolished language, asked to remain anonymous, and alleged that Civil War allegiances were still a topic too hot to handle among his neighbours and relations led Carlyle to smell a rat: 'I really wish some rational eye could get upon these old papers… I myself, driven nearly mad by similar blockheads in earlier stages of this business, am obliged to fight rather shy.'

In order to remain at arm's length from any controversy, Carlyle engaged Edward Fitzgerald to pay a visit to Squire. Rather to his surprise, Fitzgerald reported that Squire was not the elderly crank he had imagined from his correspondence, but rather, a young man of reasonable intelligence who appeared to be quite genuine. But all the doubts came welling back when it became known that apart from a few fragments, the 'original documents' from which Squire said he had quoted had been destroyed and only his transcripts remained! Even so, after careful study Carlyle eventually came to believe that the material was genuine, and in *Fraser's Magazine* for December 1847, whilst respecting Squire's wish for anonymity he published thirty-five letters. Sceptics challenged the authenticity of the material, whilst others who respected Carlyle as an historian of pre-eminent national standing defended it.

Aldis Wright's contention in 1885, four decades after these events, was that the Squire Papers might after all have been genuine. This provoked spirited denials from S. R. Gardiner, Edward Peacock and Walter himself, until the editor of *The Academy* called a halt, and it was agreed that the contributors should cool off and undertake further research.[20] Walter, who had in any case long held a dim view of Carlyle's reputation, had already been looking into this controversy himself and had written a couple of short articles confirming his belief that Carlyle had been duped.

Of the very few original documents of Squire's that survived by the mid-1880s when the revived controversy was at its height, the chief was a family prayer book of 1627, that included a number of later hand-written notes. It had by then descended to a Dr William Squire who willingly allowed British Museum and other experts including Walter to study it. Their opinions were divided as to whether all the entries could be of the date claimed.

Wright used the opportunity of the launch of the new *English Historical Review* in 1886 to publish a number of letters between Squire and Carlyle and between Carlyle and Fitzgerald which ante-dated Carlyle's publication of the transcripts. Whilst tending to respect Carlyle as an expert whose judgment should not be lightly dismissed, Wright did not express a definitive view but sought to open up a wider debate on the material's authenticity. Walter at once prepared a riposte, which he duly submitted to the editor. There was insufficient space available in the next number of the journal to carry the full article, but the editor clearly regarded this as a suitably contentious issue to fire readers of the new journal, and generously allowed Walter a couple of pages in which to summarise his argument, as a trailer for a full article in the next number. Even in the trailer, Walter was characteristically withering: 'One thing has grown upon me during my search, and that is that so far from Thomas Carlyle being "the man in all England most likely to detect the fraud", his knowledge of Cromwell and his times was superficial and inaccurate to an extreme.'[22]

Walter's main paper[23] was a substantial piece of research, and his approach merits some analysis because it shows both the strengths and weaknesses of his methods. He would later be accused of arguing from a *parti pris* and selecting only evidence that supported his case. And given the low opinion he had of Carlyle that is quite possible, though he was probably unaware of the bias that others found in his approach.

One thing must be said at the outset: whatever mistakes he may have made in his research or analysis, Walter was not in business to deceive. He can be seen to have applied his skills as both a record searcher and a lawyer, with the explicit intention that anyone who found fault with the argument or disagreed with the conclusions could see exactly how he had arrived at them.

His research, which he said had been both lengthy and costly, was impressively multi-faceted.

- He sifted through many indexes and original documents including Feet of Fines and tithe records at the PRO, as well as will registers at local probate registries, looking for Squire entries which might either chime or conflict with facts and events in the transcripts. The evidence was substantially negative.
- He put out a notice for anyone with local knowledge of Squire to contact him.[24]
- He made enquiries of many people who had known Squire in Norfolk, including a local surgeon and the staff of both the library and the museum in Norwich. These witnesses established to Walter's satisfaction that Squire was regarded locally as a prankster and a fraud, and also that, far from being the ignorant and diffident individual he claimed to be in his letters to Carlyle, he was a long-standing reader at the Norwich Library who had had plenty of opportunity to study the Civil War period. He was also a contributor of objects and compiler of catalogues for the Norwich Museum, but it transpired that the staff there had already raised queries

over the authenticity of a number of Squire's 'donations', and that as a result these had been relegated to the vaults rather than put on display.

- In an attempt to verify an allusion in the transcripts to many deaths in King's Lynn at the time of the Civil War siege – which was not borne out by local histories – Walter contacted the clergy of five Norfolk parishes to check their burial registers for any signs of an unusual number of burials at around the time of the siege. They drew a blank.

- He also consulted experts in monumental brasses to consider whether alleged transcripts by Squire from family tombs could be authentic. They were sceptical, and just as he was going to press with his article the Reverend J. R. Lunn turned up the text of an inscription on a fifteenth century brass for another family which, apart from the name, was word for word the same as those attributed to his own ancestor by Squire.

- In the course of checking on personal and place names mentioned in the transcripts, Walter came across mention of one street which did not appear to have been known at the time of the Civil War by the name ascribed to it in the transcripts. He was quite prepared to be proved wrong on this but at the end of his investigation all the evidence he could muster tended to support his case.

He certainly thought his case impregnable, yet much of his 'evidence' was either circumstantial or negative. He recognised that it was difficult to prove a negative (for example to argue that because a particular individual named Squire did not appear in certain records there could not have been such a person). But was he sufficiently alert to the possibility that his findings might need to be moderated by other documentary evidence, or witness statements, that he had not consulted or not found?

Dr William Squire, who had acquired his namesake's prayer book, argued in the next number of *EHR* that from various points of view Walter's case was defective: documents other than those in the PRO helped to support the veracity of Squire's transcripts. Walter's choice of records to inspect, he said, had therefore been too narrow. Furthermore, despite Walter's statements to the contrary, some experts were less disposed to believe that entries in the family prayer book were forged. Most poignantly of all, Dr Squire drew attention to clear errors in the details of Walter's genealogical research into the Squire family. Overall, he argued that most of the information imparted to Carlyle by Squire was in fact quite likely to be correct.

The editor gave Walter the right of reply in the following number of the journal, and then perhaps wisely brought the discussion to a close. Walter meekly admitted that his genealogical findings might be at fault: 'That in treating the family history of the Squire family a strange genealogist like I may well have made some of the slips of which Dr Squire accuses me... I do not deny.'[25]

As to the writing in the Prayer Book he agreed to differ with other experts. But as to the case as a whole he did not admit that Dr Squire's remarks had in any significant way undermined his argument. It was, perhaps, the stance of a lawyer rather than that of an historian, and it was rather typical of the endgame of several of Walter's attempts to engage in matters of historical controversy.[26]

When Walter brought together his final thoughts on this controversy and the Steward descent a further four decades on, in his *Two Cromwellian Myths* (1925),[27] H. W. Hunt, in a review in the *History Teachers' Miscellany*[28] questioned whether Carlyle could really have been as poor an historian as Walter made out. However, Walter's son J. B. Rye, the *real* historian in the family, reminded Hunt that a long list of historians had already deflated Carlyle's reputation. Another observation by Hunt, however, directed more at the Steward material, certainly hits the mark and may fairly be used to summarise Walter's method:

> One feels the marshalling of so many of the details to be unnecessary, but his idea is to lay many mines, any one of which, if successful, must demolish the whole Styward claim. That some are successful there seems little doubt.

Endnotes

1 This reached a climax in *Some new facts as to the life of St Thomas à Becket...* (1924).

2 E. M. Beloe wrote to Walter, 'What a man you are to worry poor Furnivall: why could not you state your new [? frets] without sitting on him – it is certainly very amusing, but I should not think he likes it and perhaps you did not intend he should', NRO MS4691/15.

3 Retold in W. Rye, *Chaucer, a Norfolk Man* (1915), p.1.

4 *Bury and Norwich Post*, 8 Feb. 1881, quoting *The Academy*, 29 Jan. 1881.

5 Vol.2. part 2 (c.1884).

6   p.131, 'With a chain of London Chaucers from 1226 downwards, I fear probabilities are against me.'

7   Jessopp to WR, 6 Feb. 1881: NRO, MS 4691/23.

8   See, for example WR, 'A possible Gloucestershire Origin for Geoffrey Chaucer', in *N&Q* (series 8, XII, 1897), pp.449–450, a reply to St Clair Baddeley's article of this title in *Ibid.*, p.341. On the subject of coincidences, Walter remarks that he has just come across a Chancery suit of Elizabeth I's reign of Rye v. Eyre! The correspondence continued acrimoniously. See 1898 (series 9, I) pp.189–191, 331.

9   p.viii. Two articles by Walter had appeared as appendixes to the *Life Records* in 1886, 'Chaucer's grandfather, Robert le Chaucer' (appendix I) and 'Chaucer's connection with Lynn and Norfolk' (appendix 2).

10 See, for example, a letter of 4 Oct. 1922 from W. H. Draper, Master of the Temple, who was sceptical but promised to read it: NRO, MS 4691/10.

11 WR, *Chaucer a Norfolk Man*, p.2.

12 WR, *Some Historical Essays* (vol. V, 1927), p.358.

13 *ODNB* thinks Chaucer may have been born in Thames Street, London, but admits there is no proof. See also M. M. Crow and C. C. Olsen, *Chaucer Life Records*, 1966.

14 'Oliver Cromwell's descent from the Steward family', *The Genealogist*, ns, I, 1884, p.150.

15 'The Steward genealogy and Cromwell's "Royal descent"', in *The Genealogist*, ns, II (1885).

16 See the correspondence of 1922 in NRO, MS 46091/3.

17 Letter of 10 July 1925: NRO, MS 4691/83.

18 Sir Henry Steward, 'Cromwell's Stuart descent', in *Proceedings of the Cambridge Antiquarian Society*, XXVII (1926) pp.86–122.

19 *Ibid.*, p.109.

20 *Two Cromwellian Myths; viz., the alleged royal descent of Oliver Cromwell and the Squire letters, both of which deceived Carlyle* (Norwich, 1925, p.75. This substantially reprints material already published by Walter: 'The Squire Papers', *NAM*, II/I, p.16; 'The Squire Papers', *NAM*, III, p.402; 'The Squire Papers' [Notes and Documents], *EHR*, I (1886), pp.521–2, 744–56. 'The Squire Papers', *EHR* II (1887), pp.342–3.

21 'The Squire Papers', *EHR*, I, pp.311–348.

22 *EHR*, I, pp.521–2.

23 *EHR*, I (1886), pp.744–756.

24 *EA*, I, p.93.

25 *EHR*, II, pp.342–3.

26 The ODNB article on Aldis Wright, without mentioning either Carlyle or WR, accepts that he was duped into believing the papers to be genuine. Carlyle's biographer and *ODNB* contributor, F. Kaplan, mentions nothing of this controversy or of the Squire Papers.

27 See n.1 above.

28 Vol. III, Dec. 1925 no.12 (cutting enclosed in a letter of 4 Jan. 1926 from his son J. B. Rye: NRO, MS 4691/1).

TRACK 5: PUBLISH AND BE DAMNED

'The publications of Mr Walter Rye alone must now be as numerous as
King Solomon's songs.'

Portsmouth Evening News, 8 September 1913

Introductory note

*Publishing was so central to every aspect of Walter's life that most Tracks of
this work feature some of his writings: Track 2 those on sport; Track 3 those
based on archives; Track 4 those on genealogy; and Track 6 those on Norfolk.
Track 5 takes an overview of the process and of his output as a whole.*

1
PUBLISHING OUTLETS

Between 1866 and 1929 Walter published some eighty books, ranging from short pamphlets to lengthy histories. In the same period he authored something like 150 articles. Those who remember him today specifically as a writer mainly recall his larger-scale publications, which for the most part were taken on and marketed by commercial publishers in London or Norwich at their own risk.

Table: Works of Walter Rye published commercially

London:
Tourists' Guide to Norfolk (Stanford's, 1879).
History of Norfolk (Elliot Stock, 1885).
The Murder of Amy Robsart (Elliot Stock, 1885).
Records and Record Searching (Elliot Stock, 1888).

Norwich:
Cromer Past and Present (Jarrolds, 1880).
In two versions: 75 copies in large imperial quarto for subscribers, and 500 in royal quarto for the general public.
Month on the Norfolk Broads… (Agas H. Goose of Norwich; Simpkin, Marshall of London;
A&W Huke of Yarmouth and Pawsey & Hayes of Ipswich, 1887).[1]
Address from the Gentry of Norfolk to General Monck (Jarrolds, 1913).
Early English Inscriptions in Norfolk (Jarrolds, 1923).

But by far the greater part of his literary output comprised:

- Articles, calendars, editions and finding aids published through journals and societies, mostly at their respective expense, but occasionally subsidised by Walter himself.
- A host of pamphlets and small books, published on a subscription basis by a variety of printers and publishers, with Walter underwriting the cost personally. This category includes all the constituent 'parts' of his own journal, the *Norfolk Antiquarian Miscellany (NAM)*.
- Personal and private works such as the *Autobiography* and *Rubbish and Nonsense* intended only for his family and intimate friends, for which Walter commissioned the whole print-run for himself.

Earliest writings

Even by his late teens he was contributing occasional articles to *Notes and Queries,* which provide evidence that he was already transcribing monumental inscriptions, undertaking genealogical research and in a modest way collecting manuscripts.[2] Already, he was exhibiting that impatience with other people's sloppy presentation that would be a trademark of his later writings. In 1865, for example, he publicly rebuked Robert Dymond junior for daring to suggest that Walter had made a mistake in one of his articles: 'Whether what he alleges to be a mistake is so or not, could have been better judged had he conformed to the rules of *N&Q* and cited some authority for his statement.'

Walter's earliest free-standing publication, his pamphlet, *What are the Legal and Advisable Ornaments of the Church of England?* (1866), was published by Rivingtons of London in 1866, presumably at his own expense. In similar vein he funded personally his first Norfolk-related pamphlet, on the history of the parishes of Shipden and Cromer (1870), written in aid of church restoration funds.[3]

Publications by learned societies and journals

His subsequent detailed work on archives led to the editions, calendars, indexes and articles already described. Several of these were published under the respective imprints of the antiquarian and archaeological societies for Norfolk, Suffolk and Cambridgeshire, in principle at the societies' cost although Walter, with a grumble, certainly subsidised a few in order to expedite them through the press. He would probably have seen the Norfolk and Norwich Archaeological Society as the publisher of choice for many of his future articles had it inspired his confidence, but that was sapped over the delays in publishing his Feet of Fines volumes.

The Norfolk and Norwich Archaeological Society (NNAS) and the *Norfolk Antiquarian Miscellany*

His delicious parody (1863) of a meeting of a local archaeological society[4] can only have been based on direct observation. Does it suggests perhaps that he was taken along to a meeting of the NNAS maybe even on his very first trip to Norwich, as the guest of someone like his mentor John L'Estrange? It was not until three years later (in July 1866 at the age of twenty-two, shortly after qualifying as a solicitor in London) that he attended the society as a member in his own right. His experience as an 'archaeologist' at that time was rather limited, although he did have several years' serious work in the PRO behind him and was already well rated as a transcriber and editor.[5]

As a young blood coming into an ageing society, he longed to see energetic officers breathe life into its publications programme, which had fallen well behind schedule. Instead, he quickly became one of the chief victims of its delays, and there was little he could do about it from his distant London base. Eventually he resigned in frustration,[6] and in 1873 resolved to take the drastic action of launching an unashamedly rival periodical, the *Norfolk Antiquarian Miscellany* (*NAM*) to show what might be done given greater energy. The volumes of *NAM*, provocatively formatted to match those of the NNAS on the shelf, appeared on a subscription basis, limited to 100 copies. Walter under-wrote the printer's costs, recovering whatever he could from subscribers and this was to become the general pattern for his subsequent small-scale publications.

NAM's primary function was of course to put Walter's own work into print quickly and under his own editorial control. But he persuaded others, including a handful of his friends and acquaintances to contribute.[7] These included John L'Estrange;[8] E. M. Beloe the historian of King's Lynn; Dr Augustus Jessopp; Revd George Crabbe, rector of Merton; Lucy Toulmin Smith, historian and record agent; his old school friend Dick Howlett, now a civil servant; and even Walter's own brother Frank.[9]

NAM is an uneven assemblage of rather bitty, unrelated pieces – but perhaps not more so than the output of many archaeological periodicals of the time. That could be what lay behind the ambiguous comments of an anonymous reviewer in *The Academy* in 1881, probably intended as a compliment: 'Mr Rye is a careful and industrious antiquary and has enlisted in his service some of the most accomplished scholars of East Anglia… There is nothing like fine writing in the book; no endeavour to be popular at the expense of sense or fact.'[10]

Three volumes of *NAM* were published, in 1877, 1880 and 1887, and all were warmly received by reviewers. In volume II, Walter could not resist a shot across the bows of the NNAS:

> In completing the Second Volume… the Editor thinks and hopes that his subscribers have no great cause to complain of him. He has, since 1873, issued 1183pp, all indexed *literatim*, printed to range with the *Original Papers of the Norfolk and Norwich Archaeological Society* and containing, he ventures to think, articles of equal interest with those contained therein, for four subscriptions; while the Society has issued 680pp, poorly indexed, for eleven similar subscriptions, or, proportionately, one-fifth of what a private individual has done…

After the completion of volume III, he decided to give the new Secretary (and subsequent editor) of NNAS, William Hudson, the chance to show his mettle, and came back into full membership of the society, where he presented papers, published articles, went on outings, served on committees, and even got new rules adopted. But as for the publications programme, there was little real change, and the situation cannot have been helped by Hudson's moving to live on the south coast. Grudgingly, Walter toed the line for nearly two decades, finding indeed other kindred spirits who agreed that something should be done, but nobody had the 'oomph' to do it! At that time he himself had many other weighty things on his mind, including his wife's serious illness, and lacked both time and energy to get more deeply involved. Finally, after almost twenty years of complaining from inside the society he felt the need to launch a 'second series' of the *Miscellany*. Again he used this as a platform to criticise the NNAS's lethargy:

Of the thirty articles printed [by NNAS] since 1901, I personally contributed four, suggested, and found material for, and obtained, eight more, and have compiled half the 'Deed Calendars', and the whole of the double part of the 'Early Depositions' and 'Court Book extracts', so it can hardly be said I have failed in my duty as a Committee man. But finding it impossible to overcome the *vis inertiae* of the authorities I have thought it best to withdraw from the Committee and after nearly twenty years to re-start the 'Norfolk Antiquarian Miscellany' so that practical stagnation should not continue in Norfolk antiquarian work...[11]

Contributions to other journals and to national bodies

Specialist journals covering genealogy, heraldry, Jewish studies and dialect studies, as well as the British Record Society's Index Library published contributions from Walter in their respective fields, and he was also a regular correspondent in a number of quality weekly and monthly magazines.

On the whole he himself was not a joiner of learned societies outside Norfolk, although he did for a time subscribe to a few, such as the Selden Society,[12] presumably in order to receive their publications, and he may well have been a member of the Index Society.[13] I have not found evidence that he became a member of any other learned body in the field of archaeology apart from the NNAS, although he was enlisted as a speaker at an archaeological congress in 1889 on 'Unpublished materials for a history of Norfolk'.[14] His friend and mentor Walford D. Selby of the PRO had already produced a volume on that same subject for the NNAS at Walter's request,[15] and another had been planned, but very disturbingly, just as Walter was about to take to the conference rostrum he received news of Selby's unexpected and tragic death, and had to preface his remarks with an impromptu tribute.[16]

Anglo-Jewish history

An early essay published in the first part of *NAM* (1877) under the title 'The alleged abduction and circumcision of a boy at Norwich in 1230'[17] discussed what was believed to be the first case of anti-Semitism documented in the public records. Walter retraced the story as told by Blomefield and others, but in a lawyerly way he poured scorn on the credence these writers had given to medieval rumours of abductions, circumcisions and even crucifixion of Christian children by the Jews. He showed a pioneering mastery of the relevant public records, and provided stepping-stones towards a history of the Jews in Norwich. It was not a topic that continued to engage his special interest, but his stance was noted with approval by the Jewish community and the article was the only reason Walter could think of that he should have been invited ten years later (May 1887) as the only Gentile to address the hugely impressive Anglo-Jewish Exhibition at the Royal Albert Hall.[18] Here he delivered a more wide-ranging lecture on the persecution of the Jews in England, in which he dismissed all rumours and charges typically laid at their door and lamented the harm done to the country's economy by their persecution.[19] If anything, he leaned uncritically in this direction to suit his audience, but it was a story well told and well documented, and as far as Jewish commentators were concerned, he did it in 'a masterly manner'.[20] Dr Furnivall, who was already known to Walter in another connection and would become one of his firm friends, put it to the editor of the *Jewish Quarterly Review* that Walter ought to be invited to write for that journal,[21] but nothing ever came of it. However, in 1893 he was persuaded to join the council of the newly established Jewish Historical Society, alongside other 'distinguished English antiquarians and historians', S. R. Gardiner, Dr Garnett and Mr Hyde Clarke.[22] His reputation as a fair-minded, non-Jewish historian lived on in that community for decades.[23]

English Dialect Society

Throughout his research on Norfolk, Walter was fascinated by the vocabulary and dialect expressions he encountered in the course of his conversations with local people, not least his boatman Tungate. From his very first morning walk in Norwich he had been impressed and affected by the local dialect. He was less impressed by the general standard of speech of the common sort with whom he shared his railway carriage! He kept notes, and from time to time published snippets of dialect in short articles, for example in the *East Anglian*,[24] rather than in any major publication. But this was enough to bring his name to the attention of the English Dialect Society, and he was commissioned to bring out an enlarged and updated edition of Robert Forby's *The Vocabulary of East Anglia* (1830), on which he worked intermittently for many years.[25] It was eventually published for the Society by OUP in 1895 as *A Glossary of Words used in East Anglia, founded on that of Forby, with numerous corrections and additions by Walter Rye.*[26] Forby was put down in the preface in much the same way as Walter later treated Blomefield. He was said to have 'collected with little discrimination, was very garrulous and often indecent, but East Anglians owe him a great debt of gratitude'.

Walter did not claim that his own approach was any better, and freely admitted it stemmed from his jackdaw-like collection of curious words and was serendipitous rather than systematic. He confessed he had 'none of the qualities necessary to be possessed by the editor of a Dialect dictionary'.

*

As his reputation grew Walter would also submit copy for other bodies with a nationwide remit, including the Historical Manuscripts Commission, the Dictionary of National Biography and the Victoria County History of Norfolk (Track 6). Each of these was responsible for its own publishing arrangements and costs.[27]

The Historical Manuscripts Commission (HMC)

The Isham manuscripts at Lamport Hall, Northamptonshire

Tantalisingly, without giving any explanation of the context of his entrée into this family, Walter records in his *Autobiography* for 1874 first making the 'antiquarian acquaintance' of Sir Charles Isham of Lamport Hall, '... a most interesting and highly educated man, though a thorough mystic, and had a great glass globe in which he thought he saw spirits.'

He was invited to Lamport, where he began calendaring the family muniments – a process that continued through many subsequent 'pleasant visits' in the 1870s and 80s.[28] The first direct result was his published transcript of *The Journal of Thomas Isham, 1671–1673,*[29] published by Miller and Leavins of Norwich in 1875. Two articles followed in *The Genealogist* in 1878 and 1879 on 'Isham family memoranda'.[30] After working for some years on a more comprehensive calendar of the Isham papers, he offered it to the HMC for publication, where it was apparently accepted in principle. But although some of his text was then set up in type, it never appeared in book form. He received a letter from J. J. Cartwright saying that the commissioners now had other priorities and had decided not to proceed. We cannot know whether this was the real, or only a diplomatic reason, but we can well imagine Walter's feelings on being told that 'the portion in type was… cancelled after a few pulls were taken, one of which I have the pleasure to send herewith'.[31]

Report on the manuscripts of the family of Gawdy (1885)

Walter was never employed as one of the regular inspectors of manuscripts for the HMC, and after the Isham affair would probably never have considered it; but after buying, in a number of private sales, certain papers formerly in Peter Le Neve's collection, he calendared them before selling them on to the British Museum,[32] and offered the calendar to the HMC with a view to publication. This time he was successful. His sub-title describes it as a *Collection of Letters and Documents formed by Peter Le Neve, Norroy King-at-arms (born 1661, died 1729), chiefly relating to the Norfolk families of Gawdy, Knyvet, Hobart, Hare and Le Neve.* It is a significant piece of work, covering papers ranging in date from 1509 to *c.*1675, although in conformity with HMC's practice it contains very few original remarks by Walter. He would have liked to include other Gawdy manuscripts in the possession of G. E. Frere, but some of those had already been calendared, as had others among Tanner MSS at the Bodleian Library.

Dictionary of National Biography

Another great national enterprise of the late Victorian era was the *Dictionary of National Biography*. The contributors' index shows that Walter wrote seven articles between 1886 and 1895, all but one of them concerning previous Norfolk antiquaries some or all of whose papers were in his own possession: Francis Blomefield; John, Peter and William Le Neve; John L'Estrange and Anthony Norris. The odd man out was Samuel Burt Howlett (Dick Howlett's father). These articles involved no extensive research: beyond the original manuscripts themselves he did not look far for additional information. For example, for John Le Neve he cited only T. D. Hardy's introduction to the edition of the *Fasti;* for Peter Le Neve[33] he acknowledged help from Bluemantle at the College of Arms. Walter's correspondence shows that he occasionally provided assistance to other *DNB* contributors, for example one of its most prolific contributors, the Revd Alexander Gordon, for his essay on William Richards. But he seems to have had an uneasy relationship with the general editor, Sidney Lee, and to have refused to send material to assist Lee's own entry on Henry Scogan or to correct the entries of other writers concerning Norfolk personages, on the grounds that, 'All this takes up a great deal of time which I can ill spare, and if, as I suppose I am, I am the specialist for Norfolk work, I might, at all events, have had the refusal of the articles in the first instance.'[34]

Subscription publication using Norwich printers

Little information has been found in Walter's correspondence concerning his earliest ventures into print, but from the 1880s the deals he struck are better documented.

His first book-length publication was a study of the Cubitt family of Norfolk, published – very likely on a subscription basis – by Messrs Miller (later Miller and Leavins) of Norwich in 1873. For a while he continued to use this firm for the smaller-scale publications that became his typical output. Many of these were large pamphlets rather than fully-fledged books,[35] and unfortunately for today's reader and librarian they were often printed on inferior quality paper and with board covers, on which time and acid have taken a heavy toll. (In some cases modern reprints have saved the day.) He once said that he suspected realistically there were only about forty people committed enough to buy the detailed local studies he was interested in publishing, so he tended to opt for modest print-runs of fifty or at the most a hundred copies. With a grumble, he had then to pick up personally the costs of those he failed to sell. The smallest documented list of subscribers for any of his publications was thirty-one, for his *Index to Norfolk Pedigrees* in 1896. Sometimes special arrangements were made, as when the whole print-run of ninety for a definitive book on Carrow Abbey was paid for not by Walter but by the Colman family who owned the house.

The first *Norfolk Antiquarian Miscellany* (1880) was printed by Agas H. Goose of Norwich in partnership with Miller and Leavins. Walter used this organ to see into print many articles and extracts that might well have found no other outlet. For example he reckoned that only seven or eight readers would have the skills to understand and use extracts from the Norfolk Pipe Rolls, but the important thing was to get them into print for the benefit of future students. In the preface to the edition of the Old Buckenham Register he thanked his friend Prince Frederick Duleep Singh for his financial contribution, and went on:

> The few subscriptions which can be obtained for a work of this sort always leave the undertaker a loser. Had I printed twenty-five numbered copies only, on thick paper and vellum binding, at £2.2s.0d., as some people do, I should have cleared my expenses, but as my object in printing is to make the Register available to all who are likely to want to refer to it, I prefer to take the loss and have done with it.[36]

This tells us much about his overall attitude to subscription publishing, and suggests that he saw his own financial contribution as *pro bono publico* and not just something to gratify his own ego.

For two decades he had used the long-suffering Goose (printers also for the NNAS) to print his Norfolk subscription publications, but after publication of the Buckenham register just mentioned he wrote to his friend P. B. Ficklin that he was about to part company with Goose over his poor treatment of staff, and was planning to transfer his custom once and for all to Jarrold's.[37] But if he ever made that approach little came of it, for after just one publication by Jarrold's we find him in 1905–6 turning to another Norwich printer, Messrs Gibbs & Waller.[38] Then, after an intermission in his publishing activities, Messrs Roberts (1915–22) and Hunt (1923–25) became successively his regular publishers, with Jarrold's agreeing only occasionally to take an individual title with wider sales potential: the *Address from the Gentry of Norfolk to General Monck* (1913), and *Some Early English Inscriptions in Norfolk* (1923) which had the remarkably generous print-run of 375 copies.

Pros and cons of subscription and small-scale publishing

A major challenge was to make the antiquarian world aware of his publications. He ensured that forthcoming titles were advertised in the flyleaves and endpapers of each new publication, and more widely in the press. At the same time he would float ideas for projects that might *perhaps* be undertaken if enough people expressed an interest in subscribing. For example, in his *Three Norfolk Armouries: A transcript (now in the library of Mr Walter Rye) made in 1753 of a manuscript by Anthony Norris Esq of Barton Turf* he included a prefatory note, dated 1st May 1886 from his home at Winchester House, Putney: 'If those who have subscribed for this Part care to continue their subscriptions, I propose from time to time to transcribe and print all the Norfolk Armorial MSS in the Library of the British Museum and elsewhere. Any suggestions will be gladly received.'[39]

However, a number of his hypothetical titles never found their way into print at all, presumably for want of a viable subscription list.[40]

On 16 September 1915 the *TLS* carried a trailer for Walter's book on Chaucer's origins, saying that he planned to publish it at 7s 6d with a limited subscription of 150. But alas, in wartime even the *Library Association Record*'s ringing endorsement in its 'Best Books of the Month' for October-November was not enough to avert a pitifully small take-up rate.[41]

*

Some of his contemporaries must certainly have read Walter Rye's publications in libraries, especially the London and Norwich libraries to which he sent them himself, and to that extent the small take-up by subscribers will not reflect the scale of the actual readership. Nevertheless, it is important to take these tiny print-runs into consideration when evaluating the impact of his work both at the time and subsequently. Outside Norfolk his subscription publications were little known, and his wider fame rested on the larger scale publications mentioned at the outset.[42] The small readership figures also undermine one of Walter's regular claims that because nobody had challenged his conclusions they had been widely accepted: it is equally probable that they had simply never been noticed!

Even so, there were some obvious advantages to subscription publishing.

- The market for antiquarian publications relating to Norfolk was limited, so in many cases a commercial publication would not be viable.
- Walter could deal directly with the printer without using editors or other middlemen, and thus speed up the production process.
- As he was footing the bill himself he could say whatever he liked, and

more or less at whatever *length* he liked, without having to submit copy for an editor's scrutiny.

- It was quite straightforward to retain a proportion of the print-run of any given title in order to give presentation copies to libraries such as those at the British Museum, the Public Record Office, London Guildhall, the Society of Antiquaries, the College of Arms and Norwich City; and also to friends, both local and national.
- He could make up his own mind as to the right time to go to press, and if necessary could continue feeding new research into his copy right up to the deadline.[43]
- He had the flexibility to cancel plans to publish any particular work if there were too few subscribers, and to issue corrections, or even new editions, to take account of comments made by subscribers in response to the initial printing.
- As he began increasingly to feel in the 1910s and 1920s that his days were numbered, he could still print papers and memoranda as often as he liked to get the last fragments of his life's work into the public domain.

His subscribers tended to be local antiquaries, many of them friends, although the fact that signed presentation copies can still be found for sale with some of the pages uncut suggests they were not always read![44] At times we find him giving away significant sets of his subscription publications to worthy students like James Hooper whom he took on as his assistant for work on the Norfolk *VCH*. Hooper's grateful acknowledgement was: 'They will not be laid aside and forgotten, I assure you.'[45]

Private publications

In the special case of his most intimate reflections – notably the anthology *Rubbish and Nonsense* (1887), and the *Autobiography* (1916)[46] – his own sponsorship of the entire print-run enabled Walter to restrict distribution to his close circle of family and friends without incurring wider critical exposure (or, for that matter, charges of libel with regard to his forthright comments on third parties!)[47]

Rubbish and Nonsense was a miscellany of Walter's prose and verse. To quote the preface, dated at Putney, 14 February 1887:

It will no doubt be asked why, while rightly admitting all that follows to be rubbish and nonsense, I should have printed it. For the sake, I say, of holding up an example to my boys of what they should *not* do, of setting up a beacon by which they may avoid falling into the evil way of bad rhyming and silly joking into which I fell; perhaps also, that when I am gone they may know the manner of man I was. The athletic and aquatic rhymes may have a little historical value some day, for they preserve some episodes which will be sought for in vain elsewhere. Their coarseness is that common to the scribblings of all young men over-brimming with animal vitality, as I was years ago.

There follow more than sixty endearing short pieces typical of Walter's boisterous and still youthful style, full of practical jokes and boyish foolishness. Also included are memoirs of his father Edward and brother Frank, as well as skittish accounts of some family events. Some sincere and polished writing is included, if at times it seems to us sentimental, and he is not averse to poking fun at himself.

A. H. Goose of Norwich, who printed it, mistakenly included this title in a list of Walter's available publications and even sold a few. James Hooper, at that point unknown to Walter, laid hands on a copy the same week and quoted from it in *Notes and Queries*. This greatly annoyed Walter who asked Goose to discover who this man was. They put him in touch:

> Goose says you want to know who I am – well, a poor pensioned civil servant with a penchant for literature... I have published a pamphlet of S Peter Mancroft which almost nobody has bought... Have you any idea of the snobbery of the Norwich 'circles'? I want to write a friendly article on *The Infinitesimals*! [48]

Walter replied next day that it was never meant for circulation and 'the property, both in all printed copies and in the copyright, belongs to me'.[49] Once the printers discovered their mistake, even enquirers like Walter's good friend the Revd H. T. Griffith were simply told 'it was not to be had for money but only for love, being printed for private circulation among friends'. He begged Walter for a copy: 'and mind, no Bowdlerizing'.[50]

Newspaper articles and correspondence

Walter's contentious 'Easterling' column for the *Sporting Gazette* is described in Track 2. As his professional and family life became more demanding he lacked the time to develop other regular journalistic outlets, although throughout his life he would write copious letters to the press on matters of topical interest, and in retirement he had all the more time to do so. A great many of these, on a remarkable range of subjects, survive as cuttings among his papers.[51] Marion Diamond has characterised him as an 'arch reactionary... [fulminating] against most aspects of the modern world – including both working women and the women's vote.'[52] But, as is often the case with reactionaries down to the present day, he seems to have articulated what many people were thinking but not quite daring to say in public.[53]

Just as in his more erudite correspondence on antiquarian and historical matters, so on matters of more general interest he was blind to other people's feelings, and lucky never to have ended up in court (or perhaps in a ditch with a black eye). One of his obituarists would later write: 'There were occasions when maybe the discretion of the editors of local newspapers saved him from possible unpleasant consequences, not that that would have worried him in the least; he loved a fight as long as it was a good one.'[54]

But the 'fights' were not always well chosen. During and after the First World War, when already in his seventies, he wrote a regular, highly controversial column for the *Norfolk Chronicle.* Soon after the outbreak of the war, he also became embroiled in correspondence in another local paper, the *Eastern Daily Press,* with David Brown who would not accept his contention that farmers and their sons had been much slower than other classes in volunteering for the armed services.[55] J. H. Bugden of Suffield joined the discussion, accusing Walter of inciting class hatred. On learning that each of these correspondents had lost a son in the war a contrite Walter wrote that he had merely made discrete inquiries as to recruitment across a sample area of East and North Norfolk, tabulating the results, which showed that only 15% of the farming class had enrolled. Anyway, his findings had been proved irrelevant as the government needed farmers to stay on the land to produce food. He cannot have reassured the (non-combatant) farmers by announcing in the same breath that he was now compiling a roll of honour of those who had signed up: officers who had joined up and other ranks who had received war honours.

Some of his friends, whilst perhaps sympathetic to the line he was taking, wondered about its wisdom or timeliness. Voelcker, for example, wrote on 9 Feb. 1917, 'I have just been reading your diatribe on the war. One cannot help recognising that there is much in its very hard sayings, and yet I venture to question whether it will do much good.'[56]

There is much more to be read in a scrapbook of Walter's press columns, now held by Norfolk Studies, where may be found such gems as:

The noisy Churchill is not the man for the serious hard work wanted from a Minister of Munitions and he is not generally trusted. But he is pertinacious...[57]

Endnotes

1 As a larger than average sale was expected for this popular title, Goose suggested printing 1,000 copies in hard covers with 500 in reserve in cloth covers. A. G. Rump of Goose's to WR, 4 May 1887: 'Mr Hunt will put it first in a new catalogue he will issue in three weeks and Flukes of Yarmouth will push it well through that district and at the Aquarium. Calculations of cost including money recovered from adverts are included.' NRO, MS 11522.

2 He refers to a manuscript life of the artist John Varley in his possession.

3 He would later do something similar for St Peter Mancroft in Norwich: *St Peter Mancroft, Norwich; its Parishe Historie in ye Sixteenth & Seventeenth Centuries* (Goose, Norwich, 1882). A battered and incomplete copy survives in NRO. Pasted in it is a notice from Walter that 'This paper forms pp.321 to 357 of Part II of the 2nd Vol of the *NAM* now in the press, and has been printed off somewhat hastily, so its readers must kindly excuse any errors and misprints, which will be corrected before the Part is issued.' NRO, SO 78/52 733x2.

4 *Rubbish and Nonsense*, pp.77–81.

5 *Autobiog.*, p.27.

6 However, his name continued to appear without a break in the published membership lists in *NA*, VIII and IX.

7 *Autobiog.*, p.40.

8 Posthumous articles assembled by Walter as *de facto* literary executor of L'Estrange.

9 Howlett, who was himself a competent researcher, had been working through the Register of Archbishop Peckham at Lambeth Palace Library and found the names of some Norfolk clergy not recorded by Blomefield, which he 'thought might interest my friend Mr Rye'. Frank had been drawn into researching and indexing Norfolk court rolls.

10 *Academy*, 29 Jan. 1881.

11 *NAM* Second Series, I, pp.167–171.

12 As a private member he protested in 1897 at their reprinting anything whilst there was a backlog of unprinted work awaiting, NRO, MS 4691/6. Correspondence in 1903 with F. K. Munton for the society (ibid.) suggests that Walter had by then resigned.

13 The *Essex Standard* of 12 Aug. 1882 reported on the fourth meeting of the society and its appeal for reports of places where Roman remains had been found. J. H. Round had offered help for Essex and Walter for Norfolk.

14 *The Genealogist*, ns VI.

15 *Norfolk Records, preserved in the Public Record Office, London.* See also Christopher Kitching, 'Walford Dakin Selby (1845–1889), Superintendent of the Round Room', in *Magazine of the Friends of the National Archives,* XXIV, no 1 (Apr. 2013), pp.18–20.

16 *Arch. J.,* XLVII, p.164.

17 *NAM* I, pp.312–44.

18 *Catalogue of Anglo-Jewish Historical exhibition, 1887, Royal Albert Hall, and of supplementary exhibitions at Public Record Office, British Museum, South Kensington Museum* (1887). There were a number of other possible explanations for his invitation. He had several friends on the General Committee, including the artist Holman Hunt, and was well known by staff at both the PRO and the BM, where supplementary exhibitions were held.

19 *A lecture delivered at the Anglo-Jewish historical exhibition, Royal Albert Hall, 26ᵗʰ May 1887,* Reprinted from the Anglo-Jewish Exhibition papers (London, *Jewish Chronicle*, 1887).

20 3 Mar. 1887, Moccata to WR: NRO, MS 4691/7.

21 Abrahams of the *Jewish Quarterly Review* to WR, 21 Dec. 1891: NRO, MS 4691/7: Furnivall has suggested WR might be willing to write an article on the history of the Jews. Also NRO, MS 4691/4.

22 *Birmingham Daily Post*, 6 October 1893.

23 See, for example a letter of 30 May 1912 from the Chief Rabbi of the Spanish and Portuguese Jews' Congregation to Prince Fred. Duleep Singh. He has read with gratitude FDS's letter to *The Times* of 28 May 'and the reference to the work of the Norfolk antiquary Mr Walter Rye. It is extremely valuable and contrasts rather favourably with the book of Jessopp and James, "St William of Norwich", where a similar blood accusation is told...' NRO, MS 4691/84/2.

24 See, for example *EA* ns II (1887–1888) pp.211–214, 'Two Norfolk dialect ballads'.

25 He had already publicised this commission in *NAM* III (1887).

26 English Dialect Society, Series C: Original glossaries no. 75.

27 He did not easily accept the subordinate role of working to a general editor. See also VCH in Track 6. Thomas Seccombe, his editor at the *DNB*, sought corrections to his entry on W. Richards the historian of Lynn, of 15 Apr. 1896: NRO, MS 4691/6.

28 For example in April and July 1879, 1883, Oct. 1885.

29 Sir Thomas Isham, Walter Rye and Robert Isham *The Journal of Thomas Isham, of Lamport... from 1st Nov. 1671 to 30th Sept 1673* (Norwich, Miller

and Leavins, 1875).

30 In vols II and III.

31 8 June 1888: NRO, MS 4691/4. Several other letters from the HMC are in the same bundle.

32 In 1885; see *Autobiog.*, p.60. See also a letter of 4 Aug. 1888 from Edward Scott of the BM, pondering the proposed sale price of £150: NRO, MS 4691/6.

33 His Le Neve entry suggests that Le N was president of an antiquarian society from as early as 1687 at an early age, and this may be substantiated from Le N's papers. The nebulous early years of what became the present Society of Antiquaries only go back to 1707 (when Le N was already in charge). In *ODNB* Thomas Woodcock is more circumspect and makes no mention of the earlier date (not even to say that it is wrong).

34 NRO, MS 4691/21.

35 Including, for example, his transcript of *The Journal of Thomas Isham of Lamport* (1875).

36 *The First Register Book of the Parish of Old Buckenham in Norfolk* (Goose, 1902), p.iii and see NRO, MS 4691/18.

37 15 Apr. 1903: NRO,MS 4691/19/1. He had previously run proposals for publications past Jarrolds, including what became his *Songs, Stories and Superstitions of Norfolk*, but either Jarrolds considered the financial risk too great or Goose gave him a better deal. See Jarrold to WR, 20 April 1893: NRO, MS 4691/6.

38 Hooper wrote on 3 Sept 1904: 'Jarrolds seem to disgust everyone who has dealings with them'. NRO, MS 4691/7.

39 Norwich, A. Goose 1886, of which fifty copies were printed.

40 An interesting list of the unsold stock of several of Walter's books published by Goose appeared in his *Calendar of the freemen of Norwich from 1307 to 1603*, (Elliot Stock). This shows that copies of the various parts of *NAM* ranged in price from 10s to £3. The very existence of the list shows how hard it was to sell even a print-run of 100 copies.

41 Stephens suggested that Walter send a review copy to *The Bookman* to help promote sales, 20 Oct. 1915: NRO, MS 4691/16.

42 Scores of copies of his minor publications are still available for sale online today, but this is not a guarantee that they have been widely read.

43 He planned *Norfolk Families* as a work in five parts of 144 pages (total 720pp) but it ended up as 1,108 pp at no extra cost to subscribers 'and so involved me in a further loss of another £100 or so'. (1913)

44 During my research one copy appeared in a bookseller's catalogue online of the *Catalogue of Fifty MSS...* still uncut and dated Old Buckenham, which suggests it was presented to Prince Frederick (who was working with him on this title: NRO, MS 4691/18). Other copies are often still to be found with owners' bookplates.

45 Hooper to WR, 6 and 10 June 1898, NRO, MS 4961/7.

46 For a number of appreciative letters from those who received copies of the *Autobiography*, see NRO, MS 4691/5/1.

47 *Rubbish and Nonsense* now seems to be very rare. Copies survive in Norwich Library and BL, but the BL one was only date-stamped twenty-five years after its original publication.

48 Hooper to WR, 20 Dec. 1895: NRO, MS 4961/7.

49 Ibid., 21 Dec. 1895.

50 Griffith to WR, 16 and 19 December 1895: NRO, MS 4691/4.

51 See in particular: NRO, MS 4691/82

52 Diamond, *Emigration and Empire,* p.267.

53 A not untypical comment was that of his friend Jessie Bannester who wrote to WR on 16 Sep. 1916: 'We were delighted to see you had a shot at that bounder Kimberley: what a cad he is': NRO, MS 4691/5/1.

54 *Norfolk Chronicle*, 1 Mar. 1929, p.3.

55 WR, *The Great War. Statistics of recruiting in East & North Norfolk among tenant farmers and their sons.* (Privately printed, Norwich, 1917)

56 NRO, MS4691/5/1.

57 Norwich Central Library, Norfolk Studies, C940.3.

2

ERRORS, EXCUSES AND BIBLIOGRAPHICAL PROBLEMS

Proneness to mistakes

Walter exposed himself to criticism, and in later life even to ridicule, for misciting or misusing evidence, and for misprints and errors which, to put it charitably, had slipped through the printer unnoticed. Friends and colleagues like Jessopp and Hudson, Hooper and Howlett, knew him well enough to say exactly what they thought of his publications, and to offer corrections after the event. Howlett would come to despair not only of the errors themselves but also of the very little notice Walter ever took of any comments he made about them.[1]

Even Walter himself admitted that all manner of mistakes did creep into his publications unchecked, but he attempted various excuses, such as:

- he was working at speed and often on several projects at once;
- he was using sources without the benefit (as yet) of indexes;
- given the vast coverage of his *oeuvre* it was natural for errors to creep in here and there;
- the 'perverse ingenuity of the compositor'… and so on.

But the foremost excuse he and others paraded was his difficult handwriting, which especially in his last two decades, was compounded by his failing eyesight. It confused even his own friends and correspondents:

I cannot read most of your letter but can form a general idea of it. Horatio writes nearly as bad a hand as you do, and I've been giving him a jacketing this morning about it. (P. B. Ficklin, 1913)[2]

Many thanks for your letter. Unfortunately I cannot read it. I was thinking of taking it to Miss Bowles to type as she knows your hand, no doubt to her sorrow. I then bethought me that I should much like to see you again and also to get a free drink… (T. Barrett Lennard, 1914)[3]

I have done my best, but your stylographic pen is an unconquerable foe. Your corrections are for the most part undecipherable and I can see that your typist has struggled in vain against insuperable difficulties. The references must be full of errors – wrong pages etc – it cannot be otherwise. I wish I had the energy to go through them but I am nearly 74. (Dick Howlett, 1915)[4]

If even regular correspondents like these could not cope, it was quite understandable that printers and publishers made unwitting mistakes, not only when setting his original manuscript but also when interpreting his written proof corrections: it was easy to introduce fresh errors even at the last moment as the work went into print:

Your MS often causes groanings which cannot be uttered in the Composing room, not to mention the Editor's chair. Sometimes, I think, you use a typewriter. Is it not possible always to do so? (A Cozens-Hardy, *Eastern Daily Press*, 1924). [5]

Handwriting, however, was not the only problem. As he aged he also became distinctly more slipshod, reading proofs too perfunctorily and leaving many errors uncorrected. This would get him into very deep water with sparring partners like Round, not least because by his own pen Walter had previously condemned many others for doing the same. [6]

As time went on he was also less thorough in his research and presentation. He would often say defensively in his prefaces that in the interests of accuracy and of the advancement of truth he would gladly stand corrected on matters of fact or interpretation by anyone who could produce reasonable evidence that he had made a mistake, citing chapter and verse.[7] And, as he did feel some conscience about leaving errors uncorrected in his work, he occasionally provided the Norwich Public Library with a copy of his latest work interleaved with blank pages so that readers could supply corrigenda and addenda.[8] But it was not at all easy to persuade him that he was indeed wrong, and even if he meekly admitted to critics from within his own circle that he had made a mistake, he did not always actually correct it: 'All I claim is that at great labour and very considerable expense I have issued a book of handy reference never attempted before in any county.'[9]

Howlett might have been right in thinking that more than handwriting was at fault, and that Walter was getting progressively more confused.[10] Yet the more established his reputation became, the more blindly self-assured were his outpourings, and the less notice did he take of adverse comments. So another favourite ploy was simply to ignore any errors and charge forward.[11]

A work that caused him more than usual angst, and did his reputation no good at all, was *A Calendar of the Feet of Fines for Suffolk* (1900) which he edited for the Suffolk Institute of Archaeology from a text supplied by W. E. Harrison acting as his record agent. Walter had been hoping to see this volume into print for many years, as a companion to his own work on Norfolk Fines, but it only became possible when he himself put up all the money for the printing. He was rightly nervous about it, and apologised even in the book that his record agent was even less familiar than himself with Suffolk place names and that he had failed to find anyone expert in that field to help. He acknowledged that there were still many unresolved ambiguous readings, and to compound matters the printer had inserted new errors at the final stage of setting. But as reviewers were quick to point out he really could not duck editorial responsibility like that! In the course of a long and highly critical review in *The Genealogist*, which attacked method and detail as well as slipshod presentation, the point was well made that: 'The value... of such work depends mainly upon the minute accuracy with which it is carried out; and for this the Editor is all too eager to disclaim responsibility.'[12]

Challenges for the reader

Walter regarded publication as the first rather than the last step in getting his material into the public domain, warts and all. A number of his essays and articles were reissued – sometimes more than once – in another form. For example, an essay which first appeared in a journal, including his own *Norfolk Antiquarian Miscellany*, might well appear again, with or without corrections and updates, as a free-standing book or booklet. Sometimes – as with certain more contentious issues such as the murder of Amy Robsart, or the question of whether Chaucer was a Norfolk man – the new 'edition' (not usually so called) could be a much-expanded version of a contentious article written initially to test the water or to set out a preliminary case for comment. Quite often the first airing of a paper was no more than a progress report on what he had unearthed to date, with the clear intention that it would be corrected and developed in the light of further research. In such cases the only way for the reader to retain his sanity and be sure what views Walter held at a given moment is to check carefully the date of each iteration consulted and be aware that subsequent iterations might differ in important respects. *Caveat lector* again!

Sometimes this approach to printing his material piecemeal was for the purely selfish reason that he would then be able in the course of future research to refer back to his own printed work rather than have to find again his spidery manuscript notes on a particular matter.[13] But there also seems to have been a real element of altruism: he was not one to keep his findings close to his chest, but genuinely wanted his research notes to be of service to others as quickly as possible. Errors (spotted, proven and corrected) were, he felt, a legitimate route to the truth. Importantly, too, there was that brooding thought already alluded to that he must get his material into print quickly in case his life was suddenly cut short. [14]

But were there other motives? Did he perhaps see himself as the king in his own castle (or the 'cock on his own dunghill', as he once put it), not to be second-guessed? Did he fear exposing his writings in draft to those who might prove better historians or antiquaries than himself? Was there even some element of flag-waving for the 'mere' antiquarian and topographer, proceeding as best he might, as distinct from the university-trained historian? Was there an element of 'publish-and-be-damned', to get material into the public domain as swiftly as possible and deal with any flak later?

In 1925–6 a critical review of Walter's *Two Cromwellian Myths* written by Charles Partridge of Stowmarket in the *Eastern Daily Press* under the pseudonym 'Silly Suffolk', and subsequent correspondence, summed up many of the problems of Walter's technique:

> For many years I have had great regard and respect for Mr Walter Rye as an East Anglian antiquary, genealogist and historian, who has now spent the greater part of his life – he is now in his 83rd year – collecting and publishing and indexing the bricks of which history is built. He delights to make true bricks, but I venture to submit that he takes equal delight in pulling down buildings built of false bricks. He and Dr Horace Round are of the same school.

So far so good, but then he went on to suggest that Walter made too many assumptions of his readers and plied them with a mass of detail without providing all the background to enable them to understand it. As the same reviewer had said on a previous occasion:

> It is not easy to follow Mr Rye's arguments, for from the beginning he assumes that everybody knows as much about his subject as he himself knows. [That is still true of this work, which is] a vast tangle of dates and names relating to numerous people named Wells, Styward, Stewart. You cannot see the wood for the trees...' [15]

With this Walter substantially agreed.

Problems with organising his material

Like many antiquaries before and since, Walter was better at garnering material than knowing quite what to do with it. Every book read, every archive studied and every site of antiquarian interest visited generated copious notes, which over the sixty years of his active research became a vast accumulation. Many of them still survive among his papers at Norfolk Record Office. He would sort, index and shuffle them many times over as they came to be required for successive publications. But as he would typically have several research projects on the stocks at any one time, and quite possibly be simultaneously preparing transcripts, calendars and editions of unrelated documents, it was no easy task to make his notes serve every possible need.

The difficulty of digesting a mass of MS material, so that all of it will fall into its right place and each fact will illustrate other parts of the book, is enormous. Frequently a topographer who in the early part of his work has deduced, quite to his own satisfaction, the descent of a manor or family, or has fixed the date of a church, finds to his vexation when he gets further on, that he has had, all the while, hidden away among his collections for another place, material which would have enabled him to correct his views.[16]

What he needed was a computer!

Endnotes

1   Jessopp to WR, 4 Feb. 1882, 'You have made rather a bungle in your opening paragraph. I append some suggestions which you may adopt or not at your pleasure.' NRO, MS 4691/23. In 1903 Hudson sent some quite robust criticism and corrections to WR's calendars: NRO, MS4691/7.
2   Ficklin to WR, 31 May 1913: NRO, MS 10612 folder 2.
3   TBL to WR, 5 Feb. 1914: NRO, MS4691/14/2.
4   Dick Howlett to WR, 30 June 1915: NRO, MS 4691/16.
5   11 Apr. 1924: NRO, MS 4691/3.
6   WR, *Norfolk Families* (1913), p.iv.
7   Some readers accepted the challenge. On 23 Aug. 1893 W. Williams of 135 Station Road, Liverpool Road, N wrote, 'May I point out, referring to your otherwise correct and always valuable "Guide to Norfolk" page 15 line 17, that Thomas Paine was a *deist* and not an atheist... Had I not found your book so useful I should not have read it so closely.' NRO, MS 4691/11.
8   E.g. WR, *A List of Norfolk Place Names* (1923).
9   WR, *Norfolk Families*, p.iii admits that his own errors are numerous but excuses himself in a work of 1,048 pages with 70,000 facts that may be challenged.
10 Howlett to WR, 10 Sep. 1915, NRO MS4691/21: 'Your letter is the effect of a bad headache. Its confusion of thought is too complete for any possible reply save on one point...'
11 Walter Rye, *Some Historical Essays* (V, 1927) p.377, 'Let us now recapitulate the plain facts as told by undoubted records.'
12 *The Genealogist*, ns, XVII.
13 In his *A Handbook to the Materials available to Students of Local History and Genealogy, arranged in order of date* (1924), he remarked: 'I should have found this compilation very useful to me had I made it before'.
14 E.g. WR, *Some Rough Materials... North Erpingham* (1883).
15 NRO MC202/2.
16 WR, *Some Rough Materials...* (1883), p.i.

3
'STUDIED DISCOURTESY'

Despite faults of presentation and detail, Walter often demonstrated a scholar's awareness of the importance of a critical, and not a credulous, approach to primary sources. He was aware of the necessity of meticulously accurate transcription and citation of references, and was critical of writers who failed either of these tests.[1] He was also genuinely anxious to ensure that others could retrace the sources on which his own findings or assertions were based. The code of conduct he set himself as a writer (in principle if not always in practice) might be summarised as follows:

- unceasing labour in the cause, with copious background reading of all available secondary sources, calendars and indexes;
- use of primary archival sources whenever possible;
- accurate citation of sources for his comments and opinions, so that anyone wishing to check them for himself might do so;
- clear differentiation between proven fact and supposition or guesswork;
- admission and correction of any errors found in his work.

All of that sounds reputable even to today's historians. But we have to remember that Walter's first training ground was the sports field, where the quest for victory and glory was paramount. He took many of the competitive values he derived from athletics into both his professional life as a lawyer (where he doubtless honed some of them) and his research and writings. In that last field, even though emulated by other writers, these attributes were not universally welcome. He could not understand why anyone would settle for lower standards than himself, and was quick to criticise laziness, research that had not covered all sources[2], gullibility and faulty reasoning.

Walter was fond of story-telling, and collected the kind of anecdotes – however far-fetched – that might be useful towards a good after-dinner speech or fireside reminiscence among friends. This affected the style and content of some of his books just as much as did his racy and outspoken prose. When playing the role of a chronicler or rapporteur, he would occasionally put on record a commonly held view, for example on reported sightings of ghosts, without comment and without necessarily believing it himself. But when in more serious vein as a transcriber or editor he could distance himself, even vehemently, from anything that was not soundly evidence-based, or that stretched the available evidence beyond reason:

> One wildly ingenious antiquary contended that Julius Caesar really landed in Britain at Cromer, a view he sustained with much perverse ingenuity.[3]

> The rustics will tell you that the 'Cobbler's Hole' leading out of the north rood turret of Cromer Church was where refractory monks were stowed away in a sort of 'little ease'; but as the monks never had an abiding place there, and the hole is clearly a service or choir book cupboard, this notion need not be seriously considered.[4]

> The *beauty* of the Broads is much exaggerated by writers with a 'Swiss-Family-Robinson sort of rubbish'.[5]

In his sharp remarks, he was no particular respecter of the dead – even the recently dead or dying. Nor did he make much allowance for other people's illness (though he expected them to make allowance for his). He was, he once said, a 'good hater'.

Walter had some favourite (human) targets when it came to inaccurate work. Among the dead, these included especially Dean Goulburn of Norwich who, in Walter's words, had an 'extreme incapacity to deal with historical matters', and whose work 'literally teemed' with errors;[6] and the nationally famous historian Thomas Carlyle, whose work, as we have seen, Walter thought 'slovenly and inaccurate'.[7] At various times he took to task almost all the previous historians of Norwich, even Blomefield who was in some ways his hero, for example for 'very ridiculously' identifying a church of the Holy Trinity mentioned in Domesday Book with St John's Maddermarket.[8] Blomefield's continuator, Parkin, was 'a most incompetent man'. And so on.[9]

He was even-handed in that he applied just the same high standards to friends as to strangers, and therefore caused occasional offence to both![10] Much as he owed to his friendship with John L'Estrange, it did not prevent him castigating L'Estrange for being late in delivering articles for the *Norfolk Antiquarian Miscellany*. Walter was no respecter of rank or status, and would happily make public criticisms of aristocrats, senior clergy, established historians, civic officials, elected members and other eminent personages. Some of them demonstrated in their response a greater gentility, charm and grace than Walter would ever muster. For example, responding to a critical letter from Walter in 1888, the legal historian F. W. Maitland expressed gratitude for his 'kind' letter, 'both because it is always pleasant and profitable to read sound criticisms of one's own work and because I am delighted to make the acquaintance of one who has laboured successfully in the field of English legal history. If I then defend myself it is in a very modest and friendly spirit.'[11]

All told, Walter made an art of what we would now call the 'put-down'; and the scorn and ridicule he poured on others at times teetered on the brink of defamation, as both friends and adversaries warned him without much effect. He could be carried away by his own rhetoric, and the desire to defend his own opinions, into sarcasm, nit-picking, and point-scoring. And, especially in his later years, his lawyerly forensic fussiness over minutiae often made it hard for readers to see what he was getting at.

Conversely, he could go out of his way to add interest for the general reader to what might have been merely dry research, through genuinely amusing asides of his own. We may take as fairly typical some of those from an article he wrote in *NAM* based on the archives of Burnham Manor. Where the records referred to a man skulking under a neighbour's window Walter interjected, 'I hope the habit died out.' He considered that, 'taken as a whole the manners of the common sort were rough and their customs beastly'. Contempt shown to the lord of the manor in the reign of Edward I, was 'specified on the roll more explicitly than it can be here'.

Despite all this, he could engage quite equably with adversaries provided they were prepared to argue on equal terms and not belittle him (as J. H. Round famously did), and he could be generous in acknowledging other people's help in his quest for 'truth'.[12]

Some accepted his barbs as fair sport, and press and journal editors doubtless saw that a bit of controversy and waspish humour was good for sales. Others were less tolerant of Walter's *braggadocio* and urged him to be more temperate. Jessopp, for example, wrote in 1884:

> Quixotic man! Who do you suppose will care two straws about the business except your enemies... You'll be tabulated 'dangerous' soon – a man to be derided as given to biting and kicking: a vicious horse – some will say a different animal – mule for instance.[13]

And the following year, responding to a critical review of one of his books by Walter he wrote again:

> We all make mistakes – all, that is, who do any good work in advance of our fellow creatures – the men that never say or write foolish things never do wise ones. We are all fallible, and all of us weak at times.[14]

A long-running exchange in the pages of the *East Anglian* in 1890–91[15] illustrates several of the above points. The Suffolk historian and genealogist J. J. Muskett unsuspectingly suggested that it would take too long to search all the Fines of a county to establish a certain point. Walter challenged him, and when invited by Muskett to show that it could be done replied that he had never said *Muskett* could do it! His answer struck other fairly offensive notes:

> I am rather surprised that Mr Muskett, who described himself as a specialist for the Eastern Counties... should not know what I fancy most Norfolk researchers know...

Muskett civilly tried in return to lecture Walter:

> Let me conclude my reply to his memorandum with a word to Mr Rye himself. Extravagance of statement serves sometimes to

emphasise facts; but he should avoid the appearance of studied discourtesy which mars so much of his literary work.

Even in the course of Walter's next, more conciliatory response there was still a goading undertone:

> I fear I have unintentionally trodden on his corns as he is climbing up his 'pied de gre', and I am sorry I was not more careful.

Endnotes

1 WR, *Carrow Abbey* (1889), e.g. Appendix, p.xxxiv-v, 'Norris says they also held 9 or 19 acres of land (I know not which, all the rolls which I have seen being erased in that place and altered from 19 to 9)...'

2 An enquiry in EA, II p.32 from Henry Wagner concerning one Giles Cutting drew a sharp response (p.48) from WR: 'What is the point of Chadwick's index to Blomefield if searchers do not consult it?'

3 WR, *Tourists' Guide*.

4 WR, *History of Norfolk*, p.170.

5 *Ibid.*, p.256.

6 *Autobiog.*, p.50; *NAM* II, p.85 etc.; WR, *Carrow Abbey* (1889); *Some Historical Essays*, II p.97 etc. Goulburn was also accused of blindly following Blomefield, 'So far from being of any use to the student of Norfolk history or antiquities it cannot fail to terribly mislead any one who refers to it', *NAM* II p.85.

7 *Autobiog.*, pp.16–17.

8 WR, *Some Historical Essays*, 2, p.96, cites other instances. For a more detailed attack on Blomefield see *NAM* II, p.17 but especially in the memo on him in *NAM* III, p.177 etc. His critical faculty is 'absolutely wanting', and he is gullible in swallowing family 'pedigrees'.

9 *NAM* III, p.181.

10 *Autobiog.* for 1905. On Trafalgar Day Jessopp attacked him for saying that Nelson was educated at N. Walsham Grammar School. WR rebutted this in the press and gained a recantation.

11 He went on to explain in some detail his use of legal terminology (against WR's criticisms), said he would be glad to be sent a copy of *NAM* and in return sent Walter a copy of his own Gloucestershire Eyre Roll: 'It is I fear not very well copied, for it was the work of a prentice hand and I have grown older and wiser since I had it printed.' Maitland to WR, 4 June 1888: NRO, MS10612 folder (1).

12 WR, *Chaucer, a Norfolk Man* (1915), p.1.

13 Jessopp to WR, 28 Feb. 1884: NRO, MS4691/23.

14 Jessopp to WR, 23 Jan. 1885. *Ibid.*

15 *EA*, IV (1890–91), pp.35–6, 47, 54, 56, 71–73 etc.

4
TWO MAJOR CONTROVERSIES:

THE DEATH OF AMY ROBSART, AND WALTER'S WAR WITH J. H. ROUND

Introduction

Through total immersion in the sources, Walter rightly became a recognised expert in the documentary heritage of Norfolk, and a county historian of repute. He could not have achieved this without also being well read in national history and archaeology. But when it came to entering into public controversies on historical matters beyond the county it was not so much his own sure grasp of the historical background that drove him on, as the challenge of grappling with unsolved mysteries. What he could bring to this pursuit, in addition to his extensive knowledge of the sources, was the forensic skill and combative argument of a lawyer, combined with the acerbic wit and overstatement of a popular columnist. These were not negligible tools for engaging public opinion, and he blazed every trail with a certain swagger, egging anyone on to prove him wrong if they could.

In short, for Walter this became another kind of sport. And as with a sport he attracted supporters for each new bout (and cultivated others by sending them copies of his publications). On the whole they were a small band of the faithful, drawn from his intimate circle of friends, but with a sprinkling of more dispassionate reviewers and historians.

He also had vocal critics of both his methods and his conclusions. We saw that in his later years he was berated even by friends like Howlett and Jessopp for hasty and slipshod work, and for laying out too many pieces of a jigsaw without assembling a clear picture. Others (correctly) singled out his penchant for using circumstantial evidence and coincidence for want of proof positive. And whilst some of his writing reached a large and informed readership by appearing in academic journals such as the *English Historical Review* or periodicals such as *The Academy* or *The Athenaeum*, many of his books and articles on controversial topics were produced in his usual small (even negligible) print-runs and were probably little read.

1. The death of Amy Robsart

Amy Dudley (née Robsart), wife of Elizabeth I's courtier and favourite Sir Robert Dudley, died in 1560 in suspicious circumstances.[1] Her body was found at the foot of a flight of stairs, with her neck broken. It was commonly said that she had long been ill with something like breast cancer, but that has not been established beyond doubt. Her almost continuous separation from Dudley, coupled with his intimacy with the Queen, might well have caused her to suffer depression. She had been seen much at her prayers, and on the fateful day had sent her servants away from the house. Was that because she wanted to take her own life? Did she in fact do so, or was her death a genuine accident? Did someone attack her first and then place her dead body where it was later found? And if so were they acting on their own behalf or under orders (and from whom?). Could they even have been carrying out a mercy killing to put the poor woman out of her misery? After long deliberation an inquest jury returned a verdict of accidental death. But was their investigation impartial, or was the jury rigged to present an expedient verdict to save the honour and reputation of Dudley or even of the Queen? This long list of unanswered questions continues to make it a compelling and mysterious story. But why did Walter become involved?

Victorian readers were familiar with Amy Robsart from Walter Scott's *Kenilworth* (first published in 1821), which embellished and fictionalised the story, introducing errors into the popular understanding of the event. These were compounded by dramatisations including one staged at the Covent Garden Theatre in the 1870s. On a more scholarly level, interest was stirred by the publication in 1865 of Gonzalez's *Documents relating to the reign of Elizabeth preserved in the Archives of the Simancas*. This quoted extensively from the letters of the Spanish ambassador, de Quadra, which left a number of questions unresolved. Then in 1878, Canon J. E. Jackson, who had been working on state papers at Longleat House, gave a paper about the incident to the Wiltshire Archaeological and Natural History Society and, by permission of the Marquess of Bath, exhibited some of the relevant papers for the first time. These tended to reinforce the jury's verdict of accidental death and to cast doubt on any complicity on the part of the Queen or Dudley.

It was at this point that Walter decided to enter the arena. He revisited the original and secondary sources cited by Jackson, including Froude's telling of the story, copied out long extracts from the published de Quadra letters, and conducted additional research at the PRO and the British Library, as well as using the newly published calendar of Cecil's papers at Hatfield House. True to form, he set out his conclusions first in his own *Norfolk Antiquarian Miscellany* before expanding them with supporting documents as a book entitled *The Murder of Amy Robsart: A brief for the prosecution*, which was published simultaneously in 1885 by Elliott Stock in London and Goose in Norwich. The title itself is enough to show his *parti pris*. It is not so much a reasoned argument for and against a historical theory as a cry of *'J'accuse'*. 'It strikes me,' he says of the reported accident, 'that a lamer story was never put forward.' There had been a 'wave of whitewash' leaving important people looking 'clean and respectable' when they were in fact (in Walter's estimation) at the minimum immoral, and more likely criminal. He rated Elizabeth, despite her grand public image, 'a very paltry woman made up of meanness, caprice and lechery', and accused her of being 'to the end of her long life… childishly vain, mean, cruel and vacillating'. She was, he thought, an accessory either before or after the fact. He called into question her morals and even her sanity, and concluded that she and Dudley both 'came from a bad stock'.

Unlike Canon Jackson, Walter was inclined to smell a rat and be persuaded by those who thought at the time that Dudley was implicated. So he gave credence to de Quadra, and also to *Leicester's Commonwealth*, a discredited libel circulating in the 1580s that had laid the blame for Amy's death squarely at Dudley's door. He found the disappearance of certain key documents altogether too convenient.

Most of this conspiracy theory can now be hit firmly on the head. We know, for example, that the Privy Council registers of the period were destroyed not deliberately at the time but in a later fire, and that the inquest jury's verdict (whose existence was unknown in Walter's day) in fact survives and does indeed conclude that Amy's death was an accident. Skidmore's recent research on the subject does not entirely rule out conspiracy and collusion, but not on the grounds put forward by Walter.

So, judged by today's historical method his exposé simply does not stand up. But is that to judge him by the wrong yardstick? It cannot be said that he had anything to gain from deliberately falsifying evidence or drawing false conclusions from it. Rather, he was pitching himself into a topic of current controversy, and calling in aid original documents to support a particular case, very much as a lawyer might be expected to do. He meticulously researched and copied relevant material from the archives, and in effect threw down the gauntlet to anyone who disagreed with him to do the same.

A number of reviewers, as well as subsequent historians, very properly took him to task. One, who for all his criticism clearly had some respect for Walter, wrote gently that he found Rye's case 'not quite to our mind'.[2] In denigrating Elizabeth and other important figures he had employed 'to a large extent gross exaggerations'. The writer was convinced that the opposite point of view could be arrived at 'in the face of all that Mr Rye has so ably written'. Sydney Lee, writing Dudley's biography for the *DNB* found Walter too gullible in relying on *Leicester's Commonwealth*, and unbalanced in 'interpreting unfavourably much neutral collateral information'. Jessopp took Walter to task for a number of errors, and Walter evidently tried to shrug off some of the responsibility for these on to Dick Howlett whom he had enlisted as proof-reader. Howlett wrote to Walter:

Some sympathy I have with your misfortune, but I don't feel any responsibility. I only read 'Amy Robsart' for language and argument – as to the facts of history at that date I am in a very poor position. You *do* work too fast: that is a point I have preached about until you won't listen to me any longer I am afraid. I've been reading Jessopp's review and I quite agree with Mr Beloe that it is a friendly smiting and is very flattering to your work. I don't think you have anything to be angry at in it: I have for such summary scanty treatment as is accorded to me.[3]

2. Walter's war with J. H. Round

J. H. Round, the pioneering historian of feudalism in England, was born in 1854 and was therefore some ten years Walter's junior. He took a first in modern history at Oxford in 1878.[4] In the late 1880s he became a regular reader at the PRO and after some preliminary research on the history of his native Essex delved deeply into the history of medieval England and its institutions, writing many articles and books, some of which are still valued today. His work was firmly rooted in the Public Records, and although Walter does not suggest that he met Round at the PRO, it cannot be ruled out. Round certainly knew of Walter and even admired his work, and they were to meet in other contexts from the 1880s onwards.

Round was of a delicate constitution and suffered bouts of serious illness. But he was so sure of himself as an historian, and later as a genealogist, that he was prepared almost literally to enter into battle, sometimes over trifling details, with academic historians with whose work he had found bones to pick. He was known to continue his attacks even after his antagonists had publicly retracted or confessed their 'errors'. His most famous victim was E. A. Freeman, whose professional integrity and reputation he seemed determined to destroy. Few other historians of the time had a taste for such venomous criticism, and friends and fellow historians tried unsuccessfully to dissuade him from his tirades, for which he became notorious. Maitland described him as 'a learned man but [with] many corns upon which one may not tread'.[5] But this did not deter Round, and in some respects he and Walter were like peas in a pod: each probably rather admiring the other's forthrightness and tenacity when it came to chasing up facts, especially in the field of genealogy, and each from time to time going public in disproving puffed-up claims by others to honourable ancestry. Walter drew his combativeness from his sporting life and his profession as a lawyer; Round did so in part from political activities.[6]

During his brief association with the VCH, from 1899[7] Walter sat with Round on the committee where, although he respected Round's scholarship, there was a certain amount of banter and sniping. Page, the general editor, once remarked of Round that: 'Many of his points of controversy were trivial and perhaps not worth the time and trouble their corrections involved. A friend once remarked… "if he would cease killing flies what valuable work he would do".'[8]

J Horace Round.
Wikipedia.

Was it at this period that seeds were sown in Walter's mind to take Round down a peg one day? It was a dangerous mission, since the man who had no qualms over publicly scything into Freeman and other renowned historians including Maitland, Froude and later Hubert Hall of the PRO was unlikely to pull his punches against smaller fry such as Walter Rye.[9]

To begin with, the overall relationship between the two was amicable, though they were never on first-name terms. Both became contributors to the *DNB*, and as Round's interest in genealogy became more central that too strengthened their common bond. There is plenty of evidence of mutual respect in their early correspondence, and Walter has even been described as 'one of Round's closest cronies until at last he flouted Round's authority.'[10] Walter regularly put Round on the mailing list for his publications, and they exchanged research notes on individual genealogies.[11] When Walter sent Round a copy of his *Norfolk Families* in 1913 he was rewarded with profuse and genuine thanks:

> It is a work which speaks volumes for your prodigious industry and the vastness of your local knowledge. Its peculiar value appears to me to consist of your unique acquaintance with the *real origins* of modern families which it is difficult if not impossible to obtain from

books and which soon passes from living memory... I like your wideness of grasp in the work...

But could praise from Round ever be unconditional? There was a sting in the tail. He was irritated by Walter's constant attacks on the inadequacies of the early heralds:

> ... your attitude towards arms is, as it always was to me, past all understanding. I and my friends have always maintained that bad heraldry is bad heraldry whether sanctioned by the heralds or not, just as a spurious pedigree is not made less spurious by receiving official sanction... and *you* while lashing out at the heralds (eg Lancaster and Buxton) make them the only arbiters of right and wrong arms.[12]

Round became bedridden for much of the rest of his life from 1915 – only two years after this exchange.[13] But that did not slake his thirst for controversy, and unfortunately it was now Walter's turn to be on the receiving end, at a time when he too was in a poor state of health. Each felt that he could not let any attack on his reputation pass unchallenged.

Minor skirmishes began in 1920, over Walter's acceptance of the authenticity of a medieval chronicle of St John's Abbey, Colchester, which Round held to be spurious.[14] In this, as in several subsequent bouts of the joust, Walter repeated with his old flawed logic that if nobody had openly challenged facts or interpretations he had laid before the public, sometimes decades previously, in his books and articles their silence proved they had been generally accepted. Round dismissed this with a surly wave: 'It may not have occurred to Mr Rye that historians have a better use for their time than writing replies to what he imagines to be convincing arguments.'[15]

In the *English Historical Review* in 1920,[16] Round published an article on the sheriffs of Norfolk, quite happily citing *Norfolk Families* and other works by Walter, and in a friendly enough spirit referring to Walter as 'the well-known local antiquary' – though even that might imply he had not made it into the ranks of reputable historians. But then he pointed out specific errors, which prickled Walter, who penned a substantial reply for the journal. The editor wisely reduced it to a few words.[17] Undeterred,

Walter printed his full response in *The Genealogist* for April 1921. His case was that the errors cited by Round had in some instances been uttered years before and had since been corrected in print, and, more generally, that Round's criticism was abusive and unsportsmanlike. ('This made matters worse between us'.)

Walter went on, in 1921 to write local press articles and a small book on Norwich Castle[18] despite, as he lamented, now suffering from heart disease and glaucoma.[19] One result was that undetected proof-reading and presentational errors abounded. His main point was that when the duty of 'castle guard' was levied on church lands this was for defensive purposes only. He acknowledged that 'Dr J Horace Round... is the greatest living authority on the subject, and... has kindly corresponded with me on it'. But then, using Round's own *Feudal England,* and the disputed Colchester chronicle referred to above, he began to challenge Round on his own turf. As he should have seen, he was quickly out of his depth: 'I am aware that the credibility of this Chronicle has been denied by Freeman and doubted (except where it suits him) by Round.'

This bracketed aside might have been friendly banter in Walter's eyes, but for Round it was a red rag. Worse, whilst admitting some errors of his own, Walter went on to point out errors and omissions in Round's latest article.

G. N. Clark, who had just taken over the editorship of *EHR* from R. L. Poole, was rashly persuaded to publish a reply from Round in 1922, in one of the longest and most vituperative articles that had ever been published in the journal, 'The legend of Eudo Dapifer'.[20] At the heart of the matter was again the spurious Colchester chronicle. Walter was still 'the well-known Norfolk antiquary', but Round deliberately set out to demolish him by citing in tedious detail all the dud references, mistranscriptions, misquotations and unsafe assumptions he could find in various of Walter's publications, and particularly resenting his personal criticism: 'Mr Rye, of course, has a right to his own opinion but it is perfectly intolerable that he should bring a baseless charge of *mala fides* against those who do not share it.'

And – oh dear! – in 1922 Walter fought back in a long diatribe, *Dr J. Horace Round and his recent attack on Mr Walter Rye as to the Colchester chronicle, Norwich castle and other matters.* He listed – which must have been easy – sixty people whom Round had abused in print. The latest article had been:

… avowedly made to injure me and my reputation; it was of course a gross libel for which I could have sued him, but at the age of 79 I had no inclination to waste some hundreds of pounds by suing a rich man for a possible farthing's damage… If such methods as these are the way to write History, I can only be grateful that I am only a local topographer.[21]

That 'only' tells its own story.

Many of Walter's friends had been cheering him on throughout the battle,[22] surely more in the manner of encouraging a wrestler than from any certainty that his facts or arguments were correct. He presumably knew he lacked the historical grounding to make a serious dent in Round's reputation, and in a sense this was not what he was trying to do, for at heart he did acknowledge Round as 'the most accurate historical writer we have ever had or [are] likely to have… what he tells you may be accepted as positive fact in 9 cases out of 10'.

But in this kind of polemic the compliments on both sides were usually a sweetener for the black eyes that were to follow, and as he went on to look at, as it were, the other 10% of cases, he accused Round of:

- turning a blind eye to facts that didn't suit him;
- being too apt to consider himself omniscient;
- venturing into fields he did not understand;
- having little power to use his 'accurate' facts to deduce arguments.

Walter did not perhaps appreciate what now seems transparent, that in most of these respects he could have been speaking into a mirror, so alike were the two men temperamentally. But he summed up his own stance thus:

I have been told that I should not defend myself because my opponent considers himself dangerously ill, but I am eleven years older than he, am worn-out with hard work, and my eyesight is fast failing, so I do not see why I should sit down and be silent under the violent attack he has made.

This time perhaps better counsels at last prevailed, for Round did not respond, although he was not permanently too ill to do so.[23] True to form, however, Walter ensured that his latest polemic was not only sent to Round but also deposited in influential libraries.[24] And later he also enlisted prominent historians to defend his reputation. As late as the end of 1923, T. F. Tout wrote:

I am much obliged for your sending me your interesting pamphlet about Round. I hold rather strongly the view that Round's attack on you in the *English Historical Review* ought never to have been printed, and I should not be surprised if the editor was not of the same view also now, but we must be tolerant to a man who is beginning a new job. I quite agree with you in reprobating Round's method of conducting a controversy, but I have always made a point of paying no attention to what he says. Once or twice he has attacked me quite unnecessarily, and I have never taken any notice. I think that is the best way and advise you to follow it up. The poor man is desperately ill, and it is very pathetic to see how he struggles on with his work. I have no very recent information, but I doubt whether he has left Brighton for many years. When I was last there he had not left the house for many months and was generally in bed...'[25]

Although their words could be as sharp as razor wire, each of these sick old men fundamentally appreciated the other's great dedication and achievement in their respective fields. Papers assembled after Round's death, and some of them posthumously published, continued to find fault with Walter's writings, but from a more friendly baseline, accepting also his achievements. It becomes apparent, for example, that Round had found Walter's Norfolk *Songs, Stories and Sayings* an 'entertaining treatise'.[26] He also noted that: 'Norfolk and the history of Norfolk families are the recognised preserve of Mr Walter Rye. Of his genealogical ardour and of his amazing industry there is ample proof in the 'list of publications'... from his busy pen, extending over more than fifty years.'

But in a posthumously published essay by Round on the Walpole family, some of the old animosity surfaces. Whilst endorsing Walter's views on spurious genealogies, he takes him to task for drawing false assumptions from undated documents and allowing his venom against those who paid for peerages to cloud his judgement even on genealogical issues. In this he was almost certainly correct.

Henry Berney put into words what many of Walter's friends must have been thinking:

It is so easy to appear clever by finding fault with the hard slogging research of an original Genealogist, and one should not only give credit for honest hard work but should be polite and not rude in any criticism. The difference between the *great* R's, is that the one makes mistakes sometimes and *always* candidly admits them, – whereas the other makes wrong guesses and *never* admits an error. I much prefer Rye, and wish him many years of good health to crack many more hard genealogical nuts.[27]

There is a footnote to this story. When Walter published his controversial book on Becket in 1924 he harked back to Round's 'bitter and uncalled for attack' and his own response. 'I am advised by my friends,' he said, 'not to reopen the dispute, at all events till he thinks fit to answer my pamphlet'. Round sallied forth against him once more, 'in the most offensive way', without having read his work. Walter's final, and unanswered, public challenge was:

When he reviews this book now that it is written, I will ask him to read pages 82 etc, which seems to me to utterly destroy his argument as to his alleged identity of the names Haldein and Hauteyn… If he has anything to say to rebut my arguments, let him do so in a decent and a scholarly way, and remember that abuse is not argument, and that pointing out my innumerable misprints and slips on minor matters does not answer main and important points I claim to have made.

Endnotes

1   This section is based on the following sources: *NAM* III, 49; J. E. Jackson, 'Amye Robsart', in *Wilts Archaeological and Natural History Magazine* 17 (1878), pp.47–93; *Nineteenth Century*, 11 (1882); I. Aird, 'The death of Amy Robsart – accident, suicide or murder – or disease?' in *EHR*, LXXI (1956), pp.69–79; C. Skidmore, *Death and the Virgin: Elizabeth, Dudley and the mysterious fate of Amy Robsart* (2010).

2   *EA*, ns I, p.148.

3   RH to WR, 2 Sept. 1885: NRO, MS 4691/21.

4   See Edmund King's article on Round in *ODNB*.

5   W. Raymond Powell, *John Horace Round: Historian and gentleman of Essex* (Essex RO, 2001), p.70.

6   *ODNB.*

7   See Track 6.

8   William Page, (ed), *Family Origins and other studies by the late J. Horace Round* (1930), p.xxi.

9   See especially Powell, *op. cit.*

10 Powell, *op. cit.*, p.70.

11 See for example Round to WR, 31 July 1907, thanking him for his 'delightful little book': NRO, MS 4691/14/1.

12 Round to WR 28 Oct. 1913: NRO, MS 4691/85A.

13 Powell, *op. cit.*, p.185. Round died in 1928, shortly before Walter.

14 See especially J. H. Round, 'The legend of "Eudo Dapifer"' in *EHR*, XXXVII (1922), pp.1–34.

15 Ibid., p.3.

16 J. H. Round, 'The early sheriffs of Norfolk', in *EHR*, XXXV (1920) pp.481–496.

17 WR, *Dr J Horace Round...* (1922), p.5: 'In the days of the former editor it would of course have been inserted.' EHR XXXVI.

18 WR, *Norwich Castle* (1921) also reprints articles by him in the *Essex County Standard*, Dec. 1920, Jan. 1921.

19 WR, *Dr J. Horace Round...* (ut supra) p.5.

20 *EHR*, XXXVII, pp.1–34,

21 WR, *Dr J. Horace Round...* (ut supra) p.7.

22 P. G. Bales to WR, 31 Dec. 1921, 'It was a great pleasure for me to meet Norfolk's foremost historian and antiquarian... I shall look forward to the crushing of Dr JH Round': NRO, MS 4691/10. Percy Hulburd to WR, 7 Apr. 1922: 'I hope you have long ere now completed your "counter-offensive" against Dr Round': NRO, MS 4691/10. B. Cozens-Hardy to WR, 12 July 1922: 'You seem to have demolished him': NRO, MS 4691/3. J. F. Drake to WR 18 Aug. 1922, 'You have certainly disposed of Mr Horace Round: "wiped the floor with him" as the boys say': NRO, MS 4691/12.

23 G. R. Potter to WR, 12 Feb. 1926: 'I was up in London yesterday for the Royal Historical Society's meeting. I learn that J. Horace Round is still well enough to write enormously long letters to many people – though he has, I fancy, never ventured to answer your pamphlet.' NRO, MS 4691/1.

24 In 1924 he was in correspondence with G. Andrews Moriarty who tried unsuccessfully to persuade Walter to become a member of the New England Society, and who showed his Round pamphlet to the librarian of Harvard. See letters of 13 Mar. and 4 Apr.: NRO, MS 4691/3.

25 T. F. Tout to WR, 20 Dec. 1923: NRO, MS 4691/3.

26 William Page, (ed), *Family Origins and other studies by the late J. Horace Round* (1930). A posthumous collection prepared from notes left by Round on his death. See for example pp.43, 46.

27 14 July 1924: NRO, MS 4691/3.

TRACK 6: NORFOLK'S CHAMPION

1
DESCRIBING THE COUNTY

The great majority of Walter Rye's published works concerned his ancestral county of Norfolk and its constituent parishes and hundreds, their history, topography, archaeology and antiquities; the genealogies (putative and actual) of the principal families; the region's landscape including the Broads; its place names, dialect, folklore, songs and customs. To a greater extent than for any of his antiquarian predecessors, his research was firmly rooted in those archives we initially found him exploring in the BM and the PRO, in official and private muniments, in monumental inscriptions and archaeological remains.

Throughout his lengthy explorations of Norfolk on the ground he travelled notebook in hand and no experience was wasted. Sheaves of loose notes accumulated, on the history and topography of particular towns, villages and hamlets, as well as on the principal families and their ancestry. These frequently consisted of small scraps of paper which could later be shuffled and used (or re-used) for other projects.[1] When he finally settled down as a citizen of Norwich there was no one else alive who knew the county so well. But decades before that, in his *Tourists' Guide to Norfolk* (1879) and *History of Norfolk* (1885) he had already shown himself a master of his county.

First steps towards a history of Cromer (1870)
Having traced his ancestry to Cromer in the sixteenth century, Walter in his twenties spent his holidays trying to flesh out his family history while

collecting wider materials for the town's history, taking cliff walks to study the flora and fauna, and participating in the town's athletics meetings.

Amazingly, it turned out that the very first candidate for baptism entered in Cromer's earliest surviving register – sadly they began only in 1689 – was one of his own ancestors. He soon learnt that Cromer's church history was complex. The first church, of Shipden, had been lost to the sea in the Middle Ages. At very low tides fragments of architectural flint were still visible in the sands far out from the shore. The second building, prudently sited further inland in present day Cromer, had itself been pulled down and rebuilt on site. And the third (the existing) church had suffered many successive indignities. Its chancel was already in severe decay by 1681 when it was demolished, and the end walls of the nave and aisles were then built up to close the gap. Decay continued in the following century, and in 1767 permission was obtained to sell off the bells and a significant quantity of the lead from the collapsing aisle roofs to raise the money to repair the building, necessarily in a much plainer style. Further unsympathetic changes had been made in the 1840s, and twenty years later when Walter first arrived on the scene an appeal was in progress to restore something of the building's former glory. So his researches came at a propitious time.

He was horrified at the way in which Cromer's old buildings had been allowed to decay, one after another, and contrasted the self-sacrificing donations of past generations to build and maintain the church with the cheap-jack way in which it had been kept up in modern times. When he began his work the rubble from the collapsed chancel was still *in situ* beyond the east wall of the nave, and he was allowed to grovel about in it to learn what he could of the earlier fabric.

It was natural that he should be fired with enthusiasm for a more dignified restoration, and in 1870 he published *An Account of the Churches of St Peter of Shipden and of St Peter and Paul of Cromer in the County of Norfolk*. The proceeds, ('if any', as he cautiously put it on the title page) were to be put towards the church restoration fund. He explained that he was intending one day to write a more extended history of the town, of which this would form a part, so he encouraged readers to send in any corrections. The rector and a Mr Sandford supplied local knowledge. Sandford had collected in his own house and garden significant pieces of masonry, glass and fittings from earlier phases of building. In his introduction Walter also mentions that he had run at least some of his text past his friend John L'Estrange in Norwich.

This was Walter's first free-standing publication on Norfolk history. In style, content and format it became the prototype for many of his later writings. He personally put up the money for the printing, and persuaded Samuel Miller of Rampant Horse Street, Norwich to issue the work. Its general style reflected considerable self-assurance for a young, self-taught writer and antiquary – he was about twenty-three. Yet although the work undoubtedly had rough edges, to a large extent his self-confidence was justified, for it was already the case that nobody else alive had studied the Public Records for Norfolk to the same extent. His footnotes bear witness to the wide range of records as well as printed sources consulted. At times he would seek both to trumpet and to ring-fence his own labours in the records. For example, in the late fourteenth-century dispute over the succession to the rectorship of Cromer, which was referred to Rome for settlement, he noted:

> The whole proceedings are set forth at great length, and with most tedious prolixity, in a Bull of Pope Urban, dated the 6th of the Kal. of July, in the third year of his pontificate, which Bull I have copied at length, and I earnestly hope no one may ever have occasion to do so again.[2]

He allowed himself the writer's privilege of an occasional unsupported and risky flight of fancy, for example in positing on no hard evidence that Shipden had once been a populous and prosperous place.[3] But his trademark characteristic, here and for ever after, was to be his outspokenness with regard to individuals and institutions of whose actions or morals, for whatever reason, he disapproved. Here are some examples:

> On the 1681 demolitions: 'The work of demolition is said to have been completed by gunpowder (I sincerely wish the reverend gentleman had been seated on the mine at the time of its explosion).'

> On the 1767 dilapidations: 'The money so raised was religiously expended in the highest style of churchwardens' architecture, to the intent of rendering the church as wind- and water-tight, and as hideous as possible for the money.'

On the consequential restorations: '… in fact nearly everything [was] done that could possibly spoil what little was left of the architectural beauty of the church.'

On the further restoration in 1840: 'They pulled down the west gallery, and not only built it up again, which was bad enough, but erected two others along the aisles, which was worse.'

Whilst one reviewer suggested that 'purchasers… will not find their shilling ill laid out,' others took a more critical view. The architect and antiquary R. M. Phipson wrote to an unknown recipient on 19 October 1870 that to anyone really familiar with architecture and its nomenclature Walter's pamphlet simply did not pass muster. He used laymen's vocabulary (key beam, dummy or imitation window, jambs to the tower buttresses, and even a 'quatrefoil window elaborately traced' – whatever that was) to describe features for which there were perfectly good architectural terms. More seriously, he challenged Walter's grasp of the buildings' history:

He is, I should imagine… more (if I may use such a term) of a manuscript archaeologist than an architectural one, or he would never have made so serious a blunder as even to leave a doubt about Cromer church being built in 1337… for it is perfectly clear to anyone who knows anything about architecture that the church must have been erected 70 or 80 years later. Blomefield, no great authority on Church architecture, thinks it was commenced in 1393 (Vol 8 page 106). To suppose for a moment it was built in the height of the Decorated period is an absurdity. This is only one of several blunders I find in Mr Rye's description of the church…[4]

This criticism probably did not reach Walter's notice.

Cromer Past and Present (1889)

Although it means leaping ahead chronologically, it is sensible to continue for the moment the story of Walter's involvement in Cromer, before turning to other works on Norfolk. He went on to publish several articles on Cromer's history, but his long-term goal was a book covering the town as well as the church, and for that his public had to wait almost two decades. In the intervening period, not only had he been working full time in London and spending only parts of his Norfolk holidays in Cromer, but he had also lost valuable research time through illness, and been distracted by seeing other major publications into print. So his research on Cromer had been sporadic. When it finally emerged its full title showed a diffidence worthy of Blomefield: *Cromer Past and Present. An attempt to describe the parishes of Shipden and Cromer and to narrate their history.*

This is a much grander production than the earlier pamphlet, containing engravings based on his brother Frank's drawings. On the strength of Walter's recent success with the best-selling *Tourists' Guide and History of Norfolk* it was undertaken commercially by Jarrolds.[5]

Even in Walter's lifetime significant changes had come about in the town's economy:

> Of late years the trade of the town dwindled away to nothing, a little timber and coal being imported by beaching the ships and carting away their contents at low tide; but this is quite extinct now that the railways have been opened. The only real business the natives now do is to attend to those who visit it as a watering hole.[6]

Those railways had much to answer for:

> No doubt they are convenient to certain people, and since the coaches have ceased to run, even those who hate [them] have to use them. Some day perhaps, now that there is a revival of coaching, we old stagers [he was 46!] may once more have a chance of reaching Cromer by coach from Norwich. The Great Eastern station has one redeeming point: it certainly has the finest view from any station I have ever seen. The line ceases on the crest of a hill, and the station stands like a fort commanding the village and sea below.[7]

The reviewer in the *East Anglian* applauded Jarrolds for taking it on:

> We do not remember ever to have met with a more choice book of local topography than Mr Rye's *Cromer*, and certainly it is one of the

most complete and satisfactory histories of a Parish that we have ever seen or for the matter of that can hope to see... Neither expense nor pains have been spared in rendering this book worthy of Mr Rye's skilful and discriminating treatment.[8]

The *London Standard* of 4 April 1890 found it 'a very beautifully got up book which ought to find an honoured place on the shelves of every topographical collector...'

Tourists' Guide to Norfolk (1879)[9]

We should now step back in time to Walter's mid-thirties, when he came to compile his *Tourists' Guide to Norfolk*. Non-resident though he was, he had by then notched up sixteen summers of systematic touring around the county in pursuit of its history, antiquities and folk memories. He knew at first hand most of the possible means and routes for getting from A to B, and their relative merits or demerits. He had had many occasions to search out hostelries and watering-holes, as well as purveyors of provisions for sailing holidays, and had strong views on which were the best. He had amassed a great horde of notes on Norfolk stories, folklore and customs, and thoroughly researched the historical and archival background to the many communities he had visited. There was plenty of material here not only for a tourists' guide, but for much else besides.

The guide – which was published by Stanfords in a series of county guides at two shillings a volume, with a fold-out map of the county in the front – was a handy-sized book of 6½ x 4 inches, designed to be carried in the traveller's pocket for reference. In it Walter identified himself principally as the 'Editor of the *Norfolk Antiquarian Miscellany*'.

To meet the publisher's specifications for the series he had to exercise more self-restraint and discipline in his writing than he was used to in his subscription-based publications. In the preface he acknowledged not only that much had had to be omitted, but also, in all humility, that errors would inevitably have crept in. Certainly his coverage of cities and towns such as Norwich, Yarmouth and Lynn is very selective – this is no proto-Pevsner when it comes to the description of individual buildings, and many that he knew very well are not even mentioned. In the countryside there is passing reference to inns, but the emphasis is very largely on the churches, of which the county had, and has, a superabundance. No doubt the reason for giving them such prominence is that they were the buildings most likely to be open to tourists. Large country houses are sometimes described, but for those the expectation was that the visitor normally saw only the exterior and/or the park, although it is clear from his passing reference to pictures that Walter himself had seen many of the interiors. Sandringham, for example, had been acquired by the Prince of Wales in 1862, but 'as there is nothing inside more than any other gentleman's house it is to be hoped that the tourist will content himself by keeping outside them and not annoy the occupants by any morbid desire to see the rooms etc just because the Prince lives there.'

Ruins were a different matter. At Castle Acre Priory: 'The domestic buildings are perfect and well worth notice. Free access is given to the tourist by the owner, the Earl of Leicester, who, however, considerately requests visitors to protect the interests of his tenant.' At Walsingham: 'All the ruins are in the park, belonging to the Lee-Warner family, and may be inspected by visitors on Wednesdays.'

Walter (and the series editor) allowed himself to express that same degree of passion for the things he liked, and distaste for the things he loathed, that had already characterised his writings as a sports journalist. And if some of his opinions were deliberately provocative, that was calculated to add to the reader's entertainment. He sailed close to the wind by saying exactly what he thought, for example in condemning bad planning or poor taste in buildings and monuments. In Norwich he found the statue of Lord Nelson in the Upper Close 'not in best taste; in fact the execution is hardly more than decent'. The west front of the cathedral had 'been undergoing a tedious but hardly happy restoration'. In the south aisle of the nave was 'a somewhat tawdry illuminated monument to the Wodehouse family', and in the north aisle an 'extremely ugly stained glass window to the memory of the late Professor Smyth'. In St Luke's chapel, the tourist should 'avoid as much as possible a most atrociously ugly stone pulpit'...

Country villages and towns fell under the same critical eye. At Westwick: 'a hideous arch over the road is in the worst possible taste and should be destroyed'. Holkham House was 'one of the ugliest if most commodious in the three kingdoms'. At the site of the castle in Castle Acre, 'much of the effect... [had] been spoiled by the erection of a hideous red-brick Baptist Chapel right up against the castle ditch'. At Billingford 'a house appropriately called Bedlam has been built by some foolish person, on an old tumulus'.

He knew from his own personal tours where the most tedious stretches of road or of flat countryside lay, and where for other reasons boredom might set in for tourists, so he occasionally went so far as to advise them to stay away, or to stay as briefly as possible: 'I can hardly advise a wayfarer who is not an excellent pedestrian or a bicyclist to take the 12 miles of extremely level road which leads due south from Lynn.'

At Wells by the Sea: '... there are several good inns... being all comfortable enough; but the town itself is extremely sleepy and quiet, and a stay of any length would have a depressing effect on the traveller.'

Not for the first, or the last, time in his writings, there is a raw contradiction between on the one hand, his desire to share as widely as possible his insights into the county's topography and the natural and built heritage – the proper function of a tourist guide – and, on the other hand, his horror at the impact of mass travel and tourism on the very environment he wanted others to enjoy and to protect. It was a reaction commonly to be found in travel guides throughout the country in the closing decades of the nineteenth century. The railways in particular came in for criticism. Whilst they had made beauty spots like the Broads, coastal towns like Cromer and Hunstanton, and tracts of hitherto rather remote coastline and countryside accessible to tourists, sailors and wildfowlers, this had been at the expense of shattering the peace of whole communities and changing their character for ever. 'Excursionism', on land or water, was for Walter the very bane of civilisation. Hunstanton, for example, 'was once a pleasant watering-hole like Cromer, but has been to a great extent spoiled by the railway, which brings to it great crowds of excursionists from Northampton and elsewhere.'

Walter also used the Tourists' Guide to take swipes at some of his own pet hates, ranging from exaggeration and falsification in family pedigrees to local scams like that at Scoulton Mere, a prolific breeding site for black-headed gulls, where 'the eggs are collected, and being sold for plover's eggs, from which they cannot be distinguished, bring in a very handsome income to the owner.'

But by no means everything was rotten in his beloved Norfolk, and his enthusiasms feature as strongly as his aversions. We get glimpses of the finest architecture, of the county's natural beauty and the abundance of its wildlife. And once or twice we can sense how awestruck Walter is himself. Of Hickling Broad, for example, he says, 'the extreme abundance of all sorts of water-fowl and other birds, and of fish, can hardly be imagined by anyone who has not seen them.' Lynn is 'one of the cleanest [towns] I have ever seen and [the] police, I may remark en passant, are extremely civil and obliging.' More surprisingly, he writes enthusiastically even about local industries such as Colman's in Norwich and the herring processing works at Yarmouth, and to be able to describe them as he does he had clearly been given first-hand tours.

Public reception of the *Tourists' Guide*[11]

The little book sold well, and Stanfords' publicity blurb was soon able to include extracts from very favourable press reviews. 'Mr Rye is an excellent guide: he teems with reminiscences of all kinds...' (*The Times*). 'Capitally arranged excursions by road or rail...' (*The Graphic*). 'Mr Rye's Guide is really a charming little volume, cheap, very handy, very readable, and very complete. It is sure to command an enormous sale among excursionists on the Great Eastern Line.' The last remark must have caused Walter to shudder![12]

A History of Norfolk (1885)

The *Tourists' Guide* by no means exhausted Walter's notes on Norfolk, and when he was commissioned six years later to write a history of the county he found the perfect opportunity to deploy more of the same kind of material in a rather different context. It says much for his reputation that a volume by him was the one chosen to launch a new county-by-county series published commercially by Elliot Stock of London. This time the book ran to over 300 pages, so he was less constrained than in the *Tourists' Guide*. And although for this new project he recycled and supplemented work he had already undertaken on individual parishes and towns, he also incorporated hitherto unpublished research on original sources in the PRO and from his own manuscript collection.[13]

Apart from a few passing allusions to later history, it did not venture further forward than the mid-eighteenth century; and by today's standards the work is quirky and episodic in its coverage. But in its day it was a trail-blazer. Walter told a good story and lightened what might have been a dry historical or antiquarian account with tales and folklore. Writing to a deadline, he naturally had to draw on topics that had already engaged his attention, particularly those where there was an element of controversy to titillate the public imagination. He restated, for example, his contentious – but up to then not contradicted – theory that the undoubted Scandinavian origin of many Norfolk place and family names pointed to a Danish invasion and settlement in East Anglia *before the arrival of the Romans*. He spoke of the persecution of the Jews in medieval Norwich, the unreliability of the Elizabethan heralds, the forgery of a story that Oliver Cromwell was descended from the Scottish royal house – all matters on which he had already expressed himself in print elsewhere; and his section on town life drew heavily on his early work on the Guild Certificates.

But here and there, on his own terms, he also had fun at the expense of other people. Kett's rebellion, for example, gave him the excuse to attack two historians at once: 'Lingard, as of late Professor Rogers, has said that Kett's rebellion had a religious origin, the former so writing from religious bias, the latter from ignorance. If ever there was a rising for purely personal grievances, this was one.'[14] And the story of the Squire Papers concerning Cromwell's descent, which had been concocted according to Walter by an 'impudent local forger', gave him the opportunity for a poke at Carlyle ('that very-much-overrated-for-historical-accuracy writer') who, he said, had been 'fairly taken in'.[15] If renowned historians could not escape Walter's barbs, what chance did the man in the street stand?

As narrator and guide, he stands not just as an observer but already the citizen of Norwich he aspired to be, basking in a long, proud tradition.[16] More than half the book is really another amplified tourist guide. Its coverage, first inland and then along the coast, follows in turn each of the recently-established railway routes radiating out from Norwich, while making the occasional necessary detour to cover less accessible places. Generally this worked well for anyone disposed to follow in his tracks, but there is the surprising consequence that a few important places, like Wymondham and its abbey which were not accessible by rail are completely omitted. The inauspicious starting point for these excursions was what Walter described as the 'dirty, small and incommodious' Thorpe Station at Norwich, but happily a 'magnificent' new one was being built.

Among the inns he recommended to his readers were the Angel at North Walsham, the Black Boys at Aylsham, the Fishmongers' Arms at Cley (for travellers and wildfowl shooters), the Railway Arms at Wells ('the Globe is dearer and no better than it used to be'), the Crown at Fakenham, the Hill House at Happisburgh and the Ship at Mundesley. He had tried them all.

He is sharply attentive to landscape, including gardens:

> Gunton Park is celebrated for its head of game and its fine gardens. Pheasants tamer than most barn-door fowls are uninteresting birds, but the greenhouses and orchard houses, though nothing in themselves, are known all over England for the flowers and fruit got out of them by the ability of Mr Allan, who has in him no trace of the reticence and incivility of most Scotch gardeners.[17]

As this extract indicates, Walter could occasionally be really enthusiastic about a place (or a person). In similar vein, Weybourne had the best anchorage along the coast; Castle Acre was 'one of the most interesting places in the county'; Scarning had 'the best preacher in the county' (his friend Augustus Jessopp); Happisburgh was good for bathing (though there was only one bathing machine available). The plaudits were sometimes spoiled by a caveat. The Happisburgh entry continues:

> There are however certain objections to the place, which should be stated by an honest chronicler. There is only one little general shop; no meat is to be bought except at arbitrary and erratic intervals; the seven miles that divide the place from North Walsham, where are the nearest railway station and doctor's are over the vilest roads that I have ever had the hap to come across, chiefly consisting of sea beach; no newspaper or book has ever been seen in the village; everyone is expected to be in bed at nine; and dullness reigns supreme over the district. I may conscientiously recommend the place to absconding city accountants, for no one would ever dream of looking here for anybody![18]

Cley perhaps got off lightly by being described merely as a 'dead-alive sort of place'. But as for Yarmouth, it was:

> ... nothing more or less than a big Margate, and... rapidly becoming

the Londoner's paradise... Once at Yarmouth they stop there, as close to the beach as they can; and I don't think I have ever seen half-a-dozen excursionists exploring the country more inland than half a dozen miles... If there is anything more unpleasant to me than Yarmouth, it is the first three miles of road out of it, which runs as straight as a die alongside – but out of sight of – the sea; for a more dusty and uninteresting walk I defy anybody to find in the county.[19]

Public reception of the *History of Norfolk*

The book was very widely reviewed in the press, and those bold enough to take issue with the author were in a small minority. One of them felt that more might have been said about folklore, and about the Marshland churches.[20] Another reasonably objected that the churches with which Walter pointedly thought the county was over-stocked were actually the pride of their respective communities. His view that there was no enmity in the Middle Ages between regular and secular clergy was challenged. For just a few his style grated: 'The latter part of the book, which treats of the watering places and "Broads" is very pleasant reading, [but] perhaps a trifle too 'chatty' even for a *popular* county history.'[21]

Then there was the unkind reviewer who in the light of comments above might have been reading another book: 'His practical good sense makes him describe accurately the best way of visiting this interesting district, but to him a primrose on the river's bank a primrose is, and nothing else.'[22]

More typically, reviewers both in the region and nationally loved the book for its breadth of knowledge and anecdote, its humour and outspokenness. The *Ipswich Journal* of 28 November 1885 noted that it had met with a 'deservedly hearty reception at the hands of the public'. Other comments included that there was a 'vigour and freshness about the whole volume'; that it was a mine of useful facts and theories for interpreting the history of the county; that Elliot Stock were to be congratulated on such a fine start to the series, a 'model in its class' which could 'not have been put into better hands'. It would make local history accessible to a much wider readership: 'He writes brightly, convincingly and well, and he illustrates his subjects delightfully, if rather fantastically from all sorts of out of the way sources.'[23]

The last word should go to the reviewer in the *London Daily News* of 14 December 1885: 'There is a certain humorous sincerity in Mr Rye's writing which inspires confidence and makes him infinitely preferable as a guide to the word-painting fraternity of holiday journalists.'

*

Walter's views on many places in Norfolk are to be found not only in the tourists' guide and history but also seeded throughout his *Autobiography* and a number of his other writings. He continued to compile historical and topographical information right to the end of his life, but the results became more fragmentary with time.

Monographs of Norwich Hamlets (1917–19)

This wartime series of pamphlets covered the five hamlets of Eaton, Earlham, Hellesdon, Heigham and Catton. On the covers, Walter advertised his work in progress on other hamlets, but the very slight take-up of these publications brought the series to a premature end. He prefaced the first with a kind of apologia:

> During the stress of this war time it is difficult for an old man who has been unable to find any useful work to do in connection with the war, and this must be my excuse for filling up enforced leisure by compiling the following pages. At least the printing of them affords some employment for local people.

They were, he admitted, partial and bitty sketches compiled jackdaw-like from material he happened to have to hand on printed and manuscript sources, newspapers and personal observations. For all their imperfections, they were issued in the (probably too optimistic) hope that a younger generation of scholars would use them as a quarry for more detailed work of their own, and that subscribers would alert him to errors and additional material. He issued the usual disclaimers, for example about not being an architectural historian,[24] but for all their faults he had nevertheless taken some pains over them, for example by consulting local antiquaries in each place, by including parish maps, and occasionally by giving a full transcript of an interesting document. Although each pamphlet was separately issued, their through-pagination looked to a future index that never came.

Some Historical Essays chiefly relating to Norfolk (Rye's Norfolk Essays) (1925–1928)

As Walter says himself, this late series of booklets was mostly assembled in order to clear his desk of unpublished material before he died. Again, he repeatedly says he is no expert but merely an indexer anxious to pass on to posterity such fragments as he has gathered while reading works on Norfolk history and topography.

The essays were published as individual pamphlets in 'Parts', through-paginated (463 pages in all) to assist ultimate indexing of the series, although at the end of the day only a general index of subjects was compiled. Walter concludes with a lament:

> I had intended to complete this part with a paper on the possible connection of Sir Francis Drake with Norfolk, but must defer this for the present at all events owing to my illness, and the same reason prevents my compiling an index of names to this series.[25]

Folklore

Story-telling and singing were familiar pastimes to Walter from his sporting soirées, and he himself wrote satirical pieces and nonsense verse purely to entertain on such occasions. Some of this material was preserved for the private amusement of friends and family in *Rubbish and Nonsense* (1887), whilst some was eventually given a more public airing in his *Recreations of a Norfolk Antiquary* (1920).[26]

On a different level, country tales and songs also served to while away long, dark winter evenings, though these also embedded folk traditions (or superstitions, as the case might be) with didactic or admonitory messages. Walter, the self-professed 'collector of words', gathered these too as he went around the county. Many of his findings on what we might broadly call 'folklore' appeared piecemeal to spice up one publication after another. Examples are seeded in the *History of Norfolk*; others were communicated through the *Norfolk Antiquarian Miscellany* and the *East Anglian*. A long essay, with a correspondingly long title, on 'The prophecies, traditions, superstitions, folklore, sayings and rhymes of Norfolk' appeared in the first volume of *NAM* (1877).[27] Here Walter admitted that much of what he had gathered was no more than gossip and tittle-tattle, and that many local rhymes were not particularly amusing. But he highlighted certain phrases he believed he had set down in writing for the first time, such as:

- the kettle calls the pot black face;
- at fifty years of age a man is either a fule or a doctor;
- he lies like a tooth drawer;
- a man who has had four wives is said to have shod the horse all round.[28]

Strange lights and luminous owls

Some of the anecdotes Walter collected, and the conclusions that could be drawn from them, are still occasionally recounted today, especially where they have an eerie or even a supernatural element. He had heard that certain marshmen, seeing strange lights, had come to believe in a Lantern Man who enticed people to death in the muddy water, and as he reported in his *History of Norfolk* he too had witnessed a mysterious light in the fields at Runton, near Cromer:

It is said to issue from a hedgerow, cross a field, and disappear in a fir-spinney. Many credible people have seen it, and a superstitious glamour is cast over the matter by a statement that it goes into the ground just where some human bones were once found.

Such stories, especially given the suggested link with bones, readily reinforced folk belief in supernatural phenomena, although Walter did his best to find rational explanations:

I believe myself that it may be the reflection of Cromer revolving light, cast on a bank of fog or vapour, which may appear under certain atmospheric conditions. But this theory, and that of 'Will-o'-the-wisps', is [discounted], because the ground is high and dry, and well drained.[29]

The boundary between fantasy and reality was not always easy to draw. In 1907–8 a large number of respectable observers reported seeing lights moving at night across the countryside. Walter himself was among them, and first described his experience in *The Field*, but without giving sufficient evidence to convince the public that this was not a hoax. Ornithologists including the renowned J. H. Gurney were convinced, 'but not,' said Walter, 'the little yapping persons who disbelieve anything they have not seen themselves'. Eventually the luminescence was attributed to barn owls, and was found to have been attested in several other parts of the country. A great deal was written about it in the press during 1908, and reports even reached the *New York Times*. Walter contributed as vigorously as ever, citing date, time and observer for sightings, beginning with himself and his son, returning to Foulsham on 3 February 1907. A practical joker attempted to discredit the reports by posing in the dark with a bicycle lamp and a pole, but was caught and exposed. The lights continued. [30]

Songs, stories, sayings and ghosts

More folk material was brought together in *Songs, Stories and Sayings of Norfolk* (Goose, 1897). Designed primarily to amuse, and presented in a humorous rather than a malicious spirit, this is a rambling but delightful compilation. Walter succeeds in capturing the spirit of the county whilst ranging widely through its history, folklore, food and recreations, dialect, crime and ghost stories.

Chapter 1, on Ballads, Songs and Rhymes, is a compilation of material from many sources including earlier published work, with some additional matter from his own collection of manuscripts, among them a satirical ballad on freemasonry (1721). A selection of epitaphs is included, with a note that more are to be found in his *History of Norfolk* and his *Fifty Norfolk MSS*. Chapter 2, on Dialect and Humorous Sayings, usefully documents a few dialect words, but is mostly light-hearted, humorous stuff. He refers to the 'good old sing-song way' in which true Norfolk people speak, and how it cannot be drummed out of them even with a good education, but yet is being slowly lost. He features dialect words and points to sections of his new edition of Forby's Glossary, 'which I may as well reproduce here, as it is a work chiefly for students and not intended for popular use'.

Chapter 5 covers Ghosts and Gruesome Stories. Walter suspected having encountered one or two real ghosts, or at least unexplained phenomena,[31] but he had also very plausibly debunked what he regarded as the best ghost story he had ever heard, Augustus Jessopp's famous tale of the ghost at Mannington,[32] which is worth a short detour here.

In the *Athenaeum* of 10 January 1880, Jessopp published 'An antiquary's ghost story', his graphic account of a ghostly presence he had experienced the year before while undertaking research late one night among the rare books in the library at Mannington Hall as the guest of Lord Orford. With nobody else still up and about in the house, Jessopp had suddenly found himself in the company of the ethereal figure of a man in historic clerical garb.[33] Now Jessopp was no practical joker, and we can take it on trust that he genuinely believed his experience. His standing as a cleric, teacher and writer was sufficient to give it wide credence, and for a while it became a *cause célèbre*. He would later point out that it was the editor's, not his own, decision to head the piece 'An antiquary's ghost story', and that he himself did not go so far as to describe the apparition as a 'ghost' – although it is hard to see what other interpretation could be placed upon it. A predictably vigorous response filled the *Athenaeum*'s correspondence columns, and Walter was not to be left out. He suggested that the most likely explanation was that his good friend Jessopp had nodded off and had a sort of daydream. For had he not written *One Generation of a Norfolk House* about Henry Walpole who in the sixteenth century had come under the influence of Fr Parsons, the leader of the Jesuit Mission in England? So he was doubtless calling to mind a portrait of Parsons in clerical garb. Not to be outdone, Walter recalled having had a similar experience himself whilst studying the Isham family papers at Lamport Hall.

> The fact common to both our experiences, that we were not at all afraid of our visitant, seems to strongly bear this out, for if, when undoubtedly wide awake, we were to meet a conventional white-robed ghost in a dark lane we should, I do not doubt, be abjectly afraid of it. But there is great virtue in the 'if'. The first disappearance of the 'spectre', as it were with a jerk at a movement of the seer's arm, and its equally jerky disappearance at the fall of a book, remind one much of incidents happening during those short sweet snatches of sleep not unusually stolen during dull sermons, snatches which cannot last more than a second or two.[34]

And so, back to Walter's *Songs, Stories and Sayings*. When it came to ghost stories circulating more widely in the countryside he was profoundly sceptical, preferring to find purely rational explanations, although he would have been the first to admit their spine-chilling entertainment value. His old skipper on the Broads, Tungate, filled many an evening with these anecdotes,[35] which caused Walter to reflect: '[I can easily believe] that the appalling loneliness of the marshes at night tends to make men nervous and superstitious. The boom of a bittern must have been very eerie to hear if one were six miles from a village.'[36]

As for the Grey Lady of Raynham, 'Never was there one with less foundation'.[37] The story 'was told me by one of the card players one windy night at the now defunct Chequers at Brandon, with a wealth of detail which made me most loth to leave the company and go down the damp corridor to a solitary bed room.'

One strand of his research, however, proved too emotionally charged to print: 'I had intended to give a list of some of the worst accidents in our local history… but I grew so sick of the sad tales that I burnt my notes.'[38]

Songs, Stories and Sayings of Norfolk (without the gruesome bits) was well received:

> It is not often [wrote the reviewer in the *Genealogist*] that when we have finished a book we could wish that it were twice its size, but Mr Walter Rye knows Norfolk so well, writes so pleasantly, and tells so many good stories, that we cannot help regretting that the little volume before us is not of greater proportions. Mr Rye has the courage of his opinions, and sometimes states his views in a manner which leads us to think that an unconquerable sense of humour has prompted his remarks.[39]

A cautionary note on place names

The study of place names was in its infancy in Walter's day. And although he became aware of their importance – and eccentricity – whilst indexing the place names of East Anglia that he found as he edited the Feet of Fines for Norfolk, Suffolk and Cambridgeshire, he was no expert in this field, and had very little to go on except intuition. By what now seems the too simple expedient of searching maps of Denmark and Sweden for names identical, or similar-sounding, to those in England, he came to suspect a Danish settlement in East Anglia even before the Roman occupation of Britain.

His theories were first set out in his prefaces to the respective Feet of Fines volumes, in an article in *NAM* I, and in the *History of Norfolk*. It was a valiant effort, and at least it can be said that later scholars found his indexes a useful trawling-ground for these names. But as the discipline of place-name studies has developed, his hunches, both as to chronology and often as to ethnicity, have largely been overtaken and he is not cited as an authority these days. In particular, some names he supposed to be Scandinavian have been shown to be of Anglo-Saxon origin. In the first of his *Norfolk Handlists* (1916) Walter included another article on 'Scandinavian names in Norfolk. Hundred courts & mote hills in Norfolk'. A wisely cautious reviewer in the *EHR* suggested that the list would be helpful to a student who had Bjorkman's *Nordische Personennamen in England* and Linkvist's *Middle English Place-names of Scandinavian origin* to hand, but warned the unwary reader not to come to Walter's work without such guidance.

However, whilst many of his own guesses were later proved to be wrong, Walter was sometimes right in his critique of other people's guesses. Over the name Heigham, for example, he noted that:

> ... the Rev G Munford's derivation of the name may be dismissed as quite ridiculous, for he takes it to come from the Anglo-Saxon 'heag' or 'high', whereas the situation is one of the lowest and most flooded in the county, and as the same remark applies to Potter Heigham, one is led to the conclusion that in both cases it must mean something totally different.

Endnotes

1   Volume I of *NAM* uses some of his notes on monumental inscriptions in articles and in his sundry parish histories. His *Tourists' Guide* and *Songs, Stories* etc. are full of anecdotal material rearranged from casually acquired notes.
2   p.9.
3   p.15n; by 1889 (see below) the 'city' had been changed to the 'port'.
4   NRO, PD 523/53.
5   It appeared in two versions, one of seventy-five copies in large imperial quarto and the other of 500 copies in royal quarto.
6   p.78.
7   p.147.
8   *EA*, II, pp.195–6.
9   Several subsequent editions were produced.

10 P. H. Emerson was another contemporary writer who lamented the risks to the existing ways of life from the growth of modern housing and the tourist trade, *Pictures of East Anglian Life* (1888), 80–81.

11 Among local reviews, see for example, the *Ipswich Journal* of 16 Aug. 1879.

12 *The Examiner* of 19 July 1879 was enthusiastic over its recommendation of places to stay, and found his reports of ghost stories pleasing, though perhaps not comprehensive.

13 Writing on the monks and friars, for example, he speaks of 'the materials before me' as: detached rolls of the Abbey of St Benet's at Holme, various dates, 1359–1509; the Bursar's account of Hempton Priory, 1500–01; the account of the Keeper of Norwich's cell at Yarmouth, 1484–85; and the Cellarer's account of Creak Abbey, 1331–2; describing these as 'a fairly representative series for nearly 200 years of the busiest time of monasticism'. (p.164)

14 p.58.

15 p.87.

16 'The "Queen's General" came down to Norwich to judge how we were getting on.' (p.82)

17 WR *History of Norfolk*, p.225. At Paston he admired not just the roses, but very specifically the 'Gloire de Dijon' roses (p.245); and he made special note of Petre's landscape gardening at Westwick and Coke's work at Holkham (p.253).

18 p.245.

19 p.242.

20 *The Graphic*, 14 Nov. 1885.

21 *EA* as cited in the text above.

22 *Morning Post*, 23 Dec. 1885.

23 *Notes and Queries*. series 6, XII (1885), p.439.

24 WR: Rye's *Monographs of Norwich Hamlets*, III, p.133.

25 Preface to WR, *Some Historical Essays chiefly relating to Norfolk*, Part VI.

26 *Recreations*, as well as revisiting a number of Walter's pet historical theories, was an *omnium gatherum* of anecdotes and popular legends that he had demolished before (for example, that nuns were bricked up alive as a punishment, or that there were tunnels from monasteries to adjacent nunneries or castles to facilitate illicit relationships). His own excavations had tended to prove that these 'tunnels' were usually no more than practical outlets such as sewers, short-cuts to the outside world, and not the romantic places of legend. More ghost stories and ballads were added for good measure, along with rhymes and nonsense.

27 pp.285–311.

28 *NAM* I, pp.308–9.

29 WR, *History*, p.290. For a recent take on this see the website http://griffmonster-walks.blogspot.co.uk/2014/10/folklore-trail-around-east-runton.html.

30 NRO, MS 4691/84/3 contains lengthy related press-cuttings. On the wider

background of luminosity in barn owls, including several references to the Norfolk sightings in 1908, see http://www.owlpages.com/articles.php?section=Studies+and+Papers&title=Min+Min

31 E.g. WR, *Rubbish and Nonsense*, pp.19–22: Prophecies and ghost stories related.

32 *Ibid.*, p.21.

33 Reprinted in his *Frivola* (1896) and electronically by gothictexts.wordpress.com

34 Frank Meeres, *Paranormal Norfolk* (Stroud, 2010), p.28 notes the story but not the press coverage and Walter's debunking of it. For a typical syndicated press report see *Freeman's Journal*, 28 Jan. 1880.

35 WR, *Songs, Stories and Sayings*, pp.64, 144ff.

36 *Ibid.*, p.66.

37 *Ibid.*, p.61.

38 *Ibid.*, p.68.

39 *The Genealogist*, ns, XIV, p.139.

40 For example he suggested a common root between Knapton and Knappen in Denmark, which scholars now accept as coming from an Old English personal name, Cnapa. Pulham (Polhohmen) and Tidsel (Tivetsnall) he also thought to be Scandinavian, but these too are now thought to be Anglo-Saxon… and so on. See the publications of the English Place Names Society.

41 *Rye's Monographs of Norwich Hamlets*, V (1919), p.173. It is now thought to be derived from hecg (hedge) or haecc (gate/floodgate/grating to catch fish at a weir).

2
THE VICTORIA COUNTY HISTORY

On the face of it there was much to recommend Walter Rye as county editor for the Victoria County History's volumes on Norfolk. A published historian of the county, he was an expert and prolific writer on Norfolk topography and local and family history and had an established reputation in the county. On the other hand, up to this point he had worked largely as an independent scholar, answerable (in his own view at any rate) to no one for his opinions. He had published much of his work privately without peer review or critique in advance. Was this really the kind of man to submit meekly to working under the direction of a general editor, and in accordance with a formula worked out for the whole country?

The general editor, Arthur Doubleday, called on him on 25 June 1899 to discuss the proposed Norfolk volumes of the history and the kind of contribution Walter might make to it. *Of course* he was interested! He was actively contemplating retirement to Norwich, so a definite research project based there was an attractive proposition. But he had serious reservations about Doubleday's initial proposal that the whole of Norfolk, like most other counties, should be treated in just four volumes. Walter wrote to G. L. Gomme a few days later saying, with some justification, that he could not possibly do justice to Norfolk in so short a span:

> I think that whoever allotted the volumes must have forgotten the fact that Norfolk has considerably the greatest number of churches and parishes of any county (York not even excepted) and had no

less than 123 religious houses, all of which, of course, will have to be noted in detail.[1]

Coming as it did from a man unused to laying aside any scrap of evidence collected in the course of his work, this did not bode at all well for the project. Walter must have aired the same reservations when he met Doubleday, J. H. Round and O. Barron at the Bath Club on 11 July to take matters further.[2] Still, they do seem to have started talking about contracts, terms of remuneration, and the sort of assistance Walter might need in preparing the Norfolk volumes, and after some legalistic nit-picking on Walter's part, a form of agreement was drafted by the autumn. But then another obstacle appeared. The proposed terms were that Walter, like other editors, should be remunerated only for material finally accepted for publication. Walter had of course issued many publications at his own expense *pro bono publico*, not expecting to make any serious income from them. But when he undertook to work under a contract for someone else, as in his legal work, he was used to being paid *pro rata* for work done and time spent. As if that were not enough of an issue, there was in the draft agreement the assumption that some of the text he submitted might not be selected for eventual publication. This part of the History's regular *modus operandi* came as quite a shock to other editors as well as Walter. And he was worried not only on his own account but on that of the man he had approached to be his assistant in Norfolk, James Hooper. As Walter reflected on these misgivings he once again became jaundiced about his involvement in the project and wrote to Doubleday:

> The more I look at the whole scheme the less I think it is likely to succeed *throughout as a series*, and I do not care to undertake any part of it unless the remuneration, which is none too high, is made absolutely safe. You may never reach Norfolk in print.

So for a time wounded professional pride put a brake on the negotiations. In any volume for which Walter was to be editor he was simply not going to have foisted on him contributors he did not already know.[3] He disliked Doubleday's generally successful strategy of having single experts tackling (for example) place names across the whole VCH when he himself had made the place names of Norfolk his special study for thirty years.[4] And whilst he would not dream of altering drafts from established experts such as Round, he reserved the right to 'differ with the smaller fry'. As for Stevenson who had publicly attacked Walter's *Index to Norfolk Topography* as 'valueless': 'If he writes a line for the History of Norfolk I will have nothing to do with it.'[5]

In the end, Doubleday came up with a compromise. He himself would act as editor for the two *general* volumes for Norfolk, and thus bear responsibility for decisions as to what was included and what omitted. Walter would still have some editorial input to the general volumes, but in particular would serve as the local (and expert) editor for the proposed topographical volumes for the county.[6]

On that basis a fragile agreement was finally signed in June 1900. Hooper wrote to Walter, 'I am glad to know that the Victoria History of Norfolk is not likely to be a fiasco after all.'[7] But fundamental disagreements continued to simmer. Walter intended to reserve to himself any writing on Norfolk pedigrees, and threatened to withdraw completely if this were not conceded. This again led him to dredge up all his original misgivings: 'Seriously speaking,' he wrote to Doubleday, 'have you any chance of carrying through your gigantic programme?' With hindsight we can see how prophetic those words were.[8]

In spite of all, by the autumn of 1900 he had settled down to do some actual drafting on the topographical volumes, although he was finding frustrating the constraint of reining back his normally expansive style.[9] In November he submitted two draft parish histories, not for approval but merely to be printed out so that he could estimate the space they would take up.[10]

Unfortunately, the VCH correspondence for 1901 is wanting, but when it resumes early in 1902[11] we find Walter submitting copy about the Norfolk coastline, and incidentally recommending his son James for work should the VCH require assistance. By now it was the penurious Hooper who was becoming disgruntled. Having been persuaded by Walter to research and write certain sections of the history, and having duly submitted a section (which was never published) on fisheries, he had asked Doubleday for his remuneration, but received no reply: 'Writing to Mr Doubleday seems very like knocking at the door of an empty house!' he wrote to Walter, requesting him to intervene on his behalf because 'I am, in a sense, sailing under your pilotage.'[12]

Friction with Doubleday and with other contributors continued. In essence, Walter could not bear to play second fiddle. He hated having his drafts amended, and whilst he wanted to see *his* name – and preferably only his name – on the title page, he could not stomach amendments which significantly altered the sense or scope of his drafts. Doubleday further delayed matters by proposing new material for inclusion.

Then suddenly another spanner was thrown in the works. In July 1902 Walter's eyesight took a turn for the worse and he genuinely feared he would be unable to complete the VCH work at all unless he did it quickly.[13] When the situation had not improved by February the following year, Doubleday paid a typist to have some of Walter's notes typed up in order to spare his eyes.[14]

By this time Round had duly submitted to Walter his drafts (never published within the scope of VCH) on the feudal baronies. Walter respected Round's scholarship but, ironically, found himself having to argue over the length and detail of Round's contributions in just the same way as Doubleday had argued with Walter himself; and he elicited precisely the same kind of reaction. Walter, somewhat two-facedly, complained to Doubleday:

[Round] won't be satisfied with anything but the most minute analysis of original matter. He bullies me like a schoolmaster when I ask him humbly for information or venture to disagree with him, but that I don't mind as I have no doubt it is all deserved. He is an able man and no mistake about it, but I hope to prove he isn't absolutely infallible.[15]

In the light of the later strained, even poisonous, relationship between Round and Rye, this last point is portentous!

Walter and Hooper pressed on with their work, but relations with the centre did not improve. On 24 January 1904 Hooper wrote to Walter:

I am greatly disappointed with the Victoria History people, though I was, and am, much obliged to you for annexing me as a contributor. No doubt you have had enough power in your elbow to get your bulk of matter passed and paid for, but I wrote Doubleday over three months ago stating that I had an awkward mass of accumulations which I wanted to reduce and proposing to get the *Norfolk biographies* typed and sent in, but he has not even replied. I was, and am, rather cornered for want of £20, and thought to get at least that for work to be sent in. I presume there is no doubt that they will take and pay for these biographies, so could you take them when ready and advance me, say £15 on them, till the VH people are ready?[16]

At this point there is another unfortunate gap in the VCH correspondence, but by February 1904 troubles over Walter's drafts and the scale of the whole enterprise were causing delays at the centre. Moreover, Walter's eye condition, now diagnosed as glaucoma, was worsening. The fact that letters asking the reasons for the delay in publication repeatedly went unanswered by Doubleday cannot have helped his blood pressure either, and he quit the VCH, ostensibly on health grounds.[17] He returned a substantial quantity of notes and drafts to Doubleday labelled, with a fastidiousness typical of the man: 'These MSS are the property of the Victoria County History Syndicate, which has paid me for their compilation. WR'.[18] At the end of the year, he wrote privately to Round: 'I know nothing of Doubleday or the History, so suppose there is some hitch somewhere. Luckily, I have done the General History, Coastline and Feudal Baronage, so the topography can well be left to someone else.'[19]

The general editor, as it turned out, had other ideas, and Walter's edited drafts for those sections were never published. He firmly believed that his glaucoma would prevent his ever returning to active work on original records. In January 1905 he wrote to William Page, a successful record agent who had joined VCH in 1902 and had now succeeded Doubleday as general editor: 'Having regard to my probable total incapacity to work, I am arranging to give all my MS and Printed Collection for the County to the Norwich Corporation, but it will take some time before an arrangement as to a room to hold them can be made.'[20]

Page enquired whether manuscripts from Walter's own collection might perhaps be sent on loan to London to be consulted by those working on the VCH. His reply, although bearing the absentminded salutation 'Dear Mr Hardy' (Page's business partner as a record agent), was as true as it was predictable: 'There is hardly a day on which someone does not come here to refer to them.'[21] But he generously offered to have anything that was specifically needed for reference copied and sent to London at his own expense. He suggested that Page might find his notes on Feudal Aids useful if typed up: 'I can still do all this sort of work, but all record work on original MSS is I fear closed to me, though with the help of dictating and typewriting I am still able to do a good deal, and am working on some old material I have done.'[22]

He had no doubt, as regards the Feudal Baronage, that Round would 'point out many things which he will want explained'. Round, however, was seriously ill and indeed this may well have been one of the unspoken reasons for the delay in publishing VCH Norfolk.[23] Hooper, when sending Walter comments on his account of Coke of Holkham, was pressing him: 'Can you not throw any light on the standstill of the Victoria History of Norfolk.' [24]

With Walter now definitively *hors de combat*, first Doubleday (who left the VCH in 1904) and then more particularly Page had been going through his drafts with a fine-tooth comb, cutting and editing them almost beyond recognition. When Walter finally received the proofs for the section on Political History that he thought he had already sufficiently edited (but which, again, was never published), he exploded: 'The alterations and omissions from my original copy are so extensive that I cannot agree to its being printed under my name.'[25]

VCH must consider how much of the work he had been paid to produce was going to be thrown away. 'I strongly object to scraps of it being used, mixed up with other men's work.' He would willingly correct anything that was patently wrong, but the excisions were another matter, and removed much that would make the history of interest to local readers.

There was then a stand-off. Walter bought time by going off on a cycling holiday, but returned with his mind unchanged.[26] By February 1906 the argument was still raging and he was promising to take Page and the VCH to task in the local press in Norfolk, which he would have been well placed to do, though at this stage it was no more than a threat.[27] Page replied, 'I deprecate a newspaper correspondence but I don't think it would do the History any harm'. Instead he proposed that it should be explained that the section had been compiled from information supplied by Walter Rye, a solution which Walter eventually accepted placidly only two days later.[29]

When VCH *Norfolk* volume II finally appeared in 1906, its preface explained that 'failing eyesight and other causes' had led Walter Rye to retire as editor and to hand over all his material to Page, and:

In consequence of certain alterations necessitated in the scheme of the article on the Political History of the county prepared by Mr Rye, which for the same reasons had to be made by other hands, Mr Rye thought it would be better that the article should not be wholly attributed to him.[30]

Endnotes

1   University of London Institute of Historical Research, VCH Archives: A56 Rye, 7 July 1899. This section draws on the generous advice of Professor John Beckett, formerly general editor of the VCH.
2   *Autobiog.*, p.108. John Beckett points out that this meeting was probably to discuss the two general volumes for Norfolk rather than the topographical ones.
3   5 Feb. 1900.
4   2 Mar. 1900.
5   *Ibid.*
6   29 May 1900.
7   NRO, MS 4961/7.
8   15 Aug. 1900.
9   11 Oct. 1900.
10 7 Nov. 1900.
11 1 Jan. 1902.
12 Hooper to WR, 20 Feb. 1902: NRO, MS 4961/7. It was Doubleday's normal practice to pay only upon publication, to protect the financial viability of the whole enterprise.
13 21 Jul. 1902.
14 10 Feb. 1903.
15 *Ibid.*
16 NRO, MS 4961/7
17 'I have an idea I might go off suddenly one day', 27 Feb. 1904.
18 Ibid.
19 2 Dec. 1904.
20 25 Jan. 1905.
21 1 Feb. 1905.
22 *Ibid.*
23 8 Mar. 1905.
24 Hooper to WR, 26 Apr. 1905: NRO, MS 4961/7. VCH has sent comments on which he would value a discussion with WR.
25 2 Jun. 1905.
26 20 Sep. 1905.
27 29 Feb. 1906.
28 1 Mar. 1906.
29 3 Mar. 1906.
30 VCH *Norfolk*, II, p.xv; [n.d.] Statement of account for WR's work done for

VCH. Payment seems to be at the rate of ten shillings per page. E.g. Feudal History, 50pp, 'Has been done a long while but has been waiting till Mr JH Round could attend to it. This I am particularly anxious to see through the press myself and hope to do so with help at home.' Statement includes 'Cheap labour at 6d an hour for indexing references from Patent and Close Rolls.' NRO, MC 1632/1. The NRO Catalogue also records among the Kenneth Allen Papers (MC 106/11, 560X6) proofs of an article by WR on Norfolk maritime history, submitted to VCH but never published.

3
SERIOUS FUN: CLUBS, LECTURES AND VISITS

Norwich clubs [See plate VII]

Long before Walter's permanent move to Norwich he had become well known and respected in the city, and made many friends there. He had long been a member of the Norfolk and Norwich Archaeological Society, but after the move he was better able to participate in more of the local clubs and societies, and became not just a member but a regular lecturer – one could even say an entertainer – at gatherings of (among others) the Woodpeckers Art Club and the Norwich Science Gossip Club. He also went on their club outings, for which he sometimes put on a lunch or tea at Lammas, as he did for the Norwich Photographic Society, the Prehistory Society and the NNAS itself.

Once Walter had devised a talk for a particular occasion, and found or commissioned lantern slides to accompany it, he would recycle his material as necessary when invited to speak elsewhere. His friend and regular collaborator over many years, Harry Brittain, should take most of the credit for preparing and presenting the slides.

Although Walter was fluent and confident as a writer, when it came to public speaking he confessed to being nervous and disorganised, so had to prepare his talks meticulously. Yet he cannot have come over as a bag of nerves because he quickly won an enthusiastic following. What was the attraction? As in his writings he had a waspish and devastating way with words about the people, places and things that irritated him, a puckish and infectious sense of humour, and a love of practical jokes. He also knew the importance of really *playing* an audience, leaving them asking for more, and he worked on the principle that even if people violently disagreed with him – as he probably hoped and expected they would – they would find it worth hearing him out for the sake of the ensuing debate and conversation. He knew from long experience that in many public gatherings speakers tended to hold the floor for too long. So after some trial and error he made it a rule never to take more than an hour on a lecture, and if possible never to speak for more than ten minutes at a time without showing a lantern slide or interpolating a joke or anecdote to keep the audience engaged and awake. He often attracted large audiences,[1] which presented the organisers with a number of challenges, from hiring a lantern slide projector[2] or even a piano,[3] to providing enough seats.

The scripts of just a few of his lectures survive among his papers. Some were published in his series of *Recreations*,[4] and there is mention of many more in the *Autobiography*. Central, of course, to his themes was the history of Norwich and Norfolk, but he also shared his passions for sport and sailing (Athletic Exaggerations; Byegone Sport and Modern Athletics; Unspoiled Waters of the Ant). There was frequently an element of social commentary (The Increase of Insanity; Taste and Want of Taste), although sometimes the emphasis was more on entertainment (Ballads; Folklore and Ghost Stories; Names and Nicknames), and sometimes a more sombre theme crept in (Aerial Navigation; War and the Weapons of War).

The Quatuor Coronati Lodge visit, 1902[5]

To illustrate what it was like to be led on an expedition by Walter, as several of the above clubs were, we can do no better than consider the well documented visit to Norwich of the Quatuor Coronati masonic lodge from London in 1902.

H. L. Clarke, (manager of the Maid's Head), was a Norwich freemason, which Walter was not. When the Quatuor Coronati Lodge which specialised in the history of freemasonry was considering an outing to Norwich it was most likely Clarke who suggested they should first get in touch with Walter. Accordingly, in 1901 the lodge secretary and long-standing masonic historian, George Speth, enlisted Walter's help to plan a trip to be spread over a summer weekend. Before it could take place, however, Speth died suddenly, and as a token of respect that year's outing was postponed.

In 1902 the plans were resurrected and the tour reinstated and advertised as from Thursday 3 to Sunday 6 July. Walter as the local historian and guru would be their guide, giving a preliminary briefing and then escorting them round the sights of Norwich on the Friday and the Broads on the Saturday. In preparation, Walter compiled and printed two booklets, a separate one for the members to carry with them on each of the two days. These contained extracts from historical documents concerning the work of masons (as opposed to freemasons), photographs of historic buildings, and drawings of scenery on the Broads by his old friend Wilfrid Ball who had illustrated *A Month on the Norfolk Broads* for Walter. After the event a report of the visit was published in the Lodge's transactions, *Ars Quatuor Coronatorum*, on which the following account is based. (Interpolations in brackets are taken from Walter's accompanying pamphlets.)

On the Thursday a substantial party of 42 Brethren caught the 3.20pm train from Liverpool Street to Ipswich, with Bro. Gotthelf Greiner, Worshipful Master, leading the tour. Afternoon tea was served in 'the saloon' at Ipswich, where Bro. Clarke was waiting to accompany them to Norwich. The party then split into two, some staying at the Royal and some at the Maid's Head. All dined together at the Royal, then went over to the Maid's Head for a briefing.

> Walter Rye Esq, who was to be the guide and interpreter during our sojourn, had prepared a most interesting entertainment. With the aid of very good lantern slides, admirably prepared by Harry Brittain Esq and Mr Algar, and shown by the former, he took us through the whole of the next day's tour of inspection of ancient and modern Norwich.

After breakfast at 9am the following morning, the party visited the Castle ('refaced last century in very bad taste' – WR) and were shown the city museum in the keep by its curator, Mr Reeve, and the city records, ('kept in the Castle where they are safe against fire, fiend and foe'), by the honorary archivist John Tingey. They moved on to the cathedral, where the dean spared an hour to hold them 'spellbound with his eloquent and learned explanations'. Then it was the turn of the grammar school, where Walter introduced them to his old friend Augustus Jessopp, the former headmaster.[6]

After lunch they walked to the Guildhall, then on to St Peter Mancroft ('The hideous spirelet was placed on the very fine tower at the recent restoration and the other day an interesting Jacobean porch was removed to make room for a presumed restoration of an older porch' – WR.) They then made their way back to the Maid's Head via St Andrew's Hall, Strangers' Hall (whose rescue by Leonard Bolingbroke Walter applauded), and finally to Walter's own property, Bacon's House. ('This house, the half-timber work of which was covered up, and the sides defaced by being turned into an advertising station, was bought and restored by me a year or two ago' – WR.)

For the sake of variety all dined this time at the Maid's Head, after which the Quatuor Coronati party were guests of the Norwich freemasons for a smoking concert of songs and amusing sketches in the Assembly Rooms of the Agricultural Hall, with Howlett's Quadrille Band. Walter – if he was there – must have felt quite at home in view of the similar festivities he had regularly put on for Thames Hare and Hounds. Hamon Le Strange, the Norfolk antiquary and collector who was also Past Grand Master of the masonic Province as well as Treasurer of the Quatuor Coronati, presided.

After revelries such as these, some Brethren must have struggled to parade in time for their early breakfast at 7am on the Saturday. It was timed so that they could proceed – very likely by train – to Wroxham to begin their day on and around the Broads: 'Mr Walter Rye and Mr Harry Brittain very kindly accompanied us throughout the day, and their unrivalled knowledge of everything connected with the Broads furnished us with interesting information about all that was worthy of note.'

On arrival at Wroxham their first obligation, however, was to pause for a group photograph, in which Walter, as guide and mentor, appeared prominently near the centre of the front row. Afterwards they boarded a tour boat, *The Queen of the Broads*, noting in passing Wroxham Bridge ('greatly spoiled of late years by the erection of bungalows and such-like atrocities' – WR), and proceeded down the river Bure 'to the landing for Bro. Clarke's natty riverside residence, where a tempting champagne snack afforded early comfort.' At St Benet's Abbey, 'the appearance of the Gateway before and after the mill was erected may be seen from drawings kindly lent, with many others, by Mr Walter Rye...' They continued until Yarmouth could be seen in the distance, but it was not visited – how pleased Walter must have been at that! The party returned via the Yare to Norwich. Dinner was again

The *Queen of the Broads* packed with trippers.
Photo by Donald Shields, by courtesy of The Broadland Memories Archive.

held at the Maid's Head, then it was time for the Quatuor Coronati to repay the Norfolk Brethren for their hospitality of the previous night by hosting another smoking concert of ballads, recitations, and this time handbells.

On the Sunday, the more devout among them attended Divine Service at the cathedral, whilst a detachment went, at Walter's invitation, to see St Leonard's Priory and his library and antiquarian collection. The Lodge Minutes record that a number of Norfolk Brethren including Brothers Clarke, A. G. Howlett (a city councillor) and Thomas Colman took the opportunity of the visit to become corresponding members of the Quatuor Coronati.

Endnotes

1   P. B. Ficklin to WR, 10 Apr. 1902 from Rome, 'Thanks for the account of your lecture which seems to have been a triumphant success... You seem to be regularly on the warpath as a lecturer.' NRO, MS 10612 folder 2. He does record one occasion, however, when he had a poor audience at St Stephens, at what he thought was a socialist hall with a red flag flying, which he insisted be taken down first.

2   H-L. Arnold, Dereham Vicarage, to WR, 19 Oct. 1902, 'We have an excellent lime light lantern and two men who are always on the spot to manage it': NRO, MS 4691/4.

3   Alex C. Tait to WR, 22 Feb. 1906 NRO, MS 4691/6.
4   *The Recreations of a Norfolk Antiquary*, 2 vols, Holt and Norwich, 1920 and 1922.
5   This account is based on the Minutes of Quatuor Coronati Lodge (QCL) at Freemason's Hall, an account of the visit in F. J. Redman, 'Summer outing, Norwich 3rd to 6th July 1902', (*Ars Quatuor Coronatorum*, XV, 1902) pp.141–152; and the two pamphlets prepared for the visit by WR (BL, bound with other 'Tracts relating to Norwich': ref. 10352.R.4/1-2). On G. W. Speth see David J. Peabody, 'George William Speth 1847–1901: The gift of historical imagination', in AQC, 120 (2007), pp.2–11.
6   'We had the pleasure of meeting there the Rev. Canon Dr Jessopp of Scarning rectory, the well-known Norfolk antiquarian who delighted the visitors with many most interesting remarks.'

4
SAVING HISTORIC BUILDINGS

While still living and working in London, Walter was already becoming an enthusiast for the preservation of Norwich and Norfolk's historic buildings. In his *History of Norfolk* (chapter XI) and *Tourists' Guide* he was highly critical of the insensitive and unthinking restorations that were sweeping away monumental inscriptions and historic features in many of the churches he visited: 'The wonder is that there is anything left of our churches, when one considers the woeful ordeal of neglect they went through in the seventeenth and eighteenth centuries, and the more terrible one of restoration under which they are now suffering.'

The worst example, he thought, might be Cromer (though he admits to being prejudiced because his ancestors' graves were affected): the lessor of the great tithes, presumably being unwilling to pay for the upkeep of the chancel, and arguing that the nave was big enough for the parishioners' needs anyway, blew up the chancel with gunpowder in 1681![1]

> Nowadays the pendulum of destruction is swinging the other way. Interesting late Perpendicular work, Jacobean pulpits and panelling, and monuments of families who have left the parish are swept away by the 'restorers', whose idea usually seems to be to construct a new-looking church (Decorated for choice) with a hammer-beam pine roof, cheap pine open seats, gaudy pattern encaustic tiles, and never a monument on wall or floor. The type is common and most uninteresting.[2]

Ecclesiologists, he said, had better make sketches of whatever is good before it has gone; and genealogists must record inscriptions, as he himself has done. On several occasions he published pamphlets on individual churches in aid of restoration projects, and when he became a sought-after lecturer his clerical friends sometimes invited him to use these talents in support of their fundraising efforts.

Walter had already purchased a number of historic properties in and around the city, intending either to live in them one day or, more usually, to save them from unsympathetic developers.[3] He records as an aside, for example, that in 1885 he restored some half-timbered cottages 'at St John's, Norwich' at a greater cost than it would have taken to demolish and rebuild them.[4]

The Maid's Head [See plate V]

The Maid's Head in Tombland near the cathedral was Walter's favourite hostelry in the city, and over the course of two decades of visits he spent many happy hours there. He recorded that it was 'the old Tory house – the nearest approach to the typical old hostel that I ever saw'.[5] In his *Tourists' Guide* (1885) he wrote:

> Here a visitor may well make his stay, for it is decidedly the most comfortable inn in the town, as may be imagined from the Bar mess patronizing it. The house is one of the very few inns now remaining where the host takes a personal interest in his guests, and a better guide than Mr Webster to the county, and especially to its fisheries one cannot have.[6]

In 1889, four years after these comments were published, the Maid's Head was up for sale. Fearing that it would fall into the hands of an uncaring brewery Walter (despite friends' telling him it was madness for someone who lived in London) decided to acquire the building on a long lease, and direct a restoration project from his home 120 miles away.[7] As with most of the houses he successively owned, he researched its history both on site and in the archives. In the course of his costly 'renovation' work he made a number of interesting archaeological discoveries, including an old fireplace in the Coffee Room and an old window in the Smoke Room: 'This fireplace was built up with brickwork and a nineteenth-century marble abomination inserted. After I had restored it I was severely criticised by a local antiquary for building (as he thought) so incongruous a fireplace – like nothing which could ever have been in the old house!'[8]

In the business of restoration, then as now, one person's 'abomination' is another's treasure. A feature or fitting of later date than the building's origins may yet have aesthetic integrity and make a valid contribution to its overall history. Josephine Tozier, in *Little Pilgrimages among English Inns* (1904) noted of the Maid's Head that: 'The fine Tudor office, the bar, and the carved wainscoted smoke-room have been saved from the vandals and beer-drinkers. The ancient gables look down through the glass of the roofed-in courtyard, and Queen Elizabeth's room, with its narrow private stairway, remains in all its pristine glory…'[9]

But the Tudor 'feel' that Walter brought to the Maid's Head is still not to everyone's liking. In the *Eastern Daily Press* in 1970 Jonathan Mardle commented:

> I think he did too much to it when he substituted a mock Tudor front for what old drawings show to have been a pleasant Georgian one. But as to the interior he discovered the Oak Room and its fine open fireplace which had previously been bricked up. He kept the old coach yard, the delightfully sociable little Jacobean snug and the fine 18th century dining room.[10]

Many an old inn has tried to boost its visitor numbers with tales of spurious historic associations with royalty or other celebrities, and the Maid's Head was no exception. But for Walter, truth must out even if it meant sweeping aside some of the romance. How, for example, did the inn get its name?

> It is generally said that its name was changed to the 'Maid's Head' because Queen Elizabeth stayed here when she visited the city. There are two objections to this, either of which will suffice, viz, that it is called the Maid's Head in the Paston Letters in 1472, and that Queen Elizabeth never stayed here, being lodged at the Bishop's Palace.[11]

And, this being Walter, of course he published several editions of a pamphlet for the edification of guests at the Maid's Head, with illustrations by Wilfrid

Ball.[12] He continued to stay there from time to time, soaking up the town gossip from the Coffee Room waiter,[13] but in 1894 he sold the building after a legal judgment (*Sharpe v. Wakefield*) required hotel licensees to be resident on their premises.[14] However, he kept its interest at heart, and in 1903, having moved to Norwich, seized an opportunity to buy the adjacent buildings at 9 and 11 Wensum Street in case the Maid's Head should ever need extending.[15]

Anguish House and Bacon's House

Walter had not bought the Maid's Head with any intention of living there. In 1897, however, he did buy and restore Anguish House, also in Tombland, specifically with his approaching retirement in mind. In the event, for practical reasons he decided against living there and moved instead (perhaps unwisely, as we have seen) to St Leonard's Priory.[16] He sold off Anguish House in 1911.

Walter also records having viewed Bacon's House on several occasions in 1897 and 1899.[17] He subsequently bought that too, perhaps encouraged by the public-spirited example of Leonard Bolingbroke who purchased and restored the ruined Strangers' Hall in 1899.[18] Bacon's House, at the junction of Colegate and Calvert Street, was of interest not only architecturally but also for the part it had played in the city's history. It had been constructed around 1548,[19] for Henry Bacon, who was to become Mayor of Norwich in 1557 and 1566. Other Mayors had lived there too, including George Cock in the seventeenth and William Wiggett in the eighteenth century. Sadly, it had long-since ceased to be a residence, and had had various reincarnations, among other things as a college and a shoe factory. Inevitably it had suffered depredations and alterations before Walter acquired it. Its original half-timbering had been covered over, 'and the sides defaced by being turned into an advertising station'.[20]

The Leper Hospital and other properties

The release of capital from the sale of his Hampstead house enabled his run of investments in historic properties to continue after he moved to Norwich, and in 1902 he bought the Magdalen or Leper Hospital chapel (Lazar House) on Sprowston Road, again to forestall demolition.[21] This he sold in 1908 to Sir Eustace Gurney who restored it – as much as possible of the old fabric being left undisturbed. In 1921 it was presented to the city for use as a branch library.

Walter also acquired properties in Elm Hill; and medieval cottages at the Rose Lane end of King Street which sadly have not survived, but we can learn something of them from his notes for an illustrated lecture on the streetscape:

[Opposite the Pied Friars college is] a block of four interesting houses which I bought and restored. They belonged (according to Mr Hudson) to Roger Favell in 1367. Some of them passed to Robert Bell, a tailor, in 1493 who was sheriff in 1511 and who left his rebus of R and a bell in it in the side entrance to Murrell's yard... Above the archway leading into Murrell's yard is a little Gothic window which I have carefully preserved.[22]

Outside Norwich, Walter bought several other properties, including riverside cottages at Horning and the so-called 'Bonner's Cottages', East Dereham, whose ornate pargetting and woodwork were described (with illustrations) in the *Norfolk Antiquarian Miscellany* by William Argent to whom he had entrusted their restoration.[23] He records supervising in September 1904 'the flaking off by Argent of the coatings of paint from the beautiful pargetting work'.

As Walter's experience as an antiquary broadened, he became aware that the history of many buildings, institutions and communities had been thwarted for want of adequate calendars and indexes to the surviving archival material that told their story.[24]

Consultant and critic

With quite a track record of conservation work, he was sometimes among those called on to give advice when a historic building was to be restored, as happened with Wymondham church in 1901, where he was in the company of other antiquarian consultants including fellow members of the NNAS, Prince Frederick Duleep Singh, Jessopp and Beloe.[25] More consultancies followed, like those at Upton, Overstrand and Cawston in 1911–12. In the all too rare case where modern restoration rescued a bad situation he was quick to give praise: 'When I first saw Salle and Cawston churches in the utter state of decay and disrepair in which they were in 1870 I never even hoped that such splendid work would ever be done to them as has recently [1904] been done.'[26]

Walter could be very critical of those (whether individuals or corporations) who paid scant regard to historic streetscapes or views, or who erected what he considered to be eyesores. In 1903 he began a crusade against the 'vandalism of the Dean and Chapter' for pulling down the old precinct wall of the Close to make room for 'some vulgar little villas which obstructed the view of the cathedral from Bishopgate Street'.[27] This led him to work up his more wide-ranging public lecture on 'Taste and Want of Taste in Norwich'. Even his friends had to brace themselves for his wrath if they made what seemed to him unwarranted changes to their homes.[28]

Nor did Walter's conservation instincts stop at buildings. As we have seen he was greatly distressed over the impact of tourism on places of natural beauty such as the Broads and the coast,[29] and made frequent references to this in his publications and in articles and letters for the press.[30] In 1904 the People's Park in Dereham Road was given to the city by Mrs Radford Pym, but in Walter's view the original beauty of its wild woodland and flowers was soon turned into a bland corporation park and ruined by the local youth: 'Most of the wild plants were at once eradicated by the city rough children – the worst and most mischievous set of little beasts I have ever come across. The London rough boys are cultivated gentlemen compared with them.'

The following year Walter attended the opening of the site of a new barracks on Mousehold Heath:

I was not impressed with Mr Arnold Forster, the War Minister, whose outward appearance and manners were those of a successful linen draper. The scheme of building having been abandoned under the radical Government I took the opportunity when I was Mayor in 1908–9 to ask Haldane (whose ludicrous fat appearance in a tight uniform I shall never forget) to give the city back the land subscribed for by its citizens, which he promised to do at once, and I don't suppose he ever thought again on the subject.

During 1906 he drafted a piece on coastal erosion for the Victoria County History and was encouraged by the editor, William Page, to give this wider publicity.[31] A conference of local authority and parliamentary representatives for Norfolk and Suffolk convened at the Maid's Head to highlight the risks to both local and national interests.

Property problems

In the years immediately following Georgina's death in 1910 Walter's property portfolio – quite apart from his own habitation – caused him some concern. The 1910 Finance Act introduced heavy taxation on the increased value of land, and under the Norwich Local Act, which Walter thought 'iniquitous', he became liable to pay the cost of paving and drainage of a yard adjacent to one of his properties. He wrote to the press complaining of this attack on those who had chosen to put their assets into bricks and mortar, and tried to sell several of his Norwich houses, but found that 'the Radical tactics had frightened away all buyers, as indeed they were probably meant to do.' He complained bitterly of the amount of form-filling required by the Land Revenue.[32]

August 1912 saw Norwich's great flood, after six inches of rain fell in twelve hours. It affected Walter directly, both at Lammas and in Norwich: 'We found immense damage done to my waterside houses. Magdalen Street was a river through which flat carts earned ransom… Next day I heard that my St George Bridge property had fallen into the river.'[33]

He surrendered this latter site to the Corporation in order to avoid being charged compensation for flood damage there, recording sadly that he had lost the appetite for entering into expensive litigation.

In 1915 it seemed for a while as if the forces of nature had again dealt him a severe blow, for a report reached him that Bonner's Cottages had been destroyed in a gale. But when he went to East Dereham to inspect them he found that it was actually a house on the other side of the road that had suffered.

Lutyens war memorial

One of Walter's last great tirades was against the Lutyens war memorial set up by the corporation in 1927 on a prominent site near the Guildhall to commemorate the dead of the First World War. He thought it 'lamentable'! The initial proposal, by Dean Beeching, had been for the war dead to be commemorated in a more utilitarian way by restoring a ruined chapel at the east end of the cathedral, but some subscribers to the memorial fund did not wish it to be associated with a church. When a memorial, pure and simple, was first proposed, the corporation rejected the idea of displaying a scale model for public comment. In 1921, Walter, then the oldest member of the NNAS, suggested that the project be deferred pending an archaeological dig. Nothing was done until 1927 when, in Walter's words, the Lord Mayor and Sheriff 'seemed morbidly anxious to push the matter through during their year of office'. The drawings were published, leading Walter to apostrophise on this 'frippery which reminds one only of a cheap jack's show at a fair... [a] clumsy mass of white stone', badly sited. It was, he said, 'the greatest piece of vandalism ever perpetrated in Norwich, and that is saying a great deal'. He strongly opposed it in the *Eastern Daily Press* throughout July 1927,[34] commenting that Lutyens's worthy reputation did not suffice to guarantee he was the right man for this job. He protested that the bishop and the city corporation were acting as if they were unaccountable, and it would not be surprising if they went on to paste advertisements or flashing lights on their buildings! Planning decisions of this kind should not be left to the local authority. It was a waste of money and an eyesore, but what could you expect from a bishop and Lord Mayor who knew so little about the history of the city!

I was called an armchair critic by one who asked what I did myself in the War, and who was ignorant that I was 71 when it broke out, and unable to serve personally.

Endnotes

1   WR, *History,* p.198.
2   *Ibid.*, p.199.
3   His reputation in this respect would become part of his *apologia* on being elected Mayor in 1908.
4   WR, *A Month on the Norfolk Broads,* p.12.
5   *Autobiog.*
6   WR, *Tourists' Guide* (1885), p.37.
7   *EA*, II, p.172. Some drawings of the Maid's Head are in NRO, MS 4691/8.
8   WR, *Norwich and the Broads: Itinerary* (1902).
9   (Boston 1904), reprinted at http://kellscraft.com/AmongEnglishInns/AmongEnglishInnscontent.html
10 *EDP,* 8 Apr. 1970.
11 'The window of the room in which she did *not* sleep is shown in illustration on page 8'. WR, *Norwich and the Broads: Itinerary* (1902). See N. Pevsner and B. Wilson, *The Buildings of England: Norfolk I: Norwich and North East,* (Yale, 2002, p.293).

12 See for example, NRO, MS 4691/84/2.

13 WR, *A Month on the Norfolk Broads...* p.89.

14 *Autobiog.*

15 *Autobiog.*

16 WR wrote from Golden Square to Teddy Beloe on 11 Oct.1897: 'I am buying a... 1575 house in Tombland at Norwich and shall go and live there permanently Xmas 4 years "if I live and be well", as Tungate used to say'. NRO, BL/BE 3/31.

17 *Autobiog.*, pp.97, 107.

18 Bolingbroke restored the building while living in it, bravely opening it up to the paying public to help cover the costs. Frank Meeres, *Norwich: A History and Celebration* (Teffont, 2014), p.73.

19 Or at any rate named for him. Pevsner suggests a fifteenth century origin (Pevsner and Wilson *op. cit.* p.285).

20 WR, *Norwich and the Broads: Itinerary* (1902). After Walter had sold it on, a major fire in 1925 destroyed a whole wing on Calvert Street, so what we see today is only a fraction of the original building. It eventually passed into the hands of the city council in the 1970s when a further restoration was undertaken. For Bacon's House see www.thecityclub.co.uk and www.georgeplunkett.co.uk/Norwich/cob.htm.

21 *Autobiog.*

22 NRO, MS 4691/76.

23 W. Argent, 'Some early pargetting work at Bonner's Cottages, East Dereham', pp.33–38. Now the museum of the Dereham Antiquarian Society.

24 WR, *Norwich Castle* (1921): Preface.

25 *Autobiog.*

26 *Autobiog.*

27 *Autobiog.*, p.129.

28 See, for example, NRO, MS 10612 folder 2, fragment of a letter of 2 Feb. 1904 to P. B. Ficklin complaining about incongruities in changes he has made to a staircase and mantel.

29 6 Jun.1906, W. Page of VCH to WR. Thanks him for his letter regarding erosion of the sea coast. 'I think it would be a very good thing for the History if you would send an account of what you have written to the local papers as you suggest'. NRO, MS 4691/81/2.

30 NRO, MS 4691/81/2. A file of press cuttings, some undated but some 1903–6 concerning coastal erosion. A conference of local authority and parliamentary reps for Norfolk and Suffolk convened at the Maid's Head to highlight the risks to both local and national interests.

31 Page to WR, 6 July 1906, with a file of related press cuttings: NRO, MS 4691/81/2.

32 *Autobiog.*, p.181.

33 *Autobiog.*

34 See particularly the issues of 19, 23 and 27 July.

5
LIBRARY AND MUSEUM COMMITTEES

While Walter remained in London his relations with the Norwich city muniments, as with the Archaeological Society, passed through periodic troubled phases. William Hudson in particular, whom he respected but with whom he had already clashed over the management of the NNAS, seems at times to have gone out of his way to cold-shoulder this no doubt demanding reader. Walter grumbled in 1880 that:

> ... the position of searchers at the City record room is very unsatisfactory. No encouragement is given to the public who desire to search, and the hope that I had that the room would form an historical centre for local research will, I fear, never be fulfilled. I [would have] given the whole of my somewhat large collection of glossaries and reference books to such a room, but it is no longer available to the public without trouble, and such books ought to be handed over to the Public Library for use there.[1]

But by the time Walter retired to Norwich in 1900 Hudson was gone and he was able to exert more direct influence on the affairs of both the city museum (by then housed in the castle alongside the muniments) and the library. In 1901 he was co-opted to the museum committee, on which he continued to serve until 1912.[12] He was also co-opted to the library committee, on which he would continue to serve until his death in 1929.

As far as the muniments were concerned, in retirement he threw himself enthusiastically into calendaring the corporation's deeds (at the rate of sixty a day)[3] and many other items from the collection in the castle.[4] Almost at once he also became a benefactor, personally buying strayed documents at auction in order to give them to the corporation. In 1901 he presented an original bond for the safe custody of a gilt ewer dish given by Archbishop Parker.[5] In 1902 he bought the Norwich Rate Book of 1633–34 'which had no doubt been stolen from the Guildhall in the bad old days'[6] and, after transcribing it (for publication by Jarrolds), presented it to the corporation. Early the following year he was instrumental in getting returned to the corporation a bundle of early documents, including the fabric roll of 1390–1400 for the building of the Guildhall, which had been 'borrowed' from the Muniment Room many years before.[7]

Walter's antennae twitched whenever old 'documents' were mentioned in passing. In 1905 the city librarian was told of an old parchment book then at Tillett's, a ham and beef shop in Rupert Street. He called Walter in to investigate:

> I went over to see it and found it was the long lost Custom Book of Norwich, the loss of which had been so much lamented. I warned him it was city property and at once reported my find to Mr Tingey, the Hon Archivist, who recovered it for £5.5s. It is now among the other city records. One would have thought that after this miraculous recovery the authorities would have taken rather more care of it than (to suit the convenience of the Editor of the 'Records of the City of Norwich' [Hudson]) to send it to him to the South of England by post. But they did, and luckily it came back all right.[8]

When he tried to be as assiduous with regard to antiquarian objects on behalf of the museum his intervention was not always welcome, but he still kept its interests at heart and occasionally handed on antiquarian items.[9]

As he began to sense that his capacity for work was fading, he decided it was time to start making a final disposition of his collections. In 1906 he therefore offered all his books and manuscripts to the corporation, on certain conditions including the challenging one that they should find a proper room in which to house them.[10] When they made a meal of this and prevaricated he decided to retain possession for the time being, and instead arranged to bequeath them to the library on his eventual death.[11] He had thought of giving the Smith collection of maps, also in his possession, to the NNAS, but was put off by the society's 'extreme lassitude', and instead gave them too to the library.[12] Nor was this the only spot of bother he encountered. He notes dolefully in the *Autobiography* in 1906:[13]

> All my rather large collection of record dictionaries and such like books as Ducange, Madox etc I later on gave to the Record Room at the Norwich Castle Museum, under the impression they would be useful to students there, a gift which I afterwards regretted, for under the new regulations as to access to the records… they are practically inaccessible and would be much better in the Free (now Public) Library.

To facilitate his editorial work Walter would ideally have liked free access for himself to the city's muniments on which he was spending so much time and money. He was on friendly terms with their *de facto* custodian, the honorary archivist John Tingey, and had the matter been entirely at Tingey's discretion that would have been that. But in 1906 the town clerk – not solely on Walter's account – tightened up the regulations, ordering that Tingey alone was to have the key to the muniment room, and nobody else was to have access or be allowed to copy anything without the town clerk's express permission. For a time, therefore, Walter had to arrange clandestine visits with Tingey, usually to coincide with the town clerk's temporary absence![14] Eventually there was a change of heart, and in 1908 we find the town clerk, after all, giving Walter permission to have a key. [15]

As for the library, Walter's friend James Hooper was among its frustrated readers and never had a high opinion of its staff or their ability to provide catalogues commensurate with the importance of the holdings, especially given the shoestring budget on which they had to operate.[16] Walter was among the first to recognise this, and volunteered to undertake some cataloguing. The powers-that-be were at first less than happy about allowing this untrained amateur to undertake even voluntary library work, but grudgingly accepted that nothing much would be done unless they agreed; so to everyone's benefit Walter made a start on a number of card catalogues. In 1907–8 he published not only a calendar of the library's topographical and genealogical books and manuscripts, but also catalogues of its portrait holdings and of the topographical and antiquarian sections.[17] During his mayoralty in 1909 Walter, now Chairman of the Museum Committee, somehow managed to find the time also to edit and publish for the museum a catalogue prepared by its assistant curator, Frank Leney, of *Antiquities found principally in East Anglia*.[18]

The appointment in 1911 of a new librarian, G. A. Stephen, offered some hope of improvement, particularly as he made it known that he wished to make the library more appealing. To assist him, in 1912 Walter (now more of a VIP having been Mayor) presented seven of his own manuscripts to the library, for which the library committee duly provided a show case.[19] In February 1915 he gave further items, and promised more on the understanding that the committee would print an up-to-date catalogue of the reference and local history portions of the library. But the exigencies of the First World War put an end to that, and there was in any case a general shortage of shelf space. After the war, Stephen's duties were diverted, as Walter put it, 'with the practical conversion of the library into a quasi-literary society, with lectures and so forth'. When no further catalogue had appeared by 1924 Walter again came to the rescue, this time with a handbook for researchers, in which he lamented that 'the Library itself suffers, and is like a ship without a rudder for the want of a printed, or even a MS, index'.[20] Thereafter, until his eventual bequests in 1929, his donations became more sporadic, although with his collaborator Harry Brittain he donated 726 lantern slides they had used in their many lectures, depicting 'interesting buildings that are now demolished'.[21] At his death he kept his promise to bequeath his remaining collections to the corporation. They comprised 81 volumes of manuscripts, 255 printed books and a large collection of letters and papers on antiquarian subjects.[22] Sadly, the antiquarian books were destroyed in the fire of 1994.

It should be noted, however, that Norwich Public Library was by no means the only recipient of Walter's largesse down the years. Letters of acknowledgement for gifts of books and manuscripts survive from a long list of grateful recipients including (in Norwich and Norfolk) the Norfolk and Norwich Naturalists' Society; the Norfolk and Norwich Hospital;[23] the Norwich Chapter Library; Thetford Museum and the Libraries of Great Yarmouth and King's Lynn; (elsewhere in East Anglia) Corpus Christi

College Cambridge[24] and Gonville and Caius College Cambridge; (in London) the Guildhall Library; the PRO; the British Museum; the London Library and the Law Society Library; (and, in Manchester) Chetham's Library and Manchester Public Library.[25]

Endnotes

1   *Autobiog.*, p.49.
2   See letter of 5 Jul. 1912 (illegible signatory): NRO, MS 4691/6 regretting his resignation. (But *Autobiog.* p.118 says it occurred in 1914 'as soon as Mr Hotblack was made a member of it.')
3   He took a short break for lunch at Grix's to save time, 'where the grill was excellent though it was a trifle embarrassing to be called upon to pay for it before one was trusted with the knife and fork.' *Autobiog.*
4   The muniments had been kept in the Guildhall until 1894 when the city acquired the castle with a view to making a museum and set about providing a muniment room there. Hudson and Tingey published a first catalogue of the muniments in 1898 (Hudson and Tingey, 1910, I, Introductory note).
5   *Autobiog.*, p.118 says Archbishop Tenison, but see W. T. Bensly, 'On a silver-gilt ewer and basin given by Archbishop Parker to the City of Norwich', *NA* XV (1904), p.227. The original was lost but the bond was among the Norris MSS in Walter's possession.
6   *Autobiog.*, p.122 for 1902.
7   *Autobiog.*, p.125 for 1903.
8   See, for example, the report in the *Wells Journal* of 11 May 1905.
9   *Autobiog.*, 1903: 'I was instrumental in getting Sir Kenneth Kemp to present to the Castle Museum a very beautiful curricle of the type mentioned in "Rodney Stone" but which the then curator relegated to the dungeons, expressing his opinion that we might as well show a city dust-cart.' 14 Feb. 1924, letter of thanks from the curator of Norwich Castle Museum for 'the quaint pair of kid slippers you were good enough to send to the Museum through Mr Stephen. They will go in the boot collection at the Bridewell Museum': NRO, MS 4691/3.
10   His conditions appear in a memo of 15 Feb.1906: NRO, MS 4691/13. This bundle also includes related correspondence about his other gifts to the library.
11   *Autobiog.*, p.147: Hooper had heard that the General Purposes Committee were to 'consider' Walter's gift: 'As if it needed consideration! The almost complete lack of interest in literary matters in Norwich is abysmal': NRO, MS 4691/7.
12   He issued in *NAM* a list of these and all other maps known to himself and Harry Brittain who compiled the list. This was later reprinted as the free-standing catalogue. The collection comprised thirty-eight portfolios of topographical drawings and photographs; six portfolios of maps; and five portfolios of photographs.

13 p.149.
14 JT to WR, 5 Apr. and 16 Aug.: NRO, MS 4691/6.
15 Letter of 10 Aug.: NRO, MS 4691/13; and another from James Reeve, Curator of the Castle Museum, 13 Oct. 1908: 'I am instructed by the Town Clerk to supply you with the enclosed key of the drawer in the Muniment Room containing the keys of the Presses, in accordance with the terms of the minutes of the City Committee': NRO, MS 10612 folder 1.
16 19 Apr. 1905, JH diatribe against the F[ree] L[ibrary] and its librarian. They have said that the library's local collection is very complete and they have been active in acquisitions but JH has often brought to their attention books they have not acquired. 'The Librarian has not the slightest personal knowledge of author etc.... He don't know Latin from French and ought to be [?psalmsinging] to a gang of old buzzards, male, &, especially, female.' And again, 3 Mar. 1911: 'It is very certain that no proper catalogue for the Free Library can be prepared by any member, or members, of the present Library Staff.' Both refs from NRO, MS 4691/7.
17 The British Library's copy of this catalogue is inscribed on the cover in Walter's own hand 'Mayor 1908–9'.
18 This had been awaiting a financial sponsor until Walter stepped in, according to the preface, 'as he realised its publication would prove of considerable antiquarian value as well as being the means of prompting the augmentation and enrichment of the collections'.
19 Report reprinted from *EDP*, 13 Feb. 1912: NRO, MS 4691/13.
20 WR, *A Handbook to the Materials available to Students of Local History and Genealogy, arranged in order of date* (Norwich, 1924).
21 *Norfolk Through a Lens: a Guide to the Photographic Collections held by Norfolk Library and Information Service.* Available online at www.norfolk.gov. uk/-/media/norfolk/downloads.
22 TNA, IR 62/1219 Exemption from Estate Duty of his bequest of books etc. to Norwich Public Library.
23 Minute Book, 1777–78.
24 A 1909 presentation copy of Robert Masters' history of the college, once in the possession of William Cole, antiquary.
25 Sixteen deeds rel. to the manor of Slyne, Lancs.

6
MAYOR OF NORWICH, 1908–1909

Norwich in the early twentieth century[1]

Norwich, which had once been Britain's second city, had been overtaken in population terms in the eighteenth century by Bristol, and later also by the large industrial cities of the Midlands and the North West. By 1901 the city's population was nevertheless over 100,000. Some of its once key industries such as weaving were by then in decline. Others including engineering and manufacturing were however rising, and there was a reasonable level of employment, albeit sustained in part by low pay. Most employers maintained an anti-union stance and Norwich was among the last places in the boot and shoe industry to agree a minimum wage. Much employment was seasonal. Colman's had a conscientious policy of welfare and relief for its workers, including (before the First World War) a programme of assisted emigration to Canada.[2]

The city had two parliamentary seats. For a time, after the 1895 election, both were temporarily held by Conservatives, but in the 1904 by-election one was recaptured by the Liberals, and then in the 1906 election George Roberts of the Independent Labour Party captured the other seat, becoming the first working-class MP to be elected for the city. On the city council the Liberals came to be dominated by new industrialists and the Conservatives by lawyers, commercial interests and bankers. Roberts first became known through his election in 1899 to the School Board, a body that also included women. The first woman to serve on the city council, however, was not elected until 1913. Nonconformists, who were strong in the city, tended to back the Liberals, although some Liberals were Anglican.[3]

Walter's politics

In a 1984 memoir for the Rye family, Barry Adams wrote of Walter:

> His political outlook was reactionary, something of a Tory Anarchist or Radical, a little like Cobbett… As one writer has observed, in some respects he seemed a figure out of the past, belonging essentially to the 18th century. In some other respects, however, he was a typical Victorian: robust, self-confident and vastly energetic.[4]

Until very recently Walter had not chosen to engage with local politics, and had certainly never stood as a candidate in either local or national elections, though as a result of his property holdings he had the franchise in three Norfolk constituencies and was meticulous in exercising it. He made no secret of his Conservative allegiances and suspicion of all things radical or socialist.

He says very little in the *Autobiography* about his political views. We may surmise that while in London he was fully preoccupied with business and research. But even from that distance he kept a detached but watchful and rather critical eye on elections and electioneering in Norfolk. He despised election bribery, and lamented the fact that Liberals and Conservatives, especially in Norwich, refused to mix socially: 'It seems absolutely impossible for men of different politics to be even decently civil to one another within months of an election.'[5]

Even while technically non-resident he would occasionally write to the Norfolk press setting out anti-radical and pro-Church of England views.[6]

Once resident in Norfolk, and with more time on his hands, he began to take more interest in party politics, though the infrequency of references to this in the *Autobiography* suggest it was not a primary passion. He was already a celebrity in the city, and as he does not reveal whether he became a paid-up member of the Conservative cause straight away it is possible that he attended such few political events as he does mention (like a meeting of the Primrose League) purely as a guest. On the other hand, he records in 1901 having to resist pressure to stand as a Conservative candidate for

Thorpe ward in a local election, and he was attending local events such as the annual Mayor's dinner, which clearly point to a deeper engagement with the cause. By 1904 it finally seems beyond doubt that he had become a paid-up Conservative, as he records speaking at a party meeting for the first time, as well as voting Conservative. In the 1906 elections he was again active in the Conservative cause and voted for them 'wherever I had votes'.

One indication that he was not deeply involved in, or savvy about, party politics comes from an anecdote he told against himself. During one election campaign in a ward in Norwich, the Liberal candidate posted his election address to Walter at Lammas, asking for his vote. As the other candidate sent no such communication Walter decided to vote for that second person, assuming him to be a Conservative, and went by train to Norwich and by cab to the polling booth only to discover that the Liberal's opponent was in fact a Socialist. He was narrowly saved from ignominy!

Then, out of the blue in 1908, despite having no record of political service, local or national, Walter was asked if he would take a year's turn as Mayor of Norwich: 'I was not unaware that I was only asked as a stop gap because the conservative party had been disappointed in prevailing on the Duke of Norfolk to fill the office, but thought the experience would be an interesting one.'[7]

After consulting the Conservative agent and his sons, he decided that being Mayor could do his reputation no harm, provided that the authorities understood he was not as rich a man as some of his predecessors, and would not be able to emulate their level of charitable support: 'This was a sore blow to the licensed cadgers, the fishing clubs, the replacers of dead donkeys, the layers of stones of dissenting chapels and the like, but I stuck to my guns.'

A friend wrote to the *Eastern Daily Press* that Walter's qualities were not altogether those associated with the mayoral office. Instead, he was: '... a brilliant and scholarly controversialist, a born fighter, full of unconventional surprises, whose genial presence is a very personification of the robust zest of life; a hater of shams and pretentiousness, with always something of the Homeric about whatever he says or does.'[8]

No doubt to Walter's relief, the local elections of November 1908, which preceded the mayor-making by a few days, returned an overall Tory majority (thirty-seven seats), with the Liberals taking twenty-one seats and the Socialists six.[9] When, on the great day itself, his nomination was formally read out to the council before Walter entered the room, it was reiterated that he had held no local office, apart from being a co-opted member of the Castle Museum and library committees. On the other hand he had many other suitable qualifications for the job. He came from an old Norfolk family and had spent every possible holiday in the county since his boyhood. He was renowned as a historian and antiquary of the county and had compiled catalogues and indexes of the library's holdings for the public benefit. His good work in buying up historic buildings in and around Norwich in order to save them from the snare of the developer was highly regarded, and indeed he was a tireless critic of those who, with less sense of history and the heritage, spoiled the streetscape by demolition, modernisation, or the erection of hideosities. He was of honest standing as a retired solicitor and had already served the city and county well in a number of celebrated legal cases, notably over Hickling Broad and the Town Close. He had often been in the public eye: as a lecturer, after-dinner speaker and controversialist on all manner of issues, thus 'known by his crisp and rugged contributions to the local press rather than by the many soft qualities which those who knew him privately knew that he possessed in a rich degree.'[10] And last, but not least, he had in his day been a renowned athlete. After all these attributes had been declaimed he was warmly welcomed.[11]

But on Walter's part there were still one or two logistical problems apart from any financial concerns. He was caring permanently for his sick wife at his home in Surrey Street, which was thus to all intents and purposes a nursing home, so he could not follow mayoral precedent and hold open house there. It was also clearly impossible for Georgina to be Mayoress, so for that he recruited his eldest daughter Muriel. Both the Mayor's reception and the customary reception for ladies by the Mayoress would have to be held in Strangers' Hall rather than at the Mayor's home.[12]

His sheriff was a long-serving Councillor, and now Alderman, A. G. Howlett. Walter would, he said, put all his charitable efforts into raising money for the Mayor's Fund for the Unemployed. Otherwise, all he could undertake was to set aside a sum of money to cover the costs of the mayoralty, keep a rigorous account, and pay any balance at the end of the year to the Miniature Rifle Club. He later reflected: 'Had it not been for the unexpected, though very welcome visit of King Edward VII, which unavoidably increased my necessary expenses, I should have had a good round sum to hand over to the Club instead of the relatively small balance that was left.'

He floated three specific ideas for his term as Mayor, subject to council and third-party approval. All of them were politely applauded as evidence of his commitment, but in the event all were blocked by the third parties! For the unemployed, as well as the Mayor's Fund already mentioned, he suggested using their labour to rebuild the old rifle range on Mousehold Heath for military training. After lengthy discussion including one or more visits by Walter to meet officials at the War Office, this was rejected. Secondly, following on from his work on access to the Norfolk Broads he proposed the appointment of a Royal Commission on this subject.[13] That too was later hit into the long grass by Asquith, pending the outcome of an application of the River Conservators for an Order under the Fisheries Act of 1907 to protect the Broads.[14] Finally, to encourage fitness, and create an alternative to mischief or crime, he proposed the designation of safe swimming places in the river for boys, and offered to donate a stretch of riverbank that he owned, if the city would accept it. This too was eventually rejected.[15]

Helping the unemployed

Thus, much of Walter's attention came to be concentrated on the Mayor's Fund for the Unemployed, an existing scheme whereby, in winter only, the government match-funded contributions raised locally for relief. He undertook to support and promote this, and we know quite a lot about its operation thanks to the publication of a detailed report and accounts for the fund after his year in office.

The number of male unemployed in the city at that time was estimated at 1,495 (compared with 844 in the previous year). Their dependent women and children totalled 3,615. Just ten days after his installation as Mayor, on 19 November 1908, Walter issued a circular appealing for not less than £2,680 in donations to the fund. He put his own reputation firmly behind the appeal, and successfully attracted donations from many of his own friends, including Dick Howlett and Beloe, and from his own old firm of Rye and Eyre. He himself made a contribution in kind 'in excess of £29' towards the fund's administrative expenses such as the printing of the appeal and the final report.

Firms in the city were exhorted to make corporate donations, and sometimes the workforce themselves had a whip-round, although results from the latter effort tended to be disappointing. Walter would comment: 'It certainly appears to me that those who were lucky enough to be in full work might have done more for their less fortunate brothers: 22,000 people gave on average less than a penny each.'

Some potential donors were evidently put off by the 'agitation of the Right to Work doctrine and the fomentation of strikes, with importunate circulars and personal appeals'.

Donations in kind – of food and clothing – were also collected (and roughly costed in cash terms for the sake of the fund's balance sheet). Muriel, as Mayoress, approached a number of local women and asked if they would provide cooked food or make a cash donation. She supervised the distribution of over a hundred meals a week at a centre in Fishergate, and in a number of local schools. Funds were also raised through highly successful entertainments arranged by Mrs Burton-Fanning, who also sold paintings for the cause at her bazaar. Sponsorship challenges were issued: for example Mr Johnson Taylor offered to give ten guineas if nine other people would do the same (which they did). There were many private donations, and the Hippodrome staged a free benefit performance that raised £30. There were dedicated cash collections in some churches and chapels but, as Walter reported, not from either the Roman Catholics or the Quakers who already did much towards relief, albeit for their own members.

Disbursements from the fund were assessed by the city's Distress Committee (chaired by the Police Court Missionary, J. W. Clarke), and from time to time the city itself also voted additional sums to provide half-time employment for the unemployed.[16] As a result, with matching funds from the government, a total of 1,438 men, a substantial proportion of the total unemployed, were put to work. But finding work for them to do proved to be an uphill task, the more so when Walter's scheme for military training was rejected. He particularly praised Colman's for offering work opportunities for the unemployed, observing that the firm might 'well be considered as giving quite half the amount out of their own pockets, for the unskilled labour of a casual man is not worth half that of a skilled workman'. As far as public works were concerned, Walter lamented that the beneficiaries often had to be employed on work for which there was no real need. With hindsight he recommended that people should in future be employed collectively on one large scheme chosen by the city engineer rather than on a lot of small ones, which required too much organisation.

The District Visiting Society was given £100, on condition that they undertook soup distribution to benefit the wives and children of the unemployed, with the help of the Soup Society. Walter commented that Mr and Mrs Campling of the soup kitchen, quite apart from doing extra, unpaid work, provided excellent soup 'which could not have been bought retail at double the price paid for it'.

The final report and accounts[17] demonstrated the fund's essential success. More than £3,000 was raised, in cash and in kind, compared with around £1,600 in the previous mayoralty. But Walter modestly played down his own role, saying that, as a retired man, he had more time to devote to this cause than his predecessors who were active businessmen.

Duties as Mayor *[See plate I]*

With such a strong sense of history, Walter felt himself to be the guardian of the city's (and within that, the Mayor's) privileges. Nobody was going to mess with him on account of his inexperience. So although he chose not to sit on the bench of magistrates except 'when there was a life-saving presentation', nor, as was customary, to become a JP for life after his term of office,[18] he did make an occasional appearance at the Mayor's court and quarter sessions in order to ensure that the Mayor's precedence was preserved. He hated civic ceremonial, and used to say that the only thing that kept him sane while Mayor was the knowledge that he had his country estate to return to. Nevertheless he worked tirelessly at the day-to-day duties expected of the Mayor.[19] He chaired council meetings, attended the civic service in the cathedral, and opened new buildings and amenities including Sewell Park, and Trowse Pumping Station,[20] even though he drew no real enjoyment from these formalities and recorded that his official visit to the Colchester Pageant was about the only amusing thing he did while Mayor! In contrast to his general dislike of ceremonial, Walter, under the slightly apprehensive eye of some landowners, in the summer of 1908 actually revived the historic ceremony of swan-upping. This (of course!) was the prelude to a gargantuan breakfast. A swan roll was exhibited to give the ceremony more credence.[21]

The visit of King Edward VII, 25 October 1909[22]

When Walter undertook the role of Mayor it was not known that during the final weeks of his mayoralty the city would be honoured with a royal visit. King Edward VII had visited Norwich previously, when Prince of Wales, to lay the foundation stone of the Norfolk and Norwich Hospital, and now as king he accepted a request to return to lay the foundation stone of its extension, but this time he would visit the city in its own right.

Meticulous planning, by the city engineer's department and others, went into making the visit a success. The streets along the royal route were cleaned and decorated, illuminations were erected for the *après-visite,* and barriers put up to contain the crowds. These proved very necessary on the day. The order of events was widely publicised in advance, in both the local and the national press. And, encouraged by bright sunshine, people turned out in force: 'Thorpe Station has never been busier... For a time it almost resembled Liverpool Street in activity and was manned by officials from a distance who supplemented the efforts of the local staff.'[23]

The King had spent the preceding weekend at Quidenham Hall as the guest of the Earl and Countess of Albemarle, from where he drove in a closed motor car past enthusiastic crowds in Attleborough, Wymondham and Hethersett, while children lining the route sang the National Anthem. Many later said that they had found it hard to make out the actual Personage through the car's windows. The planning and execution of street decorations along the entire route had been centrally coordinated rather than left to individual initiative, but there does seem to have been scope for local enterprise: it was reported, for example, that at Attleborough he passed: '... a huge banner inscribed "Gaymer's Cyder Works Employees: God Save the King!" which was held in position on the line of route, by a great crowd of the company's staff.'

Meanwhile in Norwich: '... hawkers were doing an extremely good business disposing with ease of their array of souvenirs in the shape of buttonholes, medallions and flags... [and] the occupants of each motor car were carefully scrutinised.'

Their patience was soon rewarded. The King arrived in Norwich via Cringleford Bridge and a great cheer went up when he posed in his Field Marshal's uniform to receive a general salute. The bells of St Peter Mancroft rang out.

The King's visit to Norwich, 1909. *Souvenir postcard in the author's
possession. The message reads: "This has been an exciting and memorable
day in the old city. Our good King has been amongst us and has received
a most loyal reception. C. has been to Mousehold with the children who
welcomed His Majesty by singing the National Anthem. He stopped to listen
to them and saluted."*

The focal point of the visit was St Andrew's Hall (the fifteenth-century nave of the former Blackfriars in the city centre), where the cloisters and adjacent rooms had been specially furnished by Messrs Trevor Page & Co, and a 'throne' had been purpose-built for the King from oak and pigskin, the timber having been retrieved during the restoration of the Guildhall. In a brief ceremony of no more than fifteen minutes the King was received by the Mayor and civic dignitaries. The sword bearer handed the sword to the town clerk, he to the Mayor, and he to the King. 'The king placed his hand upon the hilt and with a smile said a few words to the Mayor, who beamed his acknowledgements'.[24] A short address was then read by the Recorder, although the style and content suggest that it had been written by Walter himself:

It may interest your Majesty, who has honoured the county of Norfolk by making it your Majesty's home, to learn that it has recently been discovered that your Majesty's royal predecessors, King Henry III, King Edward I and King Edward II, had a residence and park at Burgh-by-Aylsham, and frequently visited them for hunting and shooting.[25]

The King responded, recalling his earlier visit to the hospital, and urging people to continue to support it. Lord Leicester, the Lord Lieutenant, presented the Mayor, Mayoress and Sheriff, and a long list of people of all ages, from the Scouts drilled for the purpose in the preceding days at the Artillery Barracks to the elderly inmates of the Great Hospital. To complete the panoply, the organ played.

For the next stage of the proceedings, the ride to Mousehold, carriages rather than motor cars were the order of the day. The Mayor and civic dignitaries led the way in two carriages, followed by the (now unmistakeable) King in Lord Albemarle's 'semi-state 4-horse landau with postillions and outriders'. They entered Mousehold through a ceremonial arch. A massed choir of 11,000 elementary school children sang. ('Very good, very good!' said the King.) And the King inspected the massed troops, assembled in their colourful uniforms, before proceeding to lunch with the officers of the Territorials at the Drill Hall of the 4th Bn Norfolk Regiment at Chapel Field.

The afternoon began with the King's return visit to the Norfolk and

Norwich Hospital, from where he went on to Crown Point 'where he honoured Mr and Mrs Colman by taking tea with them'. To round off the day he was driven to Lord Iveagh's seat at Elveden, and then on to his rooms at the Jockey Club at Newmarket before finally going to Moulton Paddocks for dinner with Sir Ernest Cassel. To all appearances he had much enjoyed his outing.[26]

And as far as the people were concerned, too, the visit was a huge success. The crowds that turned out all along the King's route were cheering and good-natured, and by the end of the day the police and the press were agreeably surprised that people had remained generally well-behaved throughout and that there were no presentations next day at the magistrates' court for public disorder in connection with the visit.[27] Some drunken revelry was reported but apart from the usual suspects who would stay up as long as drink was on offer, people generally seemed to disperse quietly, and earlier than expected, so that the half-hour's licensing extension granted to pubs and bars for the day was scarcely needed:[28] 'Everyone must have felt, when the last light was extinguished last night – everyone except, perhaps the threescore people or thereabouts who thought that if knighthoods were going about they might be the recipient – that the day had been a complete success.'[29]

Much has been made of the fact that for the royal visit Walter dressed in a grey worsted morning suit and bowler hat, and not a more formal morning suit or mayoral robes. Some of the citizenry were shocked,[30] and gossip abounded – and has passed into folklore – that this was why the King did not use the occasion to confer either a knighthood on Walter or a Lord Mayoralty on the city (especially as there had not been an official royal visit to the city since that of King Charles II in 1671).[31] It is clear from Walter's *Autobiography* that his behaviour was fully consistent with his hatred of dressing up, ceremony, and what we might call 'froth'. But he might well also have had in mind the historic precedent of the mayor of Norwich at the time of that earlier royal visit, who had refused to receive a knighthood, but had persuaded the King to bestow one instead upon Dr Thomas Browne. Walter, as well as providing agreeable entertainment, intended the fullest respect for His Majesty; and he had let it be known quietly behind the scenes that he dreaded being offered a knighthood, which he would have felt obliged to refuse. So he was relieved that the Palace had picked up and acted on these private signals.

He was also the one who blocked all discussion of the city's having a Lord Mayor, arguing that generations had been perfectly satisfied with a mere mayoralty, a title he thought more 'venerable and honourable'.[32] In this too the Palace respected his wishes, although Norwich was not forgotten and duly acquired its Lord Mayoralty under Walter's immediate successor, so in the end everyone was happy. In short, from Walter's viewpoint there could not have been a happier or more triumphant conclusion to his mayoralty; and the King's visit, while being stressful to Walter personally, served to reinforce the public view that Walter had been single-minded, staunch and unswerving in his devotion to the city, as well as having the stature and presence to fill the part well.[33]

Endnotes

1   This section is substantially based on the essays in Carole Rawcliffe and Richard Wilson, (eds.,) *Norwich since 1550* (Hambledon and London, 2004).
2   Christine Clark, 'Work and employment', in Rawcliffe, *op. cit.*, pp.385–408.
3   Barry Doyle, 'Politics 1834–1945', in Rawcliffe, *op. cit.*, pp.343–360.
4   I am grateful to Peter Rye for showing me this.
5   WR, *Tourists' Guide* (1885 edition), pp.8–9. In WR, *Rubbish and Nonsense* (pp.81–82) he reprinted an undated letter to the *Norwich Argus* criticising, as a non-voter, the mud-raking tactics of Norwich Liberals against Conservative candidates which he found ungentlemanly.
6   'The Coming election': letter to the editor of the *Norfolk Daily Standard,* 23 Nov. 1885. (WR, *Rubbish and Nonsense*, pp.83–87).
7   *Autobiog.*
8   Tribute by W. G. Clarke FGS, *EDP,* 25 Feb. 1929 p.4.
9   *EDP,* 3 Nov. 1908.
10   *EDP* cuttings file.
11   15 Feb. 1909, H. F. Killick congratulates WR on election as Mayor, 'and also to congratulate the citizens of that ancient Borough in their good sense in selecting a man of culture and intellectual distinction rather than a man who was distinguished more for the depth of his pocket that for any other qualification': NRO, MS 10612 folder (1).
12   NRO, MS 4691/11 contains correspondence for this period, including grateful thanks from the manager of Strangers' Hall for his liberality at a time when takings had been bad. There are also examples of the many letters soliciting donations from the Mayor's Fund and the Mayor's attendance at functions.
13   In Aug. 1909 Walter wrote to Norwich's MP, G. H. Roberts, to enlist his support for petitions to the Commons regarding pubic rights on the Broads. He had already contacted other Members, and had keen support from, among others, many angling clubs. NRO, MS 4691/92. The petition is quoted at length in the *Autobiog.*, pp.169–170.

14 *EDP*, 25 Feb.1929, pp.5–6 'Death of Mr Walter Rye, Athlete and Antiquary, Mayor of Norwich who received King Edward VII'.

15 *EDP* cuttings file and *Autobiog.*

16 Mentioned in an undated memorandum in NRO, MS 4691/11. Small grants were also awarded towards assisted emigration.

17 *The Mayor of Norwich's Unemployed Fund 1908–9. Report and Balance Sheet to June 9th, 1909.*

18 Official letter from town clerk, 11 Sept. 1909, acknowledging that WR does not wish to become a permanent JP: NRO, MS 4691/11.

19 *EDP*, 25 Feb. 1929 (as footnote 2 above).

20 The former Sewell Park website (www.sewellparknorwich.com but taken down since this chapter was written) gave an account of the Park's official opening during his mayoralty, 17 Dec. 1909. In his speech Walter had said that Norwich needed spaces like this 'for the benefit of small children and for rough boys to play about and yell in to their hearts' content, and to ease the ears of people who, like myself, are supposed to live in quiet streets'.

21 *Autobiog.*, and letter of 19 Aug. from TBL: NRO, MS 4691/14/1.

22 This section is derived from the reports of the *EDP* of 26 Oct. 1909, the day after the visit, and on syndicated reports of the *ordre du jour* from other newspapers on the day itself, including the *Manchester Courier* of 25 Oct. (BL Newspaper Archive). The East Anglian Film Archive in the Archive Centre, Norwich, holds a movie film of the visit, which may be viewed at http://www.eafa.org.uk/catalogue/900. (I am grateful to Dr John Alban for this reference.)

23 *EDP* press cuttings.

24 Ibid.

25 Walter himself alluded to the dispute between the civic officials and the Heralds' College over the city's coat of arms. The supporters, two sword-bearing angels, have been in existence for hundreds of years, but the heraldic tribunal refuses to recognise them, holding them to be mere decorative figures having nothing to do with the coat of arms.

26 'We have authority for stating that the King was very greatly pleased with his reception.' *EDP*.

27 *EDP* press cuttings.

28 However, not all were quite as blameless as the above suggests. The same page of *EDP* has a note that Sir Samuel Hoare had his pockets picked while in the crowd at St Stephen's Gate after the hospital ceremony while 'protecting Lady Hastings and Lady Talbot de Malahide: his purse and several railway tickets were stolen'.

29 *EDP*.

30 For an insight into Victorian attitudes to dress see Pamela Horn, *Pleasure and Pastimes in Victorian Britain* (1999), p.57.

31 These stories were still circulating in modern times. As late as 1986 George Piercy remembered the account of the King's visit to the drill hall in October 1909 as told by his grandfather, George Seaman, who was a policeman on duty at the time and recollected that the King was incensed by the Mayor's dress.

He repeated that word on the street was that the King deliberately refused to grant the city the honour of having a Lord Mayor until after Walter's term of office. 'It was all a great pity because he [Walter] was a fervent Royalist even though he didn't show it.' (*EDP*, 19 Feb 1986.) His son Frank is quoted as saying that as there had not been a royal visit to Norwich since the days of Charles II 'some signal honour could be expected', but Walter wore a grey worsted morning suit and the King was alleged to have been overheard saying 'Did you see the man's trousers?' J. Ryan (comp.) *The Annals of Thames Hare and Hounds 1868 to 1945, with the present generation 1946 to 1968* by Ian H. Fraser (1968), pp.45–6.

32 Jane Hales, 'I knew Walter Rye', in *Norfolk Fair*, Aug. 1984.

33 *EDP* 25 Feb. 1929, also p.4, Current Topics [anonymous]. For the formal printed vote of thanks to WR from the City Council on his year as Mayor, 9 Nov. 1909, see NRO, MS 4691/11. See also Cubitt to WR, 14 Nov. 1909: 'Every one in Norwich tells me that there has never been a Mayor who has put such a lot of hard work into his year of office'. NRO, MS 4691/23. A copy survives of a letter WR, as Mayor, wrote on 11 Feb. 1909 to Lloyd George as Chancellor of the Exchequer arguing for the tax on the award of armorial bearings to be increased except for those who can provide proof of their entitlement, in order to put off fraudsters: NRO, MS 4691/81/2. He received only a polite acknowledgement. For the official invitation to the banquet at St Andrew's Hall after the King's departure, see NRO, MS 4691/84/2. Walter managed to get his arms and fylfots onto the invitation.

PART THREE

THE FINAL STRAIGHT

1
LOOSE ENDS

'I have lived several lives at the same time and think I may say have worked hard at each of them.'

Walter Rye, *Autobiography*, 1916

The six preceding Tracks have provided strong support for the self-assessment above by Walter. Through them we have been able to explore each of his main 'lives' as far as the surviving evidence will permit, although some strands – for example his professional life and his politics – are either enigmatic or threadbare and leave scope for further speculation.

The same could be said of his religion and philanthropy, which are equally poorly documented. Then there is the strange fact that despite his eminence in the antiquarian field he never became a Fellow of either the Royal Historical Society or the Society of Antiquaries of London. This chapter picks up those loose ends, the next looks at what is, in a way, the 'elephant in the room', Walter's very particular sense of humour. Then, in order to give something of the broader context, we must explore some of Walter's lasting friendships. Once we have taken those into account it will finally be time to attempt an overall appraisal of Walter Rye.

Religion

We saw how the evangelical influence of St Luke's Chelsea and the example of his elder sister Maria in charitable work fired the young Walter to become a Sunday school and later a night school teacher. We know too that regular chapel attendance was required of its students by King's College where

Walter attended night school. So there can be little doubt that in his boyhood and youth he was a regular church attender. Whether he kept this up in later life is more difficult to establish because he tends not to talk about religion either in the *Autobiography* or in his correspondence. Quite possibly, like many of his peers, he was just an occasional church attender, although he never lost his Christian faith.

Certainly he was married in church and had his children baptised in various different churches, depending on where he was living (or perhaps on where his heart was at the time), but there is no other obvious indication of regular and active involvement in local church life in either London or Norfolk. He is not known to have held office in any of the parishes where he lived, although the signs are that he was a regular attender at Lammas on his retirement: he managed to have several memorials erected in the church and was thanked in 1905 for serving as the honorary secretary of the tower restoration fund.

He also made good friends among the clergy and must have spent many hours discussing religion with them and listening to sermons by men such as Augustus Jessopp while staying with them as a guest. He pointed out too that, over the years, he had had fruitful discussions with a number of Norwich's Roman Catholics, including Canon Husenbeth, John L'Estrange (Walter's mentor), Canon Dalton, Father Fitzgerald and Canon Drake. 'They were always courteous and willing to help a Protestant student in investigating past history.'

In his declining years a broadside he fired at the Roman Catholic Church, and in particular its senior representative in Norwich at that time, Canon Freeland, does at least have the merit of showing us what point Walter had reached in his own spiritual journey. Most strikingly, there is this *apologia*: 'All thinking men believe in a Creator, and such of them as are naturalists cannot doubt it. Real Christians, who are not blind followers of Roman Catholic religion, believe in Christianity because it is the only possible and perfect form of religion.'[1]

What elicited this statement was that Canon Freeland, rather doubting Walter's lucidity after a recent bout of press correspondence, had wisely refused to enter into public debate on the things Walter could not stomach about Roman Catholicism: clerical celibacy, the real Presence of Christ in the Mass and the intercessory role of the Blessed Virgin Mary. But for all that, Walter was impressed by some aspects of Catholicism: the discipline maintained over their flock by Roman Catholic priests, their teachings on birth control and sex, and their energy and drive in social work. (It should be said that he was equally impressed by the Salvation Army on several of these fronts.) He must surely have discussed these matters, too, with his youngest daughter and carer, Kitty, who as we learn from an annexe to Walter's will was considering becoming a Roman Catholic nun after his death.

At the opposite end of the religious spectrum, some forms of Protestantism revolted him almost as much as Roman Catholicism. In 1901 whilst staying with his old friend Voelcker he wrote: I was poisoned with dense tobacco smoke when I was not attending his Presbyterian service, and felt unwell from both causes.[2]

In the same vein we might recall the trouble he had in adjusting to being the tenant of non-conformist landlords in Norwich. Nor was the Anglican Church (or at least the Anglo-Catholic wing of it) entirely spared his criticism. He singled out for opprobrium those High Church clergy who refused burial to unbaptised babies, or marriage to 'sinless' divorcees. And he had little time for lay presentations to church livings. Overall, he felt that: '… what the Church of England wants is stronger Bishops, who will see their own laws are obeyed and not wink at breaches of them.'[3]

So, as if we could doubt it, Walter was no religious liberal! And in some ways by the end of his life the wheel had come full circle from his pamphlet on *Legal and Advisable Ornaments* (1866), where his knowledge of the Church's doctrine and practice had very largely been based on archival evidence such as the medieval Gild certificates and the Certificates of Church Goods at the Reformation. Theology and Canon Law did not really interest him, and his religious views seem rather to have stemmed from his Protestant upbringing and a sense of England's history.

Philanthropy

Throughout his life Walter was a generous supporter of charitable causes. His youthful voluntary effort in support of Sunday school and night schools gave way to enthusiastic support for athletic clubs, including their fundraising efforts. Then in middle age we find him organising a show ('Jarley's Waxworks') in aid of the Boer War effort in 1899,[4] and masterminding a large antiquarian contribution to a charity art exhibition in St Andrew's

Hall, Norwich in 1902. He was a supporter of the Society for Prevention of Cruelty to Animals from at least 1902, and in 1903 even served as a waiter at their Drovers' tea, also at St Andrew's, which sought to promote among them the idea of temperance (not notably successfully). That must surely have been a sight to behold!

In the course of his legal work in London he picked up governorships or trusteeships of several charitable/hospital institutions in which there was significant competition for places; so he was lobbied by friends to write in support or cast a vote in favour of an applicant they knew. These included the Deaf and Dumb Asylum in the Old Kent Road,[5] the Brompton Consumptive Hospital[6] and the Royal Hospital and Home for Incurables in Putney.[7] I have found no mention of his acquiring the same kind of responsibilities in Norwich, but he does mention, for example, supporting in 1903 Miss Oxley's benefit for the 'lunatics' of the Bethel Hospital (which he declared to be 'as good as ever', which suggests he was a regular attender). Frequent letters of thanks found among his papers show that he made one-off cash donations to many churches and charities, and as we have seen, during his mayoralty he threw his full force behind the Mayor's Fund for the Relief of the Unemployed in Norwich.

Throughout his adult life Walter served in a voluntary capacity on the committees of national and local sporting clubs, in which he not only paid his own subscriptions but sponsored cups and prizes, as he did for the Norwich Miniature Rifle Association. In the antiquarian world he was just as generous with his time, money and hospitality. In spite of personal differences with the officers of the NNAS he still sponsored a gold medal for the society in 1903. He served on the library and museum committees in Norwich, and his love of his adopted city led him to buy and present books and manuscripts during his lifetime, to undertake much voluntary listing and cataloguing after his retirement, and eventually to bequeath his books, maps and manuscripts to the city. Even Walter's continual financial subvention of his own local publications was partly fed by an altruistic desire to put his own and other people's research in the hands of other students and the wider public.

His charitable activities during the First World War are not well documented, but isolated references indicate how active he was, beginning near home. He records giving a piano to a local 'concentration camp' in 1914 and taking a Christmas turkey in 1915 to the war hospital at Cawston. From the beginning of the war he was also involved with the volunteer movement in Lammas. In 1915 soldiers of the Berkshire regiment were billeted opposite his house there:

> ... but had no tables or chairs, so I had to lend them some. They were a very decent lot indeed and I did my best to make them comfortable (though they were not quartered on me) by lending them books and supplying them with vegetables. Not enough was done by other local residents, in fact they did nothing at all.

Among his letters we find an acknowledgment for a donation in November 1916 of £10 to the Norwich War Hospital Supply Depot.[8] His support for the war-wounded among his family and friends necessitated some cutting back in his general charitable giving after the war. He ceased to subscribe to the SPCA in 1919 on the grounds that: 'The War has hit me very hard and I now have many of my family [and friends] who are injured... I have no money to spare.'[9]

And in January the same year a letter from Fred Henderson begging Walter's financial support towards some election expenses, received in return a smaller donation than Walter would have wished, for the same reason.[10]

On a personal level, too, we have seen the generosity with which he and Georgina opened their houses and gardens to fellow sportsmen, neighbours and visiting groups from the clubs and societies with which he was associated. He also showed himself to be a most faithful friend who did not count the cost of his help *in extremis* to people like John L'Estrange and Augustus Jessopp.

Overall, it is clear that Walter Rye was a generous-hearted benefactor to many individuals and institutions.

Relations with the Royal Historical Society and the Society of Antiquaries of London

Perhaps surprisingly, Walter appears never to have contemplated becoming a Fellow of the Royal Historical Society. He probably felt that his lack of a university education in history or any other discipline ruled him out. Even though he was on friendly terms with a number of professional historians throughout his life, he let slip from time to time that he thought of himself as a humble 'indexer', or 'topographer', implying that he was coming to the sources with rather different intentions. This did not always work to his advantage. For example, in the hope that he might be sent a copy of Hubert Hall's *Repertory*[11] published by the Royal Historical Society, he wrote in 1921 to congratulate Hall on the work, which he had consulted in the Norwich public library. Hall sent him a postcard regretting that as Walter was not a Fellow he did not qualify for a free copy, but adding that he would see if he could find him a review copy.[12]

Rather more mystery surrounds Walter and the Society of Antiquaries of London, another prestigious body of which he never became a member. Why not? Its interests were, on the face of it, right up his street. Did his busy working life as a London lawyer mean that he lacked the time to engage with a body of this kind sufficiently to make membership worthwhile? And after his retirement to Norwich, when he clearly did have more time on his hands, did he (as seems likely) lack the stamina to keep returning to London to take an active interest in their activities? Neither of these explanations seems quite sufficient. More plausibly, especially after his on-off relationship with the NNAS, we might suspect that Walter preferred to remain an independent spirit, set apart from the Antiquaries, so that he might feel free to criticise them when necessary. The *Western Mail,* reporting on archaeological periodicals in its issue of 23 January 1890 commented: 'It is to the Society of Antiquaries that Mr Walter Rye, the great archaeologist, applies the aphorism of Arthur Orton,[13] "Some folks have money and no brains, others etc. etc."'

Whatever his motives, he did not seek to become a Fellow, although he held the Society of Antiquaries in high enough regard to ensure that its library was among the regular recipients of his publications.

But out of the blue in the autumn of 1917 a person or persons unknown put about a malicious and quite untrue rumour that Walter had been put up for Fellowship of the Antiquaries but black-balled in the election. His long-standing friend and fellow antiquary P. B. Ficklin set the cat among the pigeons by telling Walter, in a postscript to a letter probably intended as no more than a humorous pleasantry, that: 'I was told the other day by a man that you had put up and been pilled for the Antiquaries. I said it was a lie to the best of my information and belief.'[14]

Walter became incandescent when Ficklin admitted, sheepishly and with considerable remorse, that he might have been overheard discussing this matter in public. Walter suspected that the originator of the rumour was another antiquary, Travers Davey, in revenge for Walter's having publicly exposed his false claim to arms. Typically of Walter, instead of treating the whole matter with the contempt and silence it surely deserved he fanned the flames by threatening Davey with an action for libel unless he made an apology and gave a sum to charity to settle the matter. Davey denied all knowledge of it, and after a further protest by Walter to the society itself the storm subsided, but not without temporary collateral damage to his friendship with Ficklin, and a wound to his own self-esteem. He berated Ficklin:

> I can't see that the fact of our having been friends for 30 years should debar me from having fair play in a matter affecting my personal credit... A statement that the premier Antiquarian Society did not think me worthy of being a member of it reflects on my capacity to write Antiquarian books, and coming as it does just as I am issuing circulars for my last and most important book on Norfolk Armoury must injure its sale and cause special damage.[15]

Endnotes

1 WR, *Some Historical Essays* (vol. 2), p.151.
2 *Autobiog.*, p.119.
3 *Ibid.*, p.156.
4 *Autobiog.*, p.110.
5 See, for example, letter from Griffith in 1888 and 1895, NRO, MS 4691/4 and 7.
6 WHE to WR, 20 May 1916: NRO, MS 4691/5/1.
7 Jane M. Pidgeon, sister of Arthur and Wilfrid Ball, asking for votes at the next election for Isabella Farger (with printed card of solicitation): 25 Sept. 1923, NRO, MS 4691/12. A later letter of 12 Nov. thanks him for his fifty votes.
8 NRO, MS 4691/5/1.
9 NRO, MS 4691/2.
10 NRO, MS 4691/12.
11 H. Hall, *A Repertory of British Archives* (1920).
12 NRO, MS 4691/2.
13 Celebrated as the claimant to the Tichborne baronetcy.
14 NRO, MS 4691/5/1.
15 For a sequence of letters from Davey and Ficklin in Oct. 1917 see NRO, MS 4691/5/1. This allusion may be to *A list of coat armour used in Norfolk before the date of the first Herald's Visitation of 1563*, Norwich, 1917/18.

2
PRACTICAL JOKES

'The art of making yourself scientifically disagreeable'

'In my opinion we can never begin to understand him unless we
remember his fondness for practical jokes.'

Tom Copeman, *Eastern Daily Press*, 1973

In his humorous collection of snippets and reprints, *Rubbish and Nonsense,*
Walter gives a distinct impression of himself as one of the lads, drinking,
swearing and cavorting with the best of them. The book, written for the
amusement of his family, contains an abundance of gags, jokes, satire and
even some passable doggerel. Walter's lively – often wicked – sense of
humour, which he developed as a teenager, endeared him to friends and
team-mates alike. His taste for the absurd found an outlet in nonsense
poems, tall stories and parody songs performed after dinner. But he also
developed a penchant for practical jokes (of the naughty schoolboy variety),
which might be tried out equally on insouciant friends and family, or on
people whose pompous egos he longed to deflate. It was a pastime widely
indulged in by his peers,[1] and he remained an enthusiastic practitioner to
the end of his life.

Already by his late teens – perhaps not entirely seriously – he was
setting out scenarios for practical jokes. Some appeared in *Rubbish and
Nonsense* under the heading 'On the art of making yourself scientifically
disagreeable'. The proposed trick might be of a simple 'April-fool' type. For
example, if you called on an acquaintance and found while you were waiting

to be announced that he had prominently displayed on his mantelpiece the calling cards of distinguished friends, these might be stealthily gathered up and removed, or else shuffled so that those from the least well-known callers were displayed most prominently. Or you could take one of those from a prominent personage and add a false postscript to the name: 'X has called for the third time for the money, will not call again.'

Among the more questionable drawing-room scenarios were knocking caged birds off their perches, turning the play-wheels of animals so fast that they became giddy, or alerting people to a supposed smell of gas where there was none. This kind of thing must surely have tested his long-suffering family and friends to near breaking point.

By the time he retired to Norwich he had played so many practical jokes on people, and collected such copious accounts of other people's pranks, that he had enough material to sustain a whole lecture on 'Practical joking considered as a fine art'. (See Track 6.) He claimed to have taken his inspiration from Theodore Hook, son of James Hook (b. Norwich 1746), who wrote, *inter alia, The Lass of Richmond Hill.*

In his mature years he mostly outgrew tired old jokes such as perching a bucket above an open door; removing the chair of an intending sitter; apple-pie beds; sewing up nightgowns; or filling smokers' pipes with an explosive mixture. But many of the jokes he recorded with more approval were not much better: for example placing teasels in a bed, or cutting off the retaining wire from a bedside bottle of soda-water so that the cork would pop in the middle of the night and give the sleeper an unexpected shower. Some of his tortures were more sophisticated and involved his active participation. He would try to convince first-time overnight guests that his house was haunted, contriving sound effects by blowing air down the plumbing that connected with their rooms; or he might open their bedroom doors in the night and pull bedding off the sleeping guest. Tom Copeman wrote:

I used to hear from [WG] Clarke of some of the house parties to which he and HH Halls were invited when [Walter] was still living at Lammas, where at Christmas there would be a specially fattened swan, and celebrities like Alfred Munnings would be in the company. At such times a guest who slept in the 'haunted room' might be urged to be sure to bolt his door, but it would slowly swing open at midnight, while in the morning bedclothes were liable to slide down inch by inch.

Walter had honed this trick in his annual children's party at Hampstead. The door frame was loosened so that it moved as a unit with the door. So although the unsuspecting guest believed he had locked his door, the room could in fact be entered at dead of night. The bedclothes were then removed by means of a string prepared in advance, attached to the bedding.

The dinner table as well as the bedroom might be the scene of a prank: it was not unknown for the 'Welsh rarebit' to be a bar of fried yellow soap! And he recorded news of the latest joke to reach him from Paris: passing a small India-rubber tube, activated from a bulb/pump, under the victim's table-setting so as to shift his plate when he was sufficiently drunk.

Walter's lecture, and his autobiographical writings, confirm that he had tried and tested many of these pranks: they were not purely hypothetical. He records, for example, that as boys he and his brother had wanted to poke fun at a neighbour they thought paranoid because he was having a burglar alarm fitted to his house. When his builders chanced to leave a ladder unattended beside his house, the two boys shinned up it after dark and attached a string to the bell of the alarm; they then climbed back over their fence and extended the string into their bedroom. At 2am the boys pulled the string to ring his new alarm bell, which brought out the neighbours and the police. They themselves emerged as apparently bleary-eyed innocents, and in the resulting confusion surreptitiously detached their string.

Cycling too provided humorous opportunities. Walter naturally preferred loose, practical clothing to more formal wear. Once he turned up at a hotel in Lynn hot, tired and dusty after a tricycle ride. The manager took one look at his visitor's scruffy appearance and told him there were no vacancies. So Walter asked if, in that case, he would kindly forward any of his mail to Lord So-and-So. The embarrassed landlord, thinking him to be the aristocrat in question, then kow-towed and offered him his own room, but Walter's response was, 'No, I won't stay at this pothouse, but go to a decent inn.'[2]

The desire for revenge or come-uppance was never very far from his mind in the jokes he played on complete strangers. While out for a solitary bike ride on New Year's Day 1898 his chain broke, and he was forced to push his bike up a slight slope, to accompanying sniggers from a 'Cockney rough' who assumed he was doing so simply because the slope had proved too much for an elderly man. Walter offered him the saddle and invited him to do better.[3] 'When he tried he naturally found the treadle rotated rapidly, and ejaculated, "Why, there ain't no chain!" upon which I politely informed him that I had previously discovered that fact many miles before.'[4]

At the time of the 1906 parliamentary election campaign a prominent radical, whom Walter branded an 'oily humbug', '… got into conversation with me and asked me the way to a certain place, and I had no scruple in directing his motor by a route which took him through a deep ford. Next day I saw he was late at a meeting, and I didn't wonder at it.'

Those unused to such goings-on could easily walk straight into one of his traps. In 1905 he undertook to complete Bateman's unfinished history of the Bethel Hospital, Norwich, on condition that he was allowed to print in it some original documents. He was offered payment, but replied in jest that he would rather have a place reserved for him in the hospital for when he needed it. He was at first taken seriously until one of the committee caught the guilty twinkle in his eye. 'It would,' said Walter, 'have been the greatest scalp I had ever raised in a long series of practical jokes.' Another misunderstanding arose with one of his boatmen who claimed to be feeling ill. Walter suspected he was just shirking some boring duty and told him he must be suffering from a 'malignant diagnosis'. This was so far beyond the man's regular vocabulary that he feared the worst and went off to hospital to have it checked out – only to be despatched with a flea in his ear![5]

There are hints that Walter infected his family with the same love of practical jokes. He noted with pleasure in the *Autobiography*, under 1909, that when his son HGR brought home his new fiancée, a Scot called Marjorie, to meet Walter he escorted her past the 'palatial buildings of the Norwich Union', and persuaded her that that was where Walter lived, before eventually bringing her to 'my cottage in the same street'. It was, he said, 'only in accordance with the bad family habit of leg-pulling, of which we are all so foolishly fond.'

Endnotes

1   Pamela Horn, *Pleasure and Pastimes in Victorian Britain* (Stroud, 1999), p.32 recalls William Morris's fondness for practical joking.
2   *Eastern Daily Press*, 25 Feb. 1929, p.4.

3   *Autobiog.*, p.148 (n).
4   *Autobiog.*, p.99.
5   He noted that watermen, though quite happy to brave the outdoors in all weathers, also have strange 'funks' from which they have to be stirred by alcoholic and other remedies: *Songs, Stories and Sayings of Norfolk* (1897) p.26.

3
FRIENDSHIPS

It is clear from his voluminous correspondence that Walter had many loyal friends, certainly more than can be mentioned here. A closer study of the archive, especially if it is arranged and catalogued more fully, would almost certainly add depth (and more names – perhaps including some whom I have unjustifiably neglected) to this analysis. Whether or not it is safe to judge a man by his friends, their identity reveals something of the man at the centre of the circle.

School and college friends

One of the names encountered most frequently in these pages is that of **Richard (Dick) Howlett**, a school-mate and thereafter a constant and lifelong chum of Walter's. Both of them attended St Peter's Collegiate School and the Chelsea Athenaeum. But Dick was of a more academic bent and went on to Cambridge, and thence to a post in the Civil Service Commission. Walter introduced him to antiquarian and historical research and he established a strong reputation in his own right as an author and transcriber, being elected a Fellow of the Society of Antiquaries of London, which Walter never was. As teenagers, the two would go on expeditions together, walking, cycling and sailing. But Dick did all of this for enjoyment, both of the exercise and of Walter's company. He was not a keen and competitive sportsman like Walter, and flatly refused to join Thames Hare and Hounds. He was one of the few people to whom Walter entrusted his closest personal thoughts; and the relationship was strong enough for Dick to be able to say exactly what he thought on any issue, from Walter's youthful amours and engagements to the sloppiness of some of his writing

Richard Howlett. *Autobiography*

and draughtsmanship! Walter often enlisted his help to proof-read articles and books before publication, and Dick begrudged this only to the extent that Walter ignored specific comments or made the unsafe assumption that Dick was checking accuracy of content as well as presentation. The task could be tedious and exasperating, especially as Walter's handwriting, which was never good, deteriorated with his failing eyesight.

Dick in time married, but in his fifties suffered the trauma of seeing one of his sons die. Fearing for the health of his other son too, he became anxious. His wife Alice wrote to Walter on 29 June 1896, turning down an invitation to a garden party at Hampstead because 'Dick is in such a state that he can hardly bear us to mention the poor boy's name. You know how intensely he feels things.'[1] He was a regular visitor to Walter in Norwich and Lammas after his retirement.

*

Walter's evening classes at King's College afforded little time for socialising and making new contacts, as the men arrived straight from work and the evening was well advanced by the time they had finished their classes. But he made up for this by joining the college's athletics club and representing it in competitions. A number of his peers went on to become famous lawyers or academics, and one, Isaac Seaman, became editor of *Public Opinion*, but Walter does not seem to have kept in touch with these men in later life.

Sporting friends

Walter's athletic activities brought him a whole host of new friends and acquaintances, some of them officials or fellow-members of the athletics and rowing clubs he joined, others competitors and opponents. Even those mentioned in passing in the *Autobiography* or represented in Walter's correspondence are too numerous to list, but they included athletes like his trainer **Nathaniel Perry**; **Walter Chinnery**, a founding member of the London Athletic Club, and his brothers **G. T. and H. J. Chinnery**; and rowers like **Mickey and Ben Slater** of Thames Rowing Club.

W. H. ('Piggy') Eyre, also of TRC, was one of the most formidable oarsmen of his day and became successively Walter's room-mate in Roehampton, his co-tenant for a while in Wandsworth and his legal partner in the firm which was then renamed Rye and Eyre. Walter greatly valued him not only as a close friend but also as a business partner. His firm grasp of legal issues and his prodigious memory for cases and clients far outstripped Walter's own.[2] They remained good friends, and long after his retirement Walter used to visit and stay with Eyre and his wife in London.

As we saw, the athletes **Arthur** and **Wilfrid W. Ball** of the London Athletic Club cheekily appeared over the horizon to go walking with Walter while he was on his honeymoon at Cromer![3] Wilfrid was an artist, and Walter commissioned illustrations from him for a number of his books including the *Autobiography* and *A Month on the Norfolk Broads* as well as his pamphlet on the Maid's Head in Norwich.

Many fellow-members of Thames Hare and Hounds naturally became Walter's good friends, including **Sydenham Dixon**, **D. M. Roberts** and **Dr Archer** of Wandsworth, the inspiration behind Thames Hare and Hounds' promotion of the first demonstration lacrosse match in England. Roberts ['DMR' to Walter] kept closely in touch with Walter throughout his life. In their later correspondence he was perhaps the only person who would dare refer to Walter as 'Dear Old Pal'. He joined Walter on both cycling and sailing expeditions, and was a frequent visitor and holiday companion in

George Lacy Hillier. *Friends of Blockley and Ladywell Cemeteries, www. foblc.org.uk.*

Norfolk; they obviously enjoyed each other's company enormously.[4] In the field of cycling, **Lacy Hillier**, **W. J. Winthrop** and **J. J. Bateman** were regular companions of Walter's. All were also athletes. Hillier became a national cycling champion, and promoter of, and writer on, the sport.[5] Walter recalled after Winthrop's death that he was a 'gentle giant' of a man, who took part in events such as the shot-put and tug-of-war.

Custodians and owners of records

Study visits to libraries and record offices put Walter in touch with many like-minded people, and he made good friends among the staff as well as their clientele. **Walford D. Selby** of the Public Record Office became a particular friend, and Walter was horribly shocked when Selby took his own life in a fit of depression following a bout of influenza.[6] Through Selby or some other intermediary he met **Sir Charles Isham** of Lamport Hall, Northamptonshire, and became a regular visitor there, working on the family muniments.

*

Clergy

We have seen how from his earliest visits to Norfolk Walter made the acquaintance of the county's antiquaries. Some of them became personal friends, including a number of clergy. Among these were **Revd H. T. Griffith**, at first of Bassingham, later of North Walsham and finally of Smallburgh, who became a regular correspondent, welcomed Walter and sometimes Georgina and one or more of their daughters as well, on holiday, and exchanged visits with them in London.[7] He assisted Walter in collecting and checking monumental inscriptions, and Walter commended him as 'one of the finest genealogists in the county'.

Walter's most distinguished clergy friend was **Revd Dr Augustus Jessopp**, another name often mentioned in these pages, who when Walter first met him (perhaps through the NNAS) was headmaster of Norwich School. At the end of 1878, shortly before Jessopp resigned to take up a country living, we find Walter spending Christmas in Norwich with him and his wife, and being introduced to John Brooke Little (who also became a friend and sailing companion) and other literary and antiquarian gentlemen. In 1879, Jessopp became rector of Scarning, where he remained until 1911 and where his memory is revered to this day.[8] He was awarded an Oxford DD in 1890, became an Honorary Fellow of both St John's College Cambridge and Worcester College Oxford, Chaplain in Ordinary to King Edward VII in 1904, and an honorary canon of Norwich in 1905. He denied being, or having the mind and skills of, an antiquary, but he was a well-rated historian and biographer who regularly wrote popular articles for *The Nineteenth Century*, many of which were later brought together to form books. Yet in most respects an antiquary indeed he was. He became a leading member and sometime Literary Secretary of the NNAS, to which he contributed over forty papers. He picked Walter's brains on antiquarian issues, and before long enlisted his help in reading old scripts, just as Walter as a youth had himself picked those of John L'Estrange. Walter and Augustus had much in common and became close friends, although Walter almost always continued to refer to him quite formally as 'Dr Jessopp'. They moved in similar circles, not only as Norfolk antiquaries but also, for example, as investigators of private papers for the Historical Manuscripts Commission and as contributors to the *Dictionary of National Biography*. Each cherished and acquired manuscript material, both for his own research and to give to

Revd Dr Augustus Jessopp. Frontispiece to his *One Generation of a Norfolk House,* 3rd ed., 1913.

other libraries. Jessopp, indeed, grew to care so strongly about the archives in which he researched that he campaigned for a better national strategy for their preservation in purpose-designed repositories.[9] Walter drew him in as a contributor to his *Norfolk Antiquarian Miscellany.* He also got on well with Augustus's wife Mary, not least through their shared interest in gardening.

The depth of Augustus's admiration for Walter, and of his pastoral concern for him, is apparent:

My dear Rye: You are a brick! 'Four square all round!' as friend Aristotle phrases it when describing the perfect man.[10]

It helps a man to keep up his faith in his fellow creatures to find one so large hearted as you.[11]

And the affection was mutual. Walter would later record: 'It was always a pleasure to look in on him and have a long antiquarian talk, for a better conversationalist than he was never lived...'[12]

Like other friends – but with equal lack of success – Jessopp regularly chided Walter for working too hard and not taking care of his eyesight or his health in general. In 1881, on hearing that Walter was having eye trouble, he invited him to Scarning. He also planned, and may have made, a visit to Walter and Georgina in Putney.[13] Their friendship did not prevent each of them writing exactly what he thought of the other's work, not only in private correspondence but also in published reviews and letters to the press. It was a game both liked to play, even though one of them invariably had to retire hurt when proved wrong. Walter was often the ultimate victor, perhaps because the priest in Augustus was more easily persuaded to beat his breast in public. H. Irwine Whitty's reminiscences in the *Evening Post*, after Jessopp's death, presented him as a kindly man: 'The doctor's criticisms were mostly trenchant and he would rise to the heights of sublimity in denouncing what was not to his taste; but underneath it all was a charity deep and wide...'

On one occasion, after Walter had publicly suggested that Lord Nelson had attended school at North Walsham, Jessopp wrote to the press:

> I am always sorry when my friend Mr Walter Rye takes up his pen to write in the worst manner – and he always does so when he writes as a dogmatist not as an antiquarian. In his letter in your issue this morning Mr Rye takes upon himself to decide a question about which he is not one whit more entitled to deliver his verdict than any 'man in the street' who may chance to swell the crowd that will assemble in the Cathedral Close this morning.[14]

Jessopp suspected that Walter had confused Walton with Walsham and had therefore come up with '[an] idle story that has, in my opinion, no real foundation; unless indeed the obstinate dreams of my magnanimous old friend Walter Rye are sufficient to account for anything.' Uncowed, Walter proceeded to cite chapter and verse, and Augustus was compelled, at least for the time being, to retract: 'Mr Rye has smitten me hip and thigh, and if he asks for an apology, here it is at his disposal. Nevertheless I cannot regret that I rushed into the fray so rashly, for the cause of truth has been served...'

There was certainly an element of tit-for-tat in all this. In 1885 Walter published a critical review of one of Jessopp's publications in the *Academy*.

Augustus, who did not subscribe to that journal, wrote to him requesting a copy, but already conceding: 'We all make mistakes – all, that is, who do any good work in advance of our fellow creatures – the men that never say or write foolish things never do wise ones. We are all fallible and all of us weak at times...'[15]

Sometimes we find them taking the same side in an argument. After Walter had written an article about Chaucer, challenging the work of Furnivall, Augustus called him 'such a very satisfactory extinguisher (*pro hac vice*) of that inflated fool Furnivall. My blessing upon you!'[16]

From the early 1900s Mary Jessopp began a slow decline into dementia. She died in 1905, leaving Augustus alone in his beloved Scarning, and evidently saved from penury only by the timely receipt of a Civil List pension as a king's chaplain. Perhaps unwisely he continued to engage in academic controversy and to entertain guests. But he too was ageing fast, and soon followed his wife into dementia. Walter was saddened to record its progress in successive years.

In 1912 the Brooke Littles helped Augustus move to a sanatorium in Virginia Water, Surrey. Walter took on himself the informal role of 'supervisor' or guarantor, and, in gratitude, knowing that he was fading fast, Augustus in effect took his leave: 'I am writing you a kind of Farewell. I feel I am a dying man! There is no man living to whom I owe so much and to whom I am so grateful.'[17]

Jessopp's library was sold off at auction. Among his books and papers were found some that he had borrowed from various libraries in the course of his researches and failed to return before his death, including some from Lord Orford. With mixed success, Walter acted on behalf of the City of Norwich and of Lord Orford to try to recover the most important items at the sale. There were no hard feelings, and when the sad day came both Walter and Lord Orford were among the very few people present at Jessopp's funeral.

Antiquaries

In London Walter became close to, among others, **Dr F. J. Furnivall**, the Chaucer expert, and although he was not averse to criticising Furnivall's work, he records that he became a distinct 'hit' with Georgina and the family as well as himself: 'I don't know any man whose loss I felt more when he died.'[18] Walter's legal partner W. H. Eyre, in a tribute after Furnivall's death, recollected meeting him frequently when he visited Walter at the Golden Square office.[19] All three shared a love of rowing, Eyre and Furnivall perhaps more than Walter. Typically, however, their first encounter ended in a spat between Rye and Furnivall over some historical issue, but at the same time it sowed the seeds of a long friendship. Walter found him a man after his own heart, one with whom, as it were, he could do literary business. They were in many respects two of a kind, Furnivall like Rye having quite a reputation for blunt speaking and for taking his adversaries to task in print. If there was a difference, it is the one captured in Eyre's observation of Furnivall that, 'there was never the slightest malice in it. I don't believe there was even much of a desire (as there is with most people) to get the best of his opponent; at least nothing equal to his enthusiastic aspiration that what he believed to be the truth should prevail.'

Surely he must have been comparing Furnivall's approach with that of his partner! Eyre went on:

> Rye was at that time on the staff of the *Athenaeum*, while Furnivall ruled the (antiquarian) roast [sic] of the *Academy*, from the columns of which two journals many knocks were interchanged. But after the conflict mentioned, they used, I think, when anything of doubt or controversy was in the [offing] (re Chaucer or Shakespeare or other matters) to meet and have a friendly discussion with a view to either diverting, or narrowing down hostilities. Now and then they found themselves in perfect agreement; and then it was generally made very warm for somebody else.

The Norfolk antiquarians of the day were not, of course, all clergymen. Walter forged particularly strong ties with **E. M. Beloe**, a Lynn solicitor and historian of the town (whom he first met in 1875), and his son Ted. Beloe, like Walter, was a contributor to the *DNB*. They became related by marriage when Walter's son FGR in 1901 took as his wife Beloe's daughter. But it was not only family flattery that led Beloe to write in 1895 admiring Walter's publications: 'Your research is wonderful, how you have done it with your practice I don't know... My literary work is done – I find yours is in full activity.'[20]

From a long list, other antiquarian friends who might be singled out

EM Beloe. *Autobiography.*   PB Ficklin. *Autobiography.*

because they are well represented in the correspondence included P. B. Ficklin, R. J. W. Purdy and Prince Frederick Duleep Singh.[21]

P. Berney Ficklin [PBF] was a lawyer of Lincoln's Inn when he first met Walter sometime in the 1880s.[22] He and his wife became Walter's great friends, and he used to visit and stay with them regularly at Tasburgh Hall near Norwich both before and after he retired. So close was the relationship that at times they exchanged letters almost daily, even when the Ficklins were abroad on holiday. Much of the correspondence is chatty and inconsequential, as might be expected between friends, and concerns such matters as lunch and dinner invitations, health or gardening. But Ficklin also had antiquarian interests, which Walter encouraged by helping him to decipher old documents. He collected prints and antiques.

Ficklin often berated Walter for his appalling handwriting,[23] and was sufficiently of his inner circle to get away with pulling his leg or even telling him the plain truth:

> You are the most splendidly rude man I ever knew – returning papers which testify to my ancestors' intimacy with Royalty with 'these do not interest me.' I would refer you to Court Etiquette p. [*blank*],

which says, 'Try and simulate an interest in the affairs of others even if you don't feel it...' However, I must say it is very refreshing to meet a real Dr Johnson in the last years of the 19th centuary [sic].[24]

At least once (not unusually between Walter and his friends) they argued spectacularly, and once Walter even threatened to terminate their friendship for good, but Ficklin's placatory response carried the day: 'My dear chap, you are one of the very few of my numerous acquaintances whose *friendship* I really value.'[25]

Ficklin organised shooting parties and sometimes sent birds from the shoot to Walter if he was unable to attend in person. Clay pigeon shooting was occasionally substituted, in which case the participants were asked to bring along their own pistols and cartridges. Ficklin also organised group visits to a nearby Roman camp, on which Walter was invited to speak.[26] After Walter's move to Norfolk the relationship became closer. Walter gave Ficklin both an antique staircase and a fireplace for his house, but was not entirely happy with the way he used them:

> You really are incorrigible. First you spoil the staircase I gave you by sticking some rubbishy eagles you had in stock on it (– a thing unheard of) and now you prepare not only to destroy the authenticity of an old stone mantel by cutting arms and dates in it [*I have no such intention* in PBF's hand] which will be quite wrong, for the Pettus had no arms at the date of such mantel, but to top it with a wooden thing which will be absolutely incongruous.[27]

During Walter's mayoralty, the Ficklins sent him a mock formal invitation on a postcard with a picture of Tasburgh Hall on the front, and on the back the message: 'Mr and Mrs Berney Ficklin will be very pleased if the Mayor of Norwich will lunch, dine and sleep here on Thursday next and will send their carriage to meet his worship by the 12.26 train at Flordon station. RSVP.'[28]

And when the King's visit to Norwich was announced they, like many others, assumed (without knowing Walter's determination that it should not be) that it would guarantee a knighthood for Walter. Ficklin headed a letter with the salutation: 'Dear Sir Walter (as every one says you will be, and I'm told you can't refuse it without insulting the King)...'[29]

The solidity of their friendship could not be better summed up than in the Ficklins' birthday greetings to Walter in 1912: 'Old Bear though you are, we are both very fond of you, and you have been a good friend to us for many years.'[30]

Ficklin was one of those favoured to receive a copy of Walter's *Autobiography* in 1916, and one of the few whose photograph appeared in the book. He lent it to 'Kiffie' who supplied notes on a house in Tombland and added:

> He says you ought to have after your name the letters O.O.T.B. and will give you a shilling if you can guess what they mean. I enclose a slip which you will open after guessing for five minutes and I don't think you will be displeased at his opinion of you, with which I coincide.[31]

*

Walter seems to have met the antiquary **R. J. W. Purdy** of Foulsham, a friend of Lord Orford's, some time after moving to Norwich. As two old men with much to natter about, from antiquities to gout, they became firm friends and spent much time together, exchanging notes and books, and going on local tricycling and motoring expeditions in pursuit not only of historic sites but also of the controversial 'luminous owls' on which Purdy would write a paper for the NNAS.[32] They brought each other mutual consolation, in Walter's case against the background of his wife's encroaching illness and death, and later the gradual departure of his children from the family home. But the companionship was mutual. Purdy too was glad of the chance to socialise, to spend an occasional weekend at Lammas, as in 1906 and 1909, or even at Selborne (1907) and to meet other like-minded spirits, 'a condition of things', he said, 'that doesn't often fall to my lot.'[33] When Walter suggested a ride in August 1913 Purdy declined: 'Since I saw you I have had a narrow shave from a motor accident. I have come to the conclusion it would be very silly of me to attempt a journey on my cycle along a road much frequented by the cursed vehicles, or rather their reckless drivers.'[34]

Purdy died about the time Walter's *Autobiography* was going through the press, and Walter wrote an affectionate memoir for the *Eastern Daily*

RJW Purdy. *Autobiography*.

Prince Frederick Duleep
Singh. *Image ©Peter Bance*:
www.duleepsingh.com.

Press which is quoted at length in the *Autobiography*, recalling his skill
as a wildfowl shooter and his wide-ranging knowledge of arboriculture
and natural history, as well as his antiquarian interests. Walter remarked
elsewhere that Purdy was 'one of our most observant antiquaries… [I] regret
his loss more than I can express'.[35]

Prince Frederick Duleep Singh ['Prince Freddy'] was the second son
of Duleep Singh, the Indian maharajah deposed by the British, who had
settled in England and been given a pension by Queen Victoria. Born in
1868, the prince was to become an East Anglian through-and-through.
He was educated at Eton and Cambridge where he obtained a degree in
Modern History, then served successively in the Suffolk, and (as an officer)
the Norfolk yeomanry (1893–1919, with interruptions). He was a keen
antiquary, a member of the NNAS as well as a number of other local and
national societies, and an enthusiast for preserving historic churches. He
would become a founder of the Prehistoric Society of East Anglia and
president of the London Society of East Anglians.

When Walter retired to Norwich, the Prince (then in his early thirties,
so a quarter of a century Walter's junior) was living at Old Buckenham Hall.
They presumably met through the NNAS. He lost no time in persuading

Walter to edit the *First Register Book of the Parish of Old Buckenham in Norfolk, 1560 to 1649* (1902), whose publication he generously sponsored. Nor was this their only collaboration; for example, Walter acknowledges the Prince's help in revising the proofs of his *Norfolk Families* (1913). Through correspondence on antiquarian topics, occasional visits to each other's homes, and no doubt meetings of the NNAS, the two men developed a friendship that lasted for the rest of Walter's life, although the Prince was always careful to respect the gap in age and status by beginning his letters with the salutation 'Dear Mr Rye'. Walter seems to have been instrumental in persuading him to accept for one year (1909–10) the honorary (and non-playing) presidency of the Fakenham and Dereham archery club while it looked for a longer-term president. During the 1920s Walter paid several visits to the Prince, who then lived at Blo' Norton, and they sometimes went on motoring excursions together.[36] In 1922 Prince Frederick purchased Ancient House in Thetford and gave it to the town as a museum. Walter gave him some drawings towards the collection.[37]

Historians

Through his work on such projects as the VCH and the *DNB* Walter developed contacts with academic historians and lawyers, and was happy to call on, or exchange correspondence with, men such as S. R. Gardiner and C. H. Firth. But he remained conscious that his world was a step removed from theirs: he was not a trained historian himself, nor a member of the Royal Historical Society, which may explain why for the most part these contacts did not turn into friendships but remained on a more formal level. One exception, in the last decade of Walter's life, was the young **G. R. Potter** (of University College, Leicester in the 1920s), who transcribed some Norfolk and Suffolk Pipe Rolls on Walter's behalf. He greatly admired his old and infirm patron and kept up a regular correspondence, some of which survives. Walter would send him his publications, and invariably received an effusive response, such as: 'You give me information which would cost me guineas in the market... you are inspiring me with your own spirit and I will try hard for (DV) the next 40 years to continue your work, then perhaps like you I can hope to rest contented.'[38]

... Or another written in Walter's eightieth year, about one of his recent publications:

I think it is an invaluable compilation and I know that you are the only person living capable of it. I hope you sell every copy. I am very grateful for mine. (7 July 1923)[39]

For me your knowledge and public spirit makes you the Norwich *stupor mundi*. (6 November 1923)[40]

Artists

Walter's connections, in both London and Norwich, extended beyond sporting and antiquarian circles. Artist friends included **Holman Hunt** in London [See Track 1.2] and, in Norfolk, **Seymour Lucas** and the young, not yet knighted, **Alfred Munnings**. Lucas introduced Walter to other artists,[41] but although Walter occasionally bought pictures himself,[42] he was evidently no connoisseur of contemporary art, for in 1904 he recorded making 'the usual penal walk round the Royal Academy'!

James Reeve, curator of Norwich Castle Museum and Art Gallery, expert on the Norwich School of Painters and an art collector in his own right, allowed Munnings access to his collection, and it may well have been through this mutual friend that Walter made the acquaintance of Munnings (then in his late twenties), who was among the guests invited to Lammas during his mayoralty. According to his biographer, 'through the first decade of the 1900s [Munnings] lived a near nomadic life within the Norfolk bounds', or, as Munnings himself later put it, 'Youth must be served. The company of artists and various friends in Norwich lured me away'.[43] Writing his autobiography in 1950, he recalled 'Buxton Lammas and the jolly parties given there', and, even though he had moved away to Cornwall in 1911, described Walter as 'an old friend'.[44]

Arthur Henry Patterson, of Great Yarmouth, born in 1857 and therefore some fourteen years younger than Walter, was a skilled amateur naturalist with a county-wide reputation. He wrote a succession of popular books about life on the Broads, especially around Breydon, several of which he illustrated with his own very accomplished pen sketches of birds. In his love of the Broads and of nature, he had much in common with Walter. His sense of humour was every bit as sharp, and like Walter he was a regular, sometimes controversial, contributor to the columns of the local press, especially the *Eastern Daily Press*. He was an expert on wildfowl, but by no means averse to eating them. Although in his youth he was a keen shot, conservation instincts finally got the better of him in 1891 and he renounced the gun in favour of field glasses.[45] He was a keen sailor on the Broads (although in a small houseboat or punt, not a pleasure wherry), and his outcry against the 'rowdyism and hankey-pankey of certain classes of yachting and boating gentry' might equally well have fallen from Walter's lips.[46] How the two men came to meet is not clear: it could have been through a mutual friend such as W. G. Clarke or William Hudson, or perhaps through the Woodpeckers Art Club or one of the other Norwich societies, but whatever the point of contact they became firm friends, and in Walter's later years Patterson occasionally called on him for tea and to cheer him up with his latest humorous illustrations. Only a few letters of his survive in Walter's correspondence, but they (and their attendant doodles) are enough to show the warmth of their affection. On Walter's eightieth birthday, under his *nom-de-plume* 'John Knowlittle', he sent greetings to Walter, 'My dear old friend: Congratulations, and prayers if you need them.' The letter ends with a cartoon sketch of a bird standing on one leg and visibly smiling at an old bearded man with a stick who is grabbing a young boy by the collar. Under the heading 'Compulsory Education' it says, 'The command: "Go ye into the Highways and hedges [and on the fish wharf] and compel them to come in!"' The envelope has a splendid black and white pen cartoon of an oystercatcher pecking at a stone or egg bearing the name W. Rye with the comment, 'And when you've caught him, by Gosh! He takes some getting at.'[47]

When Walter was invited to contribute an introduction to Patterson's *The Cruise of the 'Walrus' on the Broads* [c.1923], he revealed one reason why they got on so famously: 'He has taken up a line of his own, and his many readers enjoy him and his methods, for they feel he is saying just what he feels in his own devil-may-care way, which I share with him myself, and one which I think pays in the long run.'

He went on:

If he has a fault it is in his fatal failing for covering his envelopes with highly amusing sketches, a habit which interferes with the regular postal service, for they are so greatly enjoyed *in transitu* – sorters and postmen alike – that they are often "delayed in transmission".[48]

Endnotes

1. NRO, MS4691/22.
2. *Autobiog.*, p.42. See Geoffrey Page, *The History of Thames Rowing Club and Tideway Rowing* (1991), and R. C. Lehmann, *The Complete Oarsman* [with chapters by, among others, W. H. Eyre] (1908).
3. *Autobiog.*, p.34.
4. See, for example, NRO MS4691/14/1 for visits at Christmas 1902 and Easter 1903. 'The sight of you would do me good', he wrote.
5. See, for example, his entry in Wikipedia.
6. Several letters survive, see MS4691/86.
7. See for example NRO MC733/1 (1879); MS4691/4 (1880); MS4691/7 (1885). In 1889 he sent WR copies of Cubitt entries in the Smallburgh registers and gave hints on where to buy supplies when sailing, MS4691/4.
8. For the Arcadian Club founded in his honour and run under the auspices of Dereham Antiquarian Society see http://www.derehamhistory.com/dr-augustus-jessopp---arcadian-club-newsletter-archive.html
9. See for example his essay on 'Cathedral space for neglected records', in *The Trials of a Country Parson* (1894). NRO MS4691/23 includes several letters from AJ about papers he has acquired, as well as the reflection: 'I have been ransacking Lord Kimberley's archives. Not very much there and who would have thought of it?' (21 Aug. 1885).
10. NRO MS4691/23, 11 Feb. 1881.
11. NRO MS4691/23, 27 Sept. 1885.
12. *Autobiog.* for 1901.
13. NRO MS4691/23.
14. The Arcadian Club, newsletter 4, see link in note 10 above.
15. NRO MS4691/23.
16. NRO MS4691/23, 6 Feb. 1881.
17. NRO MS4691/23 14 Feb. 1912 and other related corresp.
18. *Autobiog.*, p.79.
19. Frowde, Henry (ed), *Frederick James Furnivall: a volume of personal record* (Oxford, 1911), pp.44ff.
20. NRO MS4691/15.
21. NRO MS4691/8 etc. Walter used to visit him at Blo' Norton and go on motoring expeditions with him. See, for example NRO MS4691/83 (1925).
22. They were already on intimate terms by 14 July 1888 when PBF wrote from 70 Lincoln's Inn Fields to WR at 16 Golden Square, 'I am now off to Scotland... to be married to Miss Mackintosh...' NRO MS4691/19/2.
23. 'I wonder if I took to a stylographic pen if I could manage to write as bad a hand as you do.' NRO MS4691/19/1, 2 Nov. 1889.
24. NRO MS4691/19/1 28 May 1889.
25. NRO MS4691/19/1.

26 'Could I have what you read, or is it in your vile handwriting and therefore no good to me?' NRO MS4691/19/1.

27 2 Feb. 1904, NRO MS10612 folder 2.

28 23 Apr. 1909, NRO MS4691/19/2.

29 Undated, NRO MS4691/19/2.

30 NRO MS4691/19/2. They could however be exasperated. Another letter (undated), after an argument over a family pedigree, reads: 'As my little wife would say, "I never knew the like of you for impudence" – you send me a pedigree of Mrs Duff exactly proving *my* case, and making out *yourself* [to be] right!!' NRO MS4691/19/1.

31 The slip is still attached and says: One Of The Best, NRO MS4691/5/1.

32 Many letters in 4691/20/1 and /2. Arthur Patterson was among those who poured scorn on the idea: 'The three fellows responsible for the joke hold good positions in Norfolk... I hear that a kite, a string and probably an electric battery, had something to do with the fraud.' Stanley A. Manning, *Broadland Naturalist...* (1948), pp.90–92.

33 13 Dec. 1906, NRO MS4691/20/2.

34 NRO MS4691/20/2.

35 Peter Rye has in the family album a photograph of WR and Purdy as old men.

36 FDS to WR, 10 Oct 1925, 'I think we had a successful little day and I was delighted to welcome you to Blo' Norton once again. I hope you prove your case against the Stywards!' NRO, MS 4691/83.

37 FDS to WR, 24 May 1922, NRO, MS 4691/12.

38 26 Mar. 1926, NRO MS4691/1.

39 NRO MS4691/83.

40 NRO MS4691/3.

41 Among them 'Crofts, RA' (*Autobiog.*, p.84), McWhirter (ibid., p.90) and many others in the course of Lucas's party to celebrate his becoming RA (ibid., p.105).

42 In 1898 he bought a late Tudor painting of 'Mr Symonds of Norfolk' on horseback, which he later sold to Prince Frederick who gave it to the Mayor and corporation of Thetford. Tate Gallery exhibition catalogue, *Dynasties* (1995), p.181. I am grateful to Jeremy Rye for this reference.

43 Reginald Pound, *The Englishman: A biography of Sir Alfred Munnings* (1962), p.36. Sir Alfred Munnings, *An Artists' Life* (3 vols, 1950), vol I, ch.XXXV.

44 Munnings, *loc. cit.* His memory was prompted by a chance encounter with one of Walter's lawyer sons, who sent him extracts from Walter's *Autobiography*.

45 A. H. Patterson, *Notes of an East Coast Naturalist* (1904), intro.

46 Stanley A. Manning, *Broadland Naturalist: The Life of Arthur H Patterson...* (Norwich, 1948), p.52.

47 NRO MS4691/12. For more, similar cartoons, see Manning *op. cit.*

48 Patterson, *The Cruise of the 'Walrus'...* pp15–16.

4
DEATH AND BEQUESTS

Walter Rye died at home, 66 Clarendon Road, Norwich, on 24 February 1929. In his will he requested a very simple funeral and burial next to Georgina in the graveyard at Lammas. A press photograph shows the funeral procession, in the snow, to the grave.[1] In advance of his death Walter had prepared their joint memorial brass and had already obtained a faculty for its installation on an inside wall in the parish church below a window he had donated containing roundels of the arms of ten lords of the manor.

The net value of his estate at probate was over £12,000, much of this presumably represented by his few remaining property holdings. As Georgina appears not to have made any will, it is unclear whether any of that sum derived from her personal estate. But, given what must have been the substantial medical costs incurred through her long illness, and also given the poverty that Walter pleaded during his mayoralty and after the war when asked for charitable donations, it seems quite probable that he had been bearing the household costs himself, whilst latterly maintaining a more frugal lifestyle.

To his son Frank he bequeathed all his athletics cups and trophies,[2] his other plate, his grant of arms and the family Bible. Arthur, who was named as sole executor and trustee, received his pictures, prints and sketches and his real estate, to be sold as necessary to pay off any outstanding debts including the rent and household expenses on Walter's leasehold house in Norwich. To his youngest daughter Kitty who had nursed him in his final years and returned to live with him he left all the furnishings and fittings in her bedroom and sitting room at 66 Clarendon Road.

As long promised, he bequeathed his antiquarian collections of books, manuscripts, maps and archives to Norwich City Library, on condition that they be made available to all and not lent out. He bequeathed £25 to the city librarian, George A. Stephen, as a token of his esteem, and also asked his help in selling off his other books and the text of his lectures, giving the proceeds to his executor minus a generous 20% commission for his pains. The British Museum was to be offered first refusal of his notes and writings on the history of the Rye family, with Norwich City Library as the fall-back recipient (which is where they eventually settled). To the Norfolk Archaeological Trust he left his rent charge of £5 per annum on Bonner's Cottages, East Dereham.

His collaborator in many a lantern-slide lecture, Harry Brittain,[3] and his servants Florence Hammond and Charles Hurry received cash legacies, whilst his chauffeur Arthur Sexton received all Walter's clothes.

When it came to the residual estate (presumably investments and cash in hand), Frank and Arthur had expressly asked to be excluded as they had already inherited the family legal firm, so Walter split the estate eight ways (slightly hedged about with provisos and trusteeships), in favour of each of his surviving children: James, Hugh, Gilly, Murie, Betty and Kitty (two shares). His son Roger having died, his portion was given to his widow Pauline and in the event of her death to her children.

Endnotes

1   *The Journal*, 2 Mar. 1929, p.4. Copy in NRO, MS 4691/95/1.
2   These are now dispersed among family members.
3   In 1928 the Public Libraries annual report records that Harry Brittain and Walter Rye donated 726 lantern slides depicting 'interesting buildings that are now demolished' bringing the collection to over 2,000 slides. There was considerable demand by lecturers for the local slides, which had been sent out all over the county and some as far as Bridlington. *Norfolk Through a Lens: A Guide to the Photographic Collections held by Norfolk Library and Information Service*, p.11.

5
APPRAISALS

During his life

In concluding his *Autobiography* (in 1916, thirteen years before his death), Walter summarised the achievements of 'a life which has been of considerable interest to myself'. He reflected a little sadly on 'how little one has accomplished in a long life'. All the evidence considered in these pages richly contradicts that verdict. His achievements were impressive, and were widely recognised and admired at the time.

We saw in Track 2 the favourable reports of his prowess as an athlete. He was not without his critics in the field, and we heard some of their voices. His flamboyant style of pedestrianism was severely criticised by some, his sturdy defence of the principle of the 'gentleman amateur' seemed to many already old-fashioned, and his venomous comments in the sporting press about other athletes were by no means to everyone's taste. Yet to most of his contemporaries Walter Rye, in his heyday, was first the great all-rounder, and then the grand old man of English sport. Dissent from this view was vanishingly small.

Similarly, his writings on antiquities, genealogy, topography and family history received almost universally favourable reviews, and we can safely say that by the standards of the day he was one of the greats in all these fields too. Some, especially those with whom he locked horns in controversy, accused him of discourtesy, sloppy and error-ridden research, and muddled thinking, and again we heard their voices (with some sympathy). They, like his sporting critics, were in a minority, although with hindsight we would want to agree with much of their criticism, not least because Walter himself actually admitted many of the faults of which he was accused, especially concerning his later writings. Certainly by today's standards of research Walter Rye's published work needs to be treated with caution for all the reasons outlined in Tracks 3 to 5. Despite all its faults it can still be used with care, especially to identify and locate the sources themselves.[1]

As an adopted son of Norwich, champion of the city and county, and Mayor [Track 6] he was held up as a shining example to all the citizenry. And in spite of his eccentricities and irritating habits, his good company was actively sought and cherished. He received plaudits and gratitude from countless people whom he had encouraged in their respective labours as sportsmen, antiquaries or researchers. Here, in chronological order, are a few of their unsolicited testimonials, which are mainly to be found among his correspondence:

Sydenham Dixon, 1894
If a general vote could be taken amongst those qualified to give an opinion on the matter, to decide upon the man who has done most for the promotion of amateur athletics, there is 'no possible doubt whatever' that Walter Rye would be returned at the head of the poll by an overwhelming majority.[2]

Augustus Jessopp, writing to Mr Ketton, 25 Apr. 1896
I am sure you know my friend Walter Rye who stands 'facile princeps' among Norfolk antiquaries. The more I know of him the more my regard for him increases as a man of absolute uprightness and deserving the fullest confidence that could be reposed in him.[3]

G. W. Speth of Quatuor Coronati Lodge, 4 Apr. 1901
I rejoice every day at having been put into communication with so ardent an antiquary as yourself, and one so eager to take upon himself the burden of being useful to others.[4]

J. B. Tooke Hales of NNAS, 19 May 1902
You know infinitely more about books and publishing than all the members of the Society put together.[5]

W. A. Copinger, 23 Dec. 1902
I have always looked upon you as the person who has done more for the county of Norfolk than any other person has done for any other county.[6]

P. B. Ficklin, 25 Jan.1906
I saw the account of your most generous and public spirited gift [of books and MSS] in the EDP & Norf. Chron. Your name, although unadorned by suffixes like FSA, FHS, JP etc. etc., will never be forgotten, whilst no one will know mine, except my family, 20 years after I'm dead.[7]

Lt-Col H. Curteis, 27 Sept. 1922
Every person interested in Norfolk history owes you a deep debt of gratitude. I have often been very kindly assisted by you. I hope you will be spared many years to continue your good work.[8]

W. G. Clarke, FGS, writing on Walter's eightieth birthday, 1923
Sincere congratulations to the greatest of Norfolk antiquaries. Not only have you done an enormous amount of original work, but you have provided the material for scores of lesser lights.[9]

W. H. Marcon, Edgefield Rectory, Melton Constable, 3 Mar. 1924
How grateful I am for the many things you have written and for the time and labour you've spent for the good of others.[10]

J. A. Venn, 11 Feb. 1925
Your name is indeed familiar to me – not only as an old friend and correspondent of my father, but also as an antiquary of unrivalled reputation.[11]

Obituaries and posthumous reflections

In some of those comments made during his lifetime, especially those from his declining years, we cannot rule out a desire to encourage – or at least, not to offend – an old man in his dotage. So perhaps a truer test of his esteem lies in the obituaries and appraisals published after his death, in the national and local press and in other formal tributes that appeared on behalf of the Norwich City Library, the Norfolk and Norwich Archaeological Society, and various sporting bodies with which Walter had been associated.

Whilst there are naturally differences of emphasis among the respective writers, they are not excessively flattering and together they give a remarkably consistent picture of the man we have met in these pages, so it is worth drawing on them to complete our picture.[12]

He did much good in his generation and he will be remembered with affection not only in Norwich. (*The Times*)

Those who had the privilege of his friendship admired him for his sterling worth, his keen brain and a likeable disposition once intimacy was established, and they will mourn him as one who it was well to know. (*Norwich Chronicle*)

To many, Walter Rye was highly esteemed; multi-faceted, multi-talented and in all respects an exceptional character; 'a fine type of Englishman, with varied tastes, a remarkable combination of athlete, naturalist and antiquary';[13] he was variously said to be irreplaceable; a man of grit, virility and determination. He had led a life that was, as he himself had hoped, 'useful to others'. A. E. Stamp of the PRO, perhaps the most detached of the obituarists, noted that: 'The desire to be useful seems to have been the keynote of his life, from the time when, a boy himself, he taught a class of ragged boys to the time when as an old man he was an active citizen of his beloved Norwich.'[14]

He was fêted as unquestionably one of the great sportsmen of his time, not only for his personal athletic achievements (national record holder, 'Father of Paper Chasing', founder of Thames Hare and Hounds...) but for the way he encouraged others to drive themselves hard on the athletics field, the paper-chasing circuit, or the long-distance walk or cycle ride. He was imbued, as a writer for the Blackheath Harriers put it, with a 'wish to further to the utmost extent... the grand sport with which we are particularly identified'.[15] It was remembered too that he had been instrumental in bringing lacrosse to England for the first time, and had continued participating in archery into his eighties.

Yet this was a life full of eccentricity, enigma and paradox. He was, in his own words, a 'great hater' as well as a warm friend (indeed, sometimes both and to the very same people). As the NNAS tribute had it, 'A somewhat blunt and outspoken manner often hid what his intimates knew to be a warm and generous spirit.' To the end of his life he jealously guarded his personal freedom to think, and fearlessly to say, whatever he believed to be true, without being bound by the tenets or shibboleths of sporting, religious, political or antiquarian societies, even those of which he was a paid-up member. For one or two of the latter, like the NNAS, he was not only a long-term member but also something of a goad or a thorn-in-the-flesh: the man who had declined a vice-presidency. And although he was described by one writer as at heart an 'old school Tory', he had not put himself forward for political or other office, but wherever he did reach a position of eminence, as in national sporting bodies and even as Mayor of Norwich, it was usually through popular pressure or the power of persuasion among his friends.

He was a kind friend to many; more generous than most people ever knew: to friends and neighbours in need, to charitable causes, and to those he considered worthy students of history and antiquities. He was a man of almost excessive good humour, sometimes of an earthy or ghoulish nature, who simply adored practical jokes and had a keen sense of the absurd. This helped to make him an exuberant and entertaining presence at any dinner party or larger social occasion to which he was invited, such as a sporting dinner. Athlete friends lamented that their gatherings were not the same once he was no longer fit enough to attend.

But there was another, steely and more abrasive side to him. As a self-made man with no hint of snobbery about him he was indifferent (even hostile) to pomp and ceremony, and to anything else that did not smack of good honest endeavour. (Hence the infrequency with which he wore his mayoral robes; his failure to dress as formally as some – perhaps even the town clerk – would have liked for the King's visit; his resistance to the grant of a lord mayoralty to the city on his watch, and his horror at the prospect of being offered a knighthood.) Diligence and hard work were his trademarks, and as a result he didn't suffer gladly anyone he rated as a fool, a time-waster or a charlatan, although some thought him too quick to place people in those categories. All this came out most clearly in his sporting and genealogical diatribes against anyone falsely asserting their superiority through spurious sporting records or spurious claims to arms or noble descent (which we might perhaps translate as seeking fame and standing but not through the honest personal effort which was the standard he set himself and others). The same essential motivation lay behind many of his controversial writings. No mercy was shown to opponents unless or until Walter accepted that they, like him, were doing their best to make a good case, express themselves well, and seek out the truth. Even his keenest supporters recognised that he frequently stooped to withering sarcasm, very nearly overstepped the mark into libel or slander, and came pretty close himself to the same failings of which he accused others. What was more, he did not always pick the most important issues on which to take someone to task. When his blood was up he tended to spoil his case with a baffling degree of detail. And, as *The Times* put it, 'as he was not himself always beyond criticism he was often involved in controversy'.

There were many developments in his time (especially the expansion of the railways and the growth of tourism) that appalled him and earned him a reputation as a reactionary and stick-in-the-mud, even if we might think him right to have regretted some of the things that had been lost in the great sweep of 'progress'.

As an antiquary he worked impressively long and hard, and his output was considered truly astonishing. More than one writer claimed for him the crown as the greatest of Norfolk antiquaries, right up there among the 'honoured Norfolk names of Le Neve, Blomefield, Martin, Kirkpatrick and Palmer'.[16] A few percipient obituarists did indeed comment on errors and inaccuracies to be found in his work. Stamp of the PRO, who was in a better position than most to know the sources Walter had used and the use he had made of them, was the most critical and yet not at all ungenerous:

> To many he was just an old gentleman, keenly interested in his own county, who had published many books and pamphlets, most of which were open to severe criticism. This view, though strictly correct, is hardly fair to the memory of Mr Rye... When it was pointed out to him that [the calendars he had published] might have been much improved by careful revision, he was quite impenitent, and maintained that they were useful to him and ought to be so to others. As, indeed, they are.[17]

It is on those concluding words that we should perhaps dwell.

On the whole much more emphasis was given in the obituaries to Walter's pioneering work in opening up the sources for Norfolk history, sharing his knowledge widely through publications, many of which he had paid for out of his own pocket, making his own collections freely available to *bona fide* researchers and then generously bequeathing them to the city of Norwich. To the citizens he was one who had 'left his mark on the annals of Norwich for all time', and there was none to equal him as a champion of public rights.[18] He genuinely loved the city and served it devotedly as Mayor.

Writing in 1973, Tom Copeman summed him up well:

Those of us who knew Rye will always remember him as a great character, a strange mixture of crustiness and kindliness. On his own admission he could be a good hater, but he could also be a good friend.[19]

Endnotes

1   This is borne out by the comments of A. E. Stamp quoted in the next section. For just one recent endorsement of this view see Nicholas Vincent, 'The Foundation of Westacre Priory', in NA XLI, p. 493: 'The account provided by W. Rye, *Some new facts as to the life of St Thomas a Becket* (Norwich, 1924, 18–20, 67–76), although confused in the extreme, does at least provide a useful list of evidences from the Public Records.'

2   'Some old-time athletes', in *Baily's Magazine of Sport and Pastimes*, 1 Aug. 1894, p.126.

3   NRO, MS 4691/23.

4   NRO, MS 4691/11.

5   NRO, MS 4691/7.

6   NRO, MS 4691/4.

7   NRO, MS 10612, folder (1).

8   NRO, MS 4961/10.

9   NRO, MS 4691/3.

10 Ibid.

11 NRO, MS 4691/83.

12 A file of obituaries and tributes survives in NRO, MS 4691/95/1. They include *The Journal*, 2 March 1929, p 4; the NNAS *Annual Report* for 1932 (NAS XXIV); *The Times*, 26 Feb. 1929; the *Norfolk Chronicle*, 1 Mar. 1929 and A. E. Stamp, in *History*, April 1929, p.45 MS 4691/95/1. Also useful are the files of the *Eastern Daily Press* and the memoir by G. A. Stephen (see Bibliography).

13 W. G. Clarke, in an obituary note prepared in advance for the *EDP* in 1919 and published 25 Feb. 1929. (EDP archives.)

14 NRO, MS 4691/95/1 from History, April 1929, p.45.
15 'Passing of the Father of Paper-Chasing', in *Blackheath Harriers Gazette and Club Record*, no 349, May, 1929.
16 Norfolk Archaeology, XXIV, (1932).
17 NRO, MS 4691/95/1 from *History*, April 1929, p.45.
18 Obituary in *Norwich Chronicle*.
19 *Eastern Daily Press* archives, date stamped 23 July 1973.

BIBLIOGRAPHY

PRIMARY SOURCES

NORWICH
Norfolk Record Office, Norwich
MS 4691: (107 pieces). Walter Rye's correspondence, comprising largely unsorted correspondence (1–24); genealogical notes on Norfolk families (32–48); historical notes, extracts and transcripts by WR (49–107).
Letters from or about WR in other people's correspondence also held by NRO are cross-referenced from his entry in the NRO catalogue.
MS11522: Material about the Norfolk Broads.
MSS RYE: Walter Rye's collection of original manuscripts.

Norfolk Heritage Centre (Norfolk and Norwich Millennium Library, Norwich)
C. Rye [OS]: Photocopy of a letter from WR to Rev H. T. Griffiths, written from 16 Golden Square, 11 Sept 1879.
C940.3; 'Norfolk and the Great War of 1914 etc.' A scrapbook of press cuttings compiled by WR himself.

Rye family archives in the possession of Peter Rye
Photographs, family album and memoir by Barry Adams, 1984.

Eastern Daily Press office
Correspondence and cuttings file.

LONDON
British Library
Two pedigrees in the hand of WR, bound into a compendium of pedigrees:
(a) Rough Sketch of Bacon of Baconsthorpe, 30 August 1895.
(b) 'A pedigree of the family of Vaughan of Leominster compiled from materials in the possession of Lady Isham of Lamport Hall and inscribed to her by W Rye, 1876'.
Hodgson's and Sotheby's Sale Catalogues of Edward Rye's books.

MS Add 50206 ff. 44–48. Papers of Walter de Gray Birch. Two letters from WR, 1889, and his draft replies.

Camden Local Studies and Archives Department, Holborn Library
A/01335: Hampstead Antiquarian and Historical Society archives.

College of Arms
Register of Grants of Arms, vol. LXX (1897–1899).
Athill Papers.

Guildhall Library, London
CLC/L/NA/MS 2818/2 and 39270/001. Needlemakers' Company archives. Registers of freemen 1790–1805 and 1756–1808.

London Cemetery Company
Kensal Green Cemetery: burial records and correspondence.

London Metropolitan Archives
CLC/B/192/F/001/MS11936/564/1256895-99: Sun Fire Insurance Registers.

Probate Registry, Family Division, London
Walter Rye's will.

Quaritch [booksellers]
Commission books.

Thames Hare and Hounds
Sports programmes, summons and letters by and concerning WR between 1866 and 1885. [Transcripts kindly supplied by the club.]

The National Archives (TNA, Kew)
PRO 6/325 Register of permissions, Literary Search Room.
IR 62/1219 Exemption from Estate Duty of WR's bequest of books etc. to Norwich Public Library.

University College London
J. H. Round papers.

University of London Institute of Advanced Legal Studies
A.LSOC 6/6 and 10/1: Law Society Registers.

University of London Institute of Historical Research
Victoria County History (VCH) archives.

WORKS BY WALTER RYE

Notes

The list is in alphabetical order of title omitting any opening 'A' or 'The' unless significant. It excludes articles contributed by WR to periodicals and newspapers.

This is not a complete list of Walter Rye's publications. For his main works to 1916 see his Autobiography; for later works see George A. Stephen, *Walter Rye: Memoir, bibliography and catalogue of his Norfolk Manuscripts in the Norwich Public Libraries* (Norwich, 1929).

The place of publication is Norwich unless otherwise stated.

Account of the Church and Parish of Cawston in the county of Norfolk (1898).
Account of the Churches of St Peter of Shipden and of St Peter and Paul of Cromer in the county of Norfolk (1870).
Account of the Family of Rye (London, 1876).
Address from the Gentry of Norfolk and Norwich to General Monck in 1660. Facsimile of a manuscript in the Norwich Public Library (1913). [WR supplied biographical notes.]
Autobiography of an Ancient Athlete and Antiquary (1916).
Calendar of Correspondence and Documents relating to the family of Oliver le Neve, of Witchingham, Norfolk, 1675–1743. [Edited by F. Rye and others including WR, (1895)].
Calendar of Norwich Deeds enrolled in the court rolls of that city, 1307–1341 [editor] (NNAS, 1915).
Calendar of the Feet of Fines for Suffolk (Ipswich, for Suffolk Inst. of Archaeology, 1900).
Calendar of the Freemen of Norwich from 1307 to 1603 (Edward II to Elizabeth inclusive) by John L'Estrange, ed. WR (London, 1888).
Carrow Abbey, otherwise Carrow Priory near Norwich in the County of Norfolk: its foundations, officers and inmates (1889).
Catalogue of Fifty of the Norfolk Manuscripts in the Library of Mr Walter Rye at Winchester House, Putney, 1889 (1889). [See also *Index Rerum* below].
Catalogue of the Topographical and Antiquarian portions of the Free Library at Norwich compiled by Walter Rye, a co-opted member of its Committee (1908).
Chaucer: A Norfolk Man (1915, with a further appendix 1916).
Collections for a history of the family of Cubitt of Norfolk (1873).
Cromer, Past and Present: or an Attempt to describe the parishes of Shipden and Cromer and to narrate their history (1889).
Depositions taken before the Mayor and Aldermen of Norwich 1549–67. Extracts from the court books of the city of Norwich, 1666–1688 (NNAS, 1905).
Dr J. Horace Round and his recent attack on Mr Walter Rye as to the Colchester Chronicle, Norwich Castle and other matters (1922).
Extracts from the Records of the Corporation of Norwich (Margate, Quatuor Coronati Lodge, 1902).
False Pedigree and Arms of the family of Bacon of Suffolk; the ancestors of Sir Nicholas

Bacon, of Francis Bacon (Lord Verulam), and of the present premier baronet, critically examined and exposed by Walter Rye (1919).

First Register Book of the parish of Lammas and Little Hautbois, with some notes from later registers (1905).

First Register Book of the parish of Old Buckenham in Norfolk, 1560–1649 (1902).

Glossary of Words used in East Anglia, founded on that of Forby, with numerous corrections and additions by Walter Rye (Oxford, English Dialect Society, 1895).

The Great War: Statistics of Recruiting in East and North Norfolk among tenant farmers and their sons (1917).

Handbook to the Materials available to students of local history and genealogy, arranged in order of date (1924).

Hickling Broad Case (Micklethwaite v. Vincent): The Judgment of the Court of Appeal considered (1894).

History of Norfolk (London, 1885).

Index of Norfolk Topography (London, for the Index Society, 1881). [See also Index to Norfolk Pedigrees below].

Index Rerum of Norfolk Antiquities (1899 or 1890) [Includes an appendix to his Catalogue of Fifty Norfolk Manuscripts above.]

'Index to marriage licences, Consistory. Norwich 1563–1588 from a MSS [sic] in the Public Library, Norwich compiled by Walter Rye'. (1926, unpublished typescript.)

Index to Norfolk Pedigrees and continuation of Index of Norfolk Topography (1896).

Journal of Thomas Isham of Langport in the county of Northampton... [WR contributed the introduction and index] (1875).

Later history of the family of Walpole of Norfolk (1920).

List of Norfolk Place Names compiled with the view of helping local students to compare them with similar names in Scandinavia and some preliminary remarks as to the probability that England was invaded by the Scandinavians before the coming of the Romans (1923).

Mayor of Norwich's Unemployed Fund 1908–9. Report and Balance Sheet to June 9th, 1909 (1909).

Monographs of Norwich Hamlets (1917–1919):
1. History of the parish of Eaton in the city of Norwich (1917).
2. History of the parish of Earlham in the city of Norwich (1917).
3. History of the parish of Hellesdon in the city of Norwich (1917).
4. History of the parish of Heigham in the city of Norwich (1917).
5. History of the parish of Catton in the city of Norwich (1919).

A Month on the Norfolk Broads on Board the Wherry, 'Zoe', and its Tender, the Tub, 'Lotus' (London, Norwich, Yarmouth and Ipswich, [1887]).

Monumental Inscriptions in the Hundred of Happing in the county of Norfolk (1886).

Monumental Inscriptions in the Hundred of Holt in the county of Norfolk (1885).

Monumental Inscriptions in the Hundred of Tunstead in the county of Norfolk (1891).

Murder of Amy Robsart: A brief for the prosecution (London and Norwich, 1885).

Norfolk Families (1913). [There is also an Index Nominum by Charles Nowell, 1915.]

Norfolk Handlists (1916–1919):

1. *Scandinavian Names in Norfolk: Hundred courts and mote hills in Norfolk.*
2. *Roman Camps and Remains in Norfolk.*
3. *Castles and Manor Houses [in Norfolk] from the Conquest.*
4. *Norwich Houses before 1600.*
5. *A List of Norfolk Fighting Men, from the Norman period to [1900].*
6. *Early Recumbent Figures on Monuments in Norfolk before 1500.*

Norwich and the Broads: Itinerary (Quatuor Coronati Lodge, 1902).

Norwich Castle (1921).

Norwich Castle Museum: Catalogue of Antiquities found principally in East Anglia, edited by Walter Rye, mayor of the City and County of Norwich, Chairman of Castle Museum Committee, compiled by Frank Leney, Assistant Curator, from the Curators' records and other sources (1909).

Norwich Rate Book from Easter 1633 to Easter 1634 (London, 1903).

Pedes Finium, or Fines relating to the county of Cambridgeshire (Cambridge, Cambridge Antiquarian Society, XXVI, 1891).

Pedes Finium: or, Fines, relating to the county of Norfolk, levied in the King's Court from the third year of Richard I to the end of the reign of John (NNAS, 1881).

Persecution of the Jews in England: a lecture delivered at the Anglo-Jewish Historical Exhibition, Royal Albert Hall, 26th May 1887 [Reprinted from the Anglo-Jewish Exhibition papers] (London, Jewish Chronicle, 1887).

Records and Record Searching (London, 1st edn. 1888, 2nd edn. 1897).

Recreations of a Norfolk Antiquary (2 vol , Holt and Norwich, 1920 and 1922).

Report on the Manuscripts of the family of Gawdy, formerly of Norfolk (London, Historical Manuscripts Commission, 1885).

Rights of Fishing, Shooting and Sailing on the Norfolk Broads (1899).

Rubbish and Nonsense (1887).

[Rye's monographs: see Monographs].

St Peter Mancroft Norwich; its Parish Historie in ye Sixteenth and Seventeenth Centuries (1882).

Short Calendar of the Deeds relating to Norwich enrolled in the Court Rolls of that city, 1285–1306 (NNAS, 1903).

Short Calendar of the Feet of Fines for Norfolk in the reigns of Richard I, John, Henry III, & Edward I (1885).

Short Calendar of the Feet of Fines for Norfolk in the reigns of Edward II to Richard III (1886).

Short List of Works relating to the biographies of Norfolk men and women, preserved in the Free Library, Norwich (1908).

Some early English Inscriptions in Norfolk before 1600 (London, 1923).

Some Historical Essays chiefly relating to Norfolk ('Rye's Norfolk Essays', 6 parts, 1925–1928). [Part I was separately published as *Two Cromwellian Myths* qv].

Some Monumental Inscriptions in Norfolk before 1600 (London, 1923).

Some new facts as to the life of St Thomas a Becket tending to show that he was probably early educated in, and closely connected in many ways with Norfolk (1924).

Some notes on the Deeds relating to the Parish and other Charities of Wandsworth in the county of Surrey (Hertford, 1881: see BL. MSS Add. 10347 ll 32/1–8).

Some Rough Materials for a history of the hundred of North Erpingham in the county of Norfolk (2 vols., 1883, 1885).

Songs, Stories and Sayings of Norfolk (1897).

Three Norfolk Armories: A transcript (now in the library of Mr Walter Rye) made in 1753 of a manuscript by Anthony Norris Esq of Barton Turf (1886).

Tourists' Guide to the county of Norfolk, with some preliminary remarks as to its natives, their names, superstitions and peculiarities (London, 1st edn. 1879).

Two Cromwellian Myths; viz. the alleged royal descent of Oliver Cromwell and the Squire letters, both of which deceived Carlye (1925).

Visitacion of Norfolk... 1563... 1613 (London, Harleian Society XXXII, 1891).

What are the Legal and Advisable Ornaments of the Church of England? (London, 1866).

GENERAL REFERENCE

Notes

Newspapers, where cited, are fully referenced in the endnotes. All except those in Guildhall Library, (London) and the *Eastern Daily Press* (Norwich), were read online at the British Library's Newsroom.

Websites, electronic resources and periodical literature, where cited, are fully referenced in the endnotes. They were correct at the time of going to press but may, of course, since have changed.

[Anglo-Jewish Exhibition]: *Catalogue of Anglo-Jewish Historical Exhibition, 1887, Royal Albert Hall, and of supplementary exhibitions at Public Record Office, British Museum, South Kensington Museum* (London, 1887).

Barton-Wood, Sarah, *Through Fire and Flood: Saving Norfolk's Archives* (Cromer, 2014).

Beaumont, Matthew, *Nightwalking: A Nocturnal History of London, Chaucer to Dickens* (2015).

Beeley, Serena, *A History of Bicycles* (London, 1992).

Blomefield, Francis (continued by Parkin, Charles), *An Essay Towards a Topographical History of the County of Norfolk...* (London, 2nd edn., 11 vols, 1805-1810).

Bray, David, *Evolution of the Norfolk Wherry* (nd c. 1980).

Bury, Viscount and Hillier, G. Lacy, *Cycling* (The Badminton Library, 1st edn. 1887).

Cantwell, J. D., *The Public Record Office 1838–1958* (London, 1991).

Clark, Roy, *Black-sailed Traders* (Newton Abbot, 1961/1972).

Clayton, Nick, *Early Bicycles* (Shire album 173, Princes Risborough, 1994).

Collins, Peter, *Fishing the Norfolk Broads* (London, 1967).

Crow, M. M., Olson, C. C., et al., *Chaucer: Life Records* (Oxford, 1966).

Darroch, Elizabeth and Taylor, Barry (comps.), *A Bibliography of Norfolk History* (UEA, 1975).

Davies, G. Christopher, *The Swan and her Crew, or the Adventures of Three Young Naturalists on the Broads and Rivers of Norfolk* (London, c. 1876).

Davies, G. Christopher, *The Handbook to the Rivers and Broads of Norfolk and Suffolk* (Jarrolds' Holiday Series, 29th edition, London, 1899).

Demans, A. B., *Victorian and Edwardian Cycling and Motoring from Old Photographs* (London, 1977).

Diamond, Marion, *Emigration and Empire: The Life of Maria S. Rye* (New York and London, 1999).

Dutt, W. A., *A Guide to the Norfolk Broads* [with a chapter by Arthur Patterson] (1923).

Ewald, A. C., *Our Public Records: A Brief Handbook to the National Archives* (London, 1873).

Fenwick, Gillian, (ed.), *The Contributors' Index to the Dictionary of National Biography 1885-1901* (St Paul's Bibliographies, Winchester, 1989).

Fletcher, Elaine, *A Norfolk Quiverful: Celebrating 100 years of archery in the Fakenham area* (Larks Press, Dereham, 1994).

Gerhold, Dorian, *Pubs of Wandsworth* (Wandsworth Historical Society, Wandsworth Papers 23, 2012).

Gerhold, Dorian, *Roehampton Village* (Wandsworth Historical Society, Wandsworth Papers 29, 2016).

Gerhold, Dorian, *Wandsworth Past* (Historical Publications, 1998).

Gough, Richard, *British Topography* (2 vols, London 1780).

Henshaw, D. J. de C., *The Worshipful Company of Needlemakers, 1656-2006: A Commemoration of 350 years* (London, 2006).

Hewson, Don, *Britain in Old Photographs: Putney and Roehampton* (1997).

Hillier, G. Lacy and Bramson, W. G. H., *Amateur Cycling, With Hints on Training* (London, 1883). [For Hillier see also Bury above.]

Howlett, Richard, *The Parish Register of Bircham Newton from 1562 to 1743* (Norwich, 1888).

Kaplan, F., *Thomas Carlyle: A Biography* (Cambridge 1983).

Lehmann, R. C., *The Complete Oarsman* (London, 1908).

Lovesey, Peter, *The Official Centenary History of the Amateur Athletic Association* (London, 1979).

Malster, Robert, *Wherries and Waterways* (Lavenham, 1986, first published 1871).

Manning, Stanley A., *Broadland Naturalist: The Life of Arthur H. Patterson...* (Norwich, 1948).

Mason, R. Hindry, *The History of Norfolk* (London, 1884).

Meeres, Frank, *A History of Norwich* (Chichester 1998).

Meeres, Frank, *Paranormal Norfolk* (Stroud, 2010).

Meeres, Frank, *Norwich: A History and Celebration* (Teffont, 2014).

Mortlock, D. P. and Roberts, C. V., *The Guide to Norfolk Churches* (Cambridge, 2nd revised edition, 2007).

Munnings, Sir Alfred, *An Artist's Life* (3 vols., 1950).

Page, Geoffrey, *Hear the Boat Sing: The History of Thames Rowing Club and Tideway Rowing* (London, 1991).

Page, William, (ed.), *Family Origins and Other Studies by the late J. Horace Round* (1930).

Palgrave-Moore, Patrick, *The Mayors and Lord Mayors of Norwich 1836–1974* (Norwich 1978).

Patterson, Arthur Henry, *Through Broadland by Sail and Motor* (London, 1930).

Patterson, Arthur Henry, ['John Knowlittle'], *Through Broadland in a Breydon Punt* (Norwich 1920).

Patterson, Arthur Henry, *The Cruise of the 'Walrus' on the Broads.* [nd.,c.1923]. With an introduction by Walter Rye.

Pevsner, Nikolaus and Wilson, Bill, *The Buildings of England: Norfolk I: Norwich and North East* (Yale, 2002).

Phillimore, W. P. W., *How to Write the History of a Family: a Guide for the Genealogist* (London, 1887); and *A supplement* (London, 2nd edn. 1900, published by the author).

[Pipe Roll Society], *Feet of Fines... Norfolk... 1198–1202* (London, new series XXVII, 1950).

Pound, Reginald, *The Englishman: A Biography of Sir Alfred Munnings* (1962).

Powell, W. Raymond, *John Horace Round: Historian and Gentleman of Essex* (Essex Record Office, Chelmsford, 2001).

Pratt, Edwin A., *Pioneer Women in Victoria's Reign* (London, 1897).

Rawcliffe, Carole and Wilson, Richard (eds.), *Norwich since 1550* (Hambledon and London, 2004).

Rhys, E., (ed.), *The Hampstead Annual 1898.* (London).

Round, J. H., *Studies on the Red Book of the Exchequer* (privately printed, 1898).

Ryan, J., (comp.), *The Annals of Thames Hare and Hounds 1868 to 1945, with the present generation 1946 to 1968 by Ian H. Fraser* (London, 1968).

Rye, Peter, *Walter Rye, Athlete and Antiquary* (Dereham, 1996).

Scott, W. S., *A Selborne Handbook* (1967), with a description of The Lyth and Dorton by Anthony Rye.

Selby, Walford D., *Norfolk Records* (Norwich, NNAS, 1886).

Shearman, Montague, *Athletics and Football* (The Badminton Library, 1889).

Sheppard, F. H. W. (ed.), *Survey of London: Volumes 31 and 32, St James Westminster, Part 2* (1963).

Skidmore, C., *Death and the Virgin: Elizabeth, Dudley and the Mysterious Fate of Amy Robsart* (London, 2010).

Stephen, George A., *Walter Rye: Memoir, Bibliography and Catalogue of his Norfolk Manuscripts in the Norwich Public Libraries* (Norwich, 1929).

Stoker, David (ed.) *The Correspondence of the Reverend Francis Blomefield (1705–52)* (London, 1992).

Thames Rowing Club Quadrille (music) by Charles Coote (British Library, 1865.)

Victoria History of the County of Middlesex, IX (Oxford, 1989).

Victoria History of the County of Norfolk, I and II (Westminster, 1901, 1906).

Wade, Christopher, *The Streets of Hampstead* (London, Camden History Society, 2000).

Wade, Christopher, with Usborne, Ann, *A Portrait of Hampstead* (London, 1984).

Wilson, A. N., *The Victorians* (London, 2003).

Woodforde, John, *The Story of the Bicycle* (London, 1970).

INDEX

PRINCIPAL ENTRIES, IN BOLD, MAY EXTEND FOR MORE THAN ONE PAGE

NORWICH, named places in:

Agricultural Hall 311; Anguish House 7, **317;** Artillery barracks 338; Bacon's House 8, 311 **317, Plate VI**; Bethel Hospital 348, 355; Castle 310; Cathedral 26, 285, 310, 312, 319; Christchurch Road 84; Clarendon Road 84, 375; Colman's works 140, 287, 334; Cringleford bridge 336; Elm Hill 318; Gas Hill 60, 64, 66; gasworks 63; Grammar School 310; Great Hospital 338; Guildhall 25, 311; King Street 151, 318; leper hospital (Lazar house) 8, 317; library and museum 8, 181, 194, 255, **323**, 332; London Street 63; Lutyens war memorial **320**; Maid's Head hotel 8, 310-12, **315**, 320, **Plate VI**; Mill Hill Road 83; Mousehold Heath 39, 319, 333, 337, 338; Norfolk and Norwich Hospital 326, 336, 338-9; Old Norfolk hotel 44; Oxford hotel 25(n); People's Park 319; Royal hotel 310; Sewell Park 335; St Andrew's Hall 311, 338, 347; St George's bridge 320; St Leonard's Priory 60, 63, 66, 122, 203, 312, 317; St Peter Mancroft 311, 336; Strangers' Hall 311, 317, 340(n.12); Surrey Street 67, 332; Thorpe station 288, 336; Trowse Pumping Station 335; War Hospital Supply Depot 349

NORWICH, other references:

clubs and societies **308;** Horticultural Society 66; Miniature Rifle Association 151, 332, 348; Photographic Society 66, 308; Prehistory Society 66, 308, 369; Science Gossip Club 8, 65, 66, 308; Woodpeckers Art Club 8, 66, 308, **Plate VII**

floods (1912) 79, 320

printers: Gibbs & Waller 244; Goose, Agas H **243**; Hunt 244; Jarrold 244, 283; Miller [& Leavins] 243, 281; Roberts 244

royal visit of Edward VII 332, **336**

unemployment 332, **333**

O

Old Buckenham, Norfolk 182, 194, 244, 369

Orford, Lord 198. 295, 368

Oulton Broad, [Suffolk] 155(n.1)

Overstrand, Norfolk 70, 318

owls, luminous **293**

Oxford, Bodleian Library 170, 181, 218

P

Page, Trevor & Co 338

Page, William, of VCH 268, 304, 319

Palling, Norfolk 125

Parkin, Revd Charles, antiquary 163, **164**, 179, 261

Patterson, Arthur Henry, artist 371

Peacock, Edward 228

Peake, Edward, archer 154

pedigrees **210**

Perry, Nathaniel, athlete 359

Phillimore, WPW, antiquary 184

Phipson, RM, architect and antiquary 282

place-names, study of 288, 296, 302

Plaskett, sailing companion of WR 140

Potter, GR, historian 191, **370**

Potter Heigham, Norfolk 130, 297
Preston family pedigree 182, 212
Pretoria [S Africa], procession for relief of 63
Procter, Revd F, antiquary 122, 180
Public Record Office 6, 76, **169**, 246; records in general 6, 165, **169**, **184**, 192, 218, 222, 229, 266, 268, 281, 287; Feet of Fines **173**, 185, 194, **Plate II**; Guild Certificates **172**, 288, 194; Inventories of Church Goods 172, **Plate II**
Pulham, Norfolk 43, 119
Purdy, RJW, naturalist and antiquary 69, 123, 124, 128(n.14), **368**
Putney 41, 92, 199; Red Lion 41, 91; St Mary's church 41, 43; Winchester House **47**, 55

Q

Quaritch, Bernard, bookseller 58, 187, 196-7, 224
Quatuor Coronati Lodge 64, 194, 309
Queen of the Broads, 311-2

R

railways: journeys by WR 25, 39, 83, 288; reaction to 283, 286, 382
Ranworth, Norfolk 140, 145
Raynham, Norfolk 296
record agents 200, 215, 237, 304
Reeve, James, curator 310, 328(n.15) 371
Ringstead Down, Norfolk 70
Roberts, DM 83, 122, 133, 146, **359**
Roberts, George, MP 329
Robinson, Revd WW 22-3
Robsart, Amy, murder of, *see* Rye, Walter, publications

Roehampton, Surrey, King's Head 41-2, 101
Rollesby Hall, Norfolk 123
Round, J Horace, historian 211, 225, 227, 254, 257, 262, **268**, 301-5 *passim*
Royal Historical Society 349
Rugby School and paper-chasing 95
Runton, Norfolk 70

RYE FAMILY **210**, 216
ancestors of WR: 6, 12; Edward, grandfather 12-13; Edward, father 3, 5, 13-14, 26, 29, 35 -7, 247; his books 17-18, 26, 27, 37, 196; death 37, 131; Maria (née Tuppen), mother 14, 27, 29, 38
siblings of WR: Charles 16, 17; Clara Louise 17, 29; Edward Caldwell 14, 17-19, 29, 38, 51, 90 , 91, 129, 133; Elizabeth (Bessie) 14, 17, 29; Francis (Frank) 17, 18, 29, 45, 51, 131, 133, 237, 247, 283; Maria Susan 14, 17, 23, 29, 345; Mary Anne (Annie) 16, 17, 29

RYE, GEORGINA, wife of WR 4, 5, 38, 43, **49**, **59**, 63, 64, 67-8, 72, 77, 117, 119, 132, 332, 375
children of WR and Georgina: Arthur Lockyer 45, 59, 63, 64, 74, 75, 76, 77, 80, 117; Barbara Valentine Catherine (Kitty) 51, 63, 64, 67, 76, 77, 84, 347, 375-6; Frances Elizabeth (Betty) 51, 59, 76, 77, 376; Francis (Frank Gibbs) 45, 52, 63, 74, 75, 76, **117**, 365, 375; Gilbert Walter (Gilly) 75, 76, 81, 147(n.10), 376; Hubert (Hugh) Gould 51, 75,